Microsoft®

Windows® 98

Illustrated Complete

Microsoft®

Windows® 98

Illustrated Complete

Joan Carey
Steven M. Johnson
Neil J. Salkind

COURSE
TECHNOLOGY

ONE MAIN STREET, CAMBRIDGE, MA 02142

an International Thomson Publishing company I(T)P®

Cambridge • Albany • Bonn • Boston • Cincinnati • London • Madrid • Melbourne • Mexico City
New York • Paris • San Francisco • Singapore • Tokyo • Toronto • Washington

Microsoft Windows 98—Illustrated Complete

is published by Course Technology

Managing Editor:	Nicole Jones Pinard
Senior Product Manager:	Jeanne Herring
Product Manager:	Jennifer Thompson
Production Editor:	Ellina Beletsky
Developmental Editors:	Mary Kemper, Jennifer Duffy
Composition House:	GEX, Inc.
QA Manuscript Reviewers:	Alex White
Text Designer:	Joseph Lee
Cover Designer:	Joseph Lee

© 1999 by Course Technology — I(T)P®

For more information contact:

Course Technology
One Main Street
Cambridge, MA 02142

ITP Europe
Berkshire House 168-173
High Holborn
London WCIV 7AA
England

Nelson ITP, Australia
102 Dodds Street
South Melbourne, 3205
Victoria, Australia

ITP Nelson Canada
1120 Birchmount Road
Scarborough, Ontario
Canada M1K 5G4

International Thomson Editores
Seneca, 53
Colonia Polanco
11560 Mexico D.F. Mexico

ITP GmbH
Königswinterer Strasse 418
53227 Bonn
Germany

ITP Asia
60 Albert Street, #15-01
Albert Complex
Singapore 189969

ITP Japan
Hirakawacho Kyowa Building, 3F
2-2-1 Hirakawacho
Chiyoda-ku, Tokyo 102
Japan

ISBN 0-7600-5485-1

Printed in the United States of America

1 2 3 4 5 6 7 8 9 BM 02 01 00 99

Exciting New Illustrated Products

The Illustrated Projects™ Series: The Quick, Visual Way to Apply Computer Skills

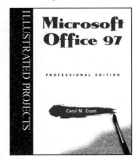

Looking for an inexpensive, easy way to supplement almost any application text and give your students the practice and tools they'll need to compete in today's competitive marketplace? Each text includes more than 50 real-world, useful projects—like creating a resume and setting up a loan worksheet—that let students hone their computer skills. These two-color texts have the same great two-page layout as the Illustrated Series.

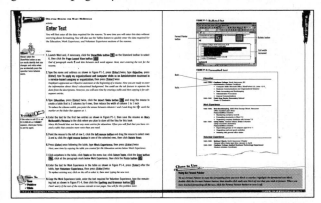

Illustrated Projects titles are available for the following:

- ▶ Microsoft Access
- ▶ Microsoft Excel
- ▶ Microsoft Office Professional
- ▶ Microsoft Publisher
- ▶ Microsoft Word

- ▶ Creating Web Sites
- ▶ World Wide Web
- ▶ Adobe PageMaker
- ▶ Corel WordPerfect

Illustrated Interactive™ Series: The Safe, Simulated Way to Learn Computer Skills

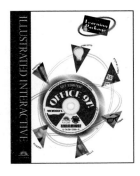

The Illustrated Interactive Series uses multimedia technology to teach computer concepts and application skills. Students learn via a CD-ROM that simulates the actual software and provides a controlled learning environment in which every keystroke is monitored. Plus, all products in this series feature the same step-by-step instructions as the Illustrated Series. An accompanying workbook reinforces the skills that students learn on the CD.

Illustrated Interactive titles are available for the following applications:*

- ▶ Microsoft Office 97
- ▶ Microsoft Word 97
- ▶ Microsoft Excel 97

- ▶ Microsoft Access 97
- ▶ Microsoft PowerPoint 97
- ▶ Computer Concepts

Standalone & networked versions available. Runs on Windows 3.1, 95, and NT. CD-only version available for Computer Concepts and Office 97.

CourseKits™: Offering You the Freedom to Choose

Balance your course curriculum with Course Technology's mix-and-match approach to selecting texts. CourseKits provide you with the freedom to make choices from more than one series. When you choose any two or more Course Technology products for one course, we'll discount the price and package them together so your students pick up one convenient bundle at the bookstore.

Contact your sales representative to find out more about these Illustrated products.

Preface

Welcome to *Microsoft Windows 98 – Illustrated*! This book in our highly visual design offers new users a hands-on introduction to Microsoft Windows 98 and also serves as an excellent reference for future use.

▶ Organization and Coverage

The Complete book contains fifteen units that cover basic through advanced Microsoft Windows 98 skills. In these units students learn basic Windows skills along with how to work with programs and manage files using both My Computer and Windows Explorer. They also learn how to access the Internet and explore the World Wide Web using Internet Explorer, work with Windows 98 on a network, manage hardware, create Web pages using FrontPage Express, and much more!

▶ About this Approach

What makes the Illustrated approach so effective at teaching software skills? It's quite simple. Each skill is presented on two facing pages, with the step-by-step instructions on the left page, and large screen illustrations on the right. Students can focus on a single skill without having to turn the page. This unique design makes information extremely accessible and easy to absorb, and provides a great reference for students after the course is over. This hands-on approach also makes it ideal for both self-paced or instructor-led classes. The modular structure of the book also allows for great flexibility; you can cover the units in any order you choose.

Each lesson, or "information display," contains the following elements:

Each two-page spread focuses on a single skill.

Concise text that introduces the basic principles in the lesson and integrates the brief case study.

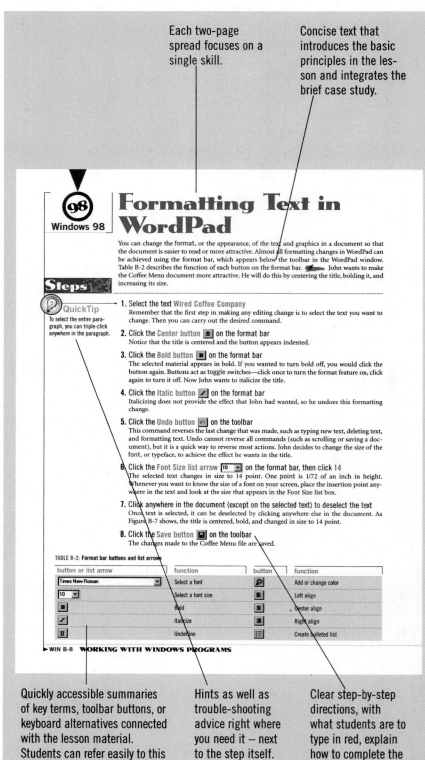

Quickly accessible summaries of key terms, toolbar buttons, or keyboard alternatives connected with the lesson material. Students can refer easily to this information when working on their own projects at a later time.

Hints as well as trouble-shooting advice right where you need it – next to the step itself.

Clear step-by-step directions, with what students are to type in red, explain how to complete the specific task.

Every lesson features large, full-color representations of what the screen should look like as students complete the numbered steps.

Other Features

The two-page lesson format featured in this book provides the new user with a powerful learning experience. Additionally, this book contains the following features:

▶ **Real-World Case**
The case study used throughout the textbook, a fictitious coffee company called Wired Coffee Company, is designed to be "real-world" in nature and introduces the kinds of activities that students will encounter when working with Microsoft Windows 98. With a real-world case, the process of solving problems will be more meaningful to students.

▶ **End of Unit Material**
Each unit concludes with a Concepts Review that tests students' understanding of what they learned in the unit. A Skills Review follows the Concepts Review and provides students with additional hands-on practice of the skills they learned in the unit. The Skills Review is followed by Independent Challenges, which pose case problems for students to solve. The Visual Workshop that follows the Independent Challenges helps students to develop critical thinking skills. Students are shown a completed screen or document and are asked to recreate it from scratch.

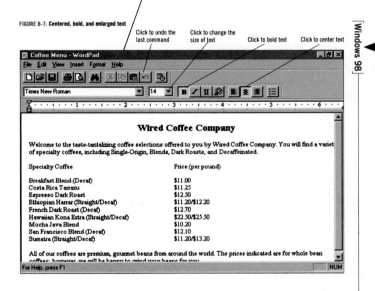

FIGURE B-7: Centered, bold, and enlarged text

Click to undo the last command
Click to change the size of text
Click to bold text
Click to center text

Windows 98

Coffee Menu - WordPad
File Edit View Insert Format Help

Times New Roman   14   B I U

Wired Coffee Company

Welcome to the taste-tantalizing coffee selections offered to you by Wired Coffee Company. You will find a variety of specialty coffees, including Single-Origin, Blends, Dark Roasts, and Decaffeinated.

Specialty Coffee   Price (per pound)

Breakfast Blend (Decaf) $11.00
Costa Rica Tarrazu $11.25
Espresso Dark Roast $12.50
Ethiopian Harrar (Straight/Decaf) $11.20/$12.20
French Dark Roast (Decaf) $12.70
Hawaiian Kona Extra (Straight/Decaf) $22.50/$25.50
Mocha Java Blend $10.20
San Francisco Blend (Decaf) $12.10
Sumatra (Straight/Decaf) $11.20/$13.20

All of our coffees are premium, gourmet beans from around the world. The prices indicated are for whole bean coffees; however, we will be happy to grind your beans for you.

For Help, press F1   NUM

CLUES TO USE

Formatting text as you type

As you've learned in the Steps, one way to format text is to select it, and then apply a change of format. Another way is to first select the formatting you want, and then enter text. This approach is helpful when you are starting a new document and are familiar with the effect that different formatting options create. For example, if you were creating a new list of items and knew that you wanted the title to be 24-point, underlined text, you would click the Underline button [U] on the format bar, and then select 24 from the Font Size list box. Anything that you type from that point will have those format characteristics. When you finish typing the title, you can change the font back to a smaller point size and click the Underline button to toggle the option off, then continue typing.

WORKING WITH WINDOWS PROGRAMS WIN B-9 ◀

Clues to Use Boxes provide concise information that either expands on the major lesson skill or describes an independent task that in some way relates to the major lesson skill.

The page numbers are designed like a road map. WIN indicates that it's a Windows unit, B indicates Unit B, and 9 indicates the page within the unit. This map allows for the greatest flexibility in content — each unit stands completely on its own.

Instructor's Resource Kit

The Instructor's Resource Kit is Course Technology's way of putting the resources and information needed to teach and learn effectively into your hands. With an integrated array of teaching and learning tools that offer you and your students a broad range of technology-based instructional options, we believe this kit represents the highest quality and most cutting edge resources available to instructors today. Many of these resources are available at www.course.com. The resources available with this book are:

Course Test Manager Designed by Course Technology, this cutting-edge Windows-based testing software helps instructors design, administer, and print tests and pre-tests. A full-featured program, Course Test Manager also has an online testing component that allows students to take tests at the computer and have their exams automatically graded.

Instructor's Manual Quality assurance tested and includes:
•Solutions to all lessons and end-of-unit material
•Detailed lecture topics for each unit with teaching tips
•Information for each unit about the differences between Windows 95 and Windows 98
•Extra Independent Challenges
•Task References
•Transparency Masters

WWW.COURSE.COM We encourage students and instructors to visit our Web site at www.course.com to find articles about current teaching and software trends, featured texts, interviews with authors, demos of Course Technology's software, Frequently Asked Questions about our products, and much more. This site is also where you can gain access to the Faculty Online Companion for this text — see below for more information.

Course Faculty Online Companion Available at www.course.com, this World Wide Web site offers Course Technology customers a password-protected Faculty Lounge where you can find everything you need to prepare for class including the Instructor's Manual in an electronic Portable Document Format (PDF) file and Adobe Acrobat Reader software. Periodically updated items include any updates and revisions to the text and Instructor's Manual, links to other Web sites, and access to student files, X-tra files, and solution files. This site will continue to evolve throughout the semester. Contact your Customer Service Representative for the site address and password.

Student Files To use this book students must have the Student Files. See the inside front or inside back cover for more information on the Student Files. Adopters of this text are granted the right to post the Student Files on any stand-alone computer or network.

X-tra files Now it's even easier to teach the skills **you** want to teach! Every two-page spread requiring a student file now includes a student file **or** an X-tra file. A student file is a file you open at the beginning of the unit and use to work through all, or a group of the lessons in that unit. An X-tra file is a student file in the exact format needed to work through that one particular lesson. X-tra files are not available for lessons in which student files are not needed, or in which a student file is explicitly opened as part of the lesson steps.

The filename of each X-tra file is the page number for the lesson with an "X" in front of it. For instance, the X-tra file for the lesson on page WIN B-6 is **XWIN B-6**. As the name implies, these files are "extra" and you can choose whether or not to make them available to your students. The X-tra files for this book are provided separately from the student files in the Instructor's Resource Kit and on the Faculty Online Companion.

Brief Contents

Contents

 ► [Windows 98]

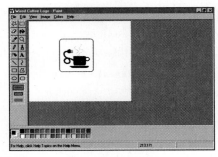

Contents

Managing Folders and Files Using Windows Explorer

Customizing Windows 98 Using the Control Panel

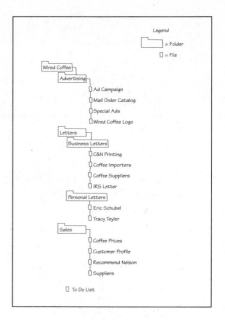

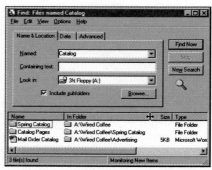

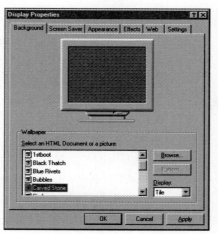

Exploring the Internet with Microsoft Internet Explorer

Exchanging Mail and News

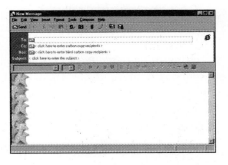

Managing Shared Files Using Network Neighborhood

Contents

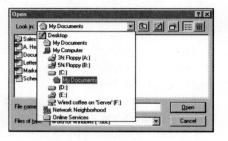

Creating a Web Page with FrontPage Express   WIN I-1

Creating a Docucentric Desktop   WIN J-1

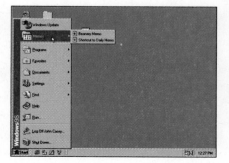

Contents

Backing Up Your Disk   WIN N-1

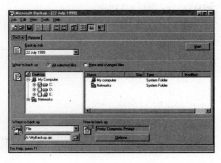

Exploring Windows 98
Communication Features   WIN O-1

Getting
Started with Windows 98

Objectives

- ► **Start Windows and view the Windows Active Desktop**
- ► **Use the mouse**
- ► **Get started with the Windows desktop**
- ► **Move and resize windows**
- ► **Use menus and toolbars**
- ► **Use scroll bars**
- ► **Use dialog boxes**
- ► **Use Windows Help**
- ► **Shut down Windows**

Microsoft Windows 98 is an **operating system**, a computer program that controls the basic operation of your computer and the programs you run on it. **Programs**, also known as **applications**, are task-oriented software you use to accomplish specific tasks, such as word processing, managing files on your computer, and performing calculations. When you work with Windows 98, you will notice many **icons**, small pictures on your screen intended to be meaningful symbols of the items they represent. You will also notice **windows** (thus the name of the operating system), rectangular frames on your screen that can contain several icons, the contents of a file, or other usable data. A **file** is an electronic collection of information, such as a resume or a database of addresses. This use of icons and windows is called a **graphical user interface** (**GUI**, pronounced "gooey"), meaning that you interact ("interface") with the computer through the use of graphics: icons and other meaningful words, symbols, and windows. This unit introduces you to basic Windows skills.

Starting Windows and Viewing the Windows Active Desktop

When you first start Windows, you see the Windows Active Desktop. The **Active Desktop** is an on-screen version of a regular desk, containing all the information and tools you need to accomplish your tasks. From the desktop, you can access, store, share, and explore information in a seamless manner, whether it resides on your computer, a network, or the Internet. (The **Internet** is a worldwide collection of over 40 million computers linked together to share information.) The desktop is called "active" because (unlike other Windows desktops) it allows you to access the Internet and view Internet content directly from it. Figure A-1 shows what the desktop looks like when you start Windows 98 for the first time. The bar at the bottom of your screen is called the **taskbar**, which allows you to start programs and switch among currently running programs. (At the moment, none are running.) At the left end of the taskbar is the **Start button**, which you use to start programs, find and open files, access Windows Help, and so on. Next to the Start button on the taskbar is the **Quick Launch toolbar**, which contains buttons you use to quickly start Internet related programs and show the desktop. The bar on the right side of your screen is called the **Channel Bar**, which shows buttons you use to access the Internet and view channels (like those on television) that display Internet content. Use Table A-1 to identify the icons and other elements you see on your desktop. Windows 98 automatically starts when you turn on your computer. If Windows is not currently running, follow the steps below to start it now.

1. **Turn on your computer**
   Windows automatically starts, and the desktop appears, as shown in Figure A-1. If you are working on a network at school or at an office, you might see a network password dialog box. If so, continue to Step 2. If not, continue to the next lesson.

2. **Type your password in the Password box**
   When you enter a valid password, you are given privileges to use the network.

3. **Click OK**
   Once the password is accepted, the Windows desktop appears on your screen, as shown in Figure A-1.

Trouble?

If you don't know your password, ask your instructor or technical support person for assistance.

FIGURE A-1: Windows Active Desktop

Icons

Start button

Channel Bar

Active Desktop

Quick Launch toolbar

Taskbar

Mouse pointer

TABLE A-1: Elements of the Windows Active Desktop

desktop element	allows you to
My Computer	Work with different disk drives and printers on your computer system
Network Neighborhood	Work with different disk drives and printers on a network
Outlook Express	Start Outlook Express, an electronic mail program
Connect to the Internet	Create a connection to the Internet using a phone or network
Recycle Bin	Delete and restore files
Internet Explorer	Start Internet Explorer, a program you use to access the Internet
My Documents folder	Store programs, documents, graphics, or other files
Online Services folder	Store programs to access online services such as CompuServe, America Online, and Prodigy
Upgrade The Microsoft Network	Start setup program for The Microsoft Network, an online service
Taskbar	Start programs and switch among open programs
Start button	Start programs, open documents, find a file, and more
Channel Bar	Start Internet Explorer and open channels
Quick Launch toolbar	Start Internet Explorer, start Outlook Express, show the desktop, and view channels

Use the Mouse

A **mouse** is a handheld input device you roll across a flat surface (such as a desk or a mousepad) to position the **mouse pointer**, the small symbol that indicates the pointer's relative position on the desktop. When you move the mouse, the mouse pointer on the screen moves in the same direction. The shape of the mouse pointer changes to indicate different activities. Table A-2 shows some common mouse pointer shapes. Once you move the mouse pointer to a desired position on the screen, you use the **mouse buttons**, shown in Figure A-2, to "tell" your computer what you want it to do. Table A-3 describes the basic mouse techniques you'll use frequently when working in Windows. 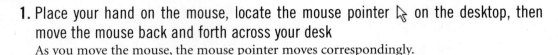 Try using the mouse now to become familiar with these navigational skills.

1. Place your hand on the mouse, locate the mouse pointer ⍅ on the desktop, then move the mouse back and forth across your desk
   As you move the mouse, the mouse pointer moves correspondingly.

QuickTip

This book assumes you are using Windows 98 default mouse settings.

2. Move the mouse to position the mouse pointer over the **My Computer icon** in the upper-left corner of the desktop
   Positioning the mouse pointer over an icon or over any specific item on the screen is called **pointing**.

3. Press and release the **left mouse button**
   The act of pressing a mouse button once and releasing it is called **clicking**. The icon is now highlighted, or shaded differently than the other icons on the desktop. The act of clicking an item, such as an icon, indicates that you have **selected** it to perform some future operation on it. To perform any type of operation on an icon (such as moving it), you must first select it. Now try a skill called **dragging**, which you use to move icons and other Windows elements.

4. Point to the **My Computer icon**, press and hold down the **left mouse button**, move the mouse down and to the right, then release the mouse button
   The icon moves with the mouse pointer. This is called dragging. Next you will use the mouse to display a shortcut menu.

5. Point to the **My Computer icon**, then press and release the **right mouse button**
   Clicking the right mouse button is known as **right-clicking**. Right-clicking an item on the desktop displays a **pop-up menu**, shown in Figure A-3. This menu displays the commands most commonly used for the item you have clicked; the available commands are not therefore the same for every item.

QuickTip

When a step tells you to "click," it means, by default, to left-click. The direction will say "right-click" if you are to click with the right mouse button.

6. Click anywhere outside the menu to close the pop-up menu

7. Move the **My Computer icon** back to its original position in the upper-left corner of the desktop using the pointing and dragging skills you have just learned

8. Point to the **My Computer icon**, then click the **left mouse button** twice quickly
   The My Computer window opens, containing several icons. Clicking the mouse button twice is known as **double-clicking**, and it allows you to open a window, program, or file that an icon represents. Leave the desktop as it is, and move on to the next lesson.

FIGURE A-2: The mouse

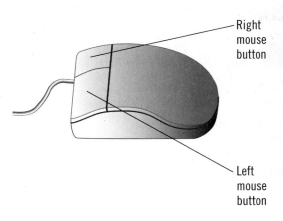

Right
mouse
button

Left
mouse
button

FIGURE A-3: Displaying a pop-up menu

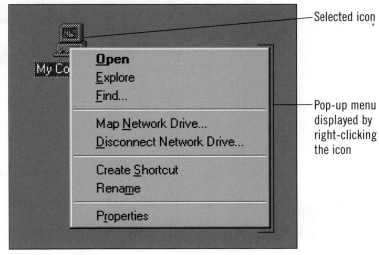

Selected icon

Pop-up menu
displayed by
right-clicking
the icon

TABLE A-2: Common mouse pointer shapes

shape	used to
⬉	Select items, choose commands, start programs, and work in programs
I	Position mouse pointer for editing or inserting text; called the insertion point or cursor
⬉⧗	Indicate Windows is busy processing a command
↔	Position mouse pointer on the border of a window for changing the size of a window
🖑	Position mouse pointer for selecting and opening Web-based content

TABLE A-3: Basic mouse techniques

task	what to do
Pointing	Move the mouse to position it over an item on the desktop
Clicking	Press and release the left mouse button
Double-clicking	Press and release the left mouse button twice quickly
Dragging	Point to an item, press and hold the left mouse button, move the mouse to a new location, then release the mouse button
Right-clicking	Point to an item, then press and release the right mouse button

CLUES TO USE

Using the mouse with the Internet

When you use the standard Windows operating system, you click an item to select it and double-click the item to open it. However, when you use the Internet, you point to an item to select it and single-click the item to open it. Because Windows 98 integrates use of the Internet with its other functions, it allows you to choose whether you want to extend the way you click on the Internet to the rest of your computer work. Therefore,

Windows 98 gives you two choices for selecting and opening icons using the mouse buttons: single-click (known as the Internet or Web style) or double-click (known as the Classic style). To change from one style to the other, click the Start button on the taskbar, point to Settings, click Folder Options, then click the Web style, Classic style, or Custom option. Windows 98 is set by default to double-click using custom settings.

Getting Started with the Windows Desktop

The key to getting started with the Windows desktop is learning how to use the Start button on the taskbar. Clicking the Start button on the taskbar displays the **Start menu**, which is a list of commands that allows you to start a program, open a document, change a Windows setting, find a file, or display Help information. Table A-4 describes the available commands on this menu that are installed with Windows 98. As you become more familiar with Windows you might want to customize the Start menu to include additional items that you use most often and change Windows settings in the Control Panel to customize your Windows desktop. Begin by viewing the Start menu and opening the **Control Panel**, a window containing various programs that allow you to specify how your computer looks and performs.

1. Click the Start button on the taskbar

The Start menu opens. You use the Settings command on the Start menu to change a Windows system setting.

2. Point to Settings on the Start menu

An arrow next to a menu indicates a **cascading menu**, or a **submenu**—a list of commands for the menu item with the arrow next to it. Pointing at the arrow displays a submenu from which you can choose additional commands. The Settings submenu opens, shown in Figure A-4, listing commands to open the Control Panel and Printers; change settings for the taskbar, Start menu, folders, and icons; and customize the Windows desktop.

3. Click Control Panel on the submenu

The Control Panel opens, shown in Figure A-5, containing icons for various programs that allow you to specify how your computer looks and performs. Leave the Control Panel open for now, and continue to the next lesson.

TABLE A-4: Start menu commands

command	description
Windows Update	Connects to a Microsoft Web site and updates your Windows 98 files as necessary
Programs	Opens programs included on the Start menu
Favorites	Connects to favorite Web sites, or opens folders or documents that you previously selected
Documents	Opens a list of documents most recently opened and saved
Settings	Allows user preferences for system settings, including Control Panel, printers, taskbar, Start menu, folders, icons, and Active Desktop
Find	Locates programs, files, folders, or computers on your computer network, or finds information or people on the Internet
Help	Displays Windows Help information by topic, alphabetical index, or search criteria
Run	Opens a program or file based on a location and filename that you type or select
Log Off	Allows you to log off the system and log on as a different user
Shut Down	Provides options to shut down the computer, restart the computer in Windows mode, or restart the computer in MS-DOS mode

FIGURE A-4: Cascading menu

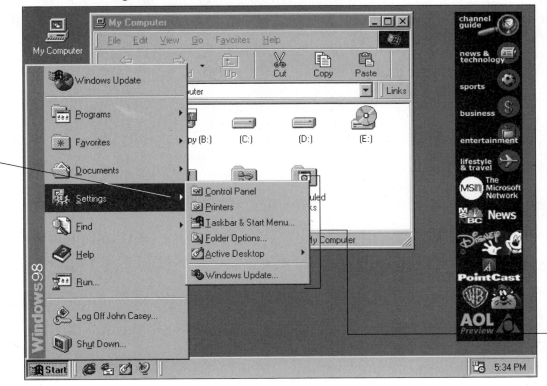

Arrow indicates submenu

Cascading menu, also called submenu

FIGURE A-5: Control Panel

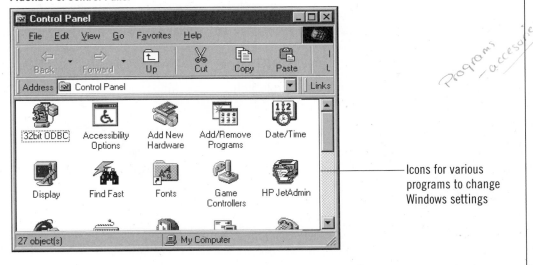

Icons for various programs to change Windows settings

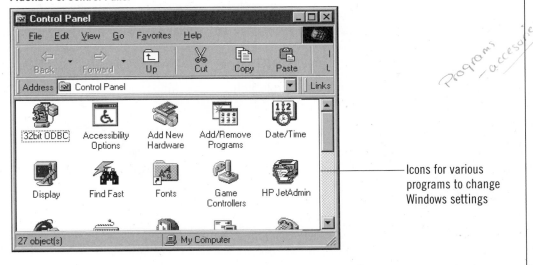

CLUES TO USE

Accessing the Internet from the Active Desktop

One of the important differences between Windows 98 and other versions of Windows is that Windows 98 allows you to access the Internet right from the desktop. This is possible because a program called Internet Explorer is integrated into the Windows 98 operating system. **Internet Explorer** is an example of a **browser**, a computer program designed to access the Internet. For example, commands on the Find submenu, On the

Internet and People, and the Favorites command on the Start menu make it easy to find and access places on the Internet you visit frequently. For additional Internet access, you can use the Quick Launch toolbar on the taskbar to launch Internet-related programs, and the Channel Bar is available on the desktop to help you view channels. Windows 98 makes it easier than ever to access the Internet.

Windows 98

Moving and Resizing Windows

One of the powerful things about the Windows operating system is that you can open more than one window or program at once. This means, however, that the desktop can get cluttered with many open windows for the various windows and programs you are using. To organize your desktop, sometimes it is necessary to change the size of a window or move it to a different location. Each window, no matter what it contains, is surrounded by a standard border that you can drag to move the window or change its size. Each window also has three standard buttons in the upper-right corner that allow you to change the size of windows. Table A-5 shows the different mouse pointer shapes that appear when resizing windows. Try moving and resizing the Control Panel window now.

1. **Click anywhere in the My Computer window or click the My Computer button on the taskbar**
   The My Computer window moves in front of the Control Panel window. The My Computer window is now **active**; this means that any actions you perform will take place in this window. At times, you might want to hide a window so that it isn't visible on the desktop but is still open.

QuickTip

You can click the Show the Desktop button on the Quick Launch toolbar to minimize all open windows and programs in order to show the desktop.

2. **Click the Minimize button** in the My Computer window
   The window no longer appears on the desktop, but you can still see a button named My Computer on the taskbar. When you **minimize** a window, you do not close it but merely reduce it to a button on the taskbar so that you can work more easily in other windows. The button on the taskbar reminds you that the program is still running.

3. **Point to the title bar on the Control Panel**
   The **title bar** is the area along the top of the window that contains the name of the file and the program used to create it. When a window is active, the title bar color changes from gray to blue. You can move any window to a new location on the desktop by dragging the window's title bar.

4. **With the mouse pointer over any spot on the title bar, click and drag the window to center it on the desktop**
   This action is similar to dragging an icon to a new location. The window is relocated.

5. **Click the Maximize button** in the Control Panel
   When you **maximize** a window, it takes up the entire screen.

6. **Click the Restore button** in the Control Panel
   The **Restore button** returns a window to its previous size, as shown in Figure A-6. The Restore button only appears when a window is maximized. Now try making the window smaller.

QuickTip

You can resize windows by dragging any corner, not just the lower left. You can also drag any border to make the window taller, shorter, wider, or narrower.

7. **Position the mouse pointer on the lower-right corner of the Control Panel window until the pointer changes to ⬉, as indicated in Figure A-6, then drag the corner up and to the left**
   The window is now resized. In the next lesson you will work with the menus and toolbars in the Control Panel, so you can close My Computer now.

8. **Click the My Computer button on the taskbar**
   The My Computer window is returned to the size it was before it was minimized and is now active. When you are finished using a window, you can close it with the Close button.

9. **Click the Close button** ☒, located in the upper-right corner of the My Computer window
   The My Computer window closes. You will learn more about My Computer in later lessons.

FIGURE A-6: **Restored Control Panel window**

Title bar   Active window   Sizing buttons

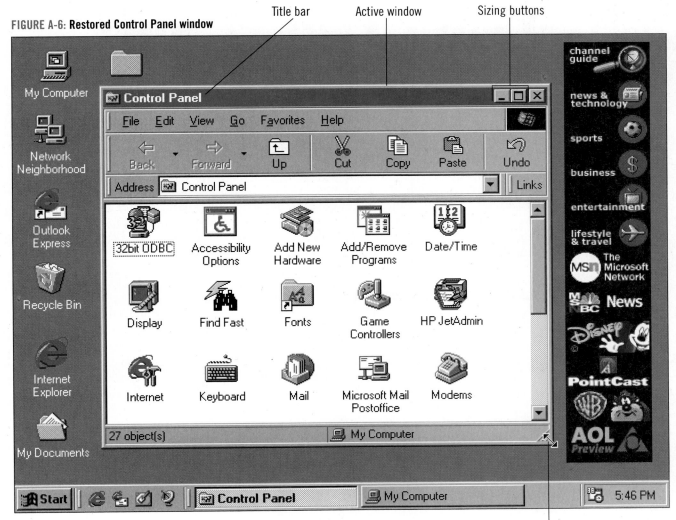

Drag here to size
both height and
width

TABLE A-5: **Mouse pointer shapes that appear when resizing windows**

mouse pointer shape	use to
↔	Drag the right or left edge of a window to change its width
↕	Drag the top or bottom edge of a window to change its height
↖ or ↗	Drag any corner of a window to change its size proportionally

Moving and resizing the taskbar

In addition to windows, you can also resize and move other elements on the desktop, such as the taskbar, using the methods in this lesson. You can move the taskbar by dragging it to any edge (right, left, top, or bottom) of the desktop. You can also change the size of the taskbar by dragging its edge.

Using Menus and Toolbars

A **menu** is a list of commands that you use to accomplish certain tasks. You've already used the Start menu to open the Control Panel. A **command** is a directive that provides access to a program's feature. Each Windows program also has its own set of menus, which are located on the menu bar along the top of the program window. The **menu bar** organizes commands into groups of related operations. Each group is listed under the name of the menu, such as "File" or "Help." To access the commands in a menu, you click the name of the menu. See Table A-6 for examples of items on a typical menu. Some of the most frequently used commands on a menu can also be carried out by clicking a button on a toolbar. A **toolbar** contains buttons that are convenient shortcuts for menu commands. Use a menu and toolbar button to change how the Control Panel window's contents are displayed.

Steps

1. Click **View** on the menu bar

The View menu appears, displaying the View commands, as shown in Figure A-7. When you click a menu name, a general description of the commands available on that menu appears in the status bar. On a menu, a **check mark** identifies a feature that is currently selected (that is, the feature is enabled or "on"). To disable ("turn off") the feature, you click the command again to remove the check mark. A **bullet mark** also indicates that an option is enabled. To disable a command with a bullet mark next to it, however, you must select another command (within the menu section) in its place. In the next step, you will select a command.

2. On the View menu, click **Small Icons**

The icons are now smaller that they were before, taking up less room in the window. Since the Control Panel window has been resized, the toolbar buttons across the top do not fit in the window. To display all the buttons, you can maximize the Control Panel window or reduce the size of the toolbar buttons. To reduce the size of the toolbar buttons, you remove the text labels at the bottom of the buttons.

3. Click **View** on the menu bar, then point to **Toolbars**

The Toolbars submenu appears, displaying check marks next to the toolbar commands. To remove the text labels on the toolbar buttons, you click Text Labels to turn the feature off.

4. Click **Text Labels**

The Control Panel toolbar appears without text labels below the menu bar. This toolbar includes buttons for the commands that you use most frequently while you are in the Control Panel. When you position the mouse pointer over a button, the name of the button, known as a **ScreenTip**, appears. Use the ScreenTip feature to explore a button on the toolbar.

5. On the Control Panel toolbar, position the pointer over the **Views button** ▦ to display the ScreenTip

Some toolbar buttons appear with an arrow, which indicates the button contains several choices. You click the button arrow to display the choices.

6. On the Control Panel toolbar, click the **Views button list arrow** ▦▾ as shown in Figure A-8, then click **Details**

The Details view includes a description of each Control Panel program. In the next lesson you will use scroll bars in the Control Panel to view and read the description of each Control Panel program.

FIGURE A-7: View menu in the Control Panel

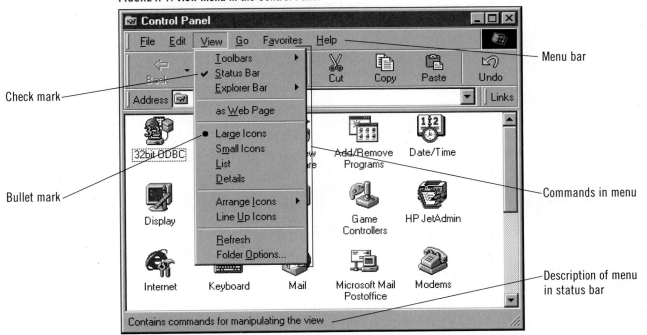

Check mark

Bullet mark

Menu bar

Commands in menu

Description of menu in status bar

FIGURE A-8: Control Panel toolbars

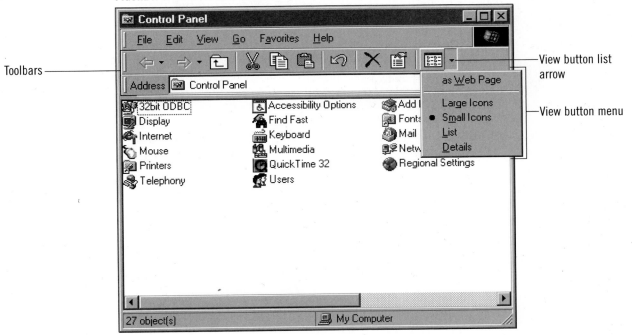

Toolbars

View button list arrow

View button menu

TABLE A-6: Typical items on a menu

item	description	example
Dimmed command	A menu command that is not currently available	Undo Ctrl+Z
Ellipsis	Indicates that a dialog box will open that allows you to select from several options	Save As...
Triangle	Indicates that a cascading menu will open containing an additional list of commands	Zoom ▶
Keyboard shortcut	An alternative to using the mouse for executing a command	Paste Ctrl+V
Underlined letter	Indicates the letter to press while holding down the [Alt] key for a keyboard shortcut	Print Preview

Using Scroll Bars

When you cannot see all of the items available in a window, scroll bars appear on the right and/or bottom edges of the window. **Scroll bars** allow you to display the additional contents of the window. See Figure A-9 for the components of the scroll bars. The vertical scroll bar moves your view up and down through a window; the horizontal scroll bar moves your view from left to right. There are several ways you can use the scroll bars. When you need to scroll only a short distance, you can use the scroll arrows. When you need to scroll more quickly, you can click in the scroll bar above or below the **scroll box**, which moves the view up or down one window's height (the line that was at the bottom of the screen is moved to the top, and vice versa). Dragging the scroll box moves you even more quickly to a new part of the window. See Table A-7 for a summary of the different ways to use scroll bars. ▸ You can use the scroll bars to view and read the description of each Control Panel program.

1. In the Control Panel, click the **down scroll arrow** in the vertical scroll bar, as shown in Figure A-9

   Clicking this arrow moves the view down one line. Clicking the up arrow moves the view up one line at a time.

2. Click the **up scroll arrow** in the vertical scroll bar

   The view moves up one line.

3. Click anywhere in the area below the scroll box in the vertical scroll bar

   The contents in the window scroll down in a larger increment.

4. Click the area above the scroll box in the vertical scroll bar

   The contents in the window scroll back up. To move in even greater increments, you can drag the scroll box to a new position.

5. Drag the **scroll box** in the horizontal scroll bar to the middle of the bar

   The scroll box indicates your relative position within the window, in this case, the halfway point. After reading the Control Panel program descriptions, you restore the Control Panel to its original display.

6. On the Control Panel toolbar, click the **Views button list arrow** ⊞▾ , then click **Large Icons**

7. Click **View** on the menu bar, point to **Toolbars**, then click **Text Labels**

   In the next lesson you will open a Control Panel program to learn how to work with dialog boxes.

FIGURE A-9: Scroll bars in Control Panel

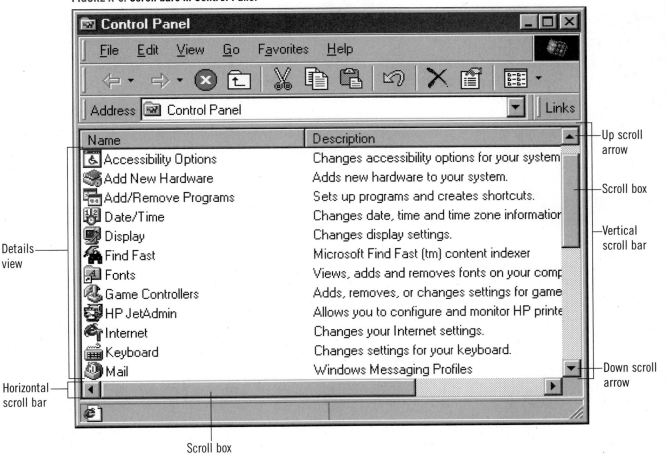

Details view

Horizontal scroll bar

Up scroll arrow

Scroll box

Vertical scroll bar

Down scroll arrow

Scroll box

TABLE A-7: Using scroll bars in a window

to	do this
Move down one line	Click the down arrow at the bottom of the vertical scroll bar
Move up one line	Click the up arrow at the top of the vertical scroll bar
Move down one window's height	Click in the area below the scroll box in the vertical scroll bar
Move up one window's height	Click in the area above the scroll box in the vertical scroll bar
Move up or down a greater distance in the window	Drag the scroll box in the vertical scroll bar
Move a short distance side to side in a window	Click the left or right arrows in the horizontal scroll bar
Move to the right one window's width	Click in the area to the right of the scroll box in the horizontal scroll bar
Move to the left one window's width	Click in the area to the left of the scroll box in the horizontal scroll bar
Move left or right a greater distance in the window	Drag the scroll box in the horizontal scroll bar

Using Dialog Boxes

A **dialog box** is a window that opens when you choose a command from a menu that is followed by an ellipsis (. . .). The ellipsis indicates that more information is required before the program can carry out the command you selected. Dialog boxes open in other situations as well, such as when you open a program in the Control Panel. In a dialog box, you specify the options you want using a variety of elements. See Figure A-10 and Table A-8 for some of the typical elements of a dialog box. ◢▬▬ Practice using a dialog box to control your mouse settings.

Steps

1. **In the Control Panel, double-click the Mouse icon** 🖱 **Mouse (you might need to scroll down the Control Panel window to find this icon)**
   The Mouse Properties dialog box opens, shown in Figure A-11. The options in this dialog box allow you to control the way the mouse buttons are configured, select the types of pointers that are displayed, choose the speed of the mouse movement on the screen, and specify what type of mouse you are using. **Tabs** at the top of the dialog box separate these options into related categories.

2. **Click the Motion tab**
   This tab has two boxes. The first, labeled Pointer speed, has a slider for you to set how fast the mouse pointer moves on the screen in relation to how you move the mouse in your hand. The second, Pointer trail, has a check box you can select to make the mouse pointer easier to see, especially on certain types of computer screens, such as laptop computers. The slider lets you specify the degree to which the option is in effect—the length of the pointer trail. You will experiment with the pointer trail options.

3. **In the Pointer trail box, click the Show pointer trails check box to select it, then drag the slider below the check box all the way to the right**
   As you move the mouse, notice the long pointer trails.

4. **Click the other tabs in the Mouse Properties dialog box and examine the options that are available in each category**
   Now, you need to select a command button to carry out the options you've selected. The two most common command buttons are OK and Cancel. Clicking OK accepts your changes and closes the dialog box; clicking Cancel leaves the original settings intact and closes the dialog box. The third command button in this dialog box is Apply. Clicking the Apply button accepts the changes you've made and keeps the dialog box open so that you can select additional options. Because you might share this computer with others, it's important to return the dialog box options back to the original settings.

5. **Click Cancel to leave the original settings intact and close the dialog box**

6. **Click the Close button in the upper-right corner of the Control Panel**

FIGURE A-10: Dialog box elements

List box —   List arrow

Option button —

Text box —

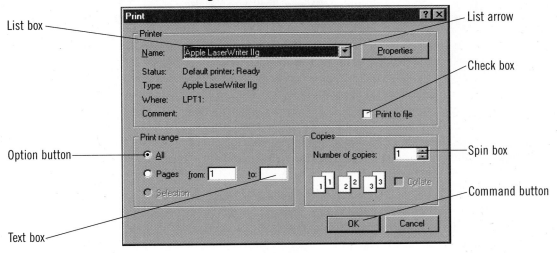

Check box

Spin box

Command button

FIGURE A-11: Mouse Properties dialog box

Tabs —

Button configuration section —

Slider

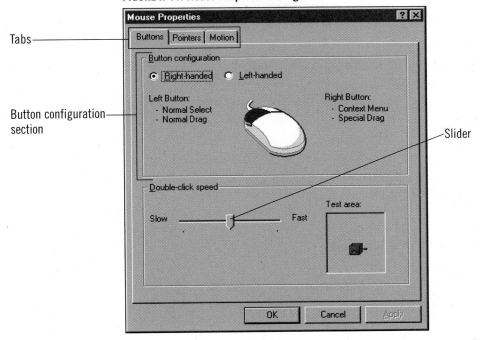

TABLE A-8: Typical items in a dialog box

item	description
Check box	A square box that turns an option on (when the box is checked) and off (when the box is blank)
Command button	A rectangular button with the name of the command on it; it carries out a command in a dialog box
List box	A box containing a list of items; to choose an item, click the list arrow, then click the desired item
Option button	A small circle that selects a single dialog box option; you cannot check more than one option button in a list
Spin box	A box with two arrows and a text box; allows you to scroll numerical increments or type a number
Slider	A shape that you drag to set the degree to which an option is in effect
Tab	A place to organize related options
Text box	A box in which you type text

Windows 98

Using Windows Help

When you have a question about how to do something in Windows 98, you can usually find the answer with a few clicks of your mouse. There are a variety of different ways to access **Windows Help**, which is like a book stored on your computer, complete with an index and a table of contents to make finding information easier. You can click Help on the Start menu to open the main Windows Help dialog box. To get help on a specific program, you can click Help on the program's menu bar. You can also access **context-sensitive help**, help specifically related to what you are doing, using a variety of methods such as pointing to or right-clicking an object. ✎ Use Help to find out about the Control Panel that comes with Windows.

Steps

1. **Click the Start button on the taskbar, then click Help**
   The main Help command is located on the Start menu. While there are other ways to get help, this is the easiest way to access the list of all Help topics that are available. The Windows Help dialog box opens, shown in Figure A-12, with the Contents tab in front. The Contents tab provides you with a list of Help categories. Each book icon has several "chapters" (subcategories) that you can see by clicking the book icon or the name of the Help category next to the book.

2. **Click the Contents tab (if necessary), point to the Exploring Your Computer category, then click to display the subcategories underneath**
   When you point to a Help category, the mouse changes to the hand pointer and the Help category text is selected. The text changes to gray and is underlined. This is similar to the way selecting on the Internet works. You continue to click subcategories to find the Help topic you want.

3. **Click the The Windows Desktop subcategory, then click the Getting Started with Windows Desktop Update topic**
   The Help topic appears in the right pane, as shown in A-13. **Panes** divide a window into two or more sections. Read the help information on the Windows desktop. You can move back and forth between Help topics you have already visited by clicking the Back button and the Forward button on the Help toolbar.

4. **Click the Index tab**
   The Index tab provides you with an alphabetical list of all the Help topics that are available, much like an index at the end of a book. You can find out about any Windows feature by either entering the topic in the text box, or by scrolling down to the topic for which you want help, selecting a topic, and then clicking Display.

5. **Click the Search tab**
   The Search tab helps you locate the topic you need using keywords. You can find a topic by entering a keyword in the text box, clicking List Topics, selecting a topic, and then clicking Display. If you cannot find the information you need, you can look on the Internet, where Microsoft has updated information on Windows 98.

6. **Click the Web Help button 🖳 on the Help toolbar**
   Windows Update Web site information appears in the right pane. You can access the Windows Update Web site by clicking the "Support Online" underlined text. When you click the underlined text, you connect to the Windows Update Web site. The Web site provides links to Internet resources, including Online Help, Troubleshooting Wizards, the Microsoft Knowledge Base, the Microsoft Technical Support for Windows Home Page, and the Windows Update Manager. Once you've read the information, you can close the window.

7. **Click the Close button in the Windows Help window**
   The Help window closes.

QuickTip

You can hide the left pane of the Help window to make reading the information easier. Click the Hide button 🖳 on the Help toolbar to hide the left pane; click the Show button 🖳 to redisplay it.

QuickTip

To print all or part of the Windows Help information, click the Options button 🖳 on the Help toolbar, then click Print.

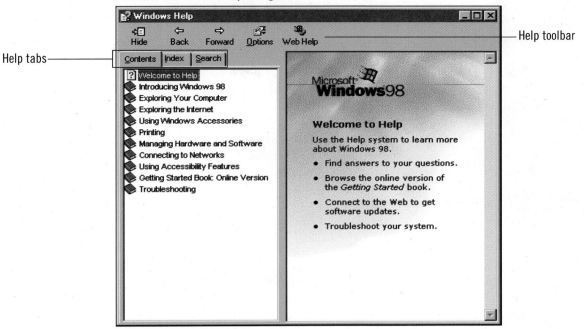

FIGURE A-12: Windows Help dialog box

Help tabs

Help toolbar

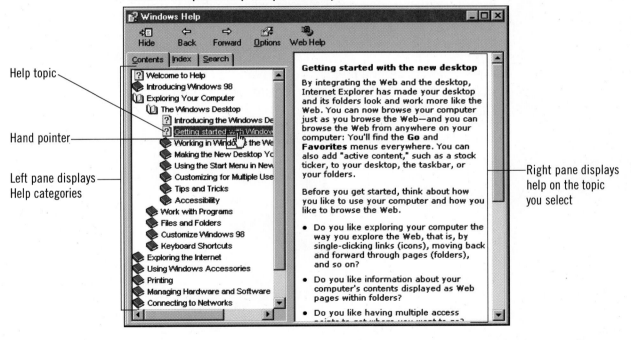

FIGURE A-13: Specific help on a particular topic

Help topic

Hand pointer

Left pane displays
Help categories

Right pane displays
help on the topic
you select

Context-sensitive help

To receive help in a dialog box, click the Help button ? in the upper-right corner of the dialog box; the mouse pointer changes to ?. Click on the item in the dialog box for which you need additional information. A pop-up window opens, providing a brief explanation of the selected feature. You can also click the right-mouse button on an item in a dialog box, then click the What's This? Button to display the explanation. In addition, when you click the right mouse button in a Help topic window, you can choose commands to annotate, copy, and print the contents of the topic. Help windows always appear on top of the currently active window, so you can see Help topics while you work.

Windows 98

Shutting Down Windows

When you are finished working at your computer, you need to make sure to **shut down**, or exit, the machine properly. This involves several steps: saving and closing all open files, closing all open windows, exiting all running programs, shutting down Windows itself, and, finally, turning off the computer. If you turn off the computer while Windows or other programs are running, you could lose important data. Once all files, windows and programs are closed, you choose the Shut Down command from the Start menu. The Shut Down Windows dialog box, shown in Figure A-14, opens with three options. See Table A-9 for a description of each option. ▰▰▰ Close all your open files, windows, and programs, and then exit Windows.

Steps 1 2 3 4

1. If you have any open windows or programs, click the **Close button** ☒ in the upper-right corner of the window
   Complete the remaining steps to shut down Windows and your computer only if you have been told to do so by your instructor.

2. Click the **Start button** on the taskbar, then click **Shut Down**
   The Shut Down Windows dialog box opens as shown in Figure A-14. In this dialog box, you have the option to shut down the computer, restart the computer in Windows mode, or restart the computer in MS-DOS mode. You choose the Shut Down option.

3. Click the **Shut Down option button**, if it isn't already selected

4. If you are working in a lab, click **Cancel** to return to the Windows desktop; if you are working on your own machine or if your instructor told you to shut down Windows, click **OK** to exit Windows

5. When you see the message "It's now safe to turn off your computer," turn off your computer and monitor

CLUES TO USE

Logging off Windows

For a quick change between users of the same computer, you can choose the Log Off command on the Start menu. This command identifies the name of the user who is currently logged on. When you choose this command, Windows 98 shuts down and automatically restarts to the Enter Network Password dialog box. When the new user enters a user name and password, Windows will provide access to network capabilities.

FIGURE A-14: Shut Down Windows dialog box

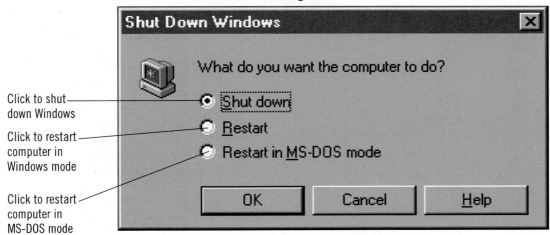

Click to shut down Windows

Click to restart computer in Windows mode

Click to restart computer in MS-DOS mode

TABLE A-9: Shut down options

shut down option	function	when to use it
Shut down	Prepares the computer to be turned off	When you are finished working with Windows and you want to shut off your computer
Restart	Restarts the computer and reloads Windows	When you want to restart the computer and begin working with Windows again; (your programs might have frozen or stopped working)
Restart in MS-DOS mode	Starts the computer in the MS-DOS mode	When you want to run programs under MS-DOS or use DOS commands to work with files

Practice

► Concepts Review

Label each of the elements of the screen shown in Figure A-15.

FIGURE A-15

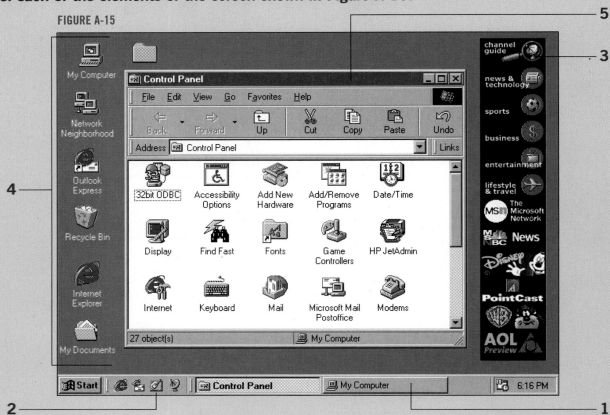

Match each of the terms with the statement that describes its function.

6. Allows for minimizing, maximizing, and restoring windows
7. The item you first click to start a program
8. Used to point at screen elements and make selections
9. Where the name of the program and file appear
10. Where deleted files are placed
11. Displays the Start button and buttons for currently open programs and windows

a. Recycle Bin
b. Sizing buttons
c. Start button
d. Taskbar
e. Title bar
f. Mouse

Select the best answer from the following list of choices.

12. The term for moving an item to a new location on the desktop is
    a. Pointing.
    b. Clicking.
    c. Dragging.
    d. Restoring.

13. **The Maximize button is used to**
    a. Return a window to its original size.
    b. Expand a window to fill the entire screen.
    c. Scroll slowly through a window.
    d. Reduce a window to a button on the taskbar.

14. **The Minimize button is used to**
    a. Return a window to its original size.
    b. Expand a window to fill the entire screen.
    c. Scroll slowly through a window.
    d. Reduce a window to a button on the taskbar.

15. **The Menu bar provides access to a program's functions through**
    a. Toolbar buttons.
    b. Scroll buttons.
    c. Commands.
    d. Dialog box elements.

16. **To move the contents of the window up one screen,**
    a. Click the up scroll arrow.
    b. Click the down scroll arrow.
    c. Click in the scroll bar above the scroll box.
    d. Click in the scroll bar below the scroll box.

17. **An ellipses after a menu command indicates**
    a. The menu command is not currently available.
    b. A dialog box will open.
    c. Another menu will display.
    d. A keyboard shortcut to that command.

18. **Which is not a method for getting Help?**
    a. Click the Start button on the taskbar, then click Help
    b. Click the question mark button in a dialog box
    c. Click Help on a program's menu bar
    d. Right-click in a dialog box, then use the Help pointer to point to what you need help with

▶ Skills Review

1. **Identify Windows items on the screen.**
    a. Identify and write down as many items on the desktop as you can, without referring to the lesson.
    b. Compare your results with Figure A-1.

2. **Practice using the mouse.**
    a. Move the mouse on your desk and watch how the mouse pointer moves across the screen.
    b. Point at the My Computer icon on the desktop.
    c. Click the My Computer icon once. Notice that the icon's title is highlighted.
    d. Press and hold down the mouse button, then drag the My Computer icon to the opposite side of the desktop. Release the mouse button when you are finished.
    e. Drag the My Computer icon back to the original location.
    f. Practice clicking and dragging other icons on the desktop.
    g. Double-click the My Computer icon.

3. **Get started with Windows.**
    a. Click the Start menu.
    b. Point to Settings.
    c. Click Control Panel.

4. **Move and resize windows.**
    a. Click the My Computer window.
    b. Click the Minimize button.
    c. Point to the title bar on the Control Panel window, then drag the window to the center of the desktop.
    d. Click the Maximize button.
    e. Click the Restore button.
    f. Position the mouse pointer on any corner of the Control Panel window, and drag to make the window smaller.
    g. Click the My Computer button on the taskbar.
    h. Click the Close button on the My Computer window.

5. **Practice working with menus and toolbars.**
    a. Click View on the menu bar, point to Toolbars, then click Text Labels.
    b. Click View on the menu bar, then click List.
    c. Click the Views button arrow on the toolbar, then click Details.

6. **Practice using scroll bars.**
    a. Click below the vertical scroll box.
    b. Click the vertical up scroll arrow.
    c. Drag the horizontal scroll box to the middle of the scroll bar.
    d. Click the View button arrow on the toolbar, then click Large Icons.
    e. Click View on the menu bar, point to Toolbars, then click Text Labels.

7. Practice using dialog boxes.

   a. Double-click the Display icon.

   b. Click the Appearance tab.

   c. Click the Scheme list arrow, then select a color scheme.

   d. Click Apply (but don't click OK yet).

   e. Click the Scheme list arrow, then click Windows Standard to return the color scheme back to the way it was.

   f. Click OK, then close the Control Panel.

8. Use Windows Help.

   a. Click the Start button, then click Help.

   b. Click the Index tab.

   c. Type "dialog boxes."

   d. Click Display.

   e. Select "To get help in a dialog box", then click Display again to see the topic.

   f. Read the Help topic in the right pane.

   g. Click the Close button.

9. Exit Windows.

   a. Click the Start button, then click Shut Down.

   b. Click the Restart option button.

   c. Click OK if you are not working in a lab or if your lab manager approves of shutting down the computer. Otherwise, click Cancel.

▶ Independent Challenges

1. Windows 98 provides extensive online help. At anytime, you can select Help from the Start menu and get the assistance you need. Use the Help options to learn about the topics listed below.

To complete this independent challenge:

1. Locate help on My Computer.
2. Locate help on adjusting the double-click speed of the mouse.
3. Locate help on changing the color of the desktop.
4. Locate help on changing the appearance of scroll bars.
5. Locate help on exiting programs.
6. If you have a printer connected to your computer, print one or more of the Help topics.
7. Close the Windows Help window.

2. You can customize many Windows features to suit your needs and preferences. One way you do this is to change the appearance of the taskbar on the desktop.

To complete this independent challenge:

1. Position the mouse pointer over the top border of the taskbar. When the pointer changes shape, drag upwards to increase the size of the taskbar.
2. Position the mouse pointer over a blank area of the taskbar, and then drag to the top of the screen to move the taskbar.
3. Click the Start button, point to Settings, and click Taskbar & Start menu. On the Taskbar Options tab, click the Show Clock check box to deselect the option, and then observe the effect on the taskbar.
4. Print the Screen (Press the Print Screen key to make a copy of the screen, open Paint, click Edit on the menu bar, click Paste to paste the screen into Paint, then click Yes to paste the large image, if necessary. Click File on the menu bar, click Print, then click OK.)
5. Restore the taskbar to its original setting, size, and location on the screen.

3. You have accepted a new job in New York City. After moving into your new home and unpacking your stuff, you decide to set up your computer. Once you set up and turn on the computer, you decide to change the date and time settings to reflect New York.

To complete this independent challenge:

1. Open the Control Panel window.
2. Double-click the Date/Time icon.
3. Click the Time Zone tab.
4. Select Eastern Time (US & Canada) from the list.
5. Click the Date & Time tab.
6. Change the month and year to September 1999, then click Apply.
7. Print the screen. (See Independent Challenge 1, Step 4 for screen printing instructions)
8. Return the date and time zone back to their original settings.
9. Click OK.
10. Close the Control Panel window.

4. You are a student in a Windows 98 course. After learning basic Windows 98 Active Desktop skills, you want to learn how to customize the desktop. Use the online version of the Getting Started Book in Windows Help to find information on customizing your desktop and then print the related Help topics.

To complete this independent challenge:

1. Open the Windows Help window.
2. Display Getting Started Book: Online Version.
3. Display Microsoft Windows 98 Getting Started.
4. Open Getting Started.
5. Display Customizing Your Desktop.
6. Display Choosing a Desktop Style.
7. Print the Overview.
8. Close the Windows Help window.

Working

with Windows Programs

Objectives

- ▶ **Start a program**
- ▶ **Open and save a WordPad document**
- ▶ **Edit text in WordPad**
- ▶ **Format text in WordPad**
- ▶ **Use Paint**
- ▶ **Copy data between programs**
- ▶ **Print a document**
- ▶ **Play a video clip**
- ▶ **Play a sound**

Now that you know how to work with common Windows graphical elements, you're ready to work with programs. Windows comes with several **Accessories**: built-in programs that, while not as feature-rich as many programs sold separately, are extremely useful for completing basic tasks. In this unit, you will work with some of these accessories. John Casey, the owner of Wired Coffee Company, will use several Accessories to prepare a coffee menu.

Starting a Program

A Windows program is software designed to run on computers using the Windows operating system. To start a program in Windows 98, you click the Start button, point to Programs to open the Programs submenu, point to a submenu (if necessary), and then click the program you want to start. ✎ In this lesson, you'll start a Windows Accessory called WordPad, a word processing program that comes with Windows. Throughout the rest of this unit, you'll work with WordPad and other Windows Accessories to learn essential Windows skills.

Steps

1. Click the Start button on the taskbar

The Start menu opens.

2. Point to Programs on the Start menu

The Programs submenu opens, listing the programs and submenus for programs installed on your computer. WordPad is in the submenu called Accessories.

3. Point to Accessories on the Programs submenu

The Accessories submenu opens, as shown in Figure B-1. Locate WordPad on this submenu.

4. Click WordPad on the Accessories submenu

Your mouse pointer will change momentarily to an hourglass, indicating that you are to wait while Windows starts the WordPad program. The WordPad window then appears on your desktop, as shown in Figure B-2. The WordPad window includes two toolbars, called the toolbar and format bar, as well as a ruler, a work area, and a status bar. A blinking cursor, known as the **insertion point**, appears in the work area of the WordPad window, indicating where new text will appear. The WordPad program button appears in the taskbar, indicating that the WordPad program is now running.

5. Click the Maximize button in the WordPad window

WordPad expands to fill the screen. In the next lesson you will open and save a document in WordPad.

FIGURE B-1: Starting WordPad using the Start menu

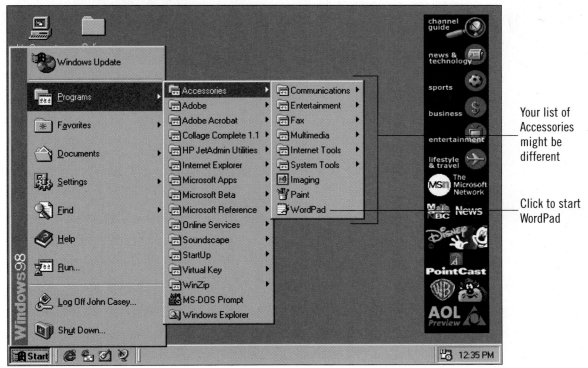

Your list of Accessories might be different

Click to start WordPad

FIGURE B-2: Windows desktop with the WordPad window open

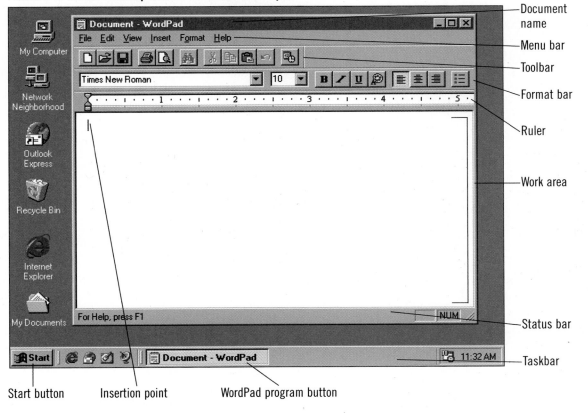

Document name

Menu bar

Toolbar

Format bar

Ruler

Work area

Status bar

Taskbar

Start button

Insertion point

WordPad program button

Windows 98

Opening and Saving a WordPad Document

A **document** is the result of your work using a word processing program. You can use WordPad to create documents such as letters, memos, and resumes. When you start WordPad, a blank document appears in the work area of the WordPad window, known as the **document window**. You can enter new information to create a new document and save the result as a file, or you can open an existing file and save the document with any changes you made. In this unit you will open a document that John created. To prevent any accidental changes to the original file, you will save it with a new name. This makes a copy of the document so you can make changes to the new document and leave the file John created unaltered. This way you can repeat a lesson. John wants to open an existing WordPad document (a coffee menu), make some changes, and then save the results.

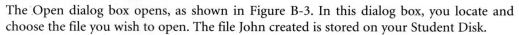

Steps

1. Insert your Student Disk into the appropriate drive, then click the **Open button** on the WordPad toolbar

   The Open dialog box opens, as shown in Figure B-3. In this dialog box, you locate and choose the file you wish to open. The file John created is stored on your Student Disk.

2. Click the **Look in list arrow**, then click the drive that contains your Student Disk

   A list of the files and folders stored on the Student Disk appears in the file list.

3. In the file list, click **Win B-1**, then click **Open**

   The file named Win B-1 opens. This is a menu for the coffee company. Save this file under a new name so you don't make any changes to the original file. You will use a more descriptive name for the file so you can identify its contents more easily.

4. Click **File** on the menu bar, then click **Save As**

   The Save As dialog box opens, as shown in Figure B-4. The Save As command allows you to save an existing document under a new name. Now specify a new name.

5. If Win B-1 is not already selected, click in the **File name text box**, then select the entire filename by dragging the mouse pointer over it

   In WordPad, as in most other Windows programs, you must select text before you can modify it. When you **select** text, the selection appears **highlighted** (white text on a black background) to indicate that it has been selected. Any action you now take will be performed on the selected text.

6. Type **Coffee Menu** to replace the selected text

   As soon as you start typing, the selected text is replaced by the text you are typing. John decides to store the Coffee Menu document on the Student Disk.

7. Click **Save**

   Once you click Save, the file is saved under the new name, Coffee Menu, which you should now see in the title bar of the WordPad window. The original file, called Win B-1, is automatically closed.

QuickTip

When an existing document is open, you can click the New button on the toolbar to create a blank new document. The original existing document is automatically closed.

FIGURE B-3: Open dialog box

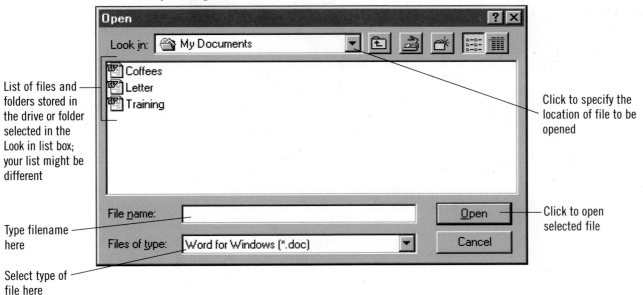

List of files and folders stored in the drive or folder selected in the Look in list box; your list might be different

Click to specify the location of file to be opened

Type filename here

Select type of file here

Click to open selected file

FIGURE B-4: Save As dialog box

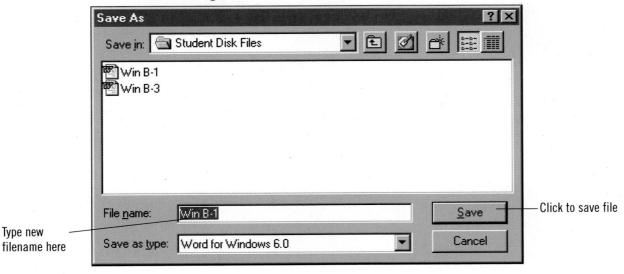

Type new filename here

Click to save file

CLUES TO USE

About saving files

Until you save them, the documents you create are stored in the computer's random access memory (RAM). **RAM** is a temporary storage space that is erased when the computer is turned off. To store a document permanently, you must save it as a file. A file is a collection of information that has a unique name, distinguishing it from other files. You can save files to a **floppy disk** that you insert into the disk drive of your computer (usually drive A: or B:) or a **hard disk**, which is built into the computer (usually drive C:). This book assumes that you will save all of your files to your Student Disk, which your instructor has provided to you. Windows 98 lets you save files using names that have up to 255 characters, including spaces.

Windows 98

Editing Text in WordPad

One of the major advantages of using a word processing program is that you can **edit**, or change, the contents of a document without having to retype it. You can also move whole sections of a document from one place to another using the Cut and Paste commands. ✎ John wants to add a greeting and change the price for a pound of coffee in the Coffee Menu document. He also wants to change the order of the menu items so that the coffees are listed in alphabetical order.

Steps 1 2 3 4

1. Press ↓ three times, or click I in the fourth line

Figure B-5 shows the insertion point in the location where you want to insert new text. Repositioning the insertion point in a document (called **navigating**) is an important skill to learn. In addition to the arrow keys, WordPad offers another set of keys and key combinations, as shown in Table B-1, that enable you to navigate a document quickly.

Trouble?

If you make a mistake while typing, press [Backspace] (which deletes the character to the left of the insertion point) until you have deleted your mistake, then retype the text.

2. Type **Welcome to the taste-tantalizing coffee selections offered to you by Wired Coffee Company. You will find a variety of specialty coffees, including Single-Origin, Blends, Dark Roasts, and Decaffeinated.**, then press **[Enter]**

WordPad automatically puts the text that won't fit on one line onto the next line, using a feature called **wordwrap**. Now John wants to change the price of the Breakfast Blend coffee from $11.90 to $11.00.

3. In the price of the Breakfast Blend coffee, click to the right of the last digit, **0**

This number needs to be changed from "11.90" to "11.00."

4. Press **[Backspace]** twice, then type **00**

Now John wants to rearrange the list so that the coffees are listed in alphabetical order. The fourth coffee in the list (Espresso Dark Roast) needs to be moved so it comes before the third (Ethiopian Harrar). To do this, John first has to select the name of the fourth coffee; only then he can move the text up the list. You can select text three different ways. You can drag the mouse to highlight the text you want to select. If you need to select just a word, you can double-click it. If you need to select a line or paragraph, you can position the pointer to the left of the first character in the line or paragraph, and then click once to select a line or twice to select an entire paragraph.

5. Position the pointer to the left of the first character in the line "Espresso Dark Roast"

The pointer changes from I to ⬈ .

QuickTip

To select the entire paragraph, you can triple-click anywhere in the paragraph.

6. Click once

The entire line is selected. Now John can move the line.

7. Click the **Cut button** ✂ on the toolbar

When selected text is **cut** from a document, Windows removes it from the document and places it on the **Clipboard**, a temporary storage place where it remains available to be pasted somewhere else. When text is **copied**, a copy of it is placed in the Clipboard to be pasted in another location, but the text also remains in its original place in the document.

8. Press ↑ once to move up one line in the list

This is where John wants to paste the line he cut.

9. Click the **Paste button** 📋 on the toolbar, then click the **Save button** 💾 on the toolbar

Figure B-6 shows the information pasted into the list with all the coffees in alphabetical order. The changes you made to the file are saved.

FIGURE B-5: Positioning the insertion point

Insertion point —

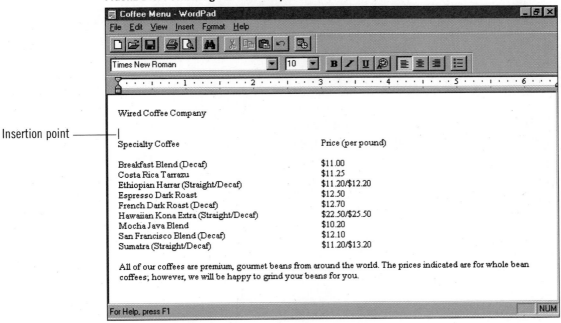

FIGURE B-6: Editing a WordPad file by cutting and pasting

Your lines may wrap differently

List is now in alphabetical order

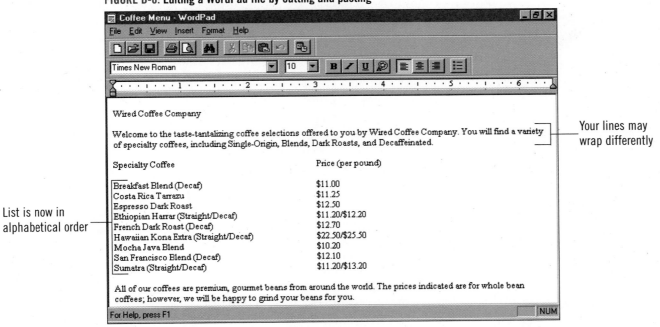

TABLE B-1: Keys to use to move around a WordPad document

key(s)	navigation	key(s)	navigation
↑	Move up one line	[PdDn]	Move to the next page
↓	Move down one line	[Ctrl][End]	Move to the end of the document
←	Move left one character	[Ctrl][Home]	Move to the beginning of the document
→	Move right one character	[Ctrl][→]	Move to the beginning of the next word to the right
[PgUp]	Move to the previous page	[Ctrl][←]	Move to the beginning of the previous word to the left

Formatting Text in WordPad

You can change the **format**, or the appearance, of the text and graphics in a document so that the document is easier to read or more attractive. Almost all formatting changes in WordPad can be achieved using the format bar, which appears below the toolbar in the WordPad window. Table B-2 describes the function of each button on the format bar. John wants to make the Coffee Menu document more attractive. He will do this by centering the title, bolding it, and increasing its size.

1. **Select the text Wired Coffee Company**
   Remember that the first step in making any editing change is to select the text you want to change. Then you can carry out the desired command.

2. **Click the Center button ▤ on the format bar**
   Notice that the title is centered and the button appears indented.

3. **Click the Bold button B on the format bar**
   The selected material appears in bold. If you wanted to turn bold off, you would click the button again. Buttons act as **toggle** switches—click once to turn the format feature on, click again to turn it off. Now John wants to italicize the title.

4. **Click the Italic button Ｚ on the format bar**
   Italicizing does not provide the effect that John had wanted, so he undoes this formatting change.

5. **Click the Undo button ↰ on the toolbar**
   This command reverses the last change that was made, such as typing new text, deleting text, and formatting text. Undo cannot reverse all commands (such as scrolling or saving a document), but it is a quick way to reverse most actions. John decides to change the size of the **font**, or typeface, to achieve the effect he wants in the title.

6. **Click the Font Size list arrow [10 ▾] on the format bar, then click 14**
   The selected text changes in size to 14 point. One **point** is 1/72 of an inch in height. Whenever you want to know the size of a font on your screen, place the insertion point anywhere in the text and look at the size that appears in the Font Size list box.

7. **Click anywhere in the document (except on the selected text) to deselect the text**
   Once text is selected, it can be deselected by clicking anywhere else in the document. As Figure B-7 shows, the title is centered, bold, and changed in size to 14 point.

8. **Click the Save button 🖫 on the toolbar**
   The changes made to the Coffee Menu file are saved.

TABLE B-2: Format bar buttons and list arrows

button or list arrow	function	button	function
Times New Roman ▾	Select a font	🖉	Add or change color
10 ▾	Select a font size	▤	Left align
B	Bold	▤	Center align
Ｚ	Italicize	▤	Right align
U	Underline	☰	Create bulleted list

FIGURE B-7: Centered, bold, and enlarged text

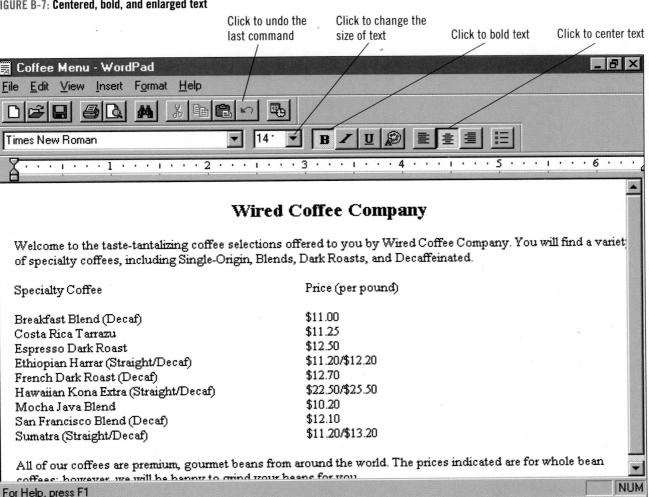

Formatting text as you type

As you've learned in the Steps, one way to format text is to select it, and then apply a change of format. Another way is to first select the formatting you want, and then enter text. This approach is helpful when you are starting a new document and are familiar with the effect that different formatting options create. For example, if you were creating a new list of items and knew that you wanted the title to be 24-point, underlined text, you would click the Underline button on the format bar, and then select 24 from the Font Size list box. Anything that you type from that point will have those format characteristics. When you finish typing the title, you can change the font back to a smaller point size and click the Underline button to toggle the option off, then continue typing.

Using Paint

You use each Windows Accessory to perform a certain task. When it comes to creating and working with images, the Windows Accessory Paint is a useful tool. You can draw images and manipulate them with commands such as rotate, stretch, and invert colors. You can open more than one Accessory at a time, so while WordPad is still running, you can open Paint and work on drawings and images. This is called **multitasking**. John already created a logo for his coffee company. Now he wants to review the logo and revise it as necessary before using it on his promotional materials.

Steps

Trouble?

If Paint doesn't appear on the Accessories submenu, see your instructor or technical support person.

1. **Click the Start button on the taskbar, point to Programs, point to Accessories, click Paint, then click the Maximize button in the Paint window**
   The Paint window opens and is maximized in front of the WordPad window. You can find buttons for frequently used commands in the Paint Toolbox, located along the left edge of the window. Table B-3 describes these tools. Now you open the file with John's logo in it.

2. **Click File on the menu bar, click Open, click the Look in list arrow, then click the drive that contains your Student Disk**
   A list of the files stored on the Student Disk appears.

3. **In the file list, click Win B-2, then click Open**
   The file named Win B-2 opens, shown in Figure B-8. If you cannot see the logo on your screen, use the scroll buttons to adjust your view. John decides the logo could use some final modifications. Before he makes any changes, he wants to save this file (using a more meaningful name) so the original file won't be affected.

4. **Click File on the menu bar, click Save As, then save the file as Wired Coffee Logo on your Student Disk**
   John wants to add a rounded border around the logo. First he selects the proper tool from the Toolbox, and then he can "draw" the border.

5. **Click the Rounded Rectangle tool ▢ in the Toolbox, then move the pointer into the Paint work area**
   When you move the mouse pointer into the work area, it changes to ┼, indicating that the Rounded Rectangle tool is active.

Trouble?

If your rounded rectangle doesn't match Figure B-9, click Edit on the menu bar, then click Undo to reverse the last command. If Undo is not available, click the Eraser tool ▨ in the Toolbox, drag to erase the rounded rectangle, then repeat Step 6.

6. **Beginning above and to the left of the logo, drag ┼ so that a rounded rectangle surrounds the image, then release the mouse button when the pointer is below and to the right of the image, as shown in Figure B-9**
   John likes this new look. The logo is complete but needs to be saved.

7. **Click File on the menu bar, then click Save**
   Now John can use the logo in his other documents.

FIGURE B-8: Company logo in Paint

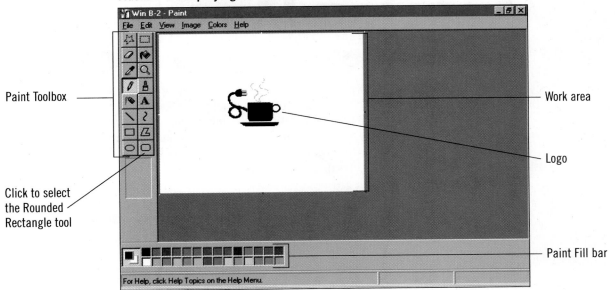

Paint Toolbox

Click to select
the Rounded
Rectangle tool

Work area

Logo

Paint Fill bar

FIGURE B-9: Company logo with rounded rectangle

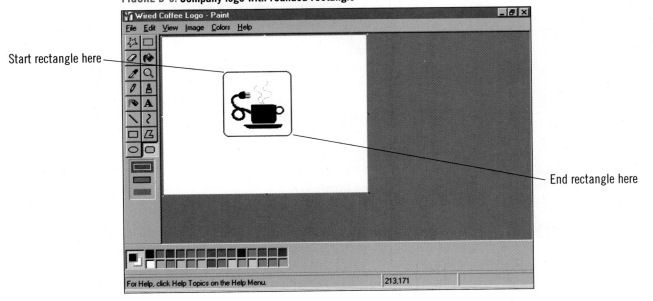

Start rectangle here

End rectangle here

TABLE B-3: Tools in the Paint Toolbox

tool	description	tool	description
	Selects a shape that is not regular		Creates dispersed lines and patterns
	Selects a shape that is regular		Enters text in drawings
	Erases part of a drawing		Draws a straight line
	Fills a shape with a color or texture		Draws a free form line
	Picks up a color from the picture for drawing		Draws a regular shape
	Magnifies part of an image		Draws an irregular shape
	Draws freehand		Draws an oval or circle
	Designates the size and shape brush to draw with		Draws a rectangle or square with rounded corners

Copying Data Between Programs

One of the most useful features that Windows offers is the ability to use data created in one document in another document, even if the two documents were created in different Windows programs. To work with more than one program or document at a time, you simply need to open them on your desktop. Any window that is open on the desktop is represented by a **program button** on the taskbar. When you want to switch from one open window to another, click the correct program button on the taskbar. Just as you worked with the Cut and Paste commands to rearrange the coffee list, you can use the same commands to move and copy data between two different documents. Table B-4 reviews the Cut, Copy and Paste commands and their associated keyboard shortcuts. ▬▬▬ John wants to add the company logo, which he created with Paint, to the Coffee Menu document, which he created with WordPad. He'll first go back to WordPad, which is still running. Then he'll copy and paste the Paint logo into the WordPad document.

Steps

Trouble?

If your windows don't appear tiled, click the program button on the taskbar for each program (Paint and WordPad) to ensure that both windows are maximized, then repeat Step 1.

QuickTip

When windows are tiled, you can drag a selected item from one program window to another to copy the item between programs.

1. Make sure both WordPad and Paint are open, place the mouse pointer on an empty area of the taskbar, right-click, then click Tile Windows Vertically on the shortcut menu
The windows (Paint and WordPad) are arranged next to one another vertically, as shown in Figure B-10, so that John can maneuver quickly between them while working.

2. Click the Paint program button on the taskbar, or click anywhere in the Paint window
The Paint program becomes the active program (the title bar changes from gray to blue). To copy the logo, John selects it first. To select an image, you need to choose the Select tool from the Toolbox and drag the mouse pointer over the image.

3. Click the Select tool ▭ in the Toolbox, then drag a rectangle around the coffee logo to select it

4. Click Edit on the Paint menu bar, then click Copy
The logo is copied to the Clipboard, but the original remains in your Wired Coffee Logo file.

5. Click the first line of the WordPad document
The WordPad program becomes active, and the insertion point is placed on the WordPad page, where John wants the logo to appear. If you cannot see enough of the page, use the scroll buttons to adjust your view.

6. Click the Paste button 📋 on the WordPad toolbar
The logo is pasted into the document, as shown in Figure B-11. Now John wants to center the logo on the page to match the title.

7. Click the Maximize button in the WordPad window, click the Center button ≡ on the format bar, then click below the logo to deselect it
The logo is centered in the document. Now save the WordPad file for future use.

8. Click the Save button 💾 on the toolbar
The document is complete and ready for John to print.

9. Click the Paint program button on the taskbar, then click the Close button in the Paint window

FIGURE B-10: **Tiled windows**

Click to activate the
Paint program

Right-click to open
pop-up menu and tile
windows vertically

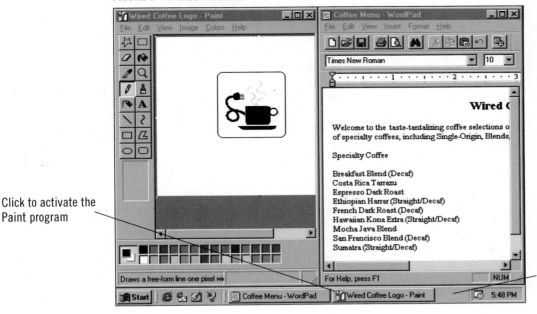

FIGURE B-11: **Copying a logo between programs**

Copy selected logo
from Paint file

Paste logo in
WordPad document

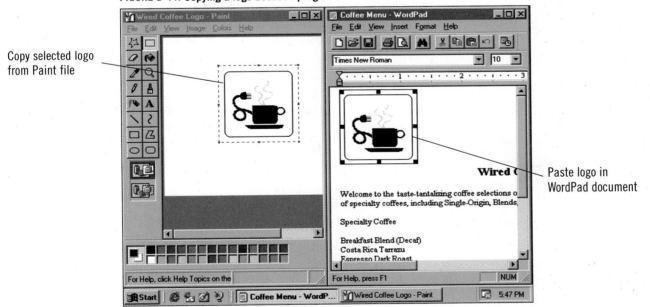

TABLE B-4: **Overview of cutting, copying, and pasting**

function	toolbar button	keyboard shortcut	drag-and-drop method *(for use within a file or between files if the windows are tiled)*
Cut: Removes selected information from a file and places it on the Clipboard	✂	[Ctrl][X]	Press and hold [Shift] as you drag selected text and it will be moved
Copy: Places a copy of selected information on the Clipboard, leaving the file intact	🗐	[Ctrl][C]	Press and hold [Ctrl] as you drag selected text and it will be copied
Paste: Inserts whatever is currently on the Clipboard into another location (within the same file or in a different file)	📋	[Ctrl][V]	Release the left mouse button

Windows 98

Printing a Document

Printing a document creates a **printout** or **hard copy**, a document on paper that you can share with others or review as a work in progress. Most Windows programs have a print option that you access through the Print dialog box and a Print button on the toolbar. Although your printing options vary from program to program, the process works similarly in all of them. It is a good idea to use the **Print Preview** feature to look at the layout and formatting of a document before you print it. You might catch a mistake, find that the document fits on more pages than you wanted, or notice formatting that you want to do differently. Making changes before you print saves paper. ✎ John decides to preview the coffee menu before printing the document. Satisfied with the result, John prints the Coffee Menu document.

Steps

1. In the WordPad window, click the **Print Preview button** 🔍 on the toolbar
A reduced but proportionate image of the page appears in the Preview window, shown in Figure B-12.

2. Click **Zoom In** in Print Preview
The preview image of the page appears larger, easier to see. John notices extra space around the dotted rectangle, the area determined by the **margin** setting. You can change the margin setting to decrease or increase the area outside the dotted rectangle with the Page Setup command. Before you can make the change, you need to close Print Preview.

3. Click **Close** in Print Preview
The Preview window closes and you return to the Coffee Menu document.

4. Click **File** on the menu bar, then click **Page Setup**
The Page Setup dialog box opens. Table B-5 describes the Page Setup dialog box options. You can change other printing options here, such as paper size, page orientation, and printer source.

5. Select the number in the Top text box, then type **1.25**, select the number in the Bottom text box, type **1.25**, then click **OK**
You should verify that you like the new margins before printing.

6. Click 🔍
The menu is displayed with smaller margins. John likes this better, so he prints the document.

7. Click **Print** in Print Preview
The Print dialog box opens, as shown in Figure B-13, showing various options available for printing. Check to make sure you are printing to the correct printer. If you need to change printers, click the Name list arrow, and then select a printer. When you are done, accept all of the settings.

8. Click **OK**
The WordPad document prints. To **close**, or quit, a program and any of its currently open files, you select the Exit command from the File menu. You can also click the Close button in the upper right corner of the program window.

9. Click the **Close button** in the WordPad window
If you have made any changes to the open file without saving them, you will be prompted to save your changes before the program quits.

QuickTip
To quickly print a document, click the Print button 🖨 on the toolbar.

FIGURE B-12: **Coffee Menu in Print Preview**

Click to print
document

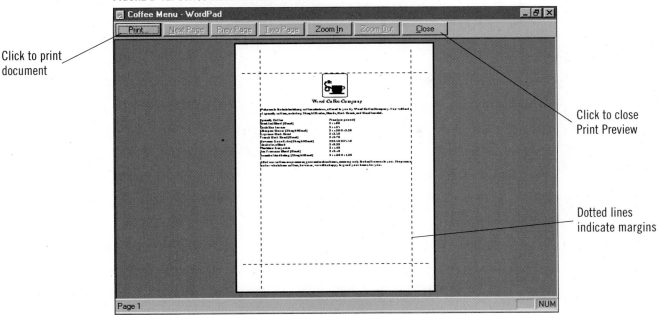

Click to close
Print Preview

Dotted lines
indicate margins

FIGURE B-13: **Print dialog box**

Click to change
printer

Printer information

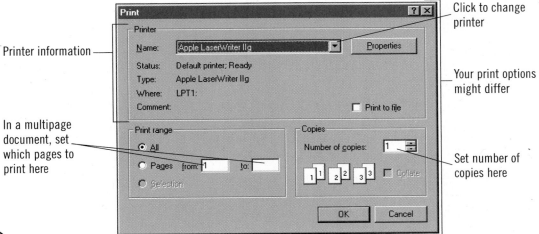

Your print options
might differ

In a multipage
document, set
which pages to
print here

Set number of
copies here

Printer properties

You can select Properties from the Print dialog box and adjust several facets of the printing operation. For example, to control the intensity with which graphics images are printed, you would click the Graphics tab, then adjust the Intensity slider. You can also adjust fonts, paper sizes and other printing dimensions in the Properties dialog box.

TABLE B-5: **Page Setup dialog box options**

page setup option	function
Size	Defines the size of the paper on which you want to print
Source	Defines the location of the paper, such as a paper tray or an envelope feeder
Orientation	Allows you to select between Portrait (the page being taller than it is wide) and Landscape (the page being wider than it is tall)
Margins	Allows you to define top, bottom, left, and right page margins

Windows 98

Playing a Video Clip

Windows 98 comes with two built-in Accessories, ActiveMovie Control and Media Player, that you can use to play video and sound files. **ActiveMovie Control** is a new media application for Windows that delivers high-quality continuous video playback. You can use it to play movies, sounds, and other multimedia files from your computer, a local network, or the Internet. The **Media Player** gives you extended capabilities over the ActiveMovie Control. With the Media Player, you can play the same ActiveMovie videos and sounds, but you can also modify the media and control the settings for multimedia hardware devices. ◆━━ John experiments using the Media Player to play a sample video.

1. **Click the Start button on the taskbar, point to Programs, point to Accessories, point to Entertainment, then click Media Player**
   Media Player opens. You can open a specific type of video or sound file by choosing a command type on the Device menu or a general type by choosing the Open command on the File menu. John decides to open a video with the ActiveMovie type.

2. **Click Device on the menu bar, then click ActiveMovie, as shown in Figure B-14**
   The Open dialog box opens. John wants to play a video located on your Student Disk.

3. **Click the Look in list arrow, then click the drive that contains your Student Disk**
   A list of the files and folders stored on the Student Disk appears in the file list.

4. **In the file list, click Coffee Cup, then click Open**
   An hourglass appears, indicating that Media Player is opening the video file. The video opens in a separate window below the Media Player window. Table B-6 describes the function of each button on the Media Player toolbar.

5. **In the Media Player window, click the Play button ▶ on the toolbar**
   The video plays in the separate window. A slider in the Media Player window indicates the progress of the video, as shown in Figure B-15. You can drag the slider backward or forward to play different parts of the video. When the video is finished, close the video window.

6. **Click File on the menu bar, then click Close**
   The video window is closed, but the Media Player window remains open. John will use the Media Player to play a sound in the next lesson.

TABLE B-6: Buttons on the Media Player toolbar

button	description
▶ or ‖	Play or pause a video or sound
■	Stop a video or sound
▲	Eject a CD-ROM
⏮	Move to the previous selection mark
◀◀	Rewind the video or sound
▶▶	Forward the video or sound
⏭	Move to next selection mark
⊻	Start the selection of a video or sound you want to copy
⊼	End the selection of a video or sound you want to copy

FIGURE B-14: **Media Player window with the Device menu**

Click to open an
ActiveMovie file

FIGURE B-15: **Media Player window and video window**

Slider indicating
current play time

Length of video
in seconds

Toolbar

Click to play video

Playing a Sound

Besides playing videos, you can also play sounds using the Media Player or the ActiveMovie Control. In order to listen to sounds, your computer must have a sound card and self-powered speakers. Media Player and ActiveMovie Control can play a variety of sounds. To play a sound, you click the Play button. If you want to pause while playing the sound, you click the Pause button. If you want to change the starting position of the sound, you drag the slider. John enjoyed playing a video, so he decided to play a sound.

Steps 1234

Trouble?

If Sound doesn't appear on the Device menu, Media Player doesn't detect a sound card on your computer. See your instructor or technical support person.

1. **Make sure Media Player is open, click Device on the menu bar, then click Sound**
   The Open dialog box opens. John decides to play a sound located on your Student Disk.

2. **Click the Look in list arrow, then click the drive that contains your Student Disk**
   A list of the files and folders stored on the Student Disk appears in the file list.

3. **In the file list, click Better Coffee, then click Open**
   The time scale appears below the slider in the Media Player window.

4. **In the Media Player window, click the Play button ▶ on the toolbar**
   The sound plays. See Figure B-16. The slider in the Media Player window moves indicating the current play time of the sound. John decides to pause the sound, change the starting position of the sound, and then resume playing.

5. **Before the sound finishes, click the Pause button ▋▋ on the toolbar**
   You can drag the slider backward or forward to play different parts of the sound. John drags the slider backward to restart the sound.

6. **Drag the slider back to the beginning, then click the Play button ▶ to restart the sound**
   When you are finished playing the sound, close the Media Player.

7. **Click the Close button in the Media Player window**

FIGURE B-16: **Media Player window playing a sound**

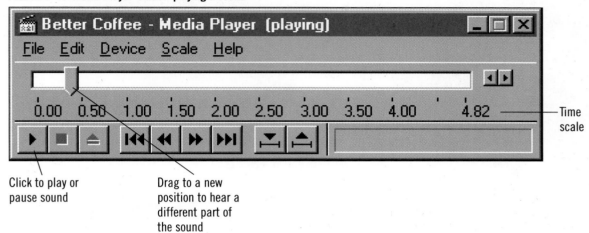

Click to play or
pause sound

Drag to a new
position to hear a
different part of
the sound

Time
scale

Playing a music CD

To accommodate the many people who like to play
audio CDs in their CD-ROM drives while working,
Windows 98 includes the CD Player program in its
accessories. The controls on the player, shown in
Figure B-17, look just like those on a regular CD
player. The Windows 98 CD Player supports many
of the same features found in CD players, such as
random play, programmable playback order, and the
ability to save programs so that users don't have to
recreate their playlists each time they play a CD. To
play an audio CD, insert the CD in your CD-ROM
drive; the CD Player will automatically start playing
the audio CD. You can click the CD Player button on
the taskbar to display the CD Player window.

FIGURE B-17: **CD Player window**

Practice

► Concepts Review

Label each of the elements of the screen shown in Figure B-18.

FIGURE B-18

Match each of the terms with the statement that describes its function.

6. Removes selected text or an image from its current location   **a.** Copy
7. Copies selected text or an image from its current location   **b.** Accessories
8. A set of characters you assign to a collection of information   **c.** Cut
9. A collection of Windows programs that enable you to perform certain tasks   **d.** Select
10. What you must first do to existing text before you can format it   **e.** Filename

Select the best answer from the following list of choices.

11. The first step in starting any Windows Accessory is to click
    a. The Start button.   **b.** The taskbar.   **c.** The Open icon.   **d.** Anywhere on the desktop.

12. What program command makes a copy of a file?
    a. Save   **b.** Save As   **c.** Copy   **d.** Duplicate

13. When WordPad automatically moves words to the next line, it is called
    a. Wordwrap.   **b.** Format insert.   **c.** Margin.   **d.** Tab.

14. Which of the following is not a way to select text?
   a. Double-click a word.
   b. Drag over the text.
   c. Click File on the menu bar, then click Select.
   d. Click to the left of the first character in a line of text.

15. What is the name of the Windows location where information is placed after it is cut or copied?
   a. Clipboard   **b.** Paint   **c.** Start Up menu   **d.** Hard drive

16. Which of the following is an option to change the size of the empty border around a document?
   a. Paper Size   **b.** Paper Source   **c.** Orientation   **d.** Margins

▶ Skills Review

1. Create, edit, and save a WordPad document.
   a. Start WordPad.
   b. Open the WordPad file named Win B-3 on your Student Disk.
   c. Save the file as "Choose Coffee" on your Student Disk.

2. Edit a WordPad document.
   a. Change the spelling of the word "neuances" to "nuances" in the first paragraph.
   b. Insert a space between the characters *r* and *a* in the word, "ora" in the second paragraph.
   c. Delete the word "heavy" in the last line of text and replace it with "medium".

3. Format WordPad text.
   a. Select all the text in the file named Choose Coffee.
   b. Change it from the present font to Garamond, and change the size to 12 point.
   c. Center the title ("Wired Coffee") and change it to bold, 16 point.
   d. Underline each title ("How to Choose a Coffee" and "How to Taste the Difference") and change them to 14 point.
   e. Click anywhere in the WordPad window outside of the selected text.
   f. Save the document.

4. Modify a Paint image.
   a. Start Paint.
   b. Open the Paint file named Win B-2 on your Student Disk (this is the same file you used in the lessons).
   c. Save this file as "Wired Coffee Logo 2" on your Student Disk.
   d. Draw a circle around the logo.
   e. Use the Undo command or Eraser tool as necessary if the circle doesn't fit around the logo.
   f. Save the file.

5. Copy data between two documents.
   a. Tile the WordPad and Paint windows vertically. (*Hint:* Maximize both windows first.)
   b. Select the logo in the Paint window.
   c. Copy it to the Clipboard.
   d. In WordPad, insert the cursor at the beginning of the document.
   e. Maximize WordPad.
   f. Paste the logo in the newly inserted blank line.
   g. Center the logo.
   h. Save the Choose Coffee file.
   i. Close the Wired Coffee Logo 2 file and Paint.

6. Print and close a document.
- **a.** Print two copies of the file named Choose Coffee.
- **b.** Close all open documents.
- **c.** Close WordPad.

7. Play a video.
- **a.** Start Media Player.
- **b.** Open the Coffee Cup video on your Student Disk.
- **c.** Play the video.
- **d.** Close the video window.

8. Play a sound.
- **a.** Open the AM Coffee sound on your Student Disk.
- **b.** Play the video.
- **c.** Pause the sound.
- **d.** Drag the slider to the beginning of the sound.
- **e.** Replay the sound.
- **f.** Close the Media Player window.

▶ Independent Challenges

1. You just opened a small, independent bookstore and are working on your inventory. You need to create a list of books that can be consulted when customers come in and want to know what kind of books you carry. Start WordPad and create a new document that lists the first 10 books in your stock, including the name of your bookstore and its street address, city, zip code, and phone number, and for each book, the author's name (last name first), the title, and the date of publication.

To complete this independent challenge:

1. Start WordPad.
2. Enter the heading (the name of the bookstore, address, city, state, zip code, and phone number).
3. Center the heading information.
4. Enter the information for at least ten books, using the Tab key to create columns for the author's name, the title, and the date of publication. Be sure that the columns line up with one another.
5. Proofread your list and correct any errors you may have made.
6. Italicize the last and first names of each author.
7. Bold the title of each book.
8. Save the list as Book Inventory on your Student Disk.
9. Print two copies of the list.
10. Close WordPad.

2. Your parents are celebrating their twenty-fifth wedding anniversary. You want to create an invitation to a party for them. Using WordPad, create an invitation, including the invitation title, your parents' names, date and time of the party, location of the party (use "35 Crow Canyon Road" for the address), written directions to the party, your name, the date to respond by, and phone number to reach you. Using Paint, you will then paste a map of the party location into the invitation. Remember that you can open more than one program at a time and you can easily switch between programs using the taskbar.

To complete this independent challenge:

1. Start WordPad and type the information needed for the invitation.
2. Select the title text and click the Center button on the toolbar.

3. Change the title text to 18 point, bold.
4. Change the rest of the text to 14-point Arial.
5. Save the WordPad document as "Invitation" on your Student Disk.
6. Start Paint, then open the "Invitation Map" file from your Student Disk.
7. Copy the map to the Clipboard.
8. Place the insertion point above the written instructions in the Invitation document.
9. Click the Paste button on the toolbar.
10. Save the document, preview the document, make any necessary changes, then print the document.
11. Close WordPad and Paint.

3. As the vice president of Things-That-Fly, a kite and juggling store, you need to design a new type of logo, consisting of three simple circles, each colored differently. This logo will be used both in the new stationery and in all advertising for the store. You'll use Paint to design the logo, and then you will paste the logo into a WordPad document and name the document Stationery.
To complete this independent challenge:

1. Start Paint and create a small circle using the [Shift] key and the Ellipse tool.
2. Use the Select tool to surround the circle (thereby selecting it), and then select Copy from the Edit menu. Now you can paste the circle so you don't have to try to redraw the exact same shape.
3. Select Paste from the Edit menu, and use the mouse to drag the second circle below the first and a bit to the right of the first.
4. Select Paste from the Edit menu again, and use the mouse to drag the third circle below the first and a bit to the left of the first.
5. For each circle, click the Fill tool in the Toolbox, click the color you want the circle to be, then click inside the circle you want filled with that color.
6. Using the Select tool, select the completed logo, click Edit on the menu bar, then click Copy.
7. Open WordPad and click the Center button on the toolbar.
8. Click the Paste button on the toolbar, click to the right of the logo to deselect it, press [Enter] twice, then type "Things-That-Fly."
9. Using the format bar, change the text to 18 point, bold.
10. Save the document as "Stationery" on your Student Disk.
11. Preview the document, make any necessary changes, then print the document.
12. Close Wordpad and Paint.

4. As the creative director at Digital Arts, a computer music company, you need to find sample sounds to include on a demo CD. You'll use Media Player to open sound files located on your computer and play each one. You'll also use WordPad to keep track of the sounds you listened to and which ones you liked the best.
To complete this independent challenge:

1. Open Media Player.
2. Open all the sound files in the Media folder (in the Windows folder) on your computer.
3. Play each sound file.
4. In WordPad, create a list of the sound files that you played and indicate the sounds you liked the best.
5. Save the list as "Sound List" on your Student Disk.
6. Print the list.
7. Close Media Player.

▶ Visual Workshop

Re-create the screen shown in Figure B-19, which displays the Windows desktop with more than one program window open. You can use the file Win B-2 for the coffee cup logo (save it as "A Cup of Coffee" on your Student Disk). Create a new WordPad document, save it as "Good Time Coffee Club" on your Student Disk, and enter the text shown in the figure. Print the screen. (Press the Print Screen key to make a copy of the screen, open Paint, click Edit on the menu bar, click Paste to paste the screen into Paint, then click Yes to paste the large image, if necessary. Click File on the menu bar, click Print, then click OK.)

FIGURE B-19

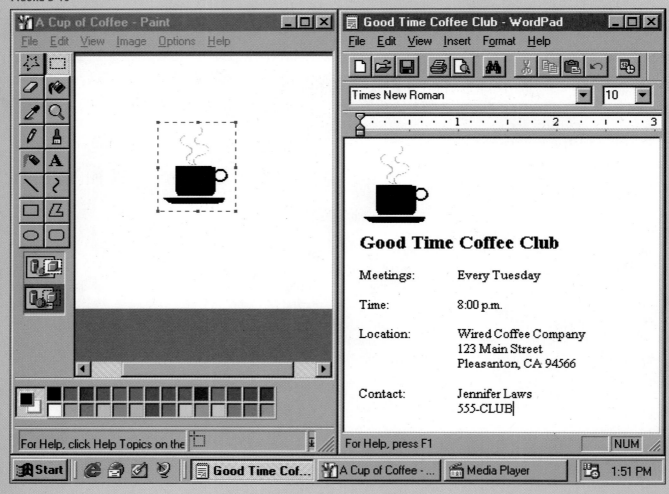

Managing
Files Using My Computer

Objectives

- ► **Understand file management**
- ► **Open and view My Computer**
- ► **View folders and files**
- ► **Create a folder**
- ► **Move files and folders**
- ► **Delete and restore files and folders**
- ► **Create a shortcut to a file**
- ► **Display drive information**

An important Windows 98 skill for you to learn is **file management**, which is being able to organize and keep track of files and folders. Windows 98 provides you with two file management programs: My Computer and Windows Explorer. You use both of these tools to view the files that are on your computer and how they are arranged. You can also use them to rearrange the files to fit the way that you work by creating new folders and by renaming and deleting files and folders. A **folder** is an electronic collection of files and other folders. This unit concentrates on My Computer while the next unit will focus on Windows Explorer.

In this unit John Casey will learn about the files on his computer and how to keep them organized using My Computer.

Understanding File Management

Managing folders and files enables you to quickly locate any file that you have already created and need to use again. Not being able to manage files is like looking for a needle in a haystack—it is frustrating and time-consuming. The way your files are organized on disk is called a **file hierarchy.**  Figure C-1 shows the files and folders that John uses in the course of running his business.

Details

As you examine the figure, note that file management can help you do the following:

 Organize folders and files in a file hierarchy, or a logical order, so that information is easy to locate and use
John stores all of his correspondence files in a folder called Letters. Within that folder are two more folders. One is named Business Letters and holds all business correspondence. The other is named Personal Letters and holds all of John's personal correspondence.

 Save files to the folder in which you want to store them for future use
John has a folder named Sales in which he stores all information about sales for the current year. He also places files related to accounting information in this folder.

 Create a new folder so you can reorganize information
Now that John is doing more advertising for Wired Coffee Company, he wants to create a new folder to store files related to these marketing efforts.

 Delete files and folders that you no longer need
John deletes files once he is sure he will no longer use them again to free up disk space and keep his disk organized.

 Create shortcuts
If a file or folder you use often is located several levels down in a file hierarchy (for example, if it is in a file within a folder within a folder), it might take you several steps to access it. To save you time in accessing the files and programs you use most frequently, you can create shortcuts to them. A **shortcut** is a link that you can place in any location that gives you instant access to a particular file, folder, or program on your hard disk or on a network. John creates a shortcut on the desktop to the Wired Coffee folder. To view or access the contents of his folder, all he will have to do is double-click the shortcut icon on the desktop.

 Find a file when you cannot remember where it is stored
John knows he created a letter to a supplier earlier this week, but now that he is ready to revise the letter, he cannot find it. Using the Find command on the Start menu, he can quickly find that letter and revise it in no time.

 Use Quick View to see the contents of a file without having to open it
John can view a WordPad file, Paint file, or almost any Windows file from My Computer using the Quick View feature, without having to first start each program and then open the file.

FIGURE C-1: How John uses Windows to organize his files

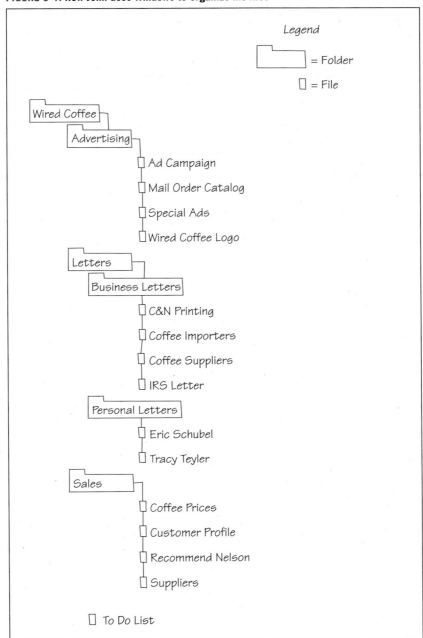

Legend

☐ = Folder

☐ = File

Wired Coffee
Advertising
☐ Ad Campaign
☐ Mail Order Catalog
☐ Special Ads
☐ Wired Coffee Logo
Letters
Business Letters
☐ C&N Printing
☐ Coffee Importers
☐ Coffee Suppliers
☐ IRS Letter
Personal Letters
☐ Eric Schubel
☐ Tracy Teyler
Sales
☐ Coffee Prices
☐ Customer Profile
☐ Recommend Nelson
☐ Suppliers
☐ To Do List

What is a file hierarchy?

Windows 98 allows you to organize folders and files into a file hierarchy, imitating the way you would actually store paper documents in real folders. Just as a filing cabinet contains several folders each containing a set of related documents, and several dividers grouping related folders together, a file hierarchy allows you to place files into folders, then folders into other folders, so that your files are neat and organized. For example, Figure C-1 shows the file hierarchy of the Wired Coffee folder on your Student Disk. At the topmost level of the hierarchy is the name of the folder, Wired Coffee. This folder contains several files and folders. The folders are named Advertising, Letters, Business Letters, Personal Letters, and Sales, each containing files and folders related to each of these topics.

Windows 98

Opening and Viewing My Computer

The key to organizing folders and files effectively within a hierarchy is storing related things together and naming folders informatively. That way, you can get a good idea of what's on your system just by looking at the higher levels of your file hierarchy, and not having to examine every individual file or memorize a coding system. 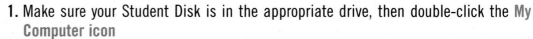 As the previous lesson showed, the file hierarchy on John's disk contains several folders and files organized by topic. Now he will use My Computer to review this organization and see if it needs to be changed.

Steps

QuickTip

Make a copy of your Student Disk before you use it. For assistance, see your instructor or technical support person.

1. Make sure your Student Disk is in the appropriate drive, then double-click the My Computer icon

This icon is usually located in the upper-left corner of the desktop. My Computer opens, displaying the contents of your computer, including all the disk drives and printers, as shown in Figure C-2. Since computers differ, your My Computer window will probably look different. There are icons that represent drives and icons that represent folders. As with most other windows, there is a toolbar, a status bar providing information about the contents of the window, a menu bar, and a list of contents in the My Computer window.

Trouble?

If the toolbar is not visible, click View on the menu bar, point to Toolbars, then click Standard Buttons.

2. If necessary, click the Maximize button in the My Computer window

This enables you to see the entire toolbar as you work. The toolbar contains a set of buttons that make using My Computer easier. Table C-1 lists what each of these buttons does and how they are used.

3. Double-click the drive that contains your Student Disk

You can see the folders that are contained on the disk drive. When you open a disk drive or folder, the Address bar changes to indicate the new location. The Address bar changed from My Computer to disk drive A (A:\) and the title bar for the My Computer window changed to 3½ Floppy (A:). To see what's contained in the folders stored on the disk drive, you need to open them. John wants to see what files are contained in the Wired Coffee folder.

4. Double-click the Wired Coffee folder

You can see the files and folders that are contained in the Wired Coffee folder. Files that are created using different applications are represented by a different type of icon. John wants to see what files are contained in the Sales folder.

QuickTip

To go from My Computer to Windows Explorer, another file management tool that comes with Windows 98, right-click any disk or folder icon, then click Explore.

5. Double-click the Sales folder

You can now see the files contained in the Sales folder. These are files that John created using WordPad and saved in the Sales folder.

FIGURE C-2: **My Computer window**

Toolbar

Floppy disk drives

Click to go to a different folder

CD-ROM drive

Your list of folders might be different

Status bar

Hard disk drives

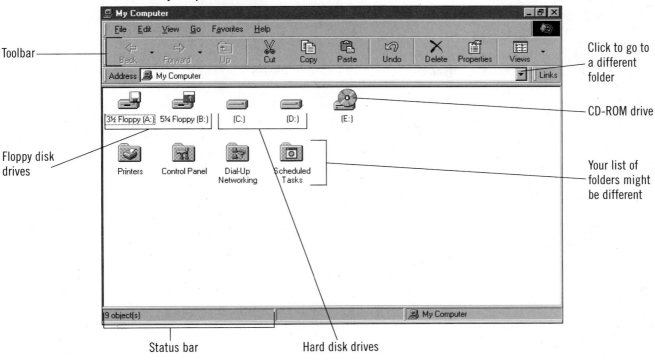

TABLE C-1: **My Computer toolbar buttons**

button	function	button	function
⬅	Moves back to the previous location you have already visited	🗐	Pastes a folder or file
➡	Moves forward to the previous location you have already visited	↩	Undoes the most recent My Computer operation
⬆	Moves up one level in the file hierarchy	✕	Deletes a folder or file
✂	Cuts a folder or file	🗐	Shows the properties of a folder or file
🗐	Copies a folder or file	▦	Lists the contents of My Computer using different views

CLUES TO USE

Formatting a disk

New floppy disks have to be formatted before they can be used. Sometimes the disk is preformatted, but if it is not, you can easily perform this function yourself. To format a floppy disk, select the disk drive in My Computer that contains the disk, click File on the menu bar, then click Format, or right-click the disk drive, then click Format. Specify the size of the disk and format type, then click Start. If you are format-

ting a disk that has never been formatted, select the Full format type. If the disk has already been formatted once and you simply want to clear its contents, select the Quick format type to reduce the time it takes. Be absolutely certain you want to format a disk before doing so, because formatting removes all the data from a disk.

Viewing Folders and Files

Once you have opened one or more folders, you can use buttons on the toolbar to help you move quickly between them in My Computer. If you want to move up one step in the hierarchy, you can click the Up One Level button. Each time you open a folder, Windows 98 keeps track of where you have been. If you want to go back or forward to a folder you have already visited, you can click the Back or Forward button. If you want to go to a folder you visited two or more locations ago, you can click the list arrow next to the Back or Forward button to display a menu of places you have been, and then select the place you want to go. When you view a folder in the My Computer window, you can use the View button on the toolbar to change the way folder and file icons are viewed. John moves between folders and changes the way he views folders and files depending upon the type of information that he needs.

QuickTip
You can also click the Address bar list arrow to move to another location up or down the file hierarchy.

1. **Click the Up One Level button 🔼 on the toolbar**
The Wired Coffee folder and its contents appear in the Wired Coffee window. Each time you click on the Up One Level button, you move up one step in the hierarchy to the folder that contains the folders and files you currently see on the screen.

2. **Click the 🔼 again**
You should now be at the topmost level of your disk drive file hierarchy showing several folders. See Figure C-3. Instead of double-clicking the Wired Coffee folder icon again to reopen the folder, you can click the Back button on the toolbar to go back to the previous folder (Wired Coffee) you visited.

3. **Click the Back button ⬅ on the toolbar**
The Wired Coffee folder and its contents appear in the My Computer window. At this point, you can open other folders. John opens the Advertising folder to see what's inside.

Trouble?
If Microsoft Word is installed on your computer, the Word icon will appear for the files, as shown in Figure C-4. If not, the WordPad icon will appear.

4. **Double-click the Advertising folder**
The Advertising folder and its contents appear in the My Computer window. John wants to go back to the Sales folder. Instead of using the Up One Level button to go back to the Wired Coffee folder and then clicking the Sales folder, you can click the list arrow next to the Back button to display a menu of places you have been, and then select the Sales folder.

5. **Click the Back button list arrow ⬅▾ on the toolbar, then click Sales**
The Back button list arrow, as shown in Figure C-4, displays the folders you have recently visited. You can click the Forward button on the toolbar to quickly return to the folder that you recently visited. In this case, you can return to the Wired Coffee folder.

QuickTip
You can click File on the menu bar, then click a folder or drive to open a location you have recently visited.

6. **Click the Forward button ➡ on the toolbar**
The Wired Coffee folder and its contents appear in the My Computer window. John wants to change the way the icons in the Wired Coffee folder are displayed.

7. **Click the Views button list arrow ▦▾ on the toolbar, then click Details**
In the Details view, the name, size of the object, type of file, and date on which each folder or file was last modified appear, as shown in Figure C-5. This might be the most useful view because it includes a great deal of information about the folder or file, in addition to the icon of the application that was used to create the file.

8. **Click the Views button ▦ on the toolbar**
The Large Icons view is displayed. Each time you click the Views button, the view changes, appearing in the following order: Large Icons, Small Icons, List, Details.

FIGURE C-3: Viewing folders and files in Large Icons view

Click to view the next level up in the folder hierarchy

Click to go back to the previous folder

Folders

Address bar changes to reflect new location

Large icons

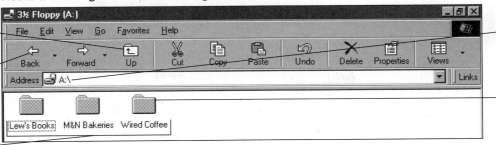

FIGURE C-4: Moving between folders

Back button list arrow

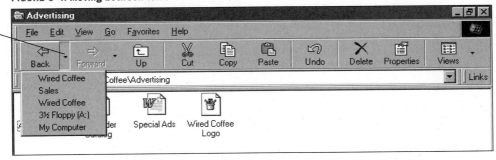

FIGURE C-5: Viewing folders and files in Details view

Click to change views

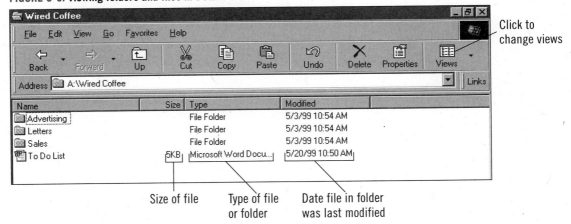

Size of file

Type of file or folder

Date file in folder was last modified

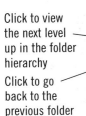

Viewing files with Quick View

Quick View allows you to view the contents of a file without having to open that file. Although you cannot edit the contents of a file in Quick View, you can open the file for editing 🖉, increase the font size for easier reading 🅰, decrease the font size 🅰⁻, or dis- play new files in the Quick View window 🖻. To open a file with Quick View, right-click the file you want to open, then click Quick View on the pop-up menu. If you do not see a Quick View option on your pop-up menu, then you probably do not have this feature installed.

Windows 98

Creating a Folder

Creating a new folder is a necessary skill for successful file management. Creating a new folder can help you organize and keep track of files and other folders. There are two ways to create a folder in Windows 98. You can select the New command on the File menu, or you can right-click anywhere in any My Computer window and then select the New command. ➤ John needs to create two new folders. One will contain his To Do List, and the other will contain information about his employees.

1. **Click File on the menu bar, point to New, then click Folder**
   A new folder appears in the Wired Coffee window, shown in Figure C-6. All new folders are initially named New Folder. A border appears around the newly created folder, meaning that it is selected and ready to be renamed. Since this folder will hold important files relating to John's work week, he decides to call the folder "Important."

2. **Type Important and press [Enter]**
   The folder is now named "Important."

3. **Place the mouse pointer anywhere in the Wired Coffee window (except on a file or folder), right-click, then point to New**
   The pop-up menu opens, as shown in Figure C-7.

4. **Click Folder**
   A new folder appears, named New Folder, where you right-clicked the mouse in the My Computer window.

5. **Type Personnel and press [Enter]**
   The My Computer window now has two new folders, shown in Figure C-8. Once you create new folders, you can quickly rearrange them into orderly rows and columns.

6. **Click the View on the menu bar, point to Arrange Icons, then click By Name**
   The folder and file icons in the Wired Coffee folder are sorted by name in alphabetical order and automatically moved in line with the other icons. You can change the way individual files and folders are sorted by using other Arrange Icons options on the View menu. Table C-2 describes these options. John is ready to move files.

QuickTip

To rename a folder, right-click the folder you want to rename, click Rename, then type a new name.

TABLE C-2: Options on the View menu for arranging files and folders

option	arranges files and folders
By Name	Alphabetically
By Type	By type, such as all documents created using the WordPad program
By Size	By size, with the largest folder or file listed first
By Date	Chronologically by the date they were last modified, with the latest modification date listed last
Auto Arrange	Automatically in orderly rows and columns

FIGURE C-6: **Creating a new folder**

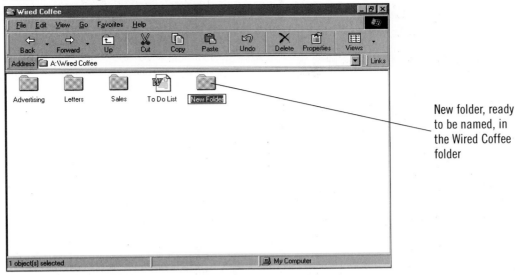

New folder, ready
to be named, in
the Wired Coffee
folder

FIGURE C-7: **Right-clicking to display a shortcut menu**

Click to create a
new folder

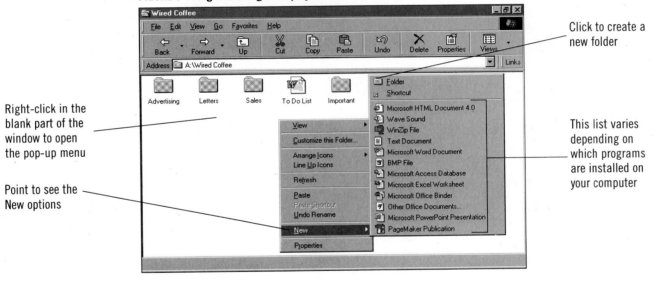

Right-click in the
blank part of the
window to open
the pop-up menu

Point to see the
New options

This list varies
depending on
which programs
are installed on
your computer

FIGURE C-8: **Two new folders**

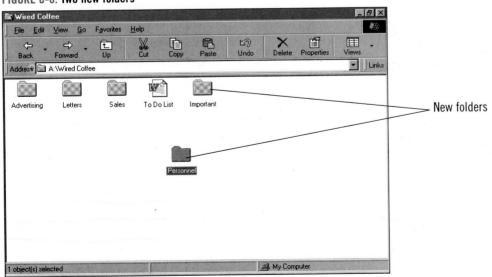

New folders

Moving Files and Folders

You can move a file or folder from one location to another using a variety of methods in My Computer (or Windows Explorer). If the file or folder and the location to which you want to move it are visible in a window or on the desktop, you can simply drag the item from one location to the other. When the location is not visible, you can use the Cut, Copy and Paste commands on the Edit menu or the buttons on the toolbar. ✎ Now that John has created a folder (which he named Important) for his weekly tasks, he is ready to move the To Do List file into it. He also needs to move a letter (a recommendation for a new marketing person) currently contained in the Sales folder to the new Personnel folder.

Steps

QuickTip

Dragging a file or folder from one place to another on the same disk will move it; whereas dragging it from one disk to another will copy it. If you want to copy the item on the same disk by dragging, simply press and hold [Ctrl] while you drag the mouse.

QuickTip

If you want to perform a file management operation such as moving or copying more than one file or folder at a time, first select all the files or folders by pressing and holding [Ctrl] and clicking each one you want to select. Then perform the operation.

1. Drag the **To Do List file** from the Wired Coffee window to the Important folder
The icon representing the To Do List file is removed from the Wired Coffee folder and is placed in the folder named Important. Folders are moved in the same manner.

2. Double-click the **Important folder** and confirm that the file has been moved
The folder named Important now contains John's To Do List. John now needs to move the file named Recommend Nelson, a personnel recommendation for one of his employees, from the Sales folder to the Personnel folder.

3. Click the **Back button list arrow** ⬅▾ on the toolbar, click **Sales**, then click the **Recommend Nelson file** to select it
Since the Personnel folder is not visible, John uses the Cut and Paste commands to move a file from one folder to another.

4. Click the **Cut button** ✂ on the toolbar
The file is removed from its original location and stored on the Windows Clipboard. When you cut or copy a file, the file icon turns gray, as shown in Figure C-9. John moves back to the Wired Coffee folder and then opens the Personnel folder to complete the file move.

5. Click the **Back button** ⬅ on the toolbar, then double-click the **Personnel folder**
John is ready to use the paste command to move the file.

6. Click the **Paste button** 📋 on the toolbar
The file is now pasted into the Personnel folder, shown in Figure C-10. After completing the move, John returns to the Wired Coffee folder.

7. Click ⬅ to return to the Wired Coffee folder

FIGURE C-9: Preparing to move a file

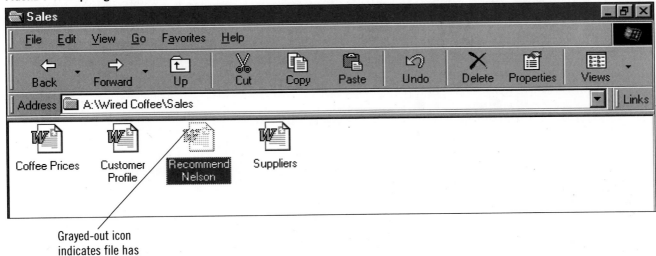

Grayed-out icon
indicates file has
been cut

FIGURE C-10: The relocated file

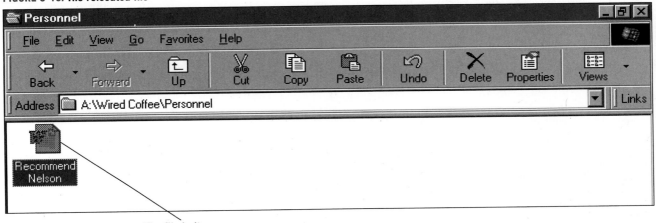

The file in its
new location

CLUES TO USE

Sending files and folders

The Send To command, located on the pop-up menu of any desktop object, lets you "send" (or move) a file or folder to a new location on your computer. For example, you can send a file or folder to a floppy disk for making a quick backup copy of the file or folder, a mail recipient for receiving electronic messages, or the desktop for creating a shortcut. You can also use the Send To command to move a file or folder from one folder to another. To send a file or folder, right-click the file or folder you want to send, point to Send To on the pop-up menu, and then click the destination you want. You can determine the options that appear in the Send To command by creating a shortcut to the program or folder you want included and moving it to the SendTo folder, located within the Windows folder.

Windows 98

Deleting and Restoring Files and Folders

When you organize the contents of a folder, disk, or the desktop, you might find files and folders that you no longer need. You can **delete** these items, or remove them from the disk. If you delete a file or folder from the desktop or from the hard disk, it goes into the Recycle Bin. The **Recycle Bin**, located on your desktop, is a temporary storage area for deleted files. If you delete a file that you still need, you can restore it by moving it from the Recycle Bin to another location. Be aware that if you delete a file from your floppy disk it will not be stored in the Recycle Bin—it will be permanently deleted. See Table C-3 for a summary of the deleting and restoring options. To demonstrate how the Recycle Bin works, John first moves a file to the desktop, deletes that file, and then restores it.

Steps

Trouble?

Click the title bar in the My Computer window, then drag the window to the right to see the Recycle Bin.

QuickTip

To quickly move files or folders from one disk to another, select the files or folder, press and hold [Shift], then drag the selected items to the new location.

QuickTip

Your deleted files remain in the Recycle Bin until you empty it. To empty the Recycle Bin, right-click the Recycle Bin icon, then click Empty Recycle Bin. This permanently removes the contents of the Recycle Bin from your hard disk.

1. **Double-click the Advertising folder, then click the Restore button in the Advertising window**
   The Advertising folder and its contents appear in the Advertising window. Before you can delete a file from a floppy disk to the Recycle Bin, you need to move it to the desktop or hard drive. If you want to delete a file directly from a floppy disk without the possibility of restoring it, you can drag the file directly to the Recycle Bin or press [Delete].

2. **Right-click and hold the Ad Campaign file, drag it to the desktop from the Advertising folder on your Student Disk, then click Move Here**
   The file now appears on the desktop and can be moved to the Recycle Bin, as shown in Figure C-11.

3. **Drag the Ad Campaign file from the desktop to the Recycle Bin (you might have to move the Advertising window), then click Yes**
   The Recycle Bin icon should now look like it contains paper.

4. **Double-click the Recycle Bin icon**
   The Recycle Bin window opens. It contains the file that was deleted. The Recycle Bin window is like most other windows in that it contains a menu bar, a toolbar, and a status bar. Because John still needs this file he decides to restore it. The contents of the folders overlap, making it difficult for John to see both windows. He will first have to rearrange the desktop.

5. **Right-click an empty area of the taskbar, then click Tile Windows Vertically**
   This option allows you to see all open windows on the desktop at one time. The Recycle Bin window and the My Computer window appear side-by-side, as shown in Figure C-12.

6. **Select the Ad Campaign file in the Recycle Bin window, then drag it back to the Advertising window**
   The file is restored—it is intact and identical to the form it was in before you deleted it.

7. **Click the Close button in the Recycle Bin window**

FIGURE C-11: Selecting a file to drag to the Recycle Bin

Drag the selected icon here to delete the file

The selected file moved from the Advertising folder to the desktop

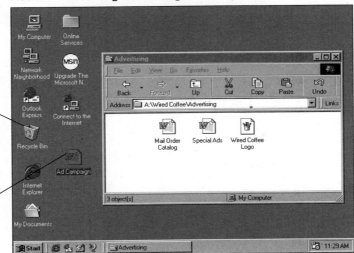

FIGURE C-12: The deleted file from the Advertising folder in the Recycle Bin

The contents of your Recycle Bin might be different

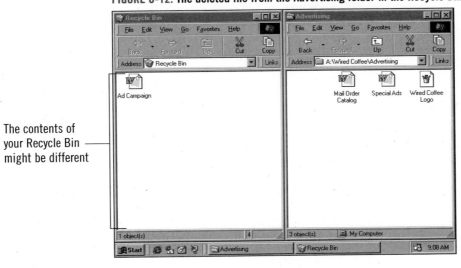

TABLE C-3: Deleting and restoring files

ways to delete a file	ways to restore a file from the recycle bin
Select the file, then click the Delete button on the toolbar	Click the Undo button on the Recycle Bin toolbar
Select the file, then press [Delete]	Select the file, click File, then click Restore
Right-click the file, then click Delete	Right-click the file, then click Restore
Drag the file to the Recycle Bin	Drag the file from the Recycle Bin to any location

CLUES TO USE

Recycle Bin properties

You can adjust several Recycle Bin settings by using the Properties option on the Recycle Bin shortcut menu. For example, if you do not want files to go to the Recycle Bin when you delete them, but, rather, want them to be immediately deleted, right-click the Recycle Bin, click Properties, then click the Do Not Move Files to the Recycle Bin check box to select the option. Also, if you find that the Recycle Bin is full and cannot accept any more files, you can increase the amount of disk space devoted to the Recycle Bin by moving the Maximum Size of Recycle Bin slider to the right. The percentage shown is of the drive on which the Recycle Bin is located.

Windows 98

Creating a Shortcut to a File

If a file or folder is buried several levels down in a file hierarchy, it could take you a while to access it. To save you time in getting to the items you use frequently, you can create shortcuts. A **shortcut** is a link between two points: a "home" folder where a file, folder, or program is actually stored and any other location where you want to access that file or program. The actual file, folder, or program remains stored in its original location, while you place the icon representing the shortcut in a convenient location, whether that is a folder or the desktop. John always uses his Wired Coffee logo in stationery, flyers, and general advertising materials. Rather than having to go through the steps to start Paint and then open the file, he'll simply place a shortcut for this Paint file on the desktop.

Steps 1 2 3 4

1. **In the Advertising folder, right-click** Wired Coffee Logo, **then click** Create Shortcut

   An icon for a shortcut to the Wired Coffee Logo now appears in the Advertising window. Compare your screen with Figure C-13. All shortcuts are named the same as the file on which they are based, but with the words "Shortcut to" in front of the original name. John wants the shortcut on his desktop for easy access to the file.

Trouble?
If you can't see an empty area of your desktop, your My Computer window is maximized. Click the Restore button to resize it.

2. **Right-click and hold the** Shortcut to Wired Coffee Logo **file, drag it from the Advertising folder to an empty area of the desktop, then click** Move Here

   The shortcut appears on the desktop, as shown in Figure C-14. A shortcut can be placed anywhere on the desktop. You should test the shortcut.

3. **Double-click the** Shortcut to Wired Coffee Logo icon

   The Paint program opens with the file named Wired Coffee Logo.

4. **Click the** Close button **in the Paint window**

   The logo file and the Paint program close. The shortcut to Wired Coffee Logo remains on the desktop until you delete it, so you can use it again and again. If you are working in a lab environment you should delete this shortcut.

5. **Right-click the** Shortcut to Wired Coffee Logo icon

   When you right-click folders and files (as opposed to the blank area in a window), a pop-up menu opens that offers several file management commands, as described in Table C-4. The commands on your pop-up menu might be different depending on the Windows 98 features installed on your computer.

6. **Click** Delete **on the pop-up menu, then click** Yes **in the Confirm File Delete dialog box**

   The shortcut is deleted from the desktop and placed in the Recycle Bin, where it will remain until John empties the Recycle Bin or restores the shortcut. When you delete a shortcut, only the shortcut is removed. The original file remains intact in its original location.

7. **Click the** Maximize button **in the Advertising window**

CLUES TO USE

Placing shortcuts on the Start menu

You can place shortcuts to your favorite files and programs on the Start menu. To do this, simply drag the folder, file, or program to the Start button, and the item will appear on the first level of the Start menu.

FIGURE C-13: **Creating a shortcut**

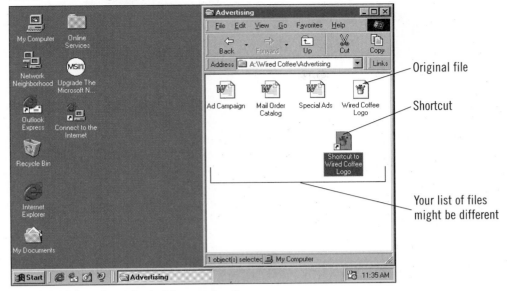

Original file

Shortcut

Your list of files
might be different

FIGURE C-14: **Dragging a shortcut to a new location**

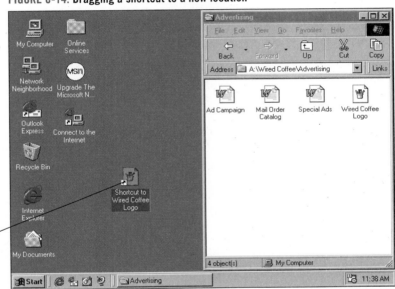

The relocated
shortcut on the
desktop

TABLE C-4: **Shortcut menu options for files and folders**

shortcut menu options	description	shortcut menu options	description
Open	Opens the file or folder	**Create Shortcut**	Creates a shortcut for the file or folder
Explore	Opens a folder or drive in Windows Explorer	**Delete**	Deletes the file or folder
Find	Finds files in a folder or drive	**Print**	Prints the file
Send To	Sends the file or folder to new location	**Quick View**	If installed, displays the contents of the file
Cut	Cuts the file or folder from its original location to the Clipboard	**Rename**	Renames the file or folder
Copy	Copies the file or folder to the Clipboard	**Properties**	Displays the properties of the file or folder
Paste	Pastes the file or folder from the Clipboard to a new location		

Displaying Drive Information

You should know as much about your system as possible. You might have to tell your instructor or technical support person certain information if you encounter a problem with your computer, or you might want to know how much space is left on a disk or want to change a **disk label** (a name you can assign to a hard or floppy disk). When you label a hard disk, the label will appear in the My Computer and Windows Explorer windows. Besides checking hard drive or floppy disk information, you can also use Windows 98 tools to check your disks for damage, optimize your disk for better performance, make copies of your disks for safe keeping, and share your disk contents with others. You can perform these activities by using the Properties command. John wants to find out how much free space is available on his floppy disk.

1. **Click the Back button list arrow** ⟨⇐ ▾⟩ **on the toolbar, then click My Computer**
John needs to display the 3½ Floppy disk icon in the My Computer window to examine property information.

2. **Right-click the icon in the My Computer window for the drive which contains your Student Disk**
The icon representing the 3½ disk drive is highlighted, and the pop-up menu opens.

3. **Click Properties on the pop-up menu**
The 3½ Floppy (A:) Properties dialog box opens with the General tab in front, as shown in Figure C-15. Click the General tab if it is not the frontmost tab. You can see a graphical representation of the amount of space being used relative to the amount available in the pie chart for the floppy disk. John reviews the chart and determines that the floppy disk contains plenty of free space. John wants to label this disk.

4. **Click the Label text box if necessary, then type StudentDisk**
A disk label can contain up to 11 characters but no spaces.

5. **Click the Tools tab**
The Tools tab becomes the frontmost tab, as shown in Figure C-16, showing you three utilities that can make Windows work more efficiently: error-checking, backup, and defragmentation. You can use the Defragmentation feature to speed up the performance of a disk. **Defragmenting** means that files will be rewritten to the disk in contiguous blocks rather than in random blocks. When you click any one of these options, Windows will update you as to when it was last used on the currently selected disk. Although these tools are mostly used for keeping a hard disk healthy, they can be used on a floppy disk as well. Table C-5 describes what each tool does.

6. **Click OK**
The Properties dialog box closes.

7. **Click the Close button in the My Computer window**

Backing up files

The more you work with a computer, the more files you'll create. To protect yourself from losing critical information, it's important to **back up** (make copies on a separate disk) your files frequently. The Backup option in the disk drive Properties dialog box walks you through a series of dialog boxes to help you back up the files on your hard disk to a floppy or tape drive. You can back up the contents of an entire disk or only certain files.

FIGURE C-15: General tab options in the 3½ Floppy (A:) Properties window

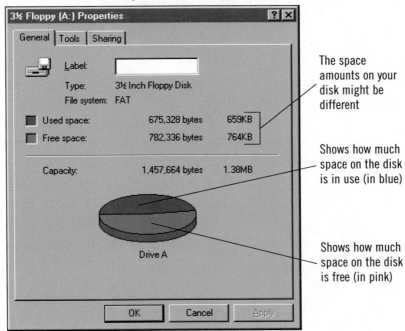

The space amounts on your disk might be different

Shows how much space on the disk is in use (in blue)

Shows how much space on the disk is free (in pink)

FIGURE C-16: Tools tab options in the 3½ Floppy (A:) Properties window

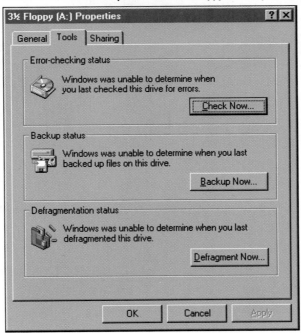

TABLE C-5: Tools in the Properties dialog box

tool	description
Error-checking status	Checks for the last time you checked the disk for damage and, if you want, attempts to correct files that are damaged
Backup status	Displays the last time you backed up the contents of the disk, and if you want, starts the Windows 98 backup program
Defragmentation status	Checks for the last time you optimized the disk, and if you want, starts the Windows 98 Defragmentation procedure

Practice

► Concepts Review

Label each of the elements of the screen shown in Figure C-17.

FIGURE C-17

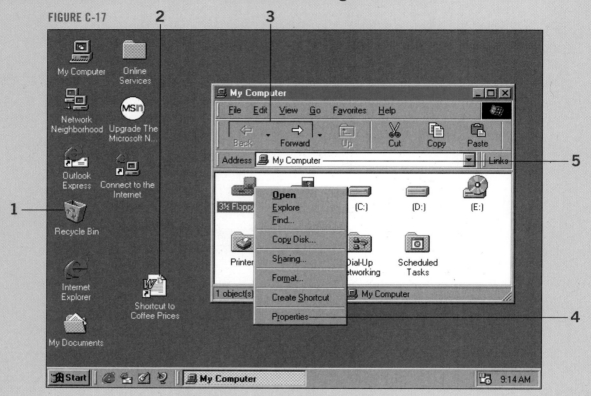

Match each of the terms with the statement that describes its function.

6. **My Computer**
7. **Shortcut**
8. **File**
9. **Recycle Bin**
10. **Folder**

a. A collection of files and folders
b. Location of deleted files
c. A file and folder management tool
d. A collection of information
e. A link to a file or folder

Select the best answer from the following list of choices.

11. **When a file is deleted, it is placed in**
    a. My Computer.
    b. Accessories.
    c. the Recycle Bin.
    d. the Desktop Container.

12. My Computer is used to
   a. manage files and folders.
   b. delete files.
   c. add folders.
   d. all of the above.

13. Which of the following is not an option for viewing files and folders?
   a. Large icons
   b. Small icons
   c. File names
   d. Details

14. When files and folders are arranged by date, they are arranged by
   a. the current date.
   b. the date they were last modified.
   c. the date they were created.
   d. the date they were last opened.

15. When right-clicking on a folder, which of the following cannot be done?
   a. Explore the folder
   b. Find a file
   c. Print the contents of the folder
   d. Create a shortcut

▶ Skills Review

1. Open and view My Computer.
   a. Insert your Student Disk in the appropriate disk drive.
   b. Double-click My Computer.
   c. Click the Maximize button in the My Computer window.
   d. Double-click the 3½ Floppy drive (A: or B:).
   e. Double-click the Wired Coffee folder.
   f. Double-click the Sales folder.

2. View files and folders.
   a. Click the Views button list arrow, then click List.
   b. Click the Up One Level button on the toolbar twice.
   c. Click the Back button on the toolbar.
   d. Open the Personnel folder.
   e. Click the Back button list arrow on the toolbar, then click Sales.
   f. Click the Forward button on the toolbar.
   g. Click View on the menu bar, then click Details.
   h. Click View on the menu bar, then click Large Icons.

3. Create folders.

   a. Right-click a blank area of the window, point to New, then click Folder.

   b. Type "Marketing" and press [Enter].

   c. Click View on the menu bar, point to Arrange Icons, then click By Name.

4. Move files.

   a. Double-click the Advertising folder.

   b. Click the Mail Order Catalog file.

   c. Click the Copy button on the toolbar.

   d. Click the Back button on the toolbar.

   e. Double-click the Marketing folder.

   f. Click the Paste button on the toolbar.

   g. Click the Back button on the toolbar.

5. Delete and restore files.

   a. Click the Marketing folder.

   b. Click the Restore button on the toolbar.

   c. Right-click the Marketing folder, drag it to the desktop, then click Move Here.

   d. Drag the Marketing folder from the desktop to the Recycle Bin, then click Yes.

   e. Double-click the Recycle Bin.

   f. Right-click an empty area of the taskbar, then click Title Windows Vertically.

   g. Click File on the Recycle Bin menu bar, click Empty Recycle Bin, then click Yes. (To restore the Marketing folder, you would drag it back to the Wired Coffee folder).

   h. Click the Close button in the Recycle Bin window.

6. Create shortcuts.

   a. Double-click the Advertising folder.

   b. Right-click the Special Ads file, then click Create Shortcut.

   c. Right-click and drag the Shortcut to Special Ads file to the desktop, then click Move Here.

   d. Right-click the Shortcut to Special Ads file, then click Delete.

   e. Click Yes.

   f. Right-click the Recycle Bin icon, then click Empty Recycle Bin.

   g. Click Yes.

7. Examine disk capacity.

   a. Click the Back button list arrow on the toolbar, then click My Computer.

   b. Right-click the icon representing your Student Disk in the My Computer window, then click Properties.

   c. Write down the capacity of the disk, how much capacity is being used, and how much is available for further use.

   d. Click OK.

   e. Click the Close button in the My Computer window.

Independent Challenges

1. As a manager at Lew's Books and Cappuccino bookstore, you need to organize the folders and files currently on the store's computer. These are located on your Student Disk in the folder named Lew's Books.

To complete this independent challenge:

1. Open My Computer, and open and view the contents of the folder called Lew's Books on your Student Disk.
2. Create a new folder called Lew's Books & Cappuccino.
3. Using paper and pencil, draw out the organization for all folders and files in Lew's Books & Cappuccino.
4. In the Lew's Books folder, create four new folders named Q1, Q2, Q3, and Q4.
5. Take the quarterly folders in the 1999 and 2000 folders and place them in the respective Q1, Q2, Q3, and Q4 folders.
6. Create a shortcut for the Collectors' Newsletter file (located in the Letters folder) and place it in the Lew's Books folder.
7. In the folder named Store Locations, create a new folder and name it New Stores.
8. Move the New Store Locations file in the Letters folder to the New Stores folder.
9. Using paper and pencil, draw out the new organization of all the folders and files in the Lew's Books folder.
10. Close My Computer.

2. You are the vice president of a small carton manufacturing company, Apex Cartons, and you need to organize your Windows 98 folders and files. As with any typical business, you have folders for correspondence (business and personal), contracts, inventory, personnel documents, and payroll information. You may have other folders as well. Your job is to organize these separate folders.

To complete this independent challenge:

1. Open My Computer and create a new folder named Apex Cartons on your Student Disk, within which the rest of the organization of files and folders for this independent challenge will appear.
2. Create a folder named Manufacturing.
3. Create a folder named Material Suppliers.
4. Create two folders; one named East Coast and one named West Coast.
5. Move (not copy) the East Coast and West Coast folders into the folder named Material Suppliers.
6. Create a file using WordPad (it doesn't have to have any text in it) and save it as "Suppliers Bid" to the Manufacturing folder on your Student Disk.
7. Move the Suppliers Bid file into the Materials Suppliers folder.
8. Using paper and pencil, draw out the new organization of all the folders and files in your Apex Cartons folder.
9. Close My Computer.

3. You and your college roommate have decided to start a mail order PC business called MO PC, and you decide to use Windows 98 to organize the files for the business. Your job is to organize the following folders and files, as well as to create shortcuts.

To complete this independent challenge:

1. Open My Computer and create a new folder named MO PC on your Student Disk, within which the rest of the organization of files and folders for this independent challenge will appear.
2. Create a new folder named Advertising.
3. Create a new folder named Customers.
4. Use WordPad to create a form letter welcoming new customers (one paragraph long), save it as "Customer Letter" and place it in the Customers folder.
5. Use WordPad to create a list of tasks that need to get done before the business opens (at least five items), save it as "Business Plan," and place it in the MO PC folder.
6. Use Paint to create a simple logo, and place it in the Advertising folder.
7. Create a shortcut for the logo.
8. Delete the Business Plan file and then restore it.
9. Using paper and pencil, draw out the new organization of all the folders and files in your MO PC folder.
10. Close My Computer.

4. M & N Bakeries just opened. You have been hired to help the owners organize their recipes into different categories and work on the design of their company logo.

For this independent challenge, use the files Icing 1, Icing 2, Brownies, Passover/Easter Torte, located in the M&N Bakeries folder on your Student Disk.

To complete this independent challenge:

1. Open My Computer and open the folder called M&N Bakeries on your Student Disk, within which the rest of the organization of files and folders for this Independent Challenge will appear.
2. Create a folder named Cakes.
3. Create a folder named Flourless Cakes, and move it into the Cakes folder.
4. Create a folder named Flour Cakes, and move it into the Cakes folder.
5. In the M&N Bakeries folder, create a folder named Cookies & Bars.
6. Place the file named Brownies in the Cookies & Bars folder.
7. Place the file named Passover & Easter Torte into the Flourless Cakes folder.
8. Move the Icing 1 recipe file to your desktop, then drag the file to the Recycle Bin.
9. Double-click to open the Recycle Bin and restore the Icing 1 recipe file to the M&N Bakeries folder on your Student Disk.
10. Using paper and pencil, draw out the new organization of all the folders and files in your M&N Bakeries folder.
11. Close My Computer.

► Visual Workshop

Re-create the screen shown in Figure C-18, which displays the My Computer window for the floppy disk drive with the Student Disk. Use Figure C-1 to help you locate the Coffee Price file on your Student Disk. Print the screen. (Press the Print Screen key to make a copy of the screen, open Paint, click Edit on the menu bar, click Paste to paste the screen into Paint, then click Yes to paste the large image, if necessary. Click File on the menu bar, click Print, then click OK.)

FIGURE C-18

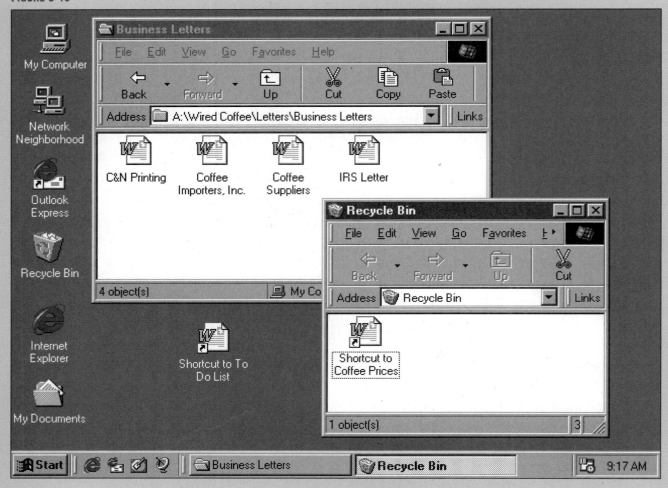

Managing

Folders and Files Using Windows Explorer

Objectives

▶ **View the Windows Explorer window**
▶ **Open and view folders in Windows Explorer**
▶ **Change the Windows Explorer window**
▶ **Create and rename folders in Windows Explorer**
▶ **Find a file**
▶ **Move and copy a file to a folder**
▶ **Restore a deleted file using Undo**
▶ **Customize a folder**

Windows 98 offers another useful feature for managing files and folders, named Windows Explorer. Windows Explorer is more powerful than My Computer, offers more features, and most importantly, allows you to work with more than one computer, folder, or file at once. This is possible because the Windows Explorer window is split into two **panes**, or frames, to accommodate a comparison of information from two different locations. You can also use Windows Explorer to copy, move, delete, and rename files and folders, as you can with My Computer. ◢ In this unit John Casey will use Windows Explorer to perform some general file management tasks and also to prepare for the upcoming Wired Coffee Spring Catalog.

Windows 98

Viewing the Windows Explorer window

The most important aspect of the Windows Explorer window is the two panes shown in Figure D-1. The pane on the left side of the screen, known as the **Explorer Bar** (or simply "the left pane"), displays all drives and folders on the computer, and the right pane displays the contents of whatever drive or folder is selected in the Explorer Bar. This arrangement enables you to simultaneously view the overall structure of the contents of your computer (the "file hierarchy") and the contents of specific folders within that structure. John wants to gain more experience working in Windows Explorer, so he starts the program and then views the contents of his computer.

Steps 1234

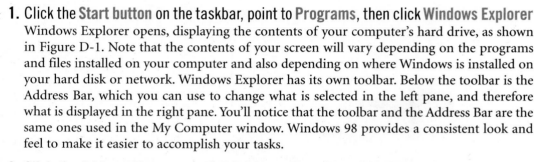

Trouble?

If you do not see the toolbar, click View on the menu bar, point to Toolbars, then click Standard Buttons to place a check mark next to it and to display the toolbar. Follow the same procedure (clicking Address Bar instead of Standard Buttons) if you don't see the Address Bar.

1. Click the Start button on the taskbar, point to Programs, then click Windows Explorer
   Windows Explorer opens, displaying the contents of your computer's hard drive, as shown in Figure D-1. Note that the contents of your screen will vary depending on the programs and files installed on your computer and also depending on where Windows is installed on your hard disk or network. Windows Explorer has its own toolbar. Below the toolbar is the Address Bar, which you can use to change what is selected in the left pane, and therefore what is displayed in the right pane. You'll notice that the toolbar and the Address Bar are the same ones used in the My Computer window. Windows 98 provides a consistent look and feel to make it easier to accomplish your tasks.

2. Click the Address list arrow on the Address Bar, then click Desktop
   The icons on the desktop are listed in the right pane. The Address Bar makes it easy to open items on the desktop and the drives, and in the folders and system folders on your computer. As an alternative to using the Address Bar, you can change what is displayed in the right pane by clicking the drive or folder in the Explorer Bar, which is the left pane. In the same way you can view the contents of your computer using the My Computer window on your desktop, you can also view the contents of your computer using Windows Explorer.

QuickTip

You can change the size of the left and right panes. Place the mouse pointer on the vertical bar that separates the two panes of the Explorer window. When the mouse changes to ←→, you can drag the line to change the size of each pane.

3. In the Explorer Bar, click the My Computer icon
   The drives and system folders on your computer are listed in the right pane.

4. Make sure your Student Disk is inserted in the appropriate disk drive, then in the right pane of Windows Explorer, double-click 3½ Floppy (A:) or (B:)
   The 3½ floppy disk drive opens, as shown in Figure D-2. The contents of the drive are shown in the right pane of Windows Explorer. You can open a folder or open a document in the right pane of Windows Explorer. When you double-click a drive or folder in the right pane, the contents of that item are shown in the right pane of the Windows Explorer. When you double-click a document, the program associated with the program starts and opens the document. You can move back and forth to the last drive or folder you displayed by using the Back and Forward buttons on the toolbar in the Explorer window just as you did in the My Computer window.

5. Click the Back button ⇐ on the toolbar
   The contents of My Computer (the last location you displayed in Step 3) are listed in the right pane of Windows Explorer.

6. Click the Forward button ⇒ on the toolbar
   The contents of the 3½ floppy disk drive reappear in the right pane of Windows Explorer. Leave Windows Explorer open and move on to the next lesson.

FIGURE D-1: Displaying the contents of your computer's hard drive

Toolbar ———

Address Bar ———

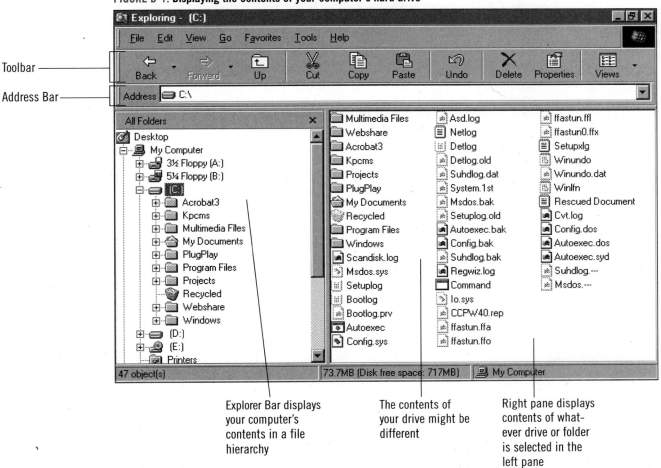

Explorer Bar displays your computer's contents in a file hierarchy

The contents of your drive might be different

Right pane displays contents of whatever drive or folder is selected in the left pane

FIGURE D-2: Contents of the 3½ floppy disk drive

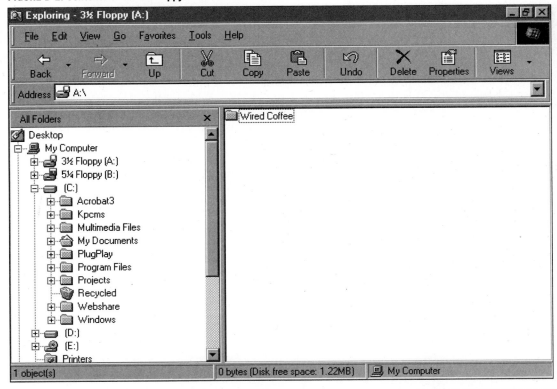

Opening and Viewing Folders in Windows Explorer

The Explorer Bar (the left pane of Windows Explorer) displays your computer's contents in file hierarchy. The top of the file hierarchy is the desktop, followed by the drives, and then the folders. The dotted gray lines indicate the different levels. You can display or hide the different levels by clicking the plus sign (+) or the minus sign (–) to the left of an icon in the Explorer Bar so that you don't always have to look at the complicated structure of your entire computer or network. Clicking the + to the left of an icon displays (or expands the drive or folder) under the icon the contents of the drive or folder, and clicking the – hides them (or "collapses" the drive or folder). Clicking the icon itself displays the contents of the item in the right pane. When neither a + nor a – appears next to an icon, it means that the item does not have any folders in it (although it might have files, which you could display in the right pane by clicking the icon). Using the + and – in the Explorer Bar allows you to quickly display the file hierarchy of the drives and folders on your computer without having to open and display the contents of each folder. John wants to open the Personnel and Letters folders without having to open and display the contents of each folder in the file hierarchy.

1. **Click the – (minus sign) next to the hard drive (C:) icon in the Explorer Bar**
   The folders on the hard drive collapse to display only the hard drive icon. The – changes to a + indicating the hard drive contains folders. Because you did not click the hard drive icon, the right pane still displays the contents of drive A as it did before. John decides to display the folders on the floppy disk drive.

2. **Click the + (plus sign) next to the 3½ Floppy drive icon in the Explorer Bar**
   The folder on the floppy disk drive, which is where your Student Disk is located, expands and appears in the Explorer Bar.

3. **Click the + next to the Wired Coffee folder in the Explorer Bar**
   The folders in the Wired Coffee folder expand and appear in the Explorer Bar, as shown in Figure D-3.

4. **Click the Personnel folder in the Explorer Bar**
   The contents of Personnel folder appear in the right pane, as shown in Figure D-4. When you click a folder in the Explorer Bar, the contents of that folder are displayed in the right pane of Windows Explorer.

5. **Click the Letters folder in the Explorer Bar, then double-click the Business Letters folder in the right pane of Windows Explorer**
   The Business Letters folder opens, as shown in Figure D-5. The contents of the Business Letters folder are shown in the right pane of Windows Explorer, and the folders in the Letters folder are expanded in the Explorer Bar.

QuickTip

Make a copy of your Student Disk before you use it. For assistance, see your instructor or technical support person.

FIGURE D-3: Folders on the 3½ floppy disk drive

Folders in the Wired Coffee folder expanded in the Explorer Bar

Contents of the 3½ floppy disk drive

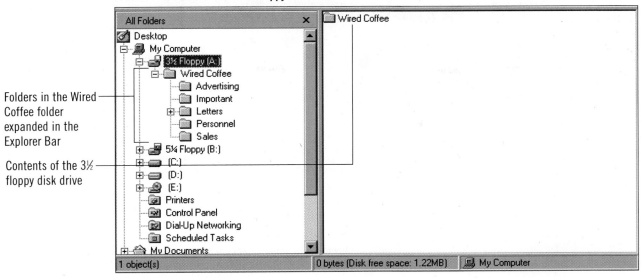

FIGURE D-4: Personnel folder

Contents of Personnel folder

Icon indicates the folder is open and its contents are displayed in the right pane

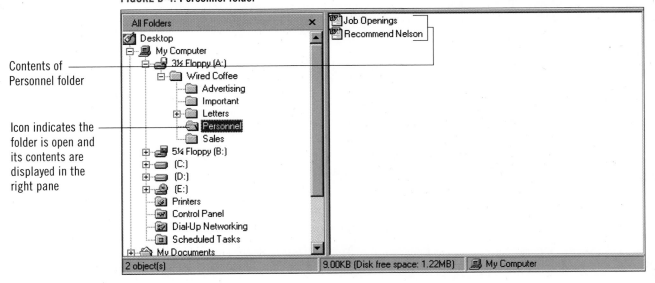

FIGURE D-5: Business Letters folder

Open folder

Contents of Business Letters folder

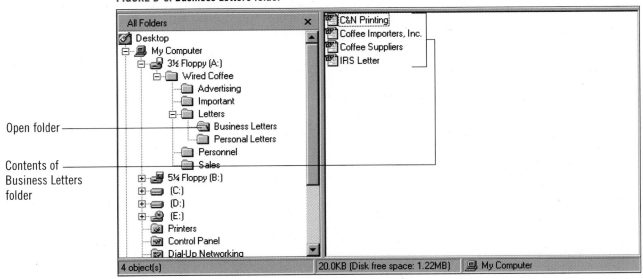

Changing the Windows Explorer Window

You can display Windows Explorer and your file hierarchy in a variety of different ways depending on what you want to see and do. For example, if you have a lot of files and folders to display, you can hide the Explorer Bar or the status bar to give you more room. If you need to change the way Windows Explorer sorts your files and folders, you can use the column indicator buttons in the right pane in Details view. When you click one of the column indicator buttons, such as Name, Size, Time, or Modified (date) in Details view, the folders and files are sorted by the type of information listed in the column. ✎ John wants to find out the date he wrote a letter to the coffee suppliers so he decides to sort the files in the Business Letters folder by date.

Steps

1. **Click the Views button list arrow 🏢▾ on the toolbar, then click Details**
   The files and folders on your Student Disk (in the 3½ floppy disk drive) are displayed in Details view, shown in Figure D-6. John wants to sort his files and folders. First, to see the file and folder information better, he closes the Explorer Bar.

2. **Click the Close button on the Explorer Bar**
   The Explorer Bar closes. You can sort by any category listed by clicking the column indicator button located at the top of the folders and files list in the right pane. The files in the Business folder are currently sorted in alphabetical order. John decides to sort the files by date.

3. **Click the Modified column indicator button**
   The files and folders are sorted by the date they were last modified, from latest to earliest, as shown in Figure D-7. You can click the Modified column indicator again to sort the list by modification date from earliest to latest.

4. **Click the Modified column indicator button again**
   The files and folders are sorted by date from earliest to latest. When you click the Name column indicator button, the list is sorted in alphabetical order from A to Z, with folders appearing before files.

5. **Click the Name column indicator button**
   The files and folders are sorted by name in alphabetical order. John finds the Coffee Suppliers file and sees the date he last modified the file. After finding the information he needs, John decides to restore the Explorer Bar.

6. **Click the View on the menu bar, point to Explorer Bar, then click All Folders**
   In the Explorer Bar, you can also display Internet-related features to search for information, list favorite Web pages, list Web pages you've visited in the past, and list channels. You'll learn more about these Internet-related features in a later lesson.

FIGURE D-6: Windows Explorer in Details view

Click to select a
different view

Column indicator
buttons

Click to close the
Explorer Bar

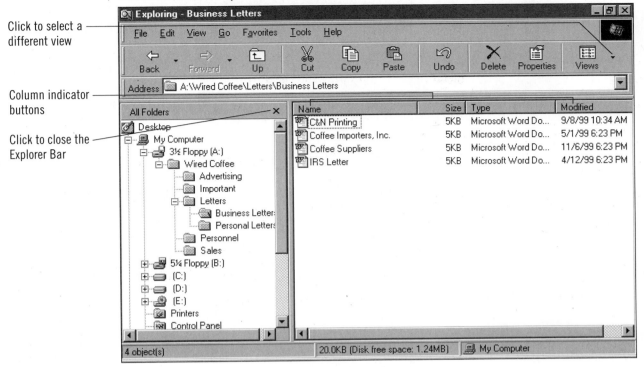

FIGURE D-7: Sorting files and folders by date

Click to sort
alphabetically
by name

Click to sort
by date

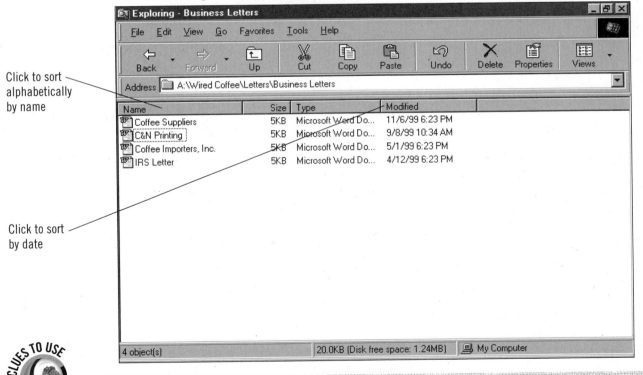

Using the status bar

The status bar at the bottom of the Windows Explorer window gives you information about drives, folders, and files on your computer. You can quickly find out how many items a drive or folder contains, the total size of its contents, where it is located on your computer and (for drives) the amount of free disk space. If you don't want to use the status bar, you can turn the status bar off by clicking View on the menu bar, then click Status Bar to remove the check mark.

Creating and Renaming Folders in Windows Explorer

To effectively manage all the files on your computer, you need folders in convenient locations to store related files. You should give each folder a meaningful name so that merely glancing at the folder reminds you what is stored there. Creating a new folder in Windows Explorer is much like doing so from My Computer. First, select the location where you want the new folder, then create the folder, and finally, name the folder. You can create a folder in Windows Explorer by using the New command on the File menu, or by right-clicking in the right pane, clicking New, then clicking folder. You can rename a folder or file in Windows Explorer using the Rename command. To do this, right-click the file or folder you want to rename, click Rename on the pop-up menu, type the new name, and then press [Enter]. John wants to create a set of new folders that will hold the files related to the creation of the Wired Coffee Spring Catalog. He then renames one of the folders.

1. Click the **Wired Coffee folder** in the Explorer Bar
To create a new folder, you must first select the drive or folder where you want the folder, which in this case is the Wired Coffee folder.

2. Click **File** on the menu bar, point to **New**, then click **Folder**
A new folder, temporarily named New Folder, appears highlighted with a rectangle around the title in the right pane of Windows Explorer, as shown in Figure D-8. To enter a new folder name, you simply type the new name. John names it "Spring Catalog".

3. Type **Spring Catalog**, then press **[Enter]** or click an empty area in the right pane
The Spring Catalog folder appears in both panes, as shown in Figure D-8. John wants to create folders within the Spring Catalog folder.

4. In the right pane, double-click the **Spring Catalog folder**
Nothing appears in the right pane because the folder is empty; there have been no new files or folders created or moved here. Because Spring Catalog is the currently selected folder, the folders that John creates will be located here.

5. Right-click anywhere in the right pane, point to **New** on the pop-up menu, then click **Folder**
A new folder, named New Folder, appears in the right pane of Windows Explorer.

6. Type **Catalog Text**, then press **[Enter]**
The folder is now named Catalog Text, as shown in Figure D-9. Notice also that there is a + (or a – if the folder is expanded) next to the Spring Catalog folder in the left pane, indicating that this folder contains other folders or files. John decides to change the name of the new folder to Catalog Pages.

7. Right-click the **Catalog Text folder** in the right pane, then click **Rename** on the pop-up menu, as shown in Figure D-10
The folder appears highlighted with a rectangle around the title in the right pane of Windows Explorer.

8. Type **Catalog Pages**, then press **[Enter]**
The folder is renamed from Catalog Text to Catalog Pages.

Trouble?

If nothing happens when you type the name, you pressed [Enter] or clicked outside the new folder. Select the folder, click the name "New Folder" so a rectangle surrounds it (with the insertion point inside), then repeat Step 3.

QuickTip

To rename a file, you can also select the item, click the name so a rectangle surrounds it, type the new name, then press [Enter].

FIGURE D-8: **Newly created folder**

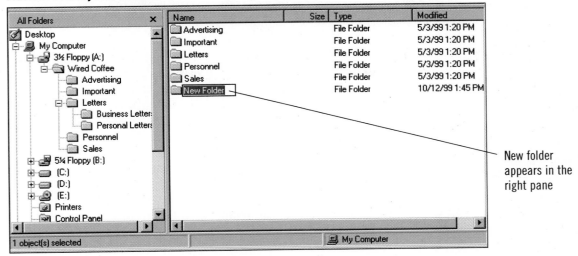

New folder appears in the right pane

FIGURE D-9: **Creating a new folder using right-click method**

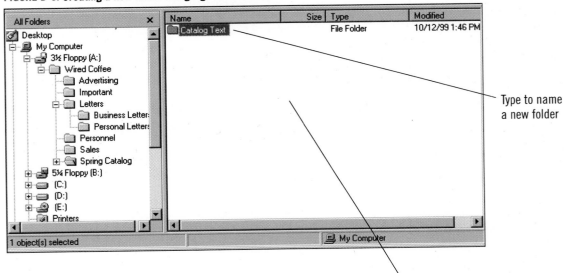

Type to name a new folder

Click an empty area to complete the folder name

FIGURE D-10: **Renaming a folder using right-click method**

Right-click to display a pop-up menu

+ (or −) indicates that this folder contains other folders

Click to rename folder

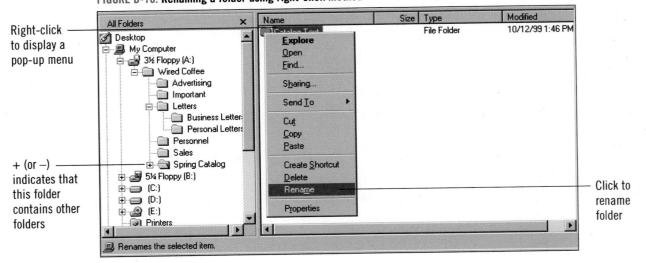

Windows 98

Finding a File

Sometimes it is difficult to remember precisely where you stored a file. Windows Explorer provides a Find program located on the Tools menu to help you find the files or folders you are looking for. The Find program gives you the option to find files or folders by name, location, size, type, and the date on which it was created or last modified. The Find program is also available on the Start menu to help you locate files and folders when you are not using Windows Explorer. To access the Find program on the Start menu, click the Start button on the taskbar, point to Find, and then click Files or Folders. ⬤ John wants to find a file he created several months ago with a preliminary outline for the Spring Catalog. He cannot remember the exact title of the file or where he stored it, so he needs to do a quick search.

Steps 1234

QuickTip

Insert the * (asterisk) wild-card symbol in a filename when you're unsure of the entire name. For example, type S*rs to find not only the file named Suppliers, but also all other files beginning with S and ending with rs (such as Stars and Sportscars).

1. **Click Tools on the menu bar, point to Find, then click Files or Folders**
   The Find: All Files window opens, shown in Figure D-11. Table D-1 lists the tabs in The Find: All Files window and describes the search options each offers. Since John remembers part of the name (but not the location) of the file he needs, he can use the Name & Location tab.

2. **Type Catalog in the Named text box**
   You can supply the full name of the folder or file you want to find, or only the part you're sure of. If, for example, John were unsure as to whether or not he had saved the file as Spring Catalog or Catalog Outline, he could type Catalog, since he's sure of that much of the name. If John didn't know the name of the file, but did know some text contained in the file, he could enter the text in the Containing text text box. Before you can start the search, you need to indicate where you want the Find program to search. The Find program initially begins searching in the open folder in Windows Explorer, but you can choose the location you want.

3. **Click the Look in list arrow, then click the drive that contains your Student Disk**

4. **Click Find Now**
   The Find program searches all the folders and files on your Student Disk and lists those folders and files whose names contain the word "Catalog" in the box at the bottom of the Find: All Files window. The full names, locations, sizes, types, and the dates on which the folders or files were created or last modified are listed.

5. **Position the pointer between the In Folder column indicator button and the Size column indicator button; when the pointer changes to ↔ drag to the right to display the location of the file, as shown in Figure D-12**
   At this point, John can either double-click the file to start the associated program and open the file, or he can note the file's location and close the Find: Files named Catalog window. He decides to note the file's location and close the window.

6. **Click the Close button in the Find: Files named Catalog window**

CLUES TO USE

Performing an Advanced Search

You can also complete an advanced search that uses criteria, or information, beyond just the name or partial name of the file. If you have no idea what the name or content of the file is, but can recall the type of file (such as a WordPad document), then use the Advanced tab in the Find: All Files window, and select a file type using the Of type list arrow, shown in Figure D-13. When you click Find Now, Windows will search for and display all the files for the type you specified. This can take a long time, although probably less time than it would take to re-create the missing file.

FIGURE D-11: Find: All Files window

Enter name or partial name of the file you are looking for here

Enter text contained in the file here

Click to include all subfolders (folders within folders)

Options for searching using criteria

After specifying what to search for, click to begin search

Specify where you think the file is here

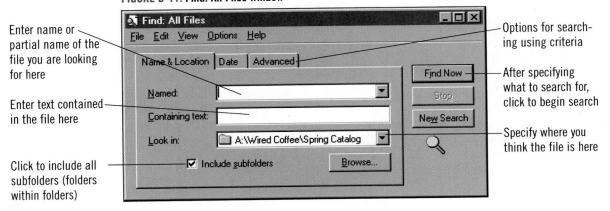

FIGURE D-12: Results of search for Catalog file

Click to start a new search

Drag to resize column size

Files that match your search

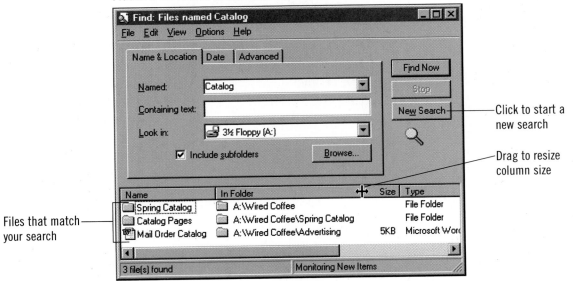

FIGURE D-13: Using advanced search features

Type of file

Size of file

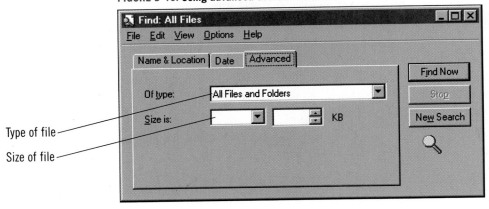

Table D-1: Tabs in the Find: All Files window

tab	use to
Name & Location	Find the file by name, location, and text the file contains; browse through directories for the file
Date	Search for files created during the previous number of days or months, or between a certain period of time that you specify
Advanced	Search for files by type (such as a WordPad file) or a file's size

Copying and Moving a File to a Folder

You should always store your files in the appropriate folders. Sometimes this means moving a file from one folder to another (removing it from the first and placing it in the second) and sometimes this means copying a file from one folder to another (leaving it in the first but placing a copy of it in the second). You can move and copy files and folders in several different ways in Windows Explorer. You can use the Cut, Copy, and Paste buttons on the Windows Explorer toolbar. Or you can "drag and drop" the file or folder while holding down a mouse button. A third way is to right-click the file or folder and choose the appropriate command from the pop-up menu. John plans to use text from the Mail Order Catalog file (currently located in the Advertising folder) in the Spring Catalog, so he wants to move the Mail Order Catalog file from the Advertising folder to the Catalog Pages folder. He also wants to make a copy of the Wired Coffee Logo file and place it in the Spring Catalog folder.

Steps

1. **Click the + next to the Spring Catalog folder in the Explorer Bar**
   The Spring Catalog folder expands displaying the folder it contains.

2. **Click the Advertising folder in the Explorer Bar**
   The contents of the folder are shown in the right pane of Windows Explorer. When moving or copying files or folders in Windows Explorer, make sure the files or folders you want to move or copy are displayed in the right pane. To move the Mail Order Catalog file, John will drag it from the right pane to the Catalog Pages folder in the Explorer Bar.

3. **Drag the Mail Order Catalog file across the vertical line separating the two panes to the Catalog Pages folder as shown in Figure D-14, then release the mouse button**
   Once you release the mouse button, the Mail Order Catalog file is relocated into the Catalog Pages folder. If you decide that you didn't want the file moved, you can move it back easily using the Undo button on the toolbar. Now John copies the Wired Coffee Logo file in the Advertising folder to the Spring Catalog folder.

4. **Point to the Wired Coffee Logo file, press and hold the right mouse button, drag the file across the vertical line separating the two panes to the Spring Catalog folder, then release the mouse button**
   As Figure D-15 shows, the pop-up menu offers a choice of options. The Copy Here option is listed second. You can also right-click a file in the right pane to open a pop-up menu—another way to copy or move the file to a new location.

5. **Click Copy Here**
   The original file named Wired Coffee Logo remains in the Advertising folder and a copy of the file has been placed in the Spring Catalog folder.

6. **Click the Spring Catalog folder in the Explorer Bar**
   The Wired Coffee Logo file was copied from the Advertising folder (where the original is still located) to the Spring Catalog folder (where the copy is located).

QuickTip

To quickly copy a file from one folder to another on the same disk, select the file, press and hold [Ctrl], then drag the file to the folder. You can also copy a file from a hard disk to a floppy disk by right-clicking the file, pointing to Send To, then clicking the appropriate disk drive icon.

FIGURE D-14: Moving a file from one folder to another

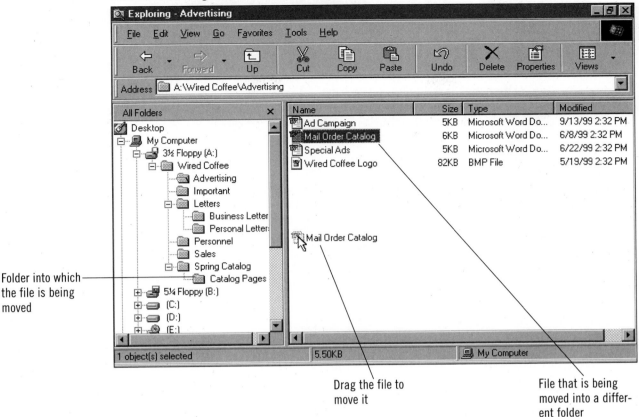

Folder into which the file is being moved

Drag the file to move it

File that is being moved into a different folder

FIGURE D-15: Copying a file from one location to another

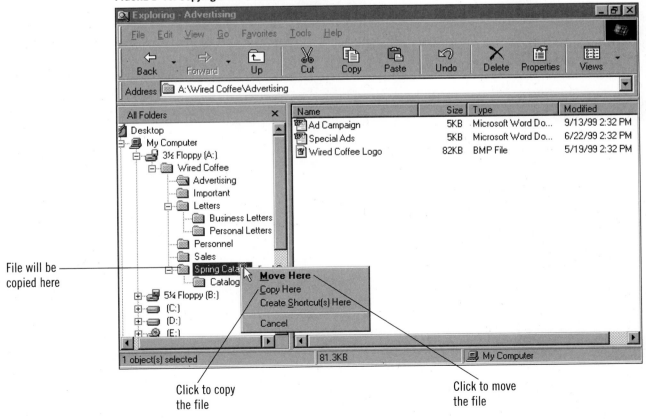

File will be copied here

Click to copy the file

Click to move the file

Windows 98

Restoring a Deleted File Using Undo

To keep your files and folders manageable, you should delete files and folders you no longer need. All the items you delete from your hard disk are stored in the Recycle Bin, so that if you accidentally delete an item, you can move it out of the Recycle Bin to restore it, or you can use the Undo command. You cannot restore files and folders that you delete from a floppy disk or that you drag from a floppy disk to the Recycle Bin. Windows does not store items deleted from a floppy disk in the Recycle Bin, rather they are deleted (after a confirmation). See Table D-2 for the various methods of deleting and restoring items. ▶ In this lesson, you'll delete a file and then restore it using the Undo command. Because you cannot restore files deleted from a floppy disk, you will start by moving a file from your Student Disk to the desktop.

1. Click the + next to the hard drive (C:) icon in the Explorer Bar

The hard drive is expanded in the left pane and the contents of the Spring Catalog folder appear in the right pane.

2. Right-click the Wired Coffee Logo file in the right pane, drag it to the My Documents folder in the Explorer Bar, then click Move Here

The Wired Coffee file is now moved to the My Documents folder.

3. Click the My Documents folder in the Explorer Bar

The My Documents folder is a general folder in which you can store files and folders. When you delete the Wired Coffee Logo file, it will be stored in the Recycle Bin, and you'll be able to restore it using the Undo command.

4. Scroll to the bottom of the Explorer Bar, then drag the Wired Coffee Logo file in the right pane to the Recycle Bin in the Explorer Bar

You can also right-click the file and then click Delete, or select the file and then press [Delete]. A confirmation dialog box appears, as shown in Figure D-16.

5. Click Yes

The Wired Coffee Logo file is now removed from the My Documents folder and is stored in the Recycle Bin.

6. Click the Undo button 🔙 on the toolbar

The Wired Coffee Logo file is now restored to the My Documents folder. The Undo command also lets you reverse multiple actions, so you can use the Undo command again to move the Wired Coffee Logo file back into the Spring Catalog folder on your Student Disk.

7. Click 🔙 again

The Wired Coffee Logo file is now moved back to the Spring Catalog folder.

8. Scroll to the top of the Explorer Bar, then click the Spring Catalog folder in the Explorer Bar

The contents of the Spring Catalog folder, including the Wired Coffee Logo file, appear in the right pane, as shown in Figure D-17.

QuickTip

Some computers are set up so that the Recycle Bin isn't used—deleted files are removed from the hard drive immediately. To check whether your Recycle Bin is being used, right-click the Recycle Bin on the desktop, then click Properties. If the Do not move files to the Recycle Bin check box has a check in it, click the check box to turn this option off.

QuickTip

Files and folders that you delete from your hard drive remain in the Recycle Bin until you either restore them or empty the Recycle Bin. To empty the Recycle Bin, right-click it (on the desktop or in Windows Explorer), then click Empty Recycle Bin.

FIGURE D-16: **Confirm File Delete dialog box**

Click to confirm delete (send file to Recycle Bin)

File dragged to Recycle Bin

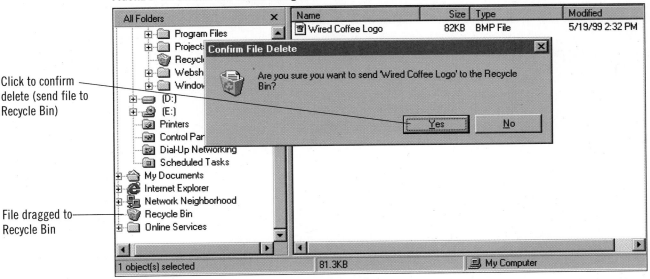

FIGURE D-17: **Using Undo to restore a file to its original location**

Wired Coffee file is restored to the Spring Catalog folder

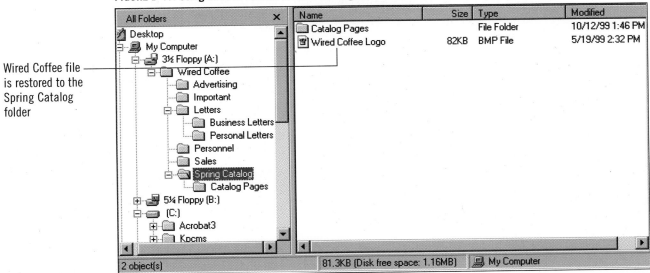

TABLE D-2: **Methods for deleting and restoring files in Windows Explorer**

action	methods
Delete	• Right-click the file or folder you want to delete, then click Delete
	• Drag the file or folder to the Recycle Bin
	• Select the file or folder, click File on the menu bar, then click Delete
	• Select the file or folder you want to delete, then press [Del]
	• Select the file or folder you want to delete, then click the Delete button on the toolbar
Restore	Open the Recycle Bin, then
	• Select the file or folder you want to restore, click File on the menu bar, then click Restore
	• Right-click the file or folder you want to restore, then click Restore
	• Drag the file or folder to a new location on the desktop

Windows 98

Customizing a Folder

To make working in Windows Explorer more interesting and appealing, you can customize the way a folder looks when it is open (when its contents are displayed in the right pane). As you have seen, by default folders appear against a white background. You can change the background color, select a picture to use as a background, or even create your own Web page view of the folder. Windows Explorer comes with a **wizard** (a series of dialog boxes) that walks you through the steps of customizing a folder. ✎ John wants to customize the background of the Wired Coffee folder to display the Wired Coffee logo.

Steps 1 2 3 4

1. **Click the Wired Coffee folder in the Explorer Bar**
   The contents of Wired Coffee folder are listed in the right pane of Windows Explorer.

2. **Click View on the menu bar, then click Customize this Folder**
   The Customize this Folder Wizard opens, as shown in Figure D-18. This wizard helps you change the background appearance of the currently displayed folder. See Table D-3 for a description of the wizard options.

3. **Click the Choose a background picture option button, then click Next**
   Now you need to select a background picture for the Wired Coffee folder. You can select a picture from the list provided, or you can click the Browse button to select a picture stored elsewhere on your computer. John wants to select the Wired Coffee Logo file, which is stored on the Student Disk, so he clicks the Browse button.

4. **Click Browse**
   The Open dialog box opens, displaying the My Documents folder. John selects the Wired Coffee Logo file on the Student Disk.

5. **Click the Look in list arrow, click the drive that contains your Student Disk, double-click the Wired Coffee folder, double-click the Advertising folder, then double-click Wired Coffee Logo**
   The Wired Coffee Logo file is displayed in the left pane of the Customize this Folder dialog box and selected in the list of available background pictures.

6. **Click Next**
   The wizard displays the filename and location of the background picture you have selected. You can click the Back button to change the picture you have selected or click the Finish button to complete the wizard with the selected picture.

7. **Click Finish**
   The right pane of Windows Explorer displays the Wired Coffee logo in the background, as shown in Figure D-19. John is finished working with Windows Explorer, so he closes the program.

8. **Click the Close button in Windows Explorer**
   Windows Explorer closes.

FIGURE D-18: Customize this Folder Wizard

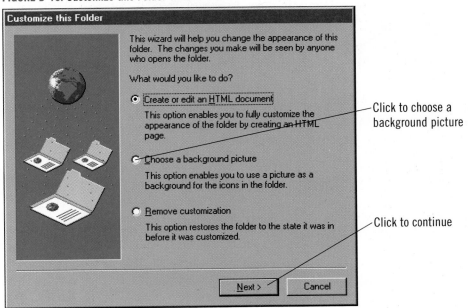

Click to choose a background picture

Click to continue

FIGURE D-19: Customized Wired Coffee folder

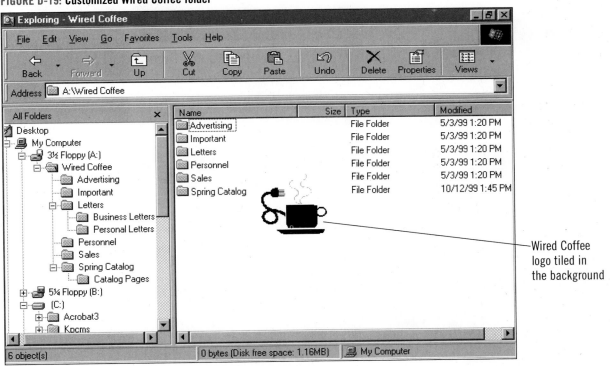

Wired Coffee logo tiled in the background

TABLE D-3: Customize this Folder Wizard options

option	allows you to...
Create or edit an HTML document	Create or edit an Internet document to view the folder as a Web page (you must know how to use HTML, a computer programming language, to use this option)
Choose a background picture	Change the background color or select a picture as a background for the folder
Remove customization	Remove the previous customization of the folder

▶ Concepts Review

Label each of the elements of the screen shown in Figure D-20.

FIGURE D-20

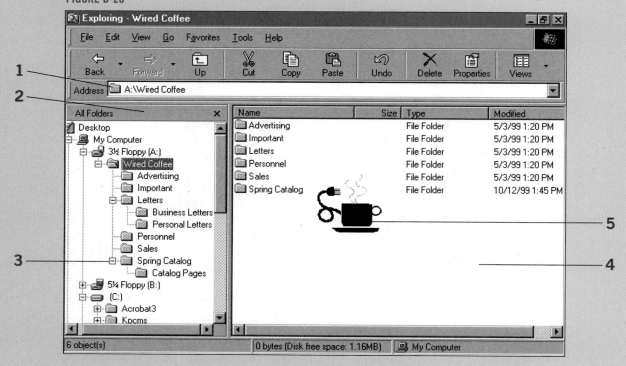

1

2

3

5

4

Match each of the terms with the statement that describes its function.

6. Move a file or folder to the Recycle Bin
7. Column indicator
8. Panes
9. + icon
10. Right-click an icon

a. Icon that is clicked to expand folder contents
b. Frames that display information from two different locations
c. Delete selected file or folder from a hard drive
d. Opens pop-up menu
e. Sorts files and folders

Select the best answer from the following list of choices.

11. Windows Explorer is different from My Computer in that it allows you to
    a. View the overall structure of your computer's contents.
    b. View the contents of a folder or drive.
    c. Change the view.
    d. Move between folders.

12. **Where is the Explorer Bar located in Windows Explorer?**
    a. Right pane
    b. Left pane
    c. Folder
    d. Hard drive

13. **In Windows Explorer, which of the following do you click to display the contents of a folder or drive in the Explorer Bar?**
    a. +
    b. −
    c. ▣
    d. ⇦

14. **To sort files and folders in Windows Explorer, click**
    a. View on the menu bar, then click Sort.
    b. A column indicator button.
    c. The Views button list arrow on the toolbar, then click List.
    d. View on the menu bar, then click Arrange.

15. **Which of the following is NOT a valid search criterion for a file using the Find program?**
    a. Name
    b. Location
    c. Date modified
    d. Date opened

16. **To copy a folder or file in Windows Explorer**
    a. Double-click the folder or file.
    b. Left-click the folder or file, then click Copy.
    c. Press [Ctrl] and drag the folder or file.
    d. Drag the folder or file.

17. **When a folder or file is moved**
    a. The original is moved.
    b. A copy of the original is created.
    c. A copy of the original is created and moved.
    d. A shortcut is created and moved.

18. **Which of the following locations is NOT a valid place from which to delete a file to the Recycle Bin?**
    a. Hard drive
    b. My Computer
    c. Floppy disk
    d. My Documents folder

19. **Which of the following is NOT a Customize this Folder Wizard option?**
    a. Choose a background picture
    b. Create and edit an HTML document
    c. Remove customization
    d. Choose a color scheme

► Skills Review

1. **View the Windows Explorer window and identify the items in it.**
   a. Insert your Student Disk in the appropriate disk drive.
   b. Click the Start button on the taskbar, point to Programs, then click Windows Explorer.
   c. Click the Address list arrow, then click My Computer.
   d. Double-click 3½ Floppy drive (A:) or (B:) to explore the contents of the floppy.
   e. Click the Back button on the toolbar.
   f. Click the Forward button on the toolbar.

2. **Open and view folders in Windows Explorer.**
   a. Click the − next to the hard drive (C:) icon in the Explorer Bar.
   b. Click the + next to the 3½ floppy drive icon in the Explorer Bar.
   c. Click the + next to the Wired Coffee folder in the Explorer Bar.
   d. Click the Personnel folder in the Explorer Bar.
   e. Click the Letters folder in the Explorer Bar.
   f. Double-click the Business Letters folder in the right pane.

3. **Change the Windows Explorer window and sort files and folders date and names.**
   a. Click the Views button list arrow on the toolbar, then click Details.
   b. Click the Close button in the Explorer Bar.
   c. Click the Modified column indicator button.
   d. Click the Name column indicator button.
   e. Click View on the menu bar, point to Explorer Bar, then click All Folders.

4. **Create and name new folders.**
   a. Click the Wired Coffee folder in the Explorer Bar.
   b. Right-click a blank area of the right pane of Windows Explorer.
   c. Point to New on the pop-up menu, then click Folder.
   d. Name the folder Money, then press [Enter].
   e. Click File on the menu bar, point to New, then click Folder.
   f. Name this folder Legal, then press [Enter].
   g. Right-click the Money folder, then click Rename.
   h. Rename this folder Financial, then press [Enter].

5. **Find a file.**
   a. Click Tools on the menu bar, point to Find, then click Files or Folders.
   b. Type "IRS" in the Named text box.
   c. Click the Look in list arrow, then click 3½ Floppy (A:) or (B:).
   d. Click Find Now.
   e. Write down the location of the IRS Letter file.
   f. Click the Close button in the Find: All Files window.

6. **Copy a file from one location to another.**
   a. Locate the IRS Letter file on your Student Disk.
   b. Drag the IRS Letter file in the right pane to the Financial folder in the Explorer Bar.
   c. Right-click and then drag the Coffee Importers, Inc. file from the Business folder in the right pane to the Legal folder in the Explorer Bar.
   d. Click Copy Here on the pop-up menu.
   e. Click the Legal folder in the Explorer Bar.

7. Restore deleted files using Undo.

a. Click the + next to the hard drive (C:) icon in the Explorer Bar.
b. Right-drag the Coffee Importers, Inc. file from the Legal folder in the right pane to the My Documents folder in the Explorer Bar, then click Move Here.
c. Click the My Documents folder in the Explorer Bar.
d. Scroll to the bottom of the Explorer Bar.
e. Drag the Coffee Importers, Inc. file from the My Documents folder in the right pane to the Recycle Bin in the Explorer Bar.
f. Click Yes.
g. Click the Undo button on the toolbar.
h. Click the Undo button on the toolbar again.
i. Scroll to the top of the Explorer Bar.

8. Customize a folder.

a. Click the Business Letters folder in the Explorer Bar.
b. Click View on the menu bar, then click Customize this Folder.
c. Click the Choose a background picture option button.
d. Click Next, then click Browse.
e. Select the Wired Coffee Logo file in the Advertising folder on your Student Disk.
f. Click Open.
g. Click Next.
h. Click Finish.
i. Click the Close button in Windows Explorer.

▶ Independent Challenges

1. You have just started Sewing Works, a sewing machine repair business, and want to use Windows 98 to organize your documents. For this challenge, you will create on your Student Disk a set of files that are relevant to the business and organize them in a set of folders that will make it easy for you to locate what you need when you need it.

To complete this independent challenge:

1. Create a WordPad file named Wilson Letter thanking Mr. Wilson for his business. Save this file and the other files you create on your Student Disk.
2. Create another WordPad file named Suppliers. List the following suppliers in the file:
Apex Sewing Machine Parts
PO Box 3645
Tempe, AZ 12345

Jones Sewing Repair
18th and 3rd Avenues
Brooklyn, NY 09091
3. Create a third WordPad file and name it Bills. List the following information in the file:

Apex	16453	$34.56
Jones	47354	$88.45
Ott	44412	$98.56

4. On your Student Disk, create a folder named Sewing Works.
5. In the Sewing Works folder, create three new folders: Letters, Contacts, and Accounts.

6. Expand the Sewing Works folder in the Explorer Bar.
7. Move the file named Wilson Letter into the Letters folder, the file named Suppliers into the Contacts folder, and the file named Bills into the Accounts folder.
8. Open the Letters folder.
9. Print the screen. (Press the Print Screen key to make a copy of the screen, open Paint, click Edit on the menu bar, click Paste to paste the screen into Paint, then click Yes to paste the large image, if necessary. Click File on the menu bar, click Print, then click OK.)
10. Close Windows Explorer.

2. As manager of the summer program at a day camp, you need to keep your folders and files organized so information can be easily and quickly found. Your files fall into two main categories: children and activities. You need to create a folder for each category and place them in a separate folder named Camp 1999, to distinguish your work this year from other years you've managed the camp.
  To complete this independent challenge:

1. On your Student Disk, create three folders: Camp 1999, Campers, and Activities.
2. Create a WordPad file named Camper Data. Save the file on your Student Disk. In this file, create information on five campers, including their name, age, bunk, and favorite sports. Here's a sample of two:

Name	Age	Bunk #	Sports
Bill Moore	11	3	Swimming, Horseshoes
Michael Morley	12	4	Basketball

3. Move the file named Camper Data into the folder named Campers.
4. Create a WordPad file named Activities Overview. Save the file on your Student Disk. In this folder, create information on five camp activities, including the name, equipment or supplies the children need to supply, number of children, and name of the activity leader. Here's a sample of two:

Activity	Children provide	Number allowed	Leader
Swimming	Swimsuit, water wings if needed	18	John Lee
Soccer	Shoes, shin guards	24	Madeline Harman

5. Move the file named Activities Overview into the folder named Activities.
6. Move the Activities folder and the Campers folder into the Camp 1999 folder.
7. Expand the Camp 1999 folder in the Explorer Bar.
8. Open the Campers folder.
9. Copy the Camper Data file to the Activities folder.
10. Open the Activities folder.
11. Print the screen. (See Independent Challenge 1, Step 9 for screen printing instructions.)
12. Close Windows Explorer.

3. The summer fine arts program that you manage has different categories of participation for young adults, including two-week and four-week programs. In order for you to keep track of who is participating in each program, you have to organize the following list into folders. For this challenge, you'll have to create new folders, create a list of participants, and then move the document lists into folders.
  To complete this independent challenge:

1. On your Student Disk, create a folder named Summer Program 1999.
2. Within the Summer Program 1999 folder, create a folder named Arts.
3. Within the Arts folder, create two other folders named 2 Weeks and 4 Weeks.

4. Create a WordPad file named 2 Weeks Art on your Student Disk with the following information:
   Leni Welitoff   2 weeks   painting
   Tom Stacey   2 weeks   ceramics and jewelry
5. Create a WordPad file named 4 Weeks Art on your Student Disk with the following information:
   Kim Dayton   4 weeks   painting and landscape design
   Sara Jackson   4 weeks   set construction
6. Move the files you created into their respective folders named 2 Weeks and 4 Weeks.
7. Rename the folder Arts to Fine Arts.
8. Collapse and expand the Summer Program 1999 folder.
9. Expand Fine Arts folders.
10. Open the 4 Weeks folder located in the Fine Arts folder.
11. Use the Print Screen key to make a copy of the screen, then print it from the Paint program (see your instructor for details).
12. Find the files on your Student Disk that contain "painting" in the text (not the title).
13. Print the screen. (See Independent Challenge 1, Step 9 for screen printing instructions.)
14. Close Windows Explorer.

4. As the head of the graphics department in a small design firm, one of your jobs is to organize the clip art images used by the company. The two categories in which you want to place an image are Lines and Shapes. You can place clip art images in more than one category as well. For this challenge, you'll have to create several folders and Paint images, then move and copy them to different folders.

To complete this independent challenge:

1. On your Student Disk, create four different Paint images and save them using the following names: Ellipses, Lines, and Curves.
2. On your Student Disk, create two folders named Lines and Shapes.
3. Move the Curves and Lines files to the Lines folder.
4. Move the Ellipses file to the Shapes folder.
5. Copy the Curves file into the Shapes folder.
6. Rename the Ellipses file to Ovals.
7. Customize the Lines folder with the Curves file.
8. Open the Lines folder.
9. Print the screen. (See Independent Challenge 1, Step 9 for screen printing instructions.)
10. Close Windows Explorer.

▶ Visual Workshop

Re-create the screen shown in Figure D-21, which displays the Windows Explorer. Print the screen. (See Independent Challenge 1, Step 9 for screen printing instructions.)

FIGURE D-21

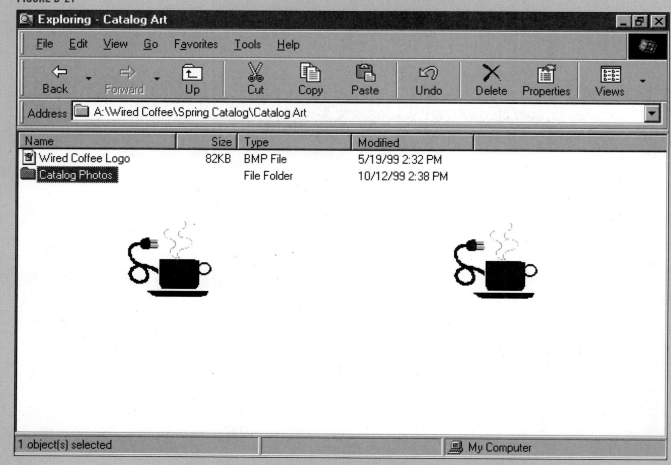

Customizing

Windows 98 Using the Control Panel

Objectives

► **Customize the Active Desktop**

► **Change the Desktop Background and Screen**

► **Saver Setting**

► **Change the Desktop Color Scheme**

► **Set the Date and Time**

► **Work with Fonts**

► **Customize Mouse Operations**

► **Examine System Properties**

► **Customize the Taskbar**

► **Add an Item to the Start Menu**

In this unit you'll learn how to customize Windows 98 to suit your personal needs and preferences. Most Windows features can be adjusted through the **Control Panel**, a central location where you can change Windows settings. The Control Panel contains several icons, each of which opens a dialog box for changing the **properties**, or characteristics, of a specific element of your computer, such as the mouse, the keyboard, or the desktop. John Casey needs to change some of the settings on his computer to make his computing environment more attractive and efficient. *If you are concerned about changing the aspects of Windows 98 at your location and do not wish to customize, simply read through this unit without completing the steps, or click the Cancel button in any dialog box where a change could be made.*

Windows 98

Customizing the Active Desktop

Because more and more people are using the Internet, Windows 98 includes the **Active Desktop**, a feature that allows you to view your desktop as you would documents on the Internet, and the Active Desktop items, such as the Channel Bar. **Active Desktop items** are elements you can place on the desktop to access or display information from the Internet. For example, you can add an Active Desktop item to continuously display stock prices or weather information. Using the Control Panel Display Properties dialog box, you can customize the desktop to display the Active Desktop items you want to use. In addition, you can also change the way you click on desktop icons. For example, you can change double-clicking to open an item to single-clicking. When you use this setting, your desktop looks and acts like a document on the Internet, known as a **Web page.** ✒ John wants to learn how to customize the Active Desktop.

Steps 1 2 3 4

QuickTip

To open the Display Properties dialog box from the Control Panel, double-click the Display icon.

1. **Right-click in an empty area on the desktop, point to Active Desktop, then click Customize my Desktop**
   The Display Properties dialog box opens, displaying the Web tab, as shown in Figure E-1. The Web tab provides a list of Active Desktop items and a preview of those items. To enable or disable (turn on or off) items on the Active Desktop, you select or deselect the Active Desktop item check boxes. John decides to disable the Internet Explorer Channel Bar on the Active Desktop.

QuickTip

You can quickly disable all Active Desktop items from the desktop by right-clicking the desktop, pointing to Active Desktop, then clicking View as Web Page to remove the check mark.

2. **Click the Internet Explorer Channel Bar check box to deselect it**
   The Internet Explorer Channel Bar is removed from the preview display. You can disable all Active Desktop items by clicking the View my Active Desktop as a Web page check box to deselect the option. John changes his mind and enables the Active Desktop item.

3. **Click the Internet Explorer Channel Bar check box to select it**
   The Internet Explorer Channel Bar is displayed in the preview display. Besides enabling and disabling Active Desktop items, you can also change the way you select and open folders and icons on the desktop and in My Computer and Windows Explorer.

QuickTip

You can open the Folder Options dialog box directly by clicking the Start button, pointing to Settings, and then clicking Folders Options.

4. **Click Folder Options, then click Yes to save and close the Display Properties dialog box**
   The Folder Options dialog box opens, displaying the General tab. The option buttons at the bottom of the dialog box determine how you click on desktop icons. Your desktop can have a classic look like it did in Windows 95, or it can have a Web page, or Internet, style look.

5. **Click the Web style option button**
   Notice the Preview box changes to show the Web style desktop view, as shown in Figure E-2. If you prefer a combination of the Web style and Classic style, you can select the Custom option. John decides to use the current custom settings.

6. **Click the Custom, based on settings you choose option button, then click Settings**
   The Custom Settings dialog box opens in which you can change the way you click items, open folders, and use the Active Desktop.

7. **Click OK, then click Close**
   The Custom Settings dialog box and the Folder Options dialog box close.

FIGURE E-1: Display Properties dialog box

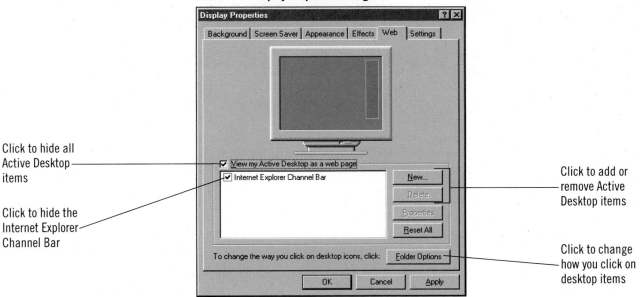

Click to hide all Active Desktop items

Click to hide the Internet Explorer Channel Bar

Click to add or remove Active Desktop items

Click to change how you click on desktop items

FIGURE E-2: Folder Options dialog box

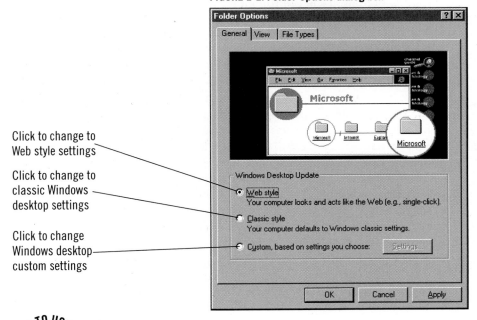

Click to change to Web style settings

Click to change to classic Windows desktop settings

Click to change Windows desktop custom settings

CLUES TO USE

Viewing a window as a Web page

If you prefer the look and feel of the Internet, you can view icons in a window as a Web page. When you view a window as a Web page, the panel along the left side of the window provides helpful information. When you select an icon, the panel displays a description or the properties of the item, as shown in the Control Panel window in Figure E-3. To view a window as a Web page, click the Views button list arrow [icon] on the toolbar, then click as Web Page. To return to the previous window view, click as Web Page again.

FIGURE E-3: Viewing the Control Panel as a Web page

Windows 98

Changing the Desktop Background and Screen Saver Settings

You can also change how your Windows desktop looks using the Display Properties dialog box. You can adjust the desktop's **background**, the basic surface on which icons and windows appear. You can use a **screen saver**, a moving display that protects your monitor from burn-in, which can occur when there is no movement on your screen for a long time. John chooses a background that he likes and makes sure that the screen saver is working. He'll select a new background and set one of the standard screen savers to start when his screen is idle for more than five minutes.

QuickTip

You can also open the Display Properties dialog box by right-clicking in an empty area of the desktop, then clicking Properties.

1. Click the **Start button** on the taskbar, point to **Settings**, then click **Control Panel**
   The Control Panel opens. Each icon represents an aspect of Windows that can be adjusted to fit your own working habits and personal needs.

2. Double-click the **Display icon** in the Control Panel
   The Display Properties dialog box opens with the Background tab active. Table E-1 describes the various tabs and what they do. John wants to experiment with wallpaper options.

3. In the Wallpaper section, click the **up** or **down scroll arrow**, click **Carved Stone** (or a wallpaper of your choosing if this one is not available on your system)
   You can preview the wallpaper you chose in the small monitor graphic, as shown in Figure E-4. **Wallpaper** is a picture that becomes your desktop's background. It is in the same format as a Paint file or an Internet document. You can use Paint to create new wallpaper designs or change existing ones. Besides the wallpaper, you can also choose a desktop **pattern**, a design that can be modified by clicking the None Wallpaper icon and then clicking the Pattern button. You can also determine how a wallpaper or pattern is displayed on the screen. Using the Display list arrow, you can select Tile, Center, or Stretch. **Tile** displays the wallpaper picture or pattern consecutively across the screen; **Center** displays the picture or pattern in the center of the screen; and **Stretch** displays the picture or pattern enlarged in the center of the screen. In addition to changing the background, John decides to change the screen saver settings.

4. Click the **Screen Saver tab**
   The default setting is for no screen saver, meaning that your screen will not be replaced by a constantly changing image no matter how long your computer remains idle. If someone else used this machine before you, a screen saver might already be set.

5. Click the **Screen Saver list arrow**, then click **3D Flying Objects**
   The 3D Flying Objects screen saver appears in the small monitor graphic, as shown in Figure E-5.

6. In the Wait box, click the **up arrow** (or **down arrow**) until it reads **5 minutes**
   This is the amount of time between when your computer detects no mouse or keyboard activity and when the screen saver begins to display.

7. Click **Preview**
   The entire desktop previews the screen saver pattern. To make it stop, move the mouse or press any key on the keyboard.

8. Click **Apply**
   The new wallpaper appears on the desktop, and the screen saver is in effect.

FIGURE E-4: Display Properties dialog box with Background tab

Preview selected wallpaper or pattern here

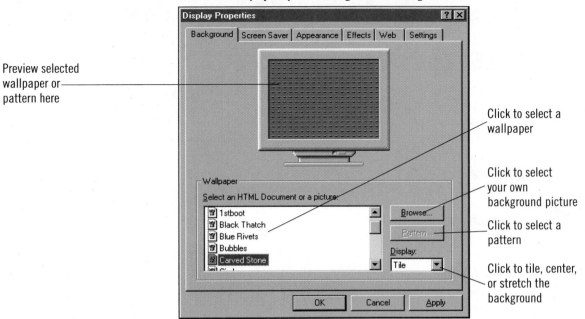

Click to select a wallpaper

Click to select your own background picture

Click to select a pattern

Click to tile, center, or stretch the background

FIGURE E-5: Display Properties dialog box with Screen Saver tab

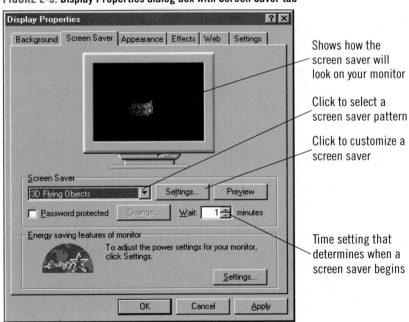

Shows how the screen saver will look on your monitor

Click to select a screen saver pattern

Click to customize a screen saver

Time setting that determines when a screen saver begins

TABLE E-1: Description of Display tab features

display tab	description
Background	Choose a picture or pattern to display on the desktop
Screen Saver	Choose and preview a screen saver pattern, and set pattern characteristics
Appearance	Choose colors, sizes, and font for Windows items
Effects	Change the appearance of desktop icons and visual settings
Web	Choose to view the desktop as a Web page, and add or delete Active Desktop items
Settings	Set the maximum number of colors viewable at one time, and change the screen resolution

Changing the Desktop Color Scheme

In addition to the background and screen saver, you can change the appearance of the color and fonts, or character designs, used for various window elements such as the title bar, icons, menus, border, and the desktop. There are thousands of custom combinations you can create in Windows. Each combination is called a **scheme**. You can select a predefined scheme or create one of your own. When you create a custom scheme, you can save the changes you make with a unique name. Other users of your computer can do the same, so each user can quickly customize the computer. ✐ Ray Adams, an employee of Wired Coffee, is visually impaired and needs a display configuration where the window elements are larger than the standard size. John can create a scheme for Ray so that Ray can switch to the scheme whenever he uses the computer.

Steps 1 2 3 4

1. Click the **Appearance tab** in the Display Properties dialog box

   The Appearance tab, as shown in Figure E-6, allows you to change the color of various desktop elements, such as the menu bar, message box, and selected text. Rather than customizing each item individually, you can select one of several predefined schemes that Windows provides and modify it as necessary.

2. Click the **Scheme list arrow**, then click **Windows Standard (extra large)**

   In Figure E-7, you can see that the size of everything in the Preview box is increased from standard size to extra large. Now Ray can work more comfortably. However, he would prefer a light gray desktop to the teal one that comes with this preset scheme. John wants to change the desktop color; first he needs to select the desktop.

3. Click the **Item list arrow**, then click **Desktop**

   The desktop color can now be changed. Notice that the Item Size option and Font option are grayed out, indicating that these options do not apply to the desktop.

4. Click the **Color list arrow**, then click **light gray color box** in the top row

   You can select from a matrix of different colors. Before John saves the scheme, he wants to apply the scheme to the desktop to see how it looks.

5. Click **Apply**

   The desktop changes, but the dialog box remains open. Use the Apply button when you want to test your changes and the OK button when you want to keep your changes and close the dialog box. John saves the changes he made so Ray can use the scheme.

6. Click **Save As**, type **Ray**, then click **OK**

   The scheme is saved with the name Ray. Now, anytime Ray wants to use the computer, he can easily select this scheme.

7. Click **Delete** to remove the selected scheme

   The scheme is deleted. John has some work to do on the computer, so he wants to return to the Windows Standard scheme, which is the one he prefers.

8. Click the **Scheme list arrow**, click **Windows Standard**, then click **Apply**

9. Click the **Screen Saver tab**, click the **Screen Saver list arrow**, then click **(None)**

10. Click the **Background tab**, click **(None)** in the Wallpaper section, then click **OK**

FIGURE E-6: Display Properties dialog box with Appearance tab

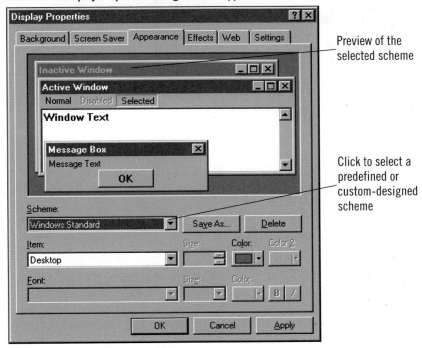

Preview of the selected scheme

Click to select a predefined or custom-designed scheme

FIGURE E-7: Changing the desktop color scheme

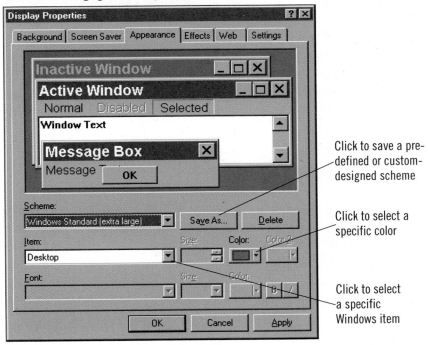

Click to save a pre-defined or custom-designed scheme

Click to select a specific color

Click to select a specific Windows item

CLUES TO USE

Changing the size of the desktop

You can change the size of the desktop that appears on your monitor. In the Display Properties dialog box, click the Settings tab, then drag the Screen Area slider to the right. The settings available depend upon the hardware that Windows detects when it is installed. In some cases, you might even have higher settings than 640 × 480 or 800 × 600 (such as 1024 × 768) available. Note that a higher setting means higher resolution, and more information can fit on the screen.

Windows 98

Setting the Date and Time

Every so often, you need to change the date and time on your computer. The date and time you set in the Control Panel appears in the lower-right corner of the taskbar and is used by programs to establish the date and time that files and folders are created and modified. To change the date and time, you modify the date and time settings in the Date/Time Properties dialog box. In addition to changing the date and time, you can also change how the date and time is displayed. This can be handy if you are working on documents from a different country or region of the world. To change the date and time display, you modify the date or time settings on the Date/Time tab in the Regional Settings Properties dialog box. ▬▬▬ John is working on an international document and wants to change his date and time settings.

Steps 1 2 3 4

1. **Double-click the Date/Time icon in the Control Panel**
   The Date/Time Properties dialog box opens with the Date & Time tab displayed, as shown in Figure E-8. To change the time, you select the hours, minutes, or seconds you want to change in the text box in the Time section, and then type the new number or click the up or down arrows to select the new time. To change the date, you select the new month and year you want in the Date section, and then click the new date you want in the calendar. John wants to set his machine three hours ahead.

2. **Double-click the current hour in the text box in the Time section, then click the up arrow three times**
   The new time appears in the running clock. Now John wants to make the change.

3. **Click Apply**
   The new time appears in the right corner of the taskbar. You can also change your computer's time zone. To change the time zone setting, click the Time Zone tab, click the list arrow, and then select the time zone you want. After making the time change, John decides to restore his computer's time setting.

4. **Double-click the current hour, click the down arrow three times, then click OK**
   You can also change how the date and time is displayed. John reviews the regional setting to make sure the date and time are set correctly.

5. **Double-click the Regional Settings icon in the Control Panel**
   The Regional Settings dialog box opens, displaying tabs for Regional Settings, Number, Currency, Time, and Date. Using these tabs, you change the format and symbols used for numbers, currency, time, and date used in your files and programs. John wants to determine the date and time settings for his computer.

6. **Click the Date tab**
   You can click the short date or long date list arrows to change the two date formats, as shown in Figure E-9. John opens the Time tab to find out what time formats are being used.

7. **Click the Time tab**
   After reviewing the date and time display formats, John decides to keep the current settings.

8. **Click OK**

FIGURE E-8: **Date/Time Properties dialog box**

Click to change the time zone

Click to change the month

Click to change the date

Click to change year

Change time here

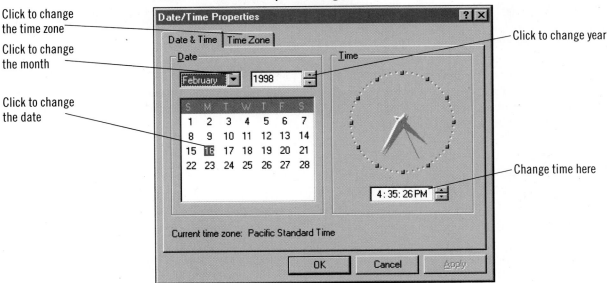

FIGURE E-9: **Regional Settings Properties dialog box**

Click to change short date display

Click to change long date display

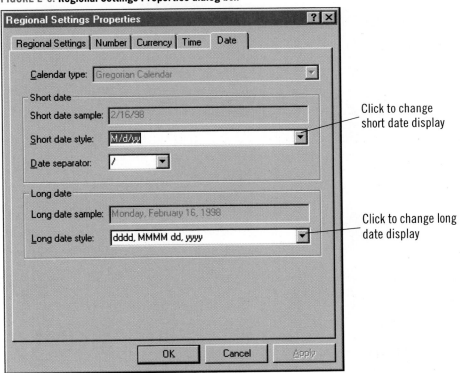

Adding a scheduled task

Task Scheduler is a tool that enables you to schedule tasks (such as Windows Tune-Up, a wizard to make your programs run faster) to run regularly, when it's most convenient for you. Task Scheduler starts each time you start Windows. When Task Scheduler is running on your computer, its icon appears next to the clock on the taskbar. You can double-click the Task Scheduler icon 🖳 on the taskbar to open Task Scheduler. With the Task Scheduler, you can schedule a task to run daily, weekly, monthly, or at certain times (such as when the computer starts or is idle), change the schedule for or turn off an existing task, or customize how a task will run at its scheduled time. To add a scheduled task, double-click the Add Scheduled Task icon and follow the step-by-step instructions.

Windows 98

Working with Fonts

Everything you type appears in a **font**, a particular design of letters. You might have heard of common font names such as Times New Roman, Arial, Courier, or Symbol. Windows comes with a variety of fonts that display and print in programs that are part of Windows, such as WordPad and Paint. Using the Fonts window, you can view these fonts, compare them to each other, see a sample of how a font would appear if printed, and even install new fonts. ◢━━━ John wants to examine different fonts in preparation for an upcoming flyer he wants to create.

1. **Double-click the Fonts icon in the Control Panel**
   The Fonts window opens, as shown in Figure E-10. The window lists the fonts available on your system and indicates whether each is a TrueType or a screen font. A **TrueType font** is based on a mathematical equation so the curves of the letters are smooth and the corners are sharp. A **screen font** consists of **bitmapped characters**, small dots organized to form a letter. Table E-2 lists the various options on the Fonts toolbar and describes what they do.

2. **If the Fonts window is not maximized, click the Maximize button in the Fonts window**

3. **Double-click the Arial font**
   As shown in Figure E-11, the window displays information about this font and shows a sample of the font in different sizes. You can print a copy of this font information to use for further reference.

4. **Click Print in the Arial (TrueType) window, then click OK**
   A copy of the font information prints.

5. **Click Done**
   The Arial (TrueType) window closes. You can also use the tools in the Fonts window to find fonts that are similar to the selected font.

6. **Click the Similarity button 🔠 on the Fonts toolbar**
   All the fonts are listed by how similar they are to Arial, the font listed in the List fonts by similarity to box. You can choose a different font to check which ones are similar to it by clicking the List fonts by similarity to list arrow and then selecting the font you want to check.

7. **Click the Large Icons button 🔲 on the Fonts toolbar, then click the Close button in the Fonts window**

TABLE E-2: **Fonts toolbar buttons**

button	description
⬅	Moves you back to a previously opened folder
➡	Moves you forward to a previously opened folder
🗁	Moves to the next level up in the hierarchy of folders
🔲	Lists fonts by large icon
🔳	Lists fonts alphabetically
🔠	Lists fonts by similarity to the selected font
🗔	Lists details of fonts, including filename, font name, size, and date last modified

FIGURE E-10: Fonts window

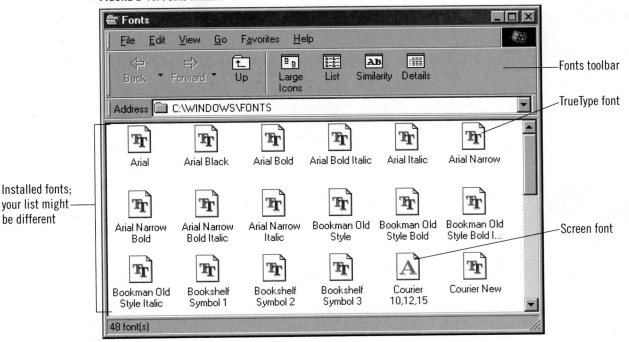

Fonts toolbar

TrueType font

Installed fonts; your list might be different

Screen font

48 font(s)

FIGURE E-11: Selected font and how it appears in different sizes

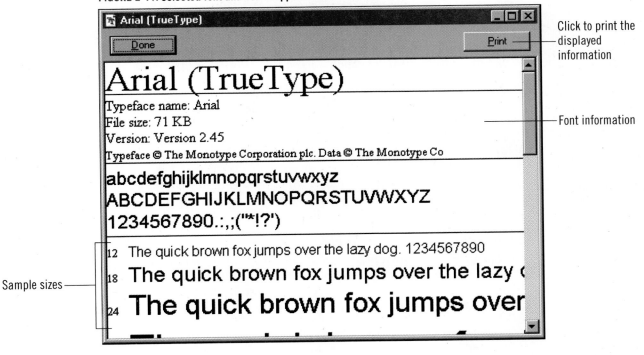

Click to print the displayed information

Font information

Sample sizes

Installing a font

Windows 98 might not come with all the fonts you need or want, but you can purchase additional fonts and easily install them. To install a new font, click Install New Font on the File menu in the Fonts window, indicate the location of the font you want to install (on the hard drive or a floppy disk drive), and then click OK. The new font will be installed and will be available in the Fonts window of the Control Panel and in all your Windows programs.

Customizing Mouse Operations

You can adjust the way your mouse works to suit your own habits and preferences. You can control which mouse button is the primary one (left or right), the size and appearance of the mouse pointer, and the speed at which the pointer moves across the screen.  John decides to change how his mouse operates, to make it easier to maneuver. Also, to make the mouse easier to see, he adds a **pointer trail**, or shadow, to the mouse pointer.

Steps

Trouble?

If you're using a mouse with a wheel, your Mouse Properties dialog box will be different. See your instructor or technical support person for assistance.

QuickTip

Restore the original mouse click speed by moving the slider back to its original position (or, if available, click Use Defaults).

1. Double-click the Mouse icon in the Control Panel (you might have to scroll to see it), then click the Buttons tab if necessary

The Mouse Properties dialog box opens, as shown in Figure E-12. In the Buttons tab you can change the primary button you'll use for most actions. Right-handed users click the left mouse button most often, and vice versa. You can also set the speed that you double-click your mouse button (the time between two clicks required for Windows to recognize the action as double-clicking and not two single clicks). John will increase the double-click speed of his mouse.

2. Drag the slider in the Double-click speed section to the right

The time between clicks is decreased. New mouse users should leave a relatively large amount of time between required clicks. As you become familiar with using the mouse, you can adjust this time to respond to the way you work. Next John tests the double-click speed.

3. Double-click the test icon in the Double-click speed Test area box

The jack-in-the-box icon opens when you use the correct click speed. You might have to double-click the Test icon again if it doesn't change. Next John changes how the pointer appears as he drags the mouse.

4. Click the Pointers tab

The Pointers tab opens, displaying different types of mouse pointers, as shown in Figure E-13. You can select from a series of schemes that will change the shape of the pointer, ranging from changing its size to adding a third dimension to it.

5. Click the Motion tab, then click the Show pointer trails check box

See Figure E-14. Now when you move the mouse, the pointer displays a trail, making it easier to see. A pointer trail is especially useful on laptop computers because it allows the user to easily track where the pointer is and not "lose it" while working.

6. Click Cancel so the settings are left unchanged

None of the changes you make occur unless you click OK in this dialog box. The Mouse Properties dialog box closes, and you return to the Control Panel.

FIGURE E-12: **Mouse Properties dialog box**

Click to configure which mouse button is primary

Click to select a different tab and different mouse options; your tabs might be different

Icon changes when you double-click it with the selected speed

Drag to change the time between clicks

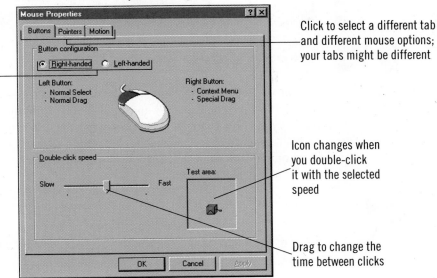

FIGURE E-13: **Changing the appearance of the mouse pointer**

Click to select a pointer scheme and change the appearance of all pointers

Scroll to view the different pointer shapes

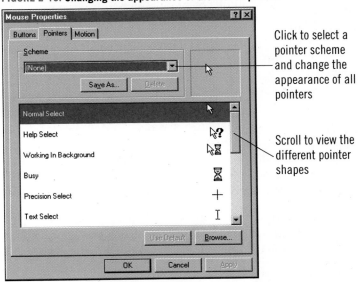

FIGURE E-14: **Changing the motion of the mouse pointer**

Drag to change pointer speed

Click to show the mouse pointer trails

Drag to change pointer trail length

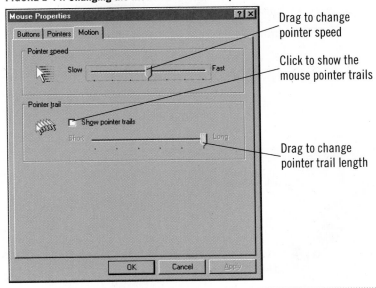

Windows 98

Examining System Properties

In this lesson, you will become familiar with the System Properties dialog box (accessed from the Control Panel), where you can view and modify your computer's hardware settings. This information helps you know more about your system in general and is important should you need to describe your system's characteristics to a technical support person. ◀━━ John's computer has been running slow, so he decides to examine the computer's system properties to find out if any performance problems exist.

Steps 1234

1. **In the Control Panel, double-click the System icon** (you might have to scroll to find it)
   The System Properties dialog box opens. Table E-3 describes the options available on each of the tabs.

2. **If it is not already selected, click the General tab**
   As Figure E-15 shows, John's computer system is running Windows 98 version 4.10.1650, and it has an Intel central processing unit and 16.0 MB of RAM.

3. **Click the Performance tab**
   The Performance tab opens, as shown in Figure E-16. This tab provides detailed information about the computer and its performance running Windows. The most important indicator in this tab is the percent of resources that are free, which, in this case, is 73%. This number reflects how much memory and other important components of the operating system are free to perform additional tasks, such as opening new programs or documents. As this number gets smaller, your computer is being asked to do more work with less energy. When this number becomes too small, the system could halt on its own and have to be restarted. To fix the problem of low system resources, you could add more memory to your computer.

4. **In the Advanced settings section, click File System**
   The File System Properties dialog box opens, providing you with a look at some of the features you can adjust to help make Windows perform at its maximum level of efficiency.

5. **Click Cancel**
   The File System Properties dialog box closes.

6. **Click OK, then click the Close button on the Control Panel**
   The Control Panel closes, and you return to the desktop.

> **QuickTip**
>
> Use the information in the System Properties dialog box to learn about your system, but don't change any settings without the advice of your instructor or technical support person.

TABLE E-3: System Properties tabs

system tab	description
General	Lists the general information about the system
Device Manager	Allows you to investigate the properties of the different hardware devices attached to your computer, such as the mouse
Hardware Profiles	Allows you to set up a particular hardware configuration you can use when you start Windows
Performance	Provides information on the computing resources that remain, the amount of memory installed, and whether disk compression is being used

FIGURE E-15: System Properties dialog box with General tab

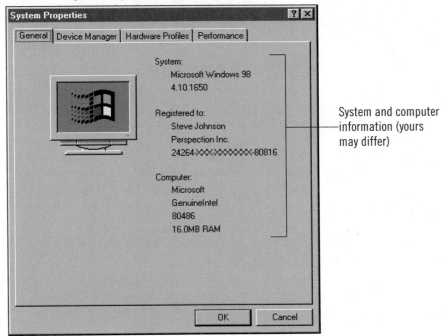

System and computer information (yours may differ)

FIGURE E-16: System Properties dialog box with Performance tab

Your properties might be different

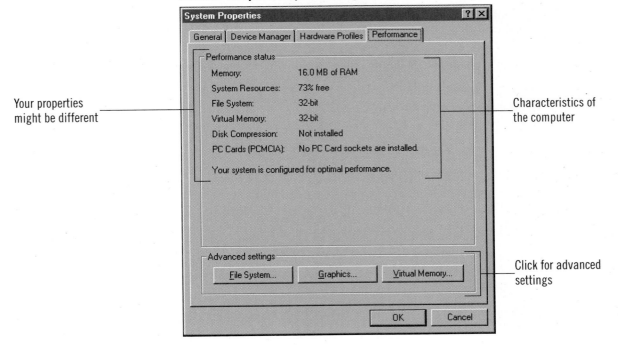

Characteristics of the computer

Click for advanced settings

CLUES TO USE

Adding new hardware and software to Windows

You can add new hardware, such as a printer, and add or remove programs by using tools on the Control Panel. The Add New Hardware and Add/Remove Programs dialog boxes walk you through the necessary steps. To start the add new hardware procedure, click the Add New Hardware icon in the Control Panel, and then click Next and follow the prompts. To add or remove a program, click the Add/Remove Program icon, click Install, and then follow the prompts. In both cases, Windows 98 should recognize that new hardware needs to be added or that an installation file needs to be executed.

Windows 98

Customizing the Taskbar

The taskbar is most often used for switching from one program to another. The taskbar is initially located at the bottom of the Windows desktop. As with other Windows elements, you can customize the taskbar; for example, you can change its size and location, or add or remove toolbars to it that help you perform the tasks you need to do. Sometimes you need more room on the screen to display a window, and it will help to hide the taskbar. You can use the **Auto hide** feature to help you automatically hide the taskbar when you don't need it. John removes and adds a toolbar to the taskbar and then learns how the Auto hide feature works.

Steps 1 2 3 4

1. **Place the mouse pointer in an empty section of the taskbar, right-click the taskbar, then point to Toolbars**
   The Toolbars submenu appears, as shown in Figure E-17. You can add or remove a variety of existing toolbars to the taskbar or create a new one.

2. **Click Quick Launch to deselect it**
   The Quick Launch toolbar is removed from the taskbar. Now you have more room on the taskbar for program buttons. John wants to try out the Auto hide feature.

3. **Click the Start button, point to Settings, then click Taskbar & Start Menu**
   The Taskbar Properties dialog box opens, displaying the Taskbar Options tab, as shown in Figure E-18. You can change how items (such as the clock and small icons on the Start menu) are displayed on the taskbar or how the taskbar is displayed on the screen.

4. **Click the Auto hide check box to select it**
   The taskbar in the Preview box is hidden.

5. **Click OK**
   The taskbar is hidden at the bottom of the screen.

6. **Move the mouse pointer to the bottom of the screen**
   While the mouse pointer is located at the bottom of the screen, the taskbar is shown. When you move the mouse pointer up, the taskbar is hidden.

7. **Right-click in an empty section of the taskbar, point to Toolbars, then click Quick Launch to select it**
   The Quick Launch toolbar is added to the taskbar. John prefers the taskbar not to move so he disables the Auto hide feature.

8. **Click the Start button, point to Settings, then click Taskbar & Start Menu**
   The Taskbar Properties dialog box opens.

9. **Click the Auto hide check box to deselect it, then click OK**

FIGURE E-17: Removing a toolbar from the taskbar

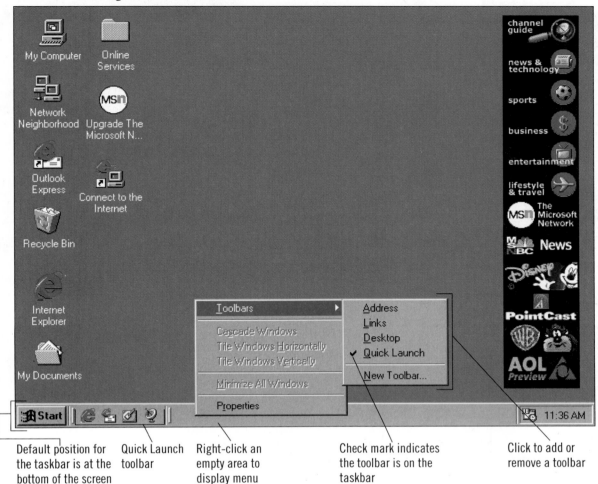

Default position for the taskbar is at the bottom of the screen

Quick Launch toolbar

Right-click an empty area to display menu

Check mark indicates the toolbar is on the taskbar

Click to add or remove a toolbar

FIGURE E-18: Taskbar Properties dialog box with Taskbar Options tab

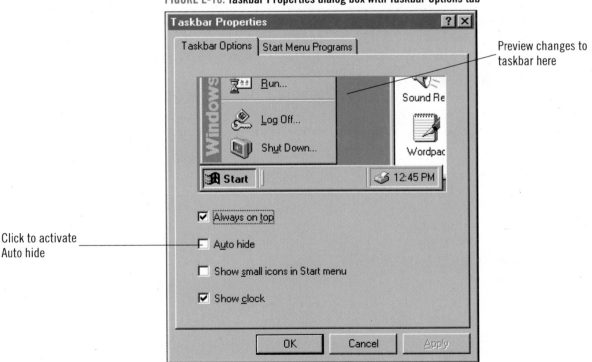

Preview changes to taskbar here

Click to activate Auto hide

Adding an Item to the Start Menu

To give you easier access to them, you can add shortcuts to programs, files, or folders to the Start menu. Instead of having to click through several levels of the Start menu to start a program or access a file, all you have to do is click the Start button and click the item you want on the Start menu. Of course, if you add too many items to the Start menu, you defeat the purpose. Because John will use the Wired Coffee logo so often in his work, he decides to add the file to the Start menu.

Steps

1. **Click the Start button, point to Settings, click Taskbar & Start Menu, then click the Start Menu Programs tab**
   The Taskbar Properties dialog box appears, as shown in Figure E-19. You can use the Start Menu Programs tab to add and delete items from the Start menu. To add the Wired Coffee Logo file to the Start menu, you need to specify where the file is located.

2. **Make sure your Student Disk is in the floppy disk drive, click Add, then click Browse**
   The Browse dialog box opens, where you can navigate to and select a file, folder, or program you want to add to the Start menu.

3. **Click the Look in list arrow, then click the drive that contains your student disk**
   You need to display all the types of files in order to view the Wired Coffee Logo file.

4. **Click the Files of type list arrow, then click All Files**
   Now you see all the files on your Student Disk.

5. **Double-click Wired Coffee Logo, then click Next**
   Once the file is located, you need to specify where to place the file on the Start menu. John wants the file on the main Start menu.

6. **Click Start Menu in the Select Program Folder dialog box, click Next, click Finish, then click OK**
   Now open the Start menu and verify that the file has been added.

7. **Click the Start button**
   The Wired Coffee Logo file now appears at the top of the Start menu, as shown in Figure E-20. To open the Wired Coffee Logo file, all you need to do is click the icon on the Start menu. Now remove this item from the Start menu to return your desktop to its original settings.

8. **Press [Esc] to close the Start menu, right-click in an empty area on the taskbar, click Properties, then click the Start Menu Programs tab**

9. **Click Remove, locate and click Wired Coffee Logo in the list, click Remove, click Close, then click OK**
   The Taskbar Properties dialog box closes, and the Wired Coffee shortcut is removed from the Start menu.

QuickTip

You can also add an item to the Start menu by creating a shortcut to it (on the desktop or in Windows Explorer, for example) and dragging the icon to the Start button.

FIGURE E-19: Taskbar Properties dialog box with Start Menu Programs tab

Click to add or remove programs to and from the Start menu

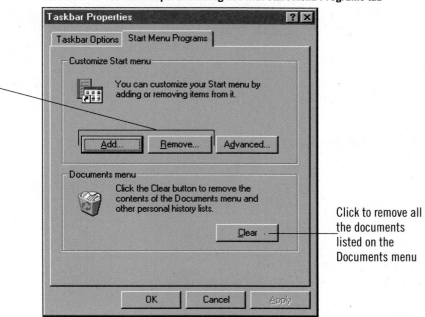

Click to remove all the documents listed on the Documents menu

If you wanted to open the file, you would click here

FIGURE E-20: File added to the Start menu

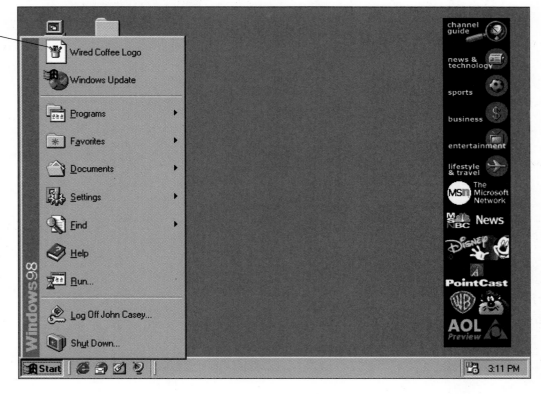

Rearranging Start menu items

If you don't like the location of an item on the Start menu, you can move the item to a different location by dragging it to the desired location. A blank line appears as you move the mouse pointer indicating the new location of the item. For example, to move the Windows Explorer menu item from the Programs sub-menu to the Start menu, open the Start menu, then drag the Windows Explorer item to the Start menu.

Practice

► Concepts Review

Label each of the elements of the screen shown in Figure E-21.

FIGURE E-21

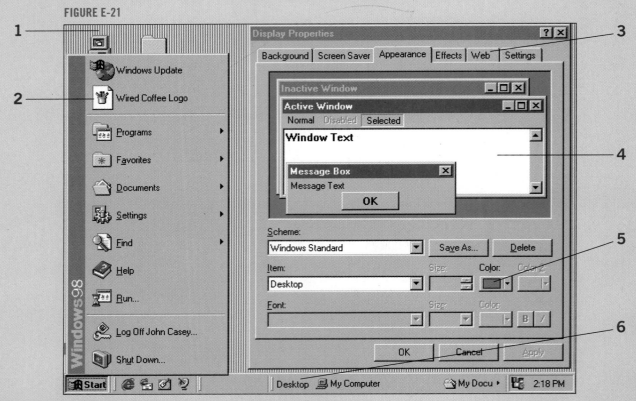

Match each of the terms with the statement that describes its function.

7. **Patterns**   a. Used to change properties of various elements of a computer
8. **Screen saver** b. Preset combinations of desktop colors
9. **Color schemes** c. Used to prevent damage to the monitor
10. **Control Panel** d. Preset designs for the desktop
11. **Start menu**   e. Used to start programs and open documents

Select the best answer from the following list of choices.

12. To customize the Active Desktop, you need to open the
    a. Folder Options dialog box.
    b. Display Properties dialog box.
    c. Desktop Settings dialog box.
    d. Custom Desktop dialog box.

13. To change the pattern on the desktop from the Display Properties dialog box in the Control Panel, click the
    a. Background tab.
    b. Screen Saver tab.
    c. Appearance tab.
    d. Settings tab.

14. **An Internet document or Paint file used as a background is called a**
   a. Pattern.
   b. Wallpaper.
   c. Display.
   d. Shortcut.

15. **To change the scheme on the desktop from the Display Properties dialog box in the Control Panel, click the**
   a. Screen Saver tab.
   b. Appearance tab.
   c. Effects tab.
   d. Background tab.

▶ Skills Review

1. **Customize the Active Desktop**
   a. Right-click in an empty area on the desktop.
   b. Point to Active Desktop, then click Customize my Desktop.
   c. Click the Web tab, if necessary.
   d. Click Folder Options, then click Yes to close the Display Properties dialog box.
   e. Click the Classic style option button, and view the change in the Preview box at the top of the dialog box.
   f. Click the Custom, based on settings you choose option button, then click the Close button.

2. **Change the desktop background and screen saver settings.**
   a. Click the Start button, point to Settings, then click Control Panel.
   b. Double-click the Display icon.
   c. Click the Background tab, if necessary, then click Blue Rivets in the Wallpaper section.
   d. Click the Screen Saver tab, click the Screen Saver list arrow, click 3D Pipes, then click Preview.
   e. Move the mouse to end the Screen Saver preview.

3. **Change the desktop color scheme.**
   a. Click the Appearance tab.
   b. Click the Item list arrow, then click Desktop.
   c. Choose any color you want for the desktop, then click Apply.
   d. Click Save As, type "Fred," then click OK.
   e. Click Delete.
   f. Click the Scheme list arrow, then click Windows Standard, then click Apply.
   g. Click the Screen Saver tab, click the Screen Saver list arrow, then click (None).
   h. Click the Background tab, click (None) in the Wallpaper section, then click OK.

4. **Set the date and time.**
   a. Double-click the Date/Time icon.
   b. Double-click the number of minutes.
   c. Click the up arrow three times, then click Apply.
   d. Double-click the number of minutes.
   e. Click the down arrow three times, then click OK.

5. **Work with fonts.**
   a. Double-click the Fonts icon.
   b. Double-click a Times New Roman icon.
   c. Click Print, click OK, click Done, then click the Close button.

6. Customize mouse operations.

   a. Double-click the Mouse icon.

   b. Click the Motion tab, then click the Show pointer trails check box.

   c. Drag the slider to the middle of the Pointer trails bar, then click Apply.

   d. Change the mouse settings back to the default, then click OK.

7. Examine system properties.

   a. Double-click the System icon.

   b. Click the Performance tab, then write down the percent of resources available.

   c. Close the System Properties dialog box.

   d. Click the Start button, open WordPad, then click the Minimize button.

   e. Reopen the System Properties dialog box, then click the Performance tab.

   f. Write down the percent of resources available.

   g. Compare the amount of resources that are now available to what you wrote in Step c, then click OK.

   h. Close the Control Panel and WordPad.

8. Customize the taskbar.

   a. Right-click the taskbar, point to Toolbars, then click Quick Launch to remove that toolbar from the taskbar.

   b. Click the Start button, point to Settings, then click Taskbar & Start Menu.

   c. Click the Auto hide check box to select it, then click OK.

   d. Move the mouse pointer to the bottom of the screen.

   e. Right-click the taskbar, point to Toolbars, then click Quick Launch to add the toolbar back to the taskbar.

   f. Click the Start button, point to Settings, then click Taskbar & Start Menu.

   g. Click the Auto hide check box to deselect it, then click Apply.

9. Add an item to the Start menu.

   a. Click the Start Menu Programs tab, click Add, then click Browse.

   b. Double-click Program Files, then double-click Accessories, double-click WordPad, then click Next.

   c. Double-click Start Menu, then click Finish.

   d. Click Remove.

   e. Click WordPad, then click Remove, click Close, then click OK.

▶ Independent Challenges

1. You have been retained as a consultant by a large law firm that has just installed Windows 98. The firm's employees need to be taught how to customize Windows 98 to fit their needs. As you prepare your presentation, you are going to customize the display so it is easier for them to see. Make the following changes, and make sure you change them back to the default setting or setup when you are finished.

  To complete this independent challenge:

1. Open the Display Properties dialog box from the Control Panel.
2. Change the background to Straw Mat.
3. Set the screen saver for 1 minute so you can show them how it works without waiting too long.
4. On the Appearance tab, set the Scheme to High contrast black (extra large).
5. Save the scheme as Demo, then apply the changes.
6. Print the screen. (Press the Print Screen key to make a copy of the screen, open Paint, click Edit on the menu bar, click Paste to paste the screen into Paint, then click Yes to paste the large image, if necessary. Click File on the menu bar, click Print, then click OK.)
7. Delete the scheme Demo, then select the Windows Standard scheme.
8. Set the screen saver for 5 minutes.

2. As the owner of a small optical laboratory, you are trying to abide by the Americans with Disabilities Act, which states that employers should make every reasonable effort to accommodate workers with disabilities. You have one worker who is visually impaired. Customize the Windows desktop for this employee so that it is easier to work in, desktop items are easier to see and read, and desktop colors are strongly contrasted with each other but still easy on the eyes. Save this custom configuration so that this employee can use it when necessary.

To complete this independent challenge:

1. Open the Display Properties dialog box from the Control Panel.
2. Change the desktop color to red.
3. Change the font size for the menu to 12.
4. Change the size and color of the text in the title bar for the Active Window to 24 and light blue (the second color in the fifth row).
5. Change the font style for the message box to bold.
6. Save the custom configuration as Visible.
7. Apply the scheme.
8. Print the screen. (See Independent Challenge 1, Step 6 for screen printing instructions.)
9. Delete the scheme Visible.
10. Select the Windows Standard scheme.

3. You've been using Windows 98 for about two weeks, and while you really like its features, it seems to be a bit sluggish. To see if you can speed it up, you need to provide certain information to your system administrator or instructor.

To complete this independent challenge:

1. Open the System Properties dialog box from the Control Panel.
2. Record what type of central processor is being used.
3. Record the percent of resources that are available.
4. Record what version of Windows you are using.
5. Record how much memory is available.
6. Print the screen. (See Independent Challenge 1, Step 6 for screen printing instructions.)

4. As the owner of Lew's Office Supply, you need to make your business computers easier for your employees to use. One way to do that is to add programs to the Start menu. Your employees use WordPad and Paint almost exclusively, and they also use the same documents quite often.

To complete this independent challenge:

1. Add a WordPad shortcut to the Start menu. (*Hint*: Select WordPad.exe located in the Accessories folder within the Program Files folder.
2. Add a Paint shortcut to the Start menu. (*Hint*: Select MSpaint.exe located in the same place as WordPad.)
3. Create a memo to employees about the upcoming company picnic using WordPad, then save the memo on your Student Disk as "Company Picnic Memo."
4. Close the memo and WordPad.
5. Add the Company Picnic Memo file to the Start menu.
6. Open the Company Picnic Memo from the Start menu.
7. Print the screen. (See Independent Challenge 1, Step 6 for screen printing instructions.)
8. Remove all the shortcuts you created.

► Visual Workshop

Re-create the screen shown in Figure E-22, which displays the Windows desktop, then print the screen. (See Independent Challenge 1, Step 6 for screen printing instructions.) You don't have to change the Log Off name on the Start menu.

FIGURE E-22

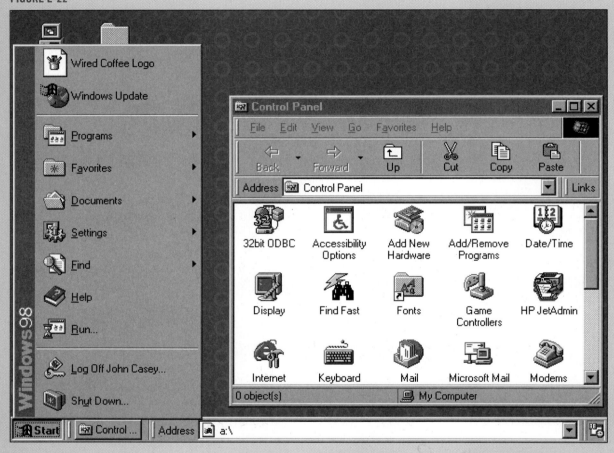

Exploring
the Internet with Microsoft Internet Explorer

Objectives

- ► **Understand Web browsers**
- ► **Start Internet Explorer**
- ► **Explore the browser window**
- ► **Open a Web page and follow links**
- ► **Add a Web page to the Favorites list**
- ► **Add an active channel to the Channels list**
- ► **Select a home page and add a link button**
- ► **Search the Web**
- ► **Print a Web page**

Another component of Windows 98 is Microsoft Internet Explorer, a software program that helps you access the World Wide Web. In this unit you will learn about the benefits of the World Wide Web, examine the basic features of Internet Explorer 4, and access Web pages. This unit requires a connection to the Internet. If your computer is not connected to the Internet, check with your instructor or technical support person to see if it's possible for you to connect. If not, simply read the lessons to learn about using Internet Explorer. ✐ Wired Coffee Company is a growing business that wants to take advantage of Internet technology. John Casey, owner of the company, uses Internet Explorer to open the company Web page and find information related to the coffee business.

Understanding Web Browsers

Windows 98

The Internet is a collection of over 40 million computers from all over the world linked together to share information. The Internet's physical structure includes telephone lines, cables, satellites, and other telecommunications media, as depicted in Figure F-1. Using the Internet, computer users can share many types of information, including text, graphics, sounds, videos, and computer programs. The **World Wide Web** (also known as the Web or WWW) is a part of the Internet that consists of Web sites located on different computers around the world. A **Web site** contains Web pages that are linked together to make looking for information on the Internet easier. **Web pages** are documents that contain highlighted words, phrases, and graphics, called **hyperlinks** (or simply links) that open other Web pages when you click them. Figure F-2 shows a sample Web page. **Web browsers** are software programs that you use to "browse the Web," or access and display Web pages. Some Web pages contain frames. A **frame** is a separate window within a Web page. Frames give you the ability to show more than one Web page at a time. Browsers make the Web easy to navigate by providing a graphical, point-and-click environment. This unit features Internet Explorer 4, a popular browser from Microsoft that comes with Windows 98. Netscape Communicator is another popular browser. John realizes that there are many applications for Internet Explorer in his company. He notes the following applications:

Details

Display Web pages from all over the world
John can look at Web pages for business purposes, such as checking the pages of other coffee companies to see how they are marketing their products.

Use links to move from one Web page to another
John can click links (which appear as either underlined text or graphics) to move from one Web page to another, investigating different sources for information. Since a Web page can contain links to any location on the Internet, you can jump to Web pages all over the world.

Play audio and video clips
John can click links that play audio and video clips, such as the sound of coffee grinding or a video of workers picking coffee beans. He can also play continuous audio and video broadcasts through radio and television stations over the Internet.

Search the Web for information
John can use search programs that allow him to look for information about any topic contained in Web pages on computers throughout the world.

Subscribe to a favorite Web page or active channel
John can create a list of his favorite Web pages to make it easy for him to return to them at a later time. He can also subscribe to a Web page or active channel. When you **subscribe** to a Web page, you are automatically notified when the Web page changes.

Print the text and graphics on Web pages
If John finds some information or images that he would like to print, he can easily print all or part of the Web page, including the graphics.

FIGURE F-1: Structure of the Internet

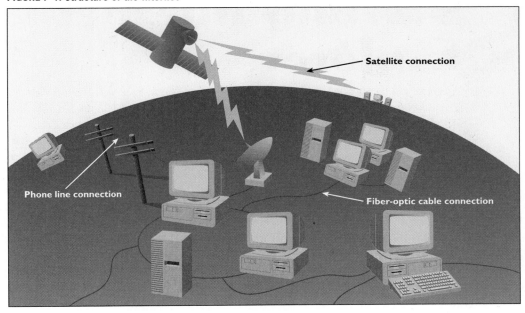

FIGURE F-2: World Wide Web page

Title of Web page and name of broswer

Graphic hyperlink you can click to view information on the President and Vice President

Text hyperlink you can click to view information on commonly requested federal services

CLUES TO USE

The history of the Internet and World Wide Web

The Internet has its roots in the Advanced Research Projects Agency Network (ARPANET), which the United States Department of Defense started in 1969. In 1986, the National Science Foundation formed NSFNET, which replaced ARPANET. NSFNET expanded the foundation of the U.S. portion of the Internet with high-speed, long distance data lines. In 1991, the U.S. Congress expanded the capacity and speed of the Internet further and opened it up to commercial use. The Internet is now accessible in over 200 countries. The World Wide Web was developed in Switzerland in 1991 to make finding documents on the Internet easier. Software programs designed to access the Web (Web browsers) use "point and click" interfaces. The first such Web browser, Mosaic, was introduced at the University of Illinois in 1993. Recently, Microsoft Internet Explorer and Netscape Communicator have become the two most popular Web browsers.

Windows 98

Starting Internet Explorer

Internet Explorer is a Web browser that you use to search the World Wide Web (you also need a physical connection to the Internet). When you install Windows 98, an icon for Internet Explorer will appear on the desktop, and a button for it will appear on the Quick Launch toolbar on the taskbar. Windows 98 also displays a Channel Bar on the desktop. The Channel Bar allows you to quickly access specialized Web pages known as active channels. An **active channel** is a specific channel on the Channel Bar, such as Disney, MSNBC, or The Microsoft Network. If you don't see the active channel you want to open, you can use the View Channels button on the Quick Launch toolbar to view an available list. If your computer is not connected to the Internet, check with your instructor or technical support person to see if it's possible for you to connect. Before John can take advantage of the many features of the World Wide Web, he must start Internet Explorer.

1. **Establish a connection to the Internet via the network or telephone**

   If you connect to the Internet through a network, follow your instructor's directions to establish your connection. If you connect by telephone, use an existing Dial-Up Networking connection, or create a new connection using the Connection Wizard to establish your connection.

2. **Locate the Internet Explorer icon on your desktop**

   The icon will probably appear on the left side of your screen, as shown in Figure F-3, but it doesn't matter where it is or even if it is not on your desktop. There are several different ways to start Internet Explorer, depending on your circumstances. See Table F-1 for a description of different ways to start Internet Explorer.

3. **Double-click the Internet Explorer icon**

   Internet Explorer opens and displays a Web page, as shown in Figure F-4. It's okay if the Web page on your screen is not the same as the one shown in Figure F-4. Later in this unit you will learn how to change the Web page that is displayed when you first start Internet Explorer. Continue with the next lesson to view the various elements of the browser window.

Trouble?

If the Internet Explorer icon isn't on your desktop, click the Start button, point to Programs, point to Internet Explorer, then click Internet Explorer.

TABLE F-1: Ways to start Internet Explorer

method	results
Double-click the Internet Explorer icon on the desktop	Starts Internet Explorer and displays the home page
Click the Launch Internet Explorer Browser button on the Quick Launch toolbar	Starts Internet Explorer and displays the home page
Click the Start button, point to Programs, point to Internet Explorer, then click Internet Explorer	Starts Internet Explorer and displays the home page
Click an active channel on the Channel Bar	Starts Internet Explorer and displays the active channel you selected
Click the View Channels button on the Quick Launch toolbar	Starts Internet Explorer and displays a list of available active channels

FIGURE F-3: Windows desktop

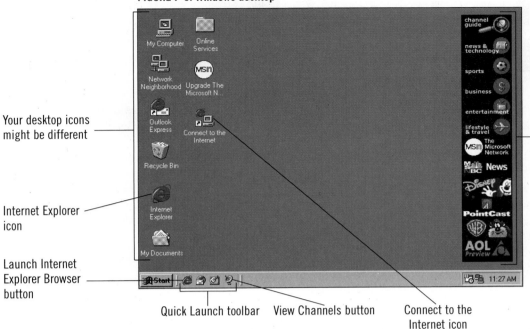

Your desktop icons might be different

Internet Explorer icon

Launch Internet Explorer Browser button

Quick Launch toolbar   View Channels button   Connect to the Internet icon

Active channels

FIGURE F-4: Web page featuring the Microsoft Corporation

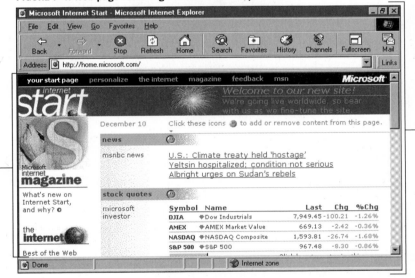

Current Web page displayed (yours might be different)

Internet Explorer window

Connecting to the Internet

Sometimes connecting your computer to the Internet can be the most difficult part of getting started. The Connection Wizard simplifies the process, whether you want to set up a new connection using an existing account or you want to select an **Internet service provider (ISP)**—a company that provides access to the Internet for a fee—and set up a new account. You might need to obtain connection information from your ISP or your system administrator. To get connected to the Internet using the Connection Wizard, double-click the Connect to the Internet icon on the desktop, then follow the step-by-step instructions. If you are on a network, you might need to use a **proxy server**, which provides a secure barrier between your network and the Internet and prevents other people from seeing confidential information on your network. To configure your computer to use a proxy server, click View on the Internet Explorer menu bar, click Internet Options, then click the Connection tab. See your system administrator for getting details to connect to your network.

Exploring the Browser Window

The elements of the Internet Explorer program window, shown in Figure F-5, allow you to view, print, and search for information on the Internet. Before exploring the Web, John decides to familiarize himself with the components of the browser window.

Details

He notes the following features:

 The **title bar** at the top of the page displays the name of the Web page and the name of the browser you are using.

 The **menu bar** provides access to a variety of commands, much like other Windows programs.

 The **toolbar** provides buttons for easy access to the most commonly used commands with Internet Explorer. See Table F-2 for a description of each toolbar button. These button commands are also available on the menus.

 The **Address bar** displays the address of the current Web page or the contents of a local or network computer drive. The **Web address**, like a postal address, is a unique place on the Internet where you can locate a Web page. The Web address is also referred to as the **URL**, which stands for Uniform Resource Locator.

 The **Links bar** displays link buttons to Web pages on the Internet or to documents on a local or network drive.

 The **status indicator** (the Windows logo) will animate while a new Web page is loading.

 The **document window** displays the current Web page or the contents of a local or network computer drive. You might need to scroll down the page to view the entire contents.

 The **vertical scroll bar** allows you to move up or down the current Web page. The **scroll box** indicates your relative position within the Web page.

 The **status bar** displays information about your connection progress with new Web pages that you open, including notification that you have connected to another site and the percentage of information that has been transferred. This bar also displays the function of the links in the document window as you move your mouse pointer over them.

FIGURE F-5: Elements of the Internet Explorer program window

Title bar
Menu bar
Toolbar
Address bar

Document window

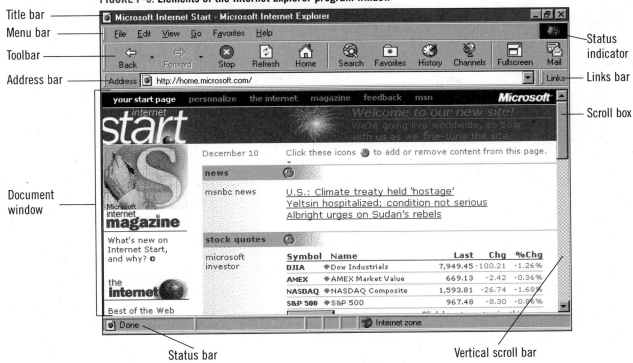

Status indicator
Links bar
Scroll box
Vertical scroll bar
Status bar

 CLUES TO USE

Displaying the entire Internet Explorer toolbar

On monitors set to a small screen size, such as 640 × 480, the Internet Explorer toolbar does not have enough room to display the Print and Edit buttons on the screen. To display all the buttons on the toolbar, you can either remove the text labels from the buttons to make them smaller or increase the screen size. To remove the text labels from the buttons, click the View menu, point to Toolbars, then click Text Labels. To increase the screen size, right-click a blank area of the desktop, click Properties, click the Settings tab, drag the Screen Area slider to 800 × 600 or higher, then click OK. (If you are working in a lab, check with your instructor or technical support person before changing the screen size.)

TABLE F-2: Internet Explorer toolbar buttons

button	description	button	description
Back	Opens the previous page	History	Opens the History list
Forward	Opens the next page; only available after you have gone back in the list of previously visited locations	Channels	Opens the Channels list
Stop	Stops loading a page	Fullscreen	Displays the Internet Explorer window using the full screen
Refresh	Refreshes the contents of the current page	Mail	Displays options for working with Mail and News
Home	Opens the home page	Print	Prints the page using current print options
Search	Opens the Search list	Edit	Opens the page in a Web page editor (only if a Web page editor is installed and selected in the Options dialog box)
Favorites	Opens the Favorites list		

Windows 98

Opening a Web Page and Following Links

You can open a Web page quickly and easily using the Address bar. To open a Web page, you select the current address in the Address bar, type the Web address, or URL, for the Web page you want to open, and then press [Enter]. If you change your mind or the Web page takes too long to **download**, to open and display on the screen, you can click the Stop button on the toolbar. If you stop a Web page while it is downloading and the page doesn't completely display, you can click the Refresh button on the toolbar to update the screen. Web pages can be connected to each other through links which you can follow to obtain more information about a topic, as shown in Figure F-6. A link can move you to another location on the same Web page, or it can open a different Web page altogether. To follow a link, simply click the highlighted word, phrase, or graphic (the mouse pointer changes to the hand pointer when it is over a link). John contracted a Web development company to create a Web site for Wired Coffee. He wants to access the new Web site and follow some of the links in order to give feedback to the developer. John knows that the URL for the Web page is http://www.course.com/illustrated/wired/.

Trouble?

If you receive an error message, type one of the URLs listed in Table F-3 in the Address bar instead.

1. Click anywhere in the Address bar

The current address is highlighted and any text you type will replace the current address. If the current address isn't highlighted, select the entire address.

2. Type http://www.course.com/illustrated/wired/, then press [Enter]

Be sure to type the address exactly as it appears. The status bar displays the connection process. After downloading for a few seconds, the Web page appears in the document window.

3. Locate the link menu, and move the mouse pointer over the link

When you move the mouse pointer over a link, the mouse pointer changes to 👆, as shown in Figure F-7. This indicates that the text or graphic is a link. The address of the link appears in the status bar.

4. Click the link menu

The status indicator animates as the new Web page is accessed and displayed. The Web page called "menu.htm" appears in the document window.

5. Move the mouse pointer over the Wired Coffee logo (the image in the upper-left corner), then click the graphic link

The Web page called "company.htm" appears in the document window. You can click the Back button on the toolbar to quickly return to the previous Web page.

6. Click the Back button 🔙 on the toolbar

The previous Web page appears in the document window. If you want to return to the Web page called company.htm you visited in Step 5, you can click the link Wired Coffee logo again or click the Forward button on the toolbar.

7. Click the Forward button 🔜 on the toolbar

The next Web page appears in the document window. If you want to go back more than one Web page, you can click the Back button list arrow, then click the Web page you want to display.

8. Click the Back button list arrow 🔙 on the toolbar, then click Home Page

The Web page called "wired_main.htm" appears in the document window. Notice that the link menu color appears in blue (your color might be different) instead of teal. When you have already visited a link, the color of the link changes.

FIGURE F-6: Web pages connected by a hyperlink

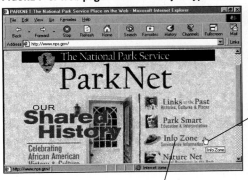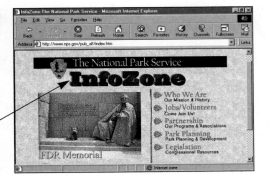

Graphic hyperlink; click to
jump to the InfoZone Web page

FIGURE F-7: Wired Coffee Company Web page

Graphic hyperlinks
appear without
any distinguishing
marks

Text hyperlinks
appear in color
with an underline
(your color might
be different)

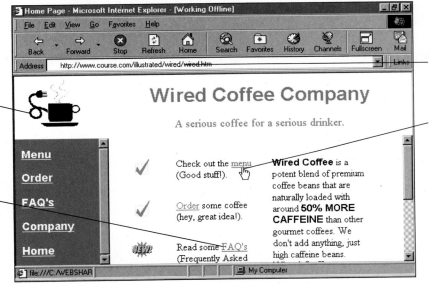

Web page address

Mouse pointer
changes to a hand
when positioned
over a link

TABLE F-3: URLs of Web sites dealing with coffee

name of company	url
Peet's Coffee & Tea	http://www.peets.com
Seattle's Best Coffee	http://www.seabest.com
Starbucks Coffee	http://www.starbucks.com

CLUES TO USE

Understanding a Web address

The address for a Web page is referred to as a URL.
Each Web page has a unique URL that begins with
"http" (HyperText Transfer Protocol) followed by a
colon, two slashes, and the name of the Web site. The
Web site is the computer where the Web pages are
located. At the end of the Web site name, another
slash might appear, followed by one or more folders

and a filename. For example, in the address,
http://www.course.com/illustrated/wired/wired_
main.htm, the name of the Web site is
www.course.com; a folder at that site is called
/illustrated/wired; and within the wired folder is a file
called *wired_main.htm*.

Windows 98

Adding a Web Page to the Favorites List

Rather than memorizing the URLs or keeping a handwritten list of Web pages you want to return to, you can use a feature called **Favorites** to store and organize the addresses. Once you add a Web page to the Favorites list, you can return to the page by opening the Favorites folder and selecting the address you want. To add a Web page to your Favorites list, display the Web page in your document window, click Favorites on the menu bar, then click Add to Favorites. You have the option to simply add the Web page to your Favorites list or to subscribe to the page. When you subscribe to a Web page, you are automatically notified when the Web page changes. ✎— John decides to subscribe to the Wired Coffee Company Web page so that he will be notified when changes are made to the Web site.

QuickTip

To view Web pages offline, click File on the menu bar, then click Work Offline. If you want to access other Web pages, you'll need to reconnect to the Internet.

Trouble?

URLs can be case-sensitive, meaning that you must type them exactly as they appear, using uppercase and lowercase letters.

1. **Click Favorites on the menu bar, then click Add to Favorites**
   The Add Favorite dialog box opens, as shown in Figure F-8. You can add the page to your Favorites list, you can subscribe to the page, or you can subscribe to the page and download it for offline viewing. When you download a Web page for **offline** viewing, the page is copied to your computer and your Internet connection is disconnected. This is helpful when you want to read a Web page without having to worry about your connect time.

2. **Click the Yes, but only tell me when this page is updated option button**
   The name of the Web page as it will appear in your Favorites list appears in the Name text box at the bottom of the Add Favorite dialog box. To change the Web page name, select the text, and type a new name. John decides to change the name to reflect the entire company name.

3. **In the Name text box, select the current text, type Wired Coffee Company, then click OK**
   The Web page is added to your Favorites list, and the subscription takes effect. When the Web page is changed, you'll be notified.

4. **Click anywhere in the Address bar, type http://www.course.com, then press [Enter]**
   Next you'll visit the Wired Coffee Company Web page using your Favorites list.

5. **Click the Favorites button 🔲 on the toolbar**
   The Explorer Bar opens on the left side of the document window and displays the Favorites list. The Favorites list contains several folders, including a Channels folder, a Links folder, the Software Updates folder, and individual favorite Web pages.

6. **Click Wired Coffee Company in the Favorites list**
   The Wired Coffee Company Web page appears in the document window, as shown in Figure F-9. The Favorites list also includes folders to help you organize your Favorites list. You can click a folder icon in the Favorites list to display its contents.

7. **Click the Links folder in the Favorites list**
   The Favorites in the Links folder expand and appear in the Explorer Bar, as shown in Figure F-10. To open a Favorite in the Links folder, position the mouse pointer over the Favorite you want to open (the mouse pointer changes to a hand and the Favorite appears underlined), then click the mouse button.

8. **Click the Links folder in the Favorites list again**
   The Favorites in the Links folder collapse to display only the Links folder icon. If you no longer use a favorite, you can delete it from the Favorites list.

9. **Right-click Wired Coffee Company in the Favorites list, click Delete, click Yes, then click the Close button in the Explorer Bar**
   The Explorer Bar with the Favorites list closes.

FIGURE F-8: Add Favorite dialog box

Subscribe options

Displays the name of the Web page as it will appear in your Favorites list

Click to change how and when you are notified of changes to the Web page

Click to save the current page in another folder

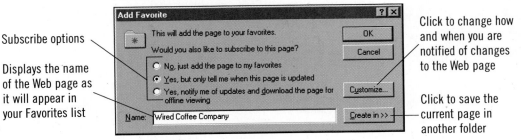

FIGURE F-9: Internet Explorer window with the Favorites list

Click to close Explorer bar

Explorer Bar displaying the Favorites list

Folders to help you organize your Favorites list

Individual Favorite Web pages

Your Favorites list might be different

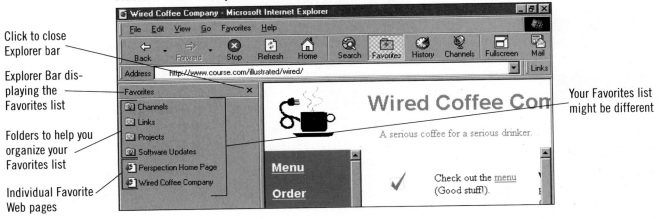

FIGURE F-10: Links folder with Favorites displayed

Click to display or collapse the list of Favorites in the Links folder

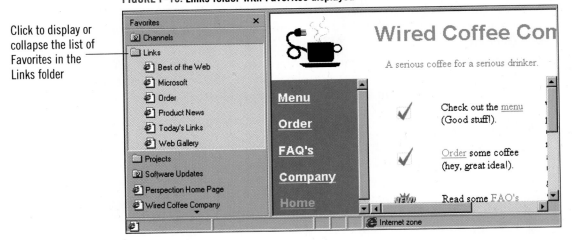

CLUES TO USE

Organizing your favorites

If your list of favorites gets too long, you can delete favorites you don't want anymore or move them into folders. To delete and move your favorites, click Favorites on the menu bar, click Organize Favorites, select one or more files from the Favorites list, then click Delete or Move. If you want to add a new folder to your Favorites list, click the Create New Folder button, type the new folder name, then press [Enter]. If you prefer to use another name for a favorite, you can select the one you want to rename, click Rename, type the new name, then press [Enter]. When you're finished making changes, click Close to exit.

Windows 98

Adding an Active Channel to the Channels List

Active channels are Web sites that deliver information to your computer in a variety of ways: through a Web page, via e-mail, as a screen saver, or directly to your desktop. Unlike cable channels on television, there are no costs involved in subscribing to Internet Explorer channels. There are hundreds of channel partners ready to deliver content to your desktop, including MSNBC, Computer Weekly, Better Homes & Gardens, Disney, and CBS Sportsline, to name a few. To view and subscribe to an active channel, click the Channels button on the Internet Explorer toolbar, click the channel you want to subscribe to, click the Add Active Channel button found on the Web site, then click the subscription option you want or click Customize to select specialized delivery options. John wants to stay abreast of the latest U.S. government policies. He decides to add the C-Span active channel to his Channels list.

Steps 1 2 3 4

1. **Click the Channels button ⊞ on the toolbar**
   The Explorer Bar opens on the left side of the document window and displays the Channels list. The Channels list contains active channels you can view and subscribe to. To view a channel, click the active channel you want in the Channels list. If you can't find the active channel you want, select the Channel Guide to view a more extensive list of active channels. John decides to view the channel guide to find C-Span.

2. **Click Microsoft active channel guide in the Channels list**
   The Microsoft active channel guide Web page appears in the document window, as shown in Figure F-11. Active channels on the Web continually change, so your active channel Web pages might look different. The Web page can be hard to read in the small window. You can use Internet Explorer's full screen button to view the page using the entire screen.

 QuickTip

To hold the Channels list in place, move the mouse pointer to the left edge of the screen to display the Channels list, then click the Pin button ⊞.

3. **Click the Fullscreen button ⊞ on the toolbar**
   The Microsoft active channel guide Web page appears using the full screen. The Channels list hides to the left side of the screen in the same way the taskbar hides to the bottom of the screen. To display the Channels list or the taskbar, move the mouse pointer to the left or bottom edge of the screen.

4. **Click the Search button on the active channel guide Web page**
   The Microsoft active channel guide search page appears, as shown in Figure F-12. You can specify a general category or enter a specific type of channel in the Keywords text box, then click the Search button to search for the active channel. John decides to search for the C-Span active channel.

5. **In the Keywords text box, type C-Span, then click the Search button**

 QuickTip

Instead of adding an active channel to the channels list, you can click the Visit Active Channel button to preview the site first.

6. **Click the link C-Span, then click Add Active Channel** [Add Active Channel ℮]
   The C-Span Web page displays a preview of the active channel. When you click Add Active Channel, the Add Active Channels dialog box opens, asking how you want to add the channel to the Channels list.

7. **Click the Yes, but only tell me when updates occur option button, then click OK**
   The C-Span active channel Web page is added to the Channels list.

8. **Click the Fullscreen button ⊞ on the toolbar**
   After viewing C-Span for awhile, John decides to remove it from the Channels list.

9. **Right-click C-Span in the Channels list, click Delete, then click Yes**
   The C-Span active channel is deleted from the Channels list.

10. **Click the Close button in the Explorer Bar**

FIGURE F-11: Explorer Bar with the Channels list

Click to view the channel guide

Your active channel page may differ

Click to scroll the Channels list

Click to view Internet Explorer window in full screen

Click to view the Channels list

Click to go to the active channel guide search page

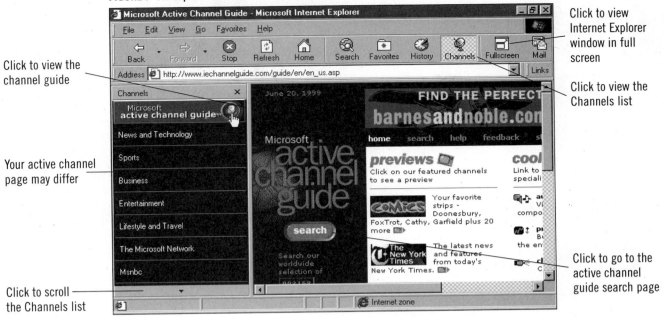

FIGURE F-12: The active channel guide in full screen

Your active channel page may differ

Toolbar in the full screen window

Enter key words for channels you want ot find here

Click to search for an active channel

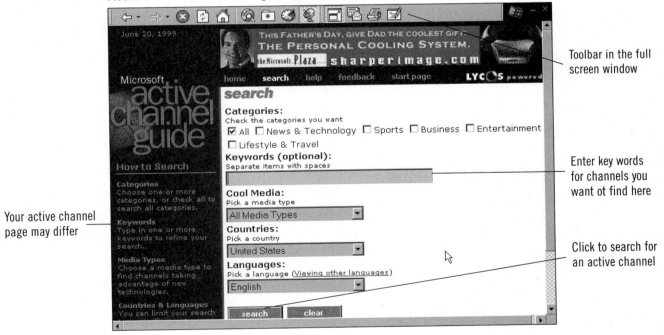

Selecting a Home Page and Adding a Link Button

A **home page** is the page that opens when you start Internet Explorer. When you first install Internet Explorer, the default home page is the Microsoft Corporation Home Web site. If you want a different page to appear when you start Internet Explorer (and whenever you click the Home button), you can click View on the menu bar, then click Internet Options. You can choose one of the millions of Web pages available through the Internet, or you can select a particular file on your hard drive. You can also change the Web pages associated with the buttons on the Links bar. John decides to change his home page to the Wired Coffee Company Web page and to add a link button to the Links bar.

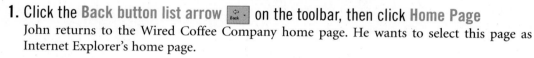

1. Click the **Back button list arrow**  on the toolbar, then click **Home Page**
John returns to the Wired Coffee Company home page. He wants to select this page as Internet Explorer's home page.

2. Click **View** on the menu bar, then click **Internet Options**
The Internet Options dialog box opens, as shown in Figure F-13. The Internet Options dialog box allows you to change a variety of Internet Explorer settings and preferences. See Table F-4 for a description of each tab.

3. Click the **General tab** (if necessary), then click **Use Current**
The address of the Wired Coffee Company Web page appears in the Address text box.

4. Click **OK**
The Home button on the toolbar is now associated with the current Web page, Wired Coffee Company. John tests the change using the Home button.

5. Click the link **FAQ's**, then click the **Home button** on the toolbar
The home page appears in the document window. Now John wants to add a link button.

6. Double-click the **Links bar** (position the mouse pointer over the word "Links")
The Links bar opens and hides the Address bar. The Links bar contains buttons with links to Web pages. You can drag a link on a page or a Web site address in the Address bar to a blank area on the Links bar to create a new Links button.

7. Drag the link **Order** to the left of the first button on the Links bar (the mouse pointer changes to a black bar to indicate the placement of the button), then release the mouse button
A new link button appears on the Links bar labeled with the name associated with the Web site, as shown in Figure F-14. You can delete or change the properties of a link button. Simply right-click the link button you want to change, then click the Delete or Properties command on the shortcut menu.

8. Right-click the **Order button** on the Links bar, click **Delete**, then click **Yes**
The home page appears in the document window. John closes the Links bar and displays the Address bar.

9. Double-click the **Links bar** to hide it

QuickTip
You will change your home page back to http://home.microsoft.com in the Skills Review exercise at the end of this unit. If you want to change it back at any other time, type "http://home.microsoft.com" in the Address bar, press [Enter], then complete Steps 1 through 3 from this lesson.

QuickTip
You can move the Links bar by dragging it to a new location.

FIGURE F-13: Internet Options dialog box

Click to use current Web page as the home page

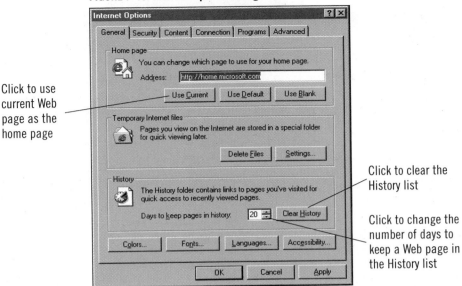

Click to clear the History list

Click to change the number of days to keep a Web page in the History list

FIGURE F-14: New button on the Links bar

Hidden Address bar (double-click to open)

New Links button

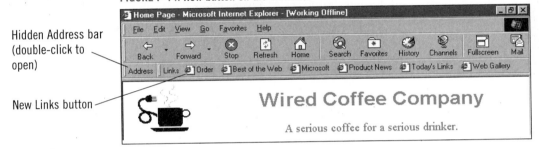

TABLE F-4: Internet Options dialog box tabs

tab	allows you to
General	Change your home page, temporary file settings, and history settings
Security	Select security levels for different parts of the Internet
Content	Set up a rating system for Internet content and information for buying items over the Internet
Connection	Change connection settings (phone and network)
Programs	Choose which programs (Mail, News, and Internet call) you want to use with Internet Explorer
Advanced	Change individual settings for browsing, multimedia, security, printing, and searching

Viewing and maintaining a History list

Sometimes you run across a great Web site and simply forget to add it to your Favorites list. With Internet Explorer there's no need to try to remember all the sites you've visited. The History feature keeps track of where you've been for days, weeks, or even months at a time. To view the History list, click the History button on the toolbar, then click a day or week in the Explorer Bar to expand the list of Web sites visited. Because the History list can grow to occupy a large amount of space on your hard drive, it's important that you control the length of time Web sites are retained in the list. Internet Explorer will delete the History list periodically based on the settings you specify in the General tab of the Internet Options dialog box, shown in Figure F-13.

Windows 98

Searching the Web

You can find all kinds of information on the Web. The best way to find information is to use a search engine. A **search engine** is a program found on a Web site that allows you to search through a collection of information found on the Internet to find what you are looking for. There are many search engines available on the Web, such as Yahoo! and Excite. When performing a search, the search engine compares the words or phrases, known as **keywords,** you submit with words that have been found on various Web sites on the Internet. If it finds your keywords in the stored database, the matched sites are listed on a Web page (these matched sites are sometimes called **hits**). The company who manages the search engine determines what information is stored in their database, so search results for different search engines will vary. John wants to search for other coffee-related Web sites to check out the competition.

Trouble?

If Excite is not in the list, click List of all search engines, click Excite to add the item to the list, then repeat step 2.

1. **Click the Search button 🔍 on the toolbar**
   A search engine appears in the Explorer Bar. If you prefer another search engine, you can choose the search engine you want using the Choose provider list arrow. John likes to use the search engine Excite.

2. **Click the Choose a Search Engine list arrow, then click Excite**
   The Excite search engine appears in the Explorer Bar, as shown in Figure F-15. To search for the information you are looking for, you need to enter keywords, usually the word or phrase that best describes what you want to retrieve, in the search text box. The more specific you are with your search criteria, the better list of matches you'll receive from the search engine. John wants to search for coffee imports on the Internet.

3. **In the search text box, type coffee imports**
   Now John is ready to start the search.

4. **Click Search in the Explorer Bar**
   The search engine retrieves and displays a list of Web sites that match your criteria, as shown in Figure F-16. The total number of Web sites found is listed at the top. The search results appear in decreasing order of relevance. The percentage next to the Web sites found indicates the degree of relevance. If the search results return too many hits, you should narrow the search criteria by adding more keywords. As you add more keywords, the search engine will find fewer Web pages that contain all of those words. See Table F-5 for other techniques to narrow a search.

5. **Click a link to a Web site in the list of matches**
   The Web site that you opened appears in the right pane of the document window. You can follow links to other pages on this Web site or jump to other Web sites. Once you are finished, close the Explorer Bar.

6. **Click the Close button in the Explorer Bar**
   The Explorer Bar closes. John returns to the Wired Coffee Company home page.

7. **Click the Back button list arrow 🔙 on the toolbar, then click Home Page**

Finding people on the Web

Internet Explorer provides several directory services to help you find people who may have access to the Internet (one service, Bigfoot, is shown in Figure F-17). To find a person on the Internet, click the Start button, point to Find, click People, select the directory service you want to use, type the person's name, then click Find Now. Each directory service accesses different databases on the Internet, so if you don't find the person you want using the first service you use, try looking with a different service.

FIGURE F-15: Explorer Bar with a search engine

Click to change
search engine

Your search engine
might be different

Type search
criteria here

Click to retrieve
Web site matches

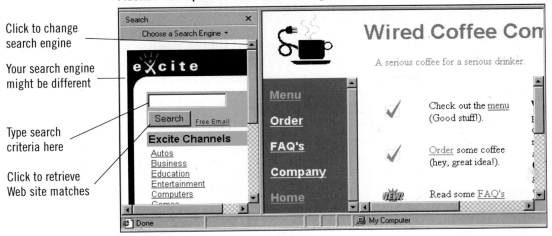

FIGURE F-16: Search engine results

Search results;
your list might
be different
(scroll down to
see entire list)

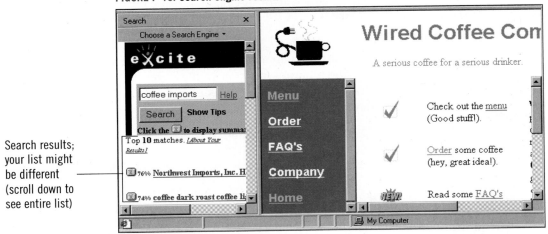

FIGURE F-17: Find People dialog box

Click to open the
Web site for the
selected directory
service

Click to choose a
different directory
service

Enter the name or
e-mail address of
person you want to
find here

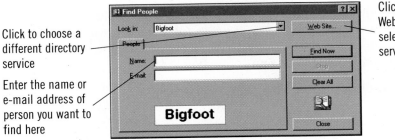

TABLE F-5: Techniques to narrow a search

technique	example
Use descriptive, specific words	beaches surfing Pacific
Use plain English phrases	Surfing beaches on the Pacific ocean
Place exact phrases and proper names in quotation marks	"Sunset Beach"
Use the plus sign (+) for words your results *must* contain	surf + beach
Use the minus sign (−) for words your results should *not* contain	surf + beach − Atlantic
Use AND to find results with all words	surf AND sea AND sand
Use OR to find results with at least one word	surf OR beach

Windows 98

Printing a Web Page

Web pages are designed to be viewed on a computer screen, but you can also print all or part of one. Internet Explorer provides many options for printing Web pages. For Web pages with frames, you can print the page just as you see it, or you can elect to print a particular frame or all frames. You can even use special Page Setup options to include the date, time, or window title on the printed page. You can also choose to print the Web addresses for the links contained in a Web page. To print a Web page, click File on the menu bar, then click Print to open the Print dialog box, then choose the appropriate print options or click the Print button on the toolbar. When you are ready to exit Internet Explorer, click the Close button in the upper-right corner of the Internet Explorer window or click File on the menu bar, then click Exit. There is no need to save before you exit, because you only view documents with Internet Explorer; you do not create or change documents. ✎ John prints a Web page and then exits Internet Explorer.

Steps

1. **Click File on the menu bar, then click Print**
   The Print dialog box opens, as shown in Figure F-18. John makes sure the printer he wants to use is selected. Make sure the printer you want to use is connected to your computer.

2. **Click the Name list arrow, then select the printer you want to use**
   When a Web page contains one or more frames, the Print dialog box gives you several options for printing the frames. You can print the Web page as it is laid out on the screen, only the selected frame, or all the frames included in the Web page individually. John decides to print all the frames of the Web page individually.

3. **Click the All frames individually option button**
   Instead of writing down the links included in a Web page, you can also automatically print the Web site addresses for each link. John wants to print the addresses of the links.

4. **Click the Print table of links check box to select the option**
   John is ready to print the frames and a table of the associated links.

5. **Click OK**
   The Web frames and a table of the links print on the selected printer.

6. **Click the Close button in the Internet Explorer window**
   Internet Explorer closes. If you connected to the Internet by telephone, a disconnect dialog box appears. If you are connected to the Internet through a network, follow your instructor's directions to close your connection.

7. **If the disconnect dialog box appears, click Yes**

Trouble?

If the disconnect dialog box doesn't appear, right-click the Connect Icon 🖳 on the right side of the taskbar, then click Disconnect.

FIGURE F-18: Printing a Web page

Click to select
which pages you
want to print

Click to select
a frame option

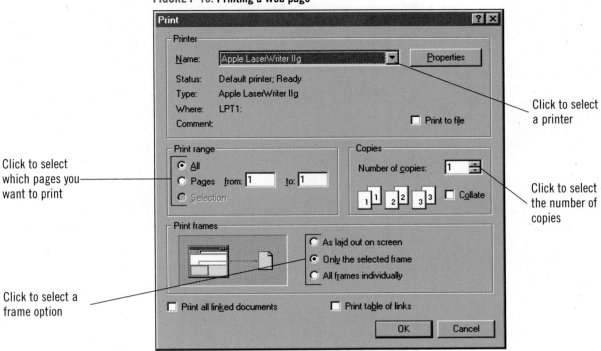

Click to select
a printer

Click to select
the number of
copies

Setting the page format

When you print a Web page, you can use the Page Setup dialog box to control the way text and graphics are printed on a page. The Page Setup dialog box, shown in Figure F-19, specifies the printer properties for page size, orientation, and paper source; in most cases, you won't want to change them. From the Page Setup dialog box, you can also change header and footer information. In the Header and Footer text boxes, you can type text that will appear as a header or footer of the Web page you print. In these text boxes, you can also use variables to substitute for information about the current page, and you can combine text and codes. For example, if you type "Page &p of &P" in the Header text box, the current page number and the total number of pages will be printed at the top of each page. Check Internet Explorer Help for a complete list of header and footer codes.

FIGURE F-19: Page Setup dialog box

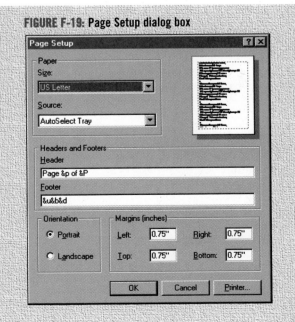

Practice

▶ Concepts Review

Label each of the elements of the screen shown in Figure F-20.

FIGURE F-20

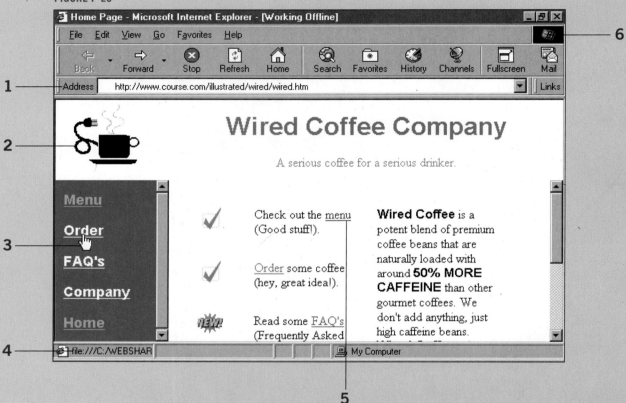

Match each of the terms with the statement that describes its function.

7. **Address bar**
8. **Toolbar**
9. **Favorites button**
10. **Status indicator**
11. **Back button**

a. Animates when Internet Explorer is loading a page
b. Displays the URL for the current page
c. Provides shortcuts for options on the menu bar
d. Displays a list of selected Web pages and folders to organize them
e. Displays the previously viewed page

Select the best answer from the following list of choices.

12. **Software programs that are used to access and display Web pages are called**
   a. Web sites.
   b. Search engines.
   c. Web utilities.
   d. Web browsers.

13. If you want to save the name and URL of a Web page in Internet Explorer and return to it later, you can add it to a list called
    a. Favorites.
    b. Bookmarks.
    c. Home pages.
    d. Preferences.

14. An international telecommunications network that consists of linked documents is called the
    a. NSFNET.
    b. Netscape Communicator.
    c. Internet Explorer.
    d. World Wide Web.

15. In Internet Explorer, where are the buttons located that perform common functions such as moving to a previous Web page?
    a. Address bar
    b. Toolbar
    c. Status bar
    d. Menu bar

16. Which of the following is a valid URL?
    a. http:/www.usf.edu/
    b. http://www.usf.edu/
    c. htp:/ww.usf.edu/
    d. http//www.usf.edu/

17. Underlined words that you click to jump to another Web page are called
    a. Explorers.
    b. Favorites.
    c. Web browsers.
    d. Hyperlinks.

18. The URL of the current Web page is displayed in the
    a. Title bar.
    b. Document window.
    c. Address bar.
    d. Status bar.

► Skills Review

1. Start Internet Explorer and explore the browser window.
   a. Connect to the Internet.
   b. Start Internet Explorer.
   c. Identify the toolbar, menu bar, Address bar, Links bar, status bar, status indicator, URL, document window, and scroll bars.
   d. In the toolbar, identify icons for searching, viewing favorites, viewing history, viewing Internet Explorer in full screen, and moving to the previous page.

2. Open a Web page and follow links.
 a. Click in the Address bar, then type "http://www.course.com".
 b. Press [Enter].
 c. Explore the Web site by using the scroll bars, toolbar, and hyperlinks.
 d. Click in the Address bar, then type "http://www.sportsline.com/".
 e. Press [Enter].
 f. Follow the links to investigate the content.

3. Add a Web page to the Favorites list.
 a. Click in the Address bar, type "http://www.loc.gov/", then press [Enter].
 b. Click Favorites on the menu bar, then click Add to Favorites.
 c. Click OK.
 d. Click the Favorites button.
 e. Click the Home button.
 f. Click Library of Congress Home Page in the Favorites list.
 g. Right-click Library of Congress Home, click Delete, then click Yes.
 h. Click the Close button in the Favorites list.

4. Add an active channel to the Channels list.
 a. Click the Channels button.
 b. Click Microsoft active channel guide.
 c. Click the Fullscreen button.
 d. Click the Search button, click the Sports checkbox, then click the Search button.
 e. Click the link ESPN SportsZone, then click Add Active Channel.
 f. Click the Yes, but only tell me when updates occur option button, then click OK.
 g. Click the Fullscreen button.
 h. Right-click the ESPN SportsZone in the Channels list, click Delete, then click Yes.
 i. Click the Close button in the Explorer Bar.

5. Select a home page and add a link button.
 a. Click in the Address bar, then type "http://home.microsoft.com/".
 b. Press [Enter].
 c. Click View on the menu bar, then click Internet Options.
 d. Click the General tab.
 e. Click Use Current.
 f. Click OK.
 g. Click the Back button.
 h. Click the Home button.

6. Search the Web.
 a. Click the Search button.
 b. Click the Choose a Search Engine list arrow, then click Yahoo.
 c. Enter "job computer training" in the Search text box.
 d. Click Search.
 e. Click a link to a Web site in the list of matches.
 f. Click the Close button in the Explorer Bar.
 g. Click the Home button.

7. Print a Web page and exit Internet Explorer.

  a. Click File on the menu bar, then click Print.

  b. Click the Name list arrow, then select a printer.

  c. Click the Pages option button (use the range 1 to 1).

  d. Click the As laid out on screen option button.

  e. Click OK.

  f. Click the Close button to exit Internet Explorer.

  g. Click Yes to disconnect, if necessary.

▶ Independent Challenges

1. You will soon graduate from college with a degree in business management. Before entering the workforce, you want to make sure that you are up-to-date on all of the advances in the field. You decide that the Web would provide the most current information. In addition, you can look for companies with employment opportunities. Use Internet Explorer to investigate the All Business Network at http://www.all-biz.com/. Follow the links, and when you find a promising site, print the page.

2. You are leaving tomorrow for a business trip in France. You want to make sure that you take the right clothes for the season, and decide that the best place to check France's weather might be the Web. Access one or two of the following weather sites and print at least two reports on the weather in Paris. (*Hint:* Web addresses are case sensitive so be sure to type capital letters where indicated.)

The Weather Channel	http://www.weather.com/
World Weather Guide	http://www.world-travel-net.co.uk./weather/
CNN Weather	http://www.cnn.com/WEATHER/

3. Your boss wants to buy a new desktop computer (as opposed to a laptop). He assigns you the task of investigating the options. You decide that it would be more expedient to look on the Web than to visit the computer stores in the area. Visit the following Web sites, and print a page from the two that you think offer the best deal.

IBM	http://www.ibm.com/
Apple	http://www.apple.com/
Dell	http://www.dell.com/

4. During the summer, you want to travel to national parks in the United States. Use one of the Internet's search engines to find Web sites with maps of the national parks. Visit four or five Web sites from the match list and print a page from the three sites that you think offer the best maps and related information for park visitors.

► Visual Workshop

Recreate the screen shown in Figure F-21, which displays the document window with a search engine and a Web site. Print the Web page and print the screen. (To print the screen, press the PrintScreen key to make a copy of the screen, open Paint, click Edit on the menu bar, click Paste to paste the screen into Paint, then click Yes to paste the larger image if necessary. Click File on the menu bar, click Print, then click OK.)

FIGURE F-21

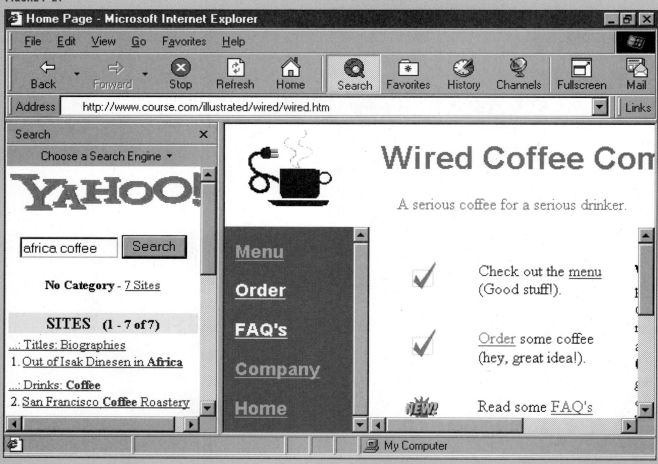

Exchanging
Mail and News

Objectives

- ► **Start Outlook Express**
- ► **Explore the Outlook Express window**
- ► **Add a contact to the Address Book**
- ► **Compose and send e-mail**
- ► **Retrieve, read, and respond to e-mail**
- ► **Manage e-mail messages**
- ► **Select a news service**
- ► **View and subscribe to a newsgroup**
- ► **Read and post news articles**

Windows 98 includes Microsoft Outlook Express, a powerful program for managing electronic mail (known as e-mail). With an Internet connection and Microsoft Outlook Express, you can exchange e-mail messages with anyone on the Internet and join any number of **newsgroups**, collections of e-mail messages on related topics posted by individuals to specified locations on the Internet. If you are not connected to the Internet, you will not be able to work the steps in this unit; however, you can read the lessons without completing the steps to learn what you can accomplish using Outlook Express. ◄━━ In this unit John Casey, owner of Wired Coffee Company, will use Outlook Express to send and receive e-mail messages and join a newsgroup about the coffee industry.

Windows 98

Starting Outlook Express

Outlook Express puts the world of online communication on your desktop. Whether you want to exchange e-mail with colleagues and friends or join newsgroups to trade ideas and information, the tools you need are here. When you install Windows 98, an icon for Outlook Express will automatically appear on the desktop, and a button will appear on the Quick Launch toolbar on the taskbar. If your computer is not connected to the Internet, check with your instructor or technical support person to see if it's possible for you to connect. ▰▰ John realizes that e-mail is a powerful way to communicate. He wants to use Outlook Express to communicate more effectively with his employees.

1. **If necessary, establish a connection to the Internet via the network or telephone**
   If you connect to the Internet through a network, follow your instructor's directions to establish your connection. If you connect by telephone, use an existing Dial-Up Networking connection, or create a new connection using the Connection Wizard to establish your connection. Once you have established a connection, you can start Outlook Express.

2. **Locate the Outlook Express icon on your desktop**
   The icon should appear on the left side of your screen, as shown in Figure G-1. You can also click the Launch Outlook Express button 📧 on the Quick Launch toolbar to start Outlook Express.

Trouble?

If a Browse For Folder dialog box appears, click OK to accept the default folder where Outlook Express should store your messages, then continue.

3. **Double-click the Outlook Express icon on your desktop**
   The Outlook Express window opens and displays the Outlook Express Start Page, as shown in Figure G-2. Continue with the next lesson to view the various elements of the Outlook Express window.

4. **If necessary, click the Maximize button to maximize the Outlook Express window**
   If you connect to the Internet through a network, follow your instructor's directions to log on. If you connect to the Internet by telephone using a Dial-Up Networking connection, continue with the following steps as necessary.

QuickTip

You can set up Outlook Express to automatically start your Dial-Up Networking connection when the program starts. In Outlook Express, click Tools on the menu bar, click Options, click the Dial Up tab, click the Dial this connection option button, then select a connection from the list box.

5. **If necessary, click the Connect button 🔗 on the toolbar to start your Dial-Up Networking connection**
   The Logon Microsoft Outlook Express dialog box opens. You need to enter your username and password to connect to the Internet. See your instructor or technical support person for this information.

6. **If necessary, enter your user name, press [Tab], enter your password, then click OK**
   A Connection dialog box opens, displaying dial-up connection status information. Upon completion of the dial-up connection, you are connected to the Internet (unless an error message appears).

FIGURE G-1: **Windows desktop**

Outlook Express icon

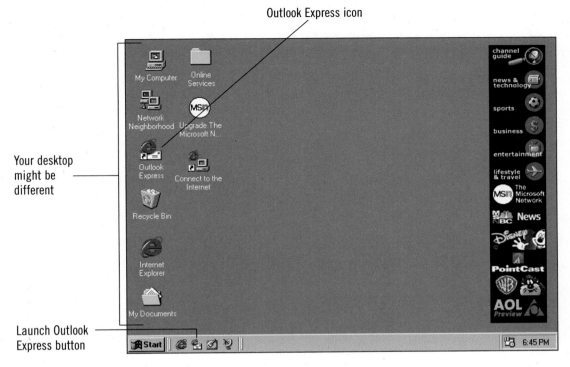

Your desktop
might be
different

Launch Outlook
Express button

FIGURE G-2: **Outlook Express window**

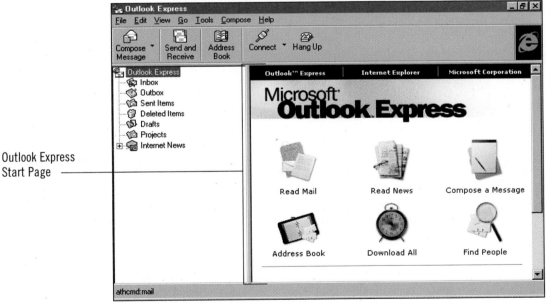

Outlook Express
Start Page

Starting Outlook Express from your Web browser

You can set Outlook Express to be your default e-mail program, so that whenever you click an e-mail link on a Web page or choose the mail command in your Web browser, Outlook Express opens. Likewise, you can set Outlook Express to be your default news reader, so that when you click a newsgroup link on a Web page or choose the news reader command in your Web browser, Outlook Express opens. To set Outlook Express to be your default e-mail or newsgroup program, start Internet Explorer, click Tools on the menu bar, click Options, click the General tab, then select the following check box(es): Make Outlook Express my default e-mail program, or Make Outlook Express my default news reader, or both.

Windows 98

Exploring the Outlook Express Window

After you start Outlook Express, the Outlook Express window displays the Outlook Express Start Page, shown in Figure G-3. The **Outlook Express Start Page** displays tools that you can use to read e-mail, download the latest newsgroup messages, read newsgroup messages, compose e-mail messages, enter and edit Address Book information, and find people on the Internet. Before reading his e-mail, John decides to familiarize himself with the components of the Outlook Express window.

He notes the following features:

 The title bar at the top of the window displays the name of the program.

 The menu bar provides access to a variety of commands, much like other Windows programs.

 The toolbar provides icons, or buttons, for easy access to the most commonly used commands. See Table G-1 for a description of each toolbar button. These button commands are also available on menus.

 The Internet Explorer link opens Microsoft Internet Explorer.

 The folder list displays folders where Outlook Express stores e-mail messages. You can also use folders to organize your e-mail messages.

 The Read Mail link jumps to the Inbox where you can read and reply to incoming e-mail messages.

 The Read News link connects to newsgroups that you can view and subscribe to.

 The Compose a Message link opens the New Message dialog box where you can compose and send e-mail messages.

 The Address Book link opens the Windows Address Book where you can enter and edit your Contact list.

 The Download All link downloads all the latest newsgroup messages.

 The Find People link opens the Find People dialog box where you can search for people on the Internet or in your Address Book.

 The status bar displays information about your Internet connection with a mail or newsgroup server.

FIGURE G-3: Outlook Express window with the Start Page

Title bar

Menu bar

Toolbar

Folder list;
your list
might be
different

Status bar

Internet
Explorer link

Outlook
Express Start
Page links

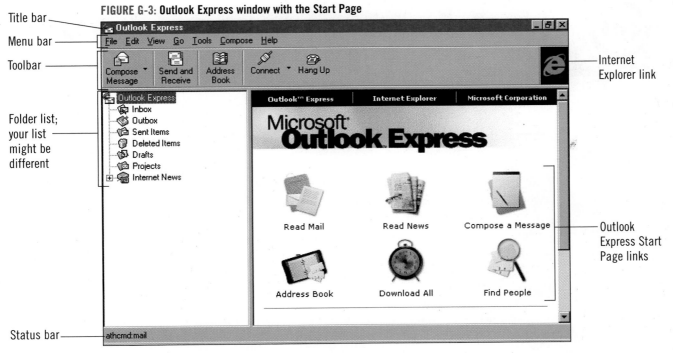

TABLE G-1: Outlook Express Start Page toolbar buttons

button	description
Compose Message	Opens the e-mail message composition window
Send and Receive	Sends e-mail messages and checks for new messages
Address Book	Opens the Address Book
Connect	Connects to the mail or newsgroup server on the Internet
Hang Up	Hangs up the Internet connection

Getting help in Outlook Express

If you need help connecting to the Internet to get mail or learning how to use Outlook Express features, you can get help from several different sources. To get Outlook Express Help, you can use the online Help system that comes with the program or view Outlook Express Web sites on the Internet. To open Outlook Express online Help, click Help on the menu bar, then click Contents and Index. To learn about Outlook Express from Web sites on the Internet, click the Outlook Express link at the top of the Outlook Express Start Page, or click Help on the menu bar, then click Learn About Microsoft Outlook. Internet Explorer starts and displays the Outlook Express Web sites.

Adding a Contact to the Address Book

A **contact** is a person or company that you communicate with. One contact can have several mailing addresses, phone numbers, e-mail addresses, or Web sites. You can store this information in the **Address Book** along with other detailed information, such as the contact's job title, cellular phone number, and personal Web page addresses. When you want to create a new contact or edit an existing one, you use the Properties dialog box to enter or change contact information. You can organize your contacts into **contact groups**, which are groups of related people you communicate with on a regular basis. One contact group might be your family members or people at work. John wants to add a new employee to his Address Book.

QuickTip

You can also click the Address Book button on the toolbar to open the Address Book.

1. **Click the Address Book link on the Outlook Express Start Page**
   The Address Book window opens, as shown in Figure G-4, displaying the current contacts in the Address Book. Your list of contacts might be different or empty. Above the list of contacts is the Address Book toolbar. See Table G-2 for a description of each toolbar button. These button commands are also available on the menus.

2. **Click the New Contact button on the Address Book toolbar**
   The Properties dialog box opens, displaying the Personal tab with empty text boxes. See Table G-3 for a description of each tab in the Properties dialog box. John types the name and e-mail address for the new employee.

3. **Type Shawn, press [Tab] twice to move to the Last name text box, then type Brooks**
   Now you can enter Shawn's e-mail address.

4. **Click the Add New text box, type shawnbrooks@course.com, then click Add**
   The e-mail address appears in the box below the Add New text box, as shown in Figure G-5. E-mail addresses are not case-sensitive (capitalization doesn't matter) and cannot contain spaces. To modify an e-mail address, select it, then click Edit. To delete an e-mail address no longer in use, select it, then click Remove.

5. **Click OK**
   The Properties dialog box closes and you return to the Address Book. Instead of opening the Properties dialog box every time you want to see a more complete listing of a contact's information, you can position the mouse pointer over a contact in the Address Book to display a ToolTip summary of the contact's information.

6. **Position the mouse pointer over Shawn Brooks in the Address Book**
   A ScreenTip summary appears on the screen. You can move the mouse pointer to remove the ScreenTip or wait. To edit a contact, simply double-click anywhere on the contact entry in the Address Book.

7. **Double-click Shawn Brooks**
   The Shawn Brooks Properties dialog box opens and displays the selected contact's information. You can use any of the tabs in this dialog box to add to or change the contact information. John adds Shawn's business phone number.

8. **Click the Business tab, click the Phone text box, type 925-555-3084, then click OK**
   Shawn's business phone number appears in the Address book. Finished making changes, John closes the Address Book.

9. **Click the Close button in the Address Book window**

FIGURE G-4: Address Book window

Address Book toolbar

Enter name here to find contact

Current contacts; your list might be different or empty

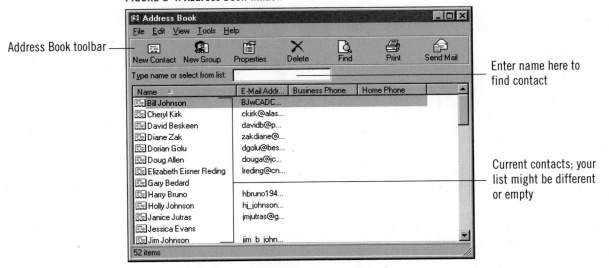

FIGURE G-5: Properties dialog box with a new contact

Enter e-mail address here

E-mail address added here

Enter name here

Click to add e-mail address

Click to edit or delete e-mail address

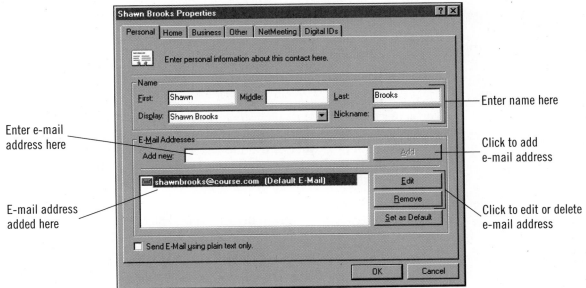

TABLE G-2: Address Book toolbar buttons

button	description	button	description
New Contact	Creates a new contact	Find	Finds a contact
New Group	Creates a new contact group	Print	Opens the Print dialog box
Properties	Opens the selected contact	Send Mail	Opens a new e-mail message addressed to selected contact
Delete	Deletes the selected contact		

TABLE G-3: New contact Properties dialog box tabs

tab	description	tab	description
Personal	Enter personal information	Other	Enter notes about contact
Home	Enter information related to the contact's home	NetMeeting	Add and modify e-mail conferencing addresses and servers
Business	Enter business related information	Digital IDs	Add, remove, and view security identification numbers for the contact

Windows 98

Composing and Sending E-mail

E-mail is quickly becoming the primary form of written communication for many people. E-mail messages follow a standard memo format with fields for the sender, recipient, date, and subject of the message. To send an e-mail message, you need to enter the recipient's e-mail address, type a subject, and then type the message itself. You can send the same message to more than one individual, or to a contact group, or a combination of individuals and groups. You can personalize your e-mail messages (and newsgroup messages) with built-in stationery, or you can design your own. ◢ John wants to send an e-mail message to the new employee whose name he entered into the Address Book in the previous lesson.

Steps 1 2 3 4

QuickTip

You can also click Compose on the menu bar, then click New Message, or click the Compose a Message link to open the New Message window.

QuickTip

To remove a name from the Message recipients list, click the person's name in the Message recipients list box, then press [Delete].

QuickTip

If you don't want to send the e-mail message right now, click File on the menu bar, then click Send Later. The e-mail message is placed in the Outbox but not sent.

1. **Click the Compose Message button list arrow** [icon] **on the toolbar, then click Ivy**
The New Message window opens, as shown in Figure G-6, displaying the Ivy stationery in the message box. You can click the Compose Message button to create a new message without stationery.

2. **Click the Select recipients from a list icon** [icon] **next to the To text box**
The Select Recipients dialog box opens, as shown in Figure G-7, displaying the contacts from the Address Book.

3. **In the list of contacts, click the down scroll arrow if necessary, then click Shawn Brooks**

4. **Click the To button**
The contact, Shawn Brooks, appears in the Message recipients list box. You can also add additional recipients to this list, select another recipient and click the Cc (carbon copy) button to send a copy of your e-mail message to that person, or click the Bcc (blind carbon copy) button to send a copy of your e-mail message to another person without displaying the names of the blind copy recipients in the e-mail message.

5. **Click OK**
Shawn Brooks's name appears in the To text box. Shawn's e-mail address is associated with the name selected even though it is not displayed. John includes a subject title.

6. **Click <click here to enter the subject>, then type Welcome aboard!**
The message title bar changes from New Message to the subject text, Welcome aboard! Now you can type your message.

7. **Click the text box at the bottom of the message window**
The Formatting toolbar, just below the Subject text box, is activated. The Formatting toolbar works just like the Formatting toolbar in WordPad or other Windows programs. You can use it to change the format of your message text at any time.

8. **Type Dear Shawn:, press [Enter] twice, type I would like to welcome you to the Wired Coffee Company. We are excited that you have joined our team. Wired Coffee is a growing company, and I believe your contributions will make a big difference. Please come to a luncheon for new employees this Thursday at 12:30 in the company cafe., press [Enter] twice, then type John**

9. **Click the Send button** [Send icon] **on the toolbar**
The New Message window closes, and the e-mail message is placed in the Outbox, a folder where outgoing messages are stored, and then automatically sent to the recipient.

FIGURE G-6: **New Message window with Ivy stationery**

Click to select a recipient from the Address Book

Ivy stationery

Click to enter subject text

Click here to begin typing message

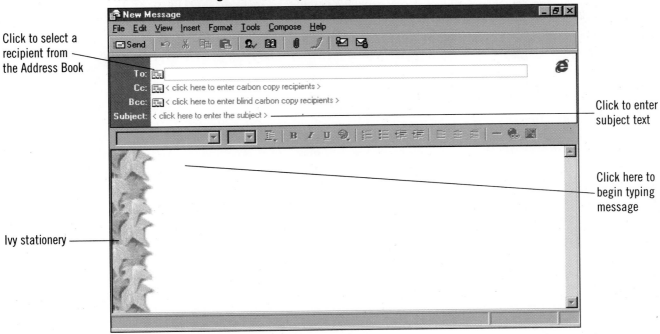

FIGURE G-7: **Selecting recipients for an e-mail message**

Enter name here to find a recipient, or click the Find button

Select a contact from this list, then click the To button (your list will differ)

Click to add a new contact

Click to choose the selected contact as a recipient for this message

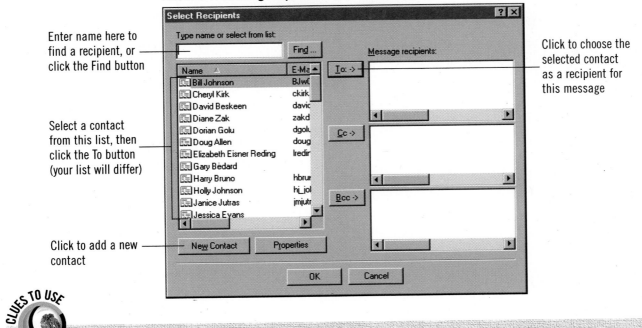

Attaching a file to an e-mail message

In addition to exchanging messages, another powerful feature of e-mail is the ability to easily share files. You can send a file, such as a picture or a document by attaching it to an e-mail message. When the e-mail is received, the recipient can open the file in the program in which it was created. For example, suppose you are working on a report that you created using WordPad and that a colleague working in another part of the country needs to present today. After you finish the report, you can attach the report file to an e-mail message and send the message to your colleague, who can then open, edit, and print the report. To attach a file to an e-mail message, create the message, click the Insert File button 📎 on the toolbar, select the file you want to attach, then click Attach. The attached file appears at the bottom of the message window as an icon that the message recipient can double-click to open the file.

Windows 98

Retrieving, Reading, and Responding to E-mail

To retrieve your e-mail, you can manually connect to the Internet or set Outlook Express to automatically retrieve your messages. New messages appear in the Inbox along with any messages you haven't yet stored elsewhere or deleted. A **message flag** appears next to any message that has a certain priority or a file attached to it and helps you determine the content of a message and its status, or whether or not the message has been read, if it has an attachment, and its priority. See Table G-4 for a description of the message flags. ✎ John forwards an e-mail message he received from Shawn Brooks to another person at the company..

Steps 1234

1. **Click the Send and Receive button [icon] on the toolbar**
   A dialog box displays the progress of the e-mail messages you are sending and receiving. After your e-mail messages have been sent or received, the dialog box closes. When you receive new e-mail, the Inbox folder in the Folder list is bold, indicating that it contains unread messages, and a number in parenthesis indicates the number of new e-mail messages you have received.

2. **In the Folder list, click Inbox**
   The Inbox folder opens as shown in Figure G-8. The **preview pane** displays the messages in your Inbox. The **display pane** displays the e-mail message that is selected in the preview pane. E-mail messages in the preview pane with the subject or heading text in bold are messages that have not been opened.

Trouble?

If you didn't receive a message from Shawn Brooks, click the Send and Receive button on the toolbar again. It may take a few minutes for the message to arrive.

3. **Click the message you received from Shawn Brooks**
   When a message you receive is short, you can quickly read the message text in the display pane. Longer messages, like the one from Shawn Brooks, are easier to open and read in a full window.

4. **Double-click the message you received from Shawn Brooks in the preview pane, then click the Maximize button in the message window**
   After reading a message, you can reply to the author, reply to all of the recipients, forward the message to another person, or simply close or delete the message. John forwards the message to his human resources administrator to ask her to add Shawn Brooks to the list of luncheon attendees. You will forward the message to your instructor or to someone else whose e-mail address you know.

5. **Click the Forward Message button [icon] on the message toolbar**
   The Forward Message window opens, as shown in Figure G-9, displaying the original e-mail message you sent. At the top of the message box, you can add additional text to the message.

Trouble?

If you don't know an e-mail address to send the forwarded message to, click the Close button in the message window, then continue with the next lesson.

6. **Click in the upper-left corner of the message box, then type Please add Shawn Brooks to Thursday's luncheon guest list.**
   Next enter the e-mail address of someone you know who won't mind receiving this message, possibly your instructor.

7. **Click <click here to enter recipients>, type the e-mail address of your instructor or someone else you know, then click the Send button [icon] on the toolbar**
   The e-mail message is sent. John deletes Shawn from his Address Book.

8. **Click the Address Book button [icon] on the toolbar, click Shawn Brooks, click the Delete button [icon], click Yes, then click the Close button**

FIGURE G-8: Outlook Express window with the Inbox

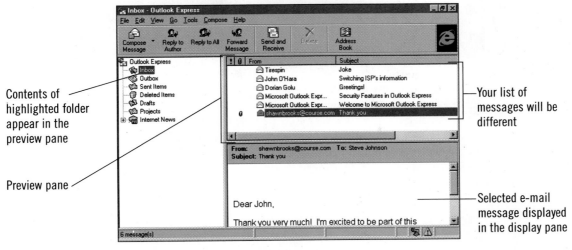

Contents of highlighted folder appear in the preview pane

Preview pane

Your list of messages will be different

Selected e-mail message displayed in the display pane

FIGURE G-9: Forward Message window

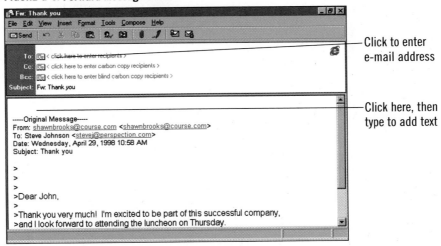

Click to enter e-mail address

Click here, then type to add text

TABLE G-4: Mail message flag icons

icon	description	icon	description
✉	Message has not been read; message heading text appears bold	!	Message has been marked as high priority by the sender
✉	Message has been read	↓	Message has been marked as low priority by the sender
📎	Message has one or more files attached to it		

CLUES TO USE

Diverting incoming e-mail to folders

Outlook Express can direct incoming messages that meet criteria that you specify to folders you specify, rather than to your Inbox. Let's say that you have a friend who loves sending you funny e-mail, but you often don't have time to read it right away. You can set the Inbox Assistant to store any messages you receive from your friend in a different folder so they won't clutter your Inbox. When you are ready to read the messages, you simply open the folder and access the messages just as you would in the Inbox. To set criteria for incoming messages, click Tools on the menu bar, click Inbox Assistant to open the Inbox Assistant dialog box, click Add to open the Properties dialog box, click the From button, select your friend's e-mail address from the Select Recipients dialog box, click the Move To check box, click Folder, and then select or create a folder where you would like your friend's messages to be stored.

Managing E-mail Messages

A common problem with using e-mail is an overcrowded Inbox. To help you keep your Inbox organized, you should move messages you want to keep to other folders and subfolders, delete messages you no longer want, and create new folders as you need them. Storing incoming messages in other folders and deleting unwanted messages make it easier to see the new messages you receive and to keep track of messages to which you have already responded. John wants to create a new folder for his important messages, move a message from the Inbox to the new folder, and then delete the messages he no longer needs.

Steps 1 2 3 4

1. **Click File on the menu bar, point to Folder, then click New Folder**
   The Create Folder dialog box opens, displaying the list of folders contained in the Outlook Express folder, as shown in Figure G-10. John will name the new folder Important.

2. **Type Important**
   Now you need to select where you want to store the new folder. John wants the new Important folder to be in the Outlook Express folder.

3. **Click Outlook Express at the top of the Folder list**
   The new folder will appear in the Folder list under Outlook Express. To create a **subfolder** (a folder in a folder), you would select one of the folders in the Folder list under Outlook Express. The Folder list works like the left pane of Windows Explorer. When a subfolder is created, a plus sign (+) is displayed next to the folder which contains the subfolder.

4. **Click OK**
   The new folder, Important, appears in the Folder list under Outlook Express.

5. **In the preview pane of the Inbox, right-click the message you received from Shawn Brooks**
   A pop-up menu appears, displaying commands, such as move, copy, delete, and print, to help you manage your e-mail messages.

6. **Click Move To on the pop-up menu**
   The Move To dialog box opens, asking you to select the folder where you want the selected message to be stored.

7. **Click the Important folder, then click OK**

8. **In the Folder list, click the Important folder**
   The e-mail message you just moved appears in the preview and display panes, as shown in Figure G-11. Next John deletes the Important folder.

9. **In the Folder list, right-click the Important folder, click Delete, then click Yes**
   The Important folder and all of its contents are deleted.

FIGURE G-10: Create Folder dialog box

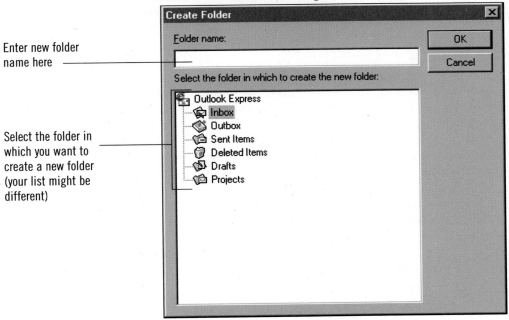

Enter new folder name here

Select the folder in which you want to create a new folder (your list might be different)

FIGURE G-11: Important folder

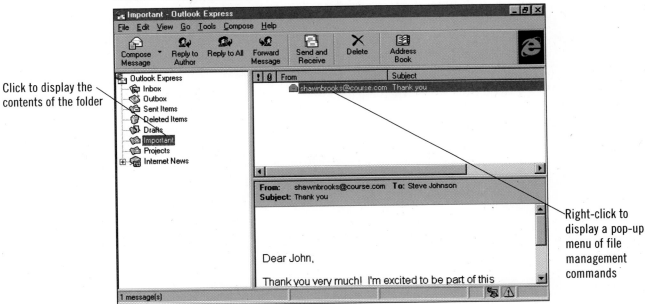

Click to display the contents of the folder

Right-click to display a pop-up menu of file management commands

Printing e-mail messages and contacts

You can print your e-mail messages from any folder at any time using Outlook Express. To print an e-mail message, open the message, then click the Print button on the toolbar. You can also open the Address Book and print contact information in a variety of formats, such as Memo, Business Card, and Phone List. The Memo style prints all the information you have for a contact with descriptive titles. The Business Card style prints the contact information without descriptive titles. The Phone List style prints all the phone numbers for a contact or for all your contacts. To print contact information, open the Address Book, select a specific contact (if desired), click the Print button on the toolbar, then select a print range, print style, and the number of copies you want to print.

Selecting a News Service

A newsgroup is an electronic forum where people from around the world with a common interest can share ideas, ask and answer questions, and comment on and discuss any subject. You can find newsgroups on almost any topic, from the serious to the lighthearted, from educational to controversial, from business to social. Before you can participate in a newsgroup, you must select a news server. A **news server** is a computer located on the Internet where newsgroup messages, called **articles**, on different topics are stored. Each news server contains several newsgroups from which to choose. The Internet Connection Wizard walks you through the process of selecting a news server. This wizard also appears the first time you use Outlook Express News. To complete the wizard and the steps in this lesson, you'll need to get the name of the news server you want to use from your instructor, network administrator, or Internet service provider (ISP), and possibly an account name and password. ▸ John wants to add a news server account so he can access coffee-related newsgroups.

Steps 1234

Trouble?

If you do not already have a news server selected, the Internet Connection Wizard will appear, and you should skip to Step 4 to complete the wizard. If you already have a news server, continue with the next step.

1. In the Folder list, click **Outlook Express**, then click the **Read News link**

2. Click **Tools** on the menu bar, then click **Accounts**

The Internet Accounts dialog box opens, as shown in Figure G-12, displaying the News tab with your list of available news servers. Using the Internet Accounts dialog box, you can add, remove, and view properties for news servers, mail servers, and directory services.

3. Click **Add**, then click **News**

The Internet Connection Wizard dialog box opens.

4. Type your **name**, then click **Next**

Individuals participating in the newsgroup need to know your e-mail address so they can reply to your news messages either by posting another news message or by sending you an e-mail message.

5. Type your **e-mail address**, then click **Next**

6. Type the name of the news server provided by your instructor, network administrator, or ISP, as shown in Figure G-13, then click **Next**

To make it easier to identify, give the news server a more friendly name.

7. Type **General News**, then click **Next**

You need to select which method you want to use to connect to the Internet. You can connect to the Internet using a phone line or a local area network (LAN), or by establishing a manual connection.

8. Click the appropriate connection type option button, then click **Next**

Some connection types require additional information. If so, see your instructor or network administrator for instructions, and then click Next to continue.

9. Click **Finish**, click **Close** if necessary, then click **No**

If the Internet Accounts dialog box is open, you'll need to close it. The news server name appears in the Folder list, as shown in Figure G-14. At this time, you'll click No to view a list of available newsgroups. In the next lesson, you'll view the list.

FIGURE G-12: Internet Accounts dialog box

Click to select server type

Click to add a server

Click to remove the selected server

Click to view properties of selected server

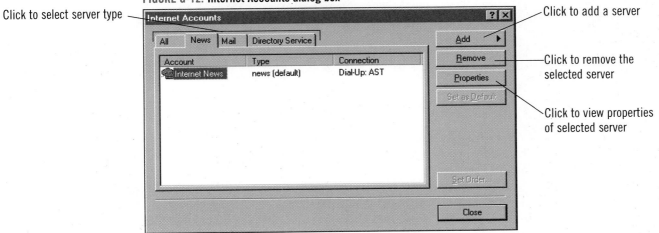

FIGURE G-13: Internet Connection Wizard dialog box

Enter news server name here

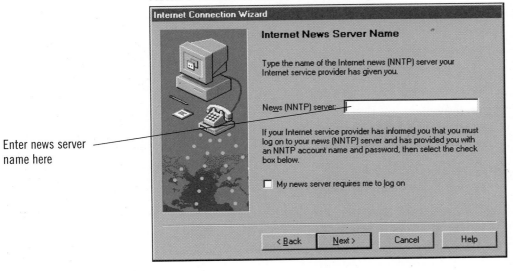

FIGURE G-14: Outlook Express window with news servers

News servers

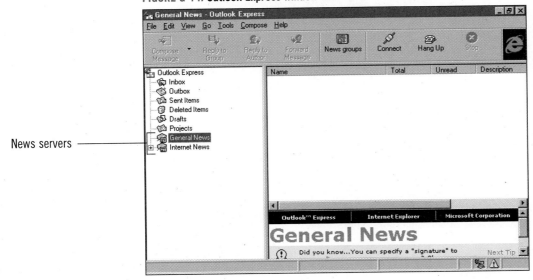

Windows 98

Viewing and Subscribing to a Newsgroup

When you add a news server account to Outlook Express, it retrieves a list of newsgroups available on that server. Often this list is quite lengthy. Rather than scroll through the entire list looking for a particular topic, you can have Outlook Express search the list for that topic. Similarly, you can search a newsgroup for a particular message from all the messages you retrieve from a newsgroup. Once you select a newsgroup, you can merely view its contents, or, if you expect to come back to the newsgroup often, you can subscribe to it. Subscribing to a newsgroup places a link to the group in the news server folder in your Outlook Express Folder list, providing easy access to the newsgroup. John wants to find and subscribe to a newsgroup for coffee drinkers, so he can keep track of what people want from a coffee company.

Trouble?

The news server list on the left in the dialog box will not appear if you have only one news server account.

QuickTip

To subscribe or unsubscribe to a newsgroup, you can also click the News groups button on the toolbar, select a newsgroup, then click Subscribe or Unsubscribe.

1. Click the News groups button 🗔 on the toolbar
   The Newsgroups dialog box opens, as shown in Figure G-15, displaying news servers on the left (if more than one exists) and related newsgroups on the right.

2. In the News server list, click General News (the news server you added in the previous lesson) if available
   A list of the newsgroups you have subscribed to appears in the preview pane. Your list might be empty.

3. Type coffee in the text box
   Newsgroups related to coffee appear in the News groups list box.

4. Scroll if necessary, click the newsgroup rec.food.drink.coffee (if available), or click a different newsgroup from your list, then click Go To
   The newsgroup name you have chosen appears selected in the Folder list and the newsgroup messages appear in the preview pane of the Outlook Express window, as shown in Figure G-16. John thinks this newsgroup looks promising, so he decides to subscribe to it.

5. Right-click the newsgroup name in the Folder list, then click Subscribe to this newsgroup
   The number of newsgroup messages appears next to the newsgroup name in the folder list.

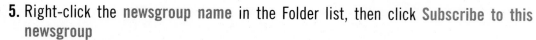

Filtering unwanted newsgroup messages

After you become familiar with a newsgroup, you might decide that you don't want to retrieve messages from a particular person, about a specific subject, of a certain length, older than a number of days. This is called **filtering** newsgroup messages. To filter unwanted messages, click Tools on the menu bar, click Newsgroup Filters, click Add, click News, select the newsgroup or new server you want to filter, then set your criteria.

FIGURE G-15: Newsgroup dialog box

Click to
select a news
server

News server
list may not
appear if you
have only one
news server
account

Click to
subscribe to
the selected
newsgroup

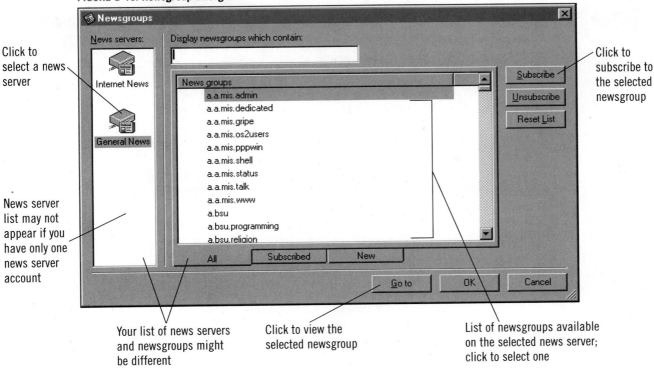

Your list of news servers
and newsgroups might
be different

Click to view the
selected newsgroup

List of newsgroups available
on the selected news server;
click to select one

FIGURE G-16: Outlook Express window with a newsgroup

Newsgroup

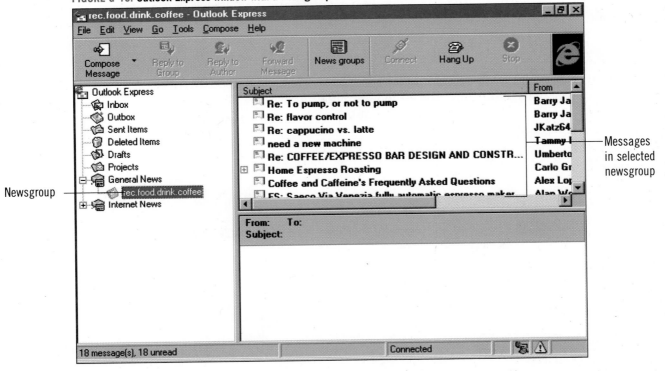

Messages
in selected
newsgroup

Windows 98

Reading and Posting News Articles

After retrieving new newsgroup messages, you can read them. Newsgroup messages appear in the preview pane, just as e-mail messages do. To view a newsgroup message in the display pane, click the title of the message in the preview pane. If a plus sign (+) in a box appears to the left of a newsgroup message, then the message contains a conversational thread. A **thread** consists of the original message on a particular topic along with any responses that include the original message. To read the responses, click the + to display the message titles, and then click the title of the message you want to read. John decides to read some of the messages in the newsgroup.

Steps 1 2 3 4

Trouble?

If a newsgroup message doesn't have a +, click a message without a +, then skip to Step 3.

1. Click a **newsgroup message** in the preview pane with a + to the left of the title, then read the message in the display pane
The newsgroup message appears in the display pane.

2. Click the + next to the newsgroup message
The titles of the responses to the original message appear under the original newsgroup message, as shown in Figure G-17.

3. Click each reply message under the original message, and read the reply
As you read each message, you have the choice to compose a new message, send a reply message to everyone viewing the newsgroup (known as **posting**), send a reply message to the author's private e-mail address (rather than posting it on the newsgroup), or forward the message you are reading to another person. John wants to post a message about the coffee business.

4. After reading the last reply message, click the **Reply To Group button** on the toolbar
John types his reply.

5. Type a response to the newsgroup message
Once you've entered your response, as shown in Figure G-18, you're ready to post the message to the news server for everyone viewing the newsgroup to download and read.

6. Click the **Post button** on the toolbar, then click **OK**
Your reply message appears in the preview pane along with the other replies to the original message. Next John unsubscribes from this newsgroup and removes the news server from the Folder list.

7. Right-click the **newsgroup** in the Folder list, click **Unsubcribe from this newsgroup**, then click **Yes**

8. Right-click **General News** in the Folder list, click **Remove Server**, then click **Yes**

9. Click **File** on the menu bar, click **Exit**, then click **Yes** if necessary to disconnect from the Internet

FIGURE G-17: Reading a newsgroup message

Click + to display or – to hide replies to newsgroup messages

Message selected in preview pane is displayed here

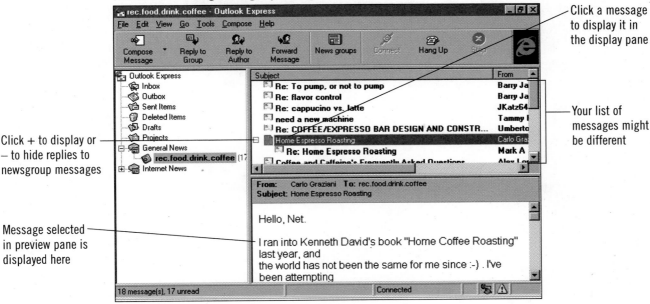

Click a message to display it in the display pane

Your list of messages might be different

FIGURE G-18: Posting a newsgroup message

Click to post message to the newsgroup

Type your reply to the newsgroup here

Your list of messages might be different

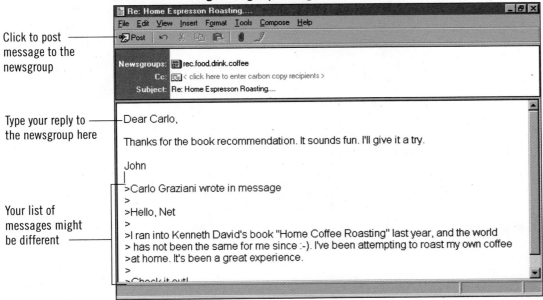

 CLUES TO USE

Deleting old news articles

Newsgroup messages are stored on your hard drive. This means you should delete messages you don't need to free up disk space. Outlook Express gives several clean up options to help you optimize your hard drive space. You can delete entire messages (titles and bodies), compress messages, remove just the message bodies (leaving the title headers), or reset the information stored for selected messages, which allows you to re-download messages. To clean up files on your local hard drive, select a news server in the Folder list, click File on the menu bar, click Clean Up Files, select the news server or newsgroup that you want to clean up, click the button for the clean up option you want, then click Close.

Practice

► Concepts Review

Label each of the elements of the screen shown in Figure G-19.

FIGURE G-19

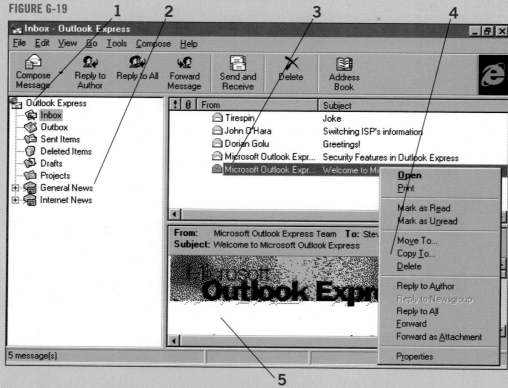

Match each of the terms with the statement that describes its function.

6. **Message flag**
7. **Outlook Express Start Page**
8. **Inbox Assistant**
9. **Outlook Express window**
10. **News server**

a. A computer on the Internet where articles are stored
b. Displays e-mail and newsgroups
c. An icon that indicates e-mail status
d. Diverts selected incoming e-mail to folders
e. Jumps to folders and opens tools

Select the best answer from the following list of choices.

11. **The location that allows you to jump to folders and open tools is called**
    a. Outlook Express window.
    b. Outlook Express Start Page.
    c. Folder list.
    d. Outlook Express Link Page.
12. **To compose a message, you can**
    a. Click the Compose a Message link.
    b. Click Compose Message button on the toolbar.
    c. Click Compose on the menu bar, then click New Message.
    d. All of the above.
13. **A contact is a**
    a. Person you communicate with.
    b. Mailing address.
    c. Newsgroup.
    d. Group you communicate with.
14. **When you click the Send button, an e-mail message is sent first to the**
    a. E-mail address.
    b. Outbox.
    c. Internet.
    d. Cc and Bcc addresses.

15. ✉ indicates that the message has
   a. Not been read.
   b. Been read.
   c. One or more files attached to it.
   d. Been marked as low priority by sender.
16. Printing styles in the Address Book include
   a. Memo.
   b. Business Card.
   c. Phone List.
   d. All of the above.
17. A location on the Internet where articles are stored is called a
   a. Newsgroup.
   b. News service.
   c. News server.
   d. News article.
18. When you subscribe to a newsgroup, you are
   a. Purchasing newsgroup messages.
   b. Linking to a newsgroup.
   c. Selecting a newsgroup.
   d. Viewing a newsgroup.

► Skills Review

1. **Start Outlook Express and explore the window.**
   a. Connect to the Internet.
   b. Double-click the Outlook Express icon.
   c. Identify the title bar, menu bar, toolbar, Internet Explorer link, Folder list, Read Mail link, Read News link, Compose a Message link, Address Book link, Download All link, Find People link, and status bar.
   d. On the toolbar, identify icons for opening the Address Book, sending and receiving e-mail messages, composing a message, connecting to the mail or news server, and hanging up the Internet connection.
   e. If necessary, click the Connect button on the toolbar, enter your username and password, then click OK.

2. **Add a contact to the Address Book.**
   a. Click the Address Book button.
   b. Click the New Contact button.
   c. Type "John", press [Tab] twice, then type "Asher".
   d. Click in the Add New box, type "JohnA@course.com".
   e. Click Add.
   f. Click OK.
   g. Click the Close button.

3. **Compose and send e-mail.**
   a. Click the Compose Message button.
   b. Click the Select recipients from a list icon.
   c. Click "John Asher".
   d. Click the To button.
   e. Click OK.
   f. Click <click here to enter the subject>.
   g. Type "Financial Update Request".
   h. Press [Tab] to move to the message window.
   i. Type "John: Please send 1998 year-end financial report ASAP. Thanks".
   j. Click the Send button.

4. **Retrieve, read, and respond to e-mail.**
   a. Click the Send and Receive button. It may take a few minutes before you receive a message from John Asher.
   b. In the Folder list, click Inbox.
   c. Click the message you just received from John Asher.
   d. Click the Forward Message button.
   e. Click <click here to enter recipients>.
   f. Enter your e-mail address.
   g. Click the Send button.

5. **Manage e-mail messages.**
   a. Click File on the menu bar, point to Folder, then click New Folder.
   b. Type "Archive".

   c. Click Outlook Express in the Folder list.

   d. Click OK.

   e. Right-click the message received from John Asher.

   f. Click Move To on the pop-up menu.

   g. Click Archive, then click OK.

   h. In the Folder list, click the Archive folder.

   i. Right-click the message received from John Asher.

   j. Click Delete on the pop-up menu.

   k. Right-click the Archive folder, click Delete, then click Yes.

   l. Click the Address Book button.

   m. Click John Asher, click the Delete button, then click Yes.

   n. Click the Close button.

6. Select a news server.

   a. In the Folder list, click Outlook Express.

   b. Click Read News link.

   c. If the Internet Connection Wizard appears, skip to Step e. Otherwise, click Tools on the menu bar, then click Accounts.

   d. Click Add, then click News.

   e. Type your name, then click Next.

   f. Type your e-mail address, then click Next.

   g. Type the name of a news server (see your instructor, technical support person, or ISP for a name), then click Next.

   h. Type another name for the news server, then click Next.

   i. Click a connection type option button, then click Next.

   j. Click Finish, click Close (if necessary), then click No.

7. View and subscribe to a newsgroup.

   a. Click the News groups button.

   b. In the News server list, click the news server you just added (if available).

   c. Type "Caffeine".

   d. Click a newsgroup.

   e. Click Go To.

   f. Right-click the newsgroup in the Folder list, then click Subscribe to this newsgroup.

8. Read and post news articles.

   a. Click a newsgroup with a +.

   b. Click the + next to the newsgroup.

   c. Click each reply and read it.

   d. Click the Reply To Group button.

   e. Type a response.

   f. Click the Post button, then click OK.

   g. Right-click the newsgroup in the Folder list.

   h. Click Unsubscribe from this newsgroup on the pop-up menu, then click Yes.

   i. Right-click the news server in the Folder list.

   j. Click Remove Server.

   k. Click Yes.

   l. Click File on the menu bar, then click Exit.

   m. Click Yes if necessary to disconnect.

► Independent Challenges

1. You are a new lawyer at Bellig & Associates. You have a computer with Windows 98 and Outlook Express. Since e-mail is an important method of communication at the law firm, you want to start Outlook Express, open the Address Book, and enter colleagues' e-mail addresses.

To complete this independent challenge:

1. Start Outlook Express.

2. Open the Address Book.

3. Enter the following names and e-mail addresses:

Gary Bellig	garyb@bellig_law.com
Greg Bellig	gregb@bellig_law.com
Jacob Bellig	jacobb@bellig_law.com
Jarod Higgins	jarodh@bellig_law.com

4. Print the Address Book in the Business Card and Memo styles.
5. Delete the names and e-mail addresses you just entered in the Address Book.

2. You are the president of Auto Metals, a manufacturing company. You have just negotiated a deal to export metal auto parts to an assembly plant in China. To complete the deal, you need to draw up contracts for each party to sign. Your lawyer is Josh Higgins at Higgins Associates. He has already worked up a preliminary contract. You want to send Josh an e-mail indicating the terms of the deal so he can finish the contract. When Josh responds, move the e-mail into the Legal folder. (*Note:* If you do not have a connection to the Internet, ask your instructor or technical support person for help in completing this challenge.)

To complete this independent challenge:

1. Open a New Message window using the stationery called Technical (*Hint:* Use More Stationery command, then select Technical.htm).
2. Type "jhiggins@course.com" in the To text box in the message window.
3. Type "China Deal Contract" in the Subject text box.
4. Type the following text in the message box:
   Dear Josh,
   I have completed the negotiations for exporting metal auto parts to an assembly plant in China. Please modify the following terms to the contract:
   1. All parts shall be inspected before shipping.
   2. Ship 10,000 units a month for 3 years with an option for 2 more years.
   Sincerely yours,
   [your name here]
5. Send the e-mail.
6. Print the e-mail you receive from Josh Higgins.
7. Create a new folder called "Legal".
8. Move the e-mail message you received from Josh Higgins to the new folder.
9. Delete the Contracts folder.

3. You are a legal assistant at Blazer, Jarvis, and Whitefield, a law firm specializing in international law. You received an e-mail message from your boss asking you to research international contracts with China. You decide to start your research with newsgroups on the Internet.

To complete this independent challenge:

1. Select a news server (see your instructor, technical support person, or ISP to provide you with a news server).
2. Subscribe to a newsgroup about China.
3. Read several newsgroup messages and replies.
4. Reply to a message.
5. Post a new message.
6. Print the newsgroup messages including the original message and replies.

4. You like all types of sports, from hockey to football, from basketball to baseball, from soccer to volleyball. You like to play sports, watch sports, read about sports, and talk about sports all the time, so you join a sports newsgroup.

To complete this independent challenge:

1. Select a news server (see your instructor or network administrator to provide you with a news server).
2. Subscribe to a newsgroup about sports.
3. Read several newsgroup messages and replies.
4. Reply to the message.
5. Post a new message.
6. Print the newsgroup messages including the original message and replies.

Visual Workshop

Re-create the screen shown in Figure G-20, which displays the Outlook Express window with a message that has been sent. Print the Outlook Express window. (To print the screen, press the Print Screen key, open Paint, click File on the menu bar, click Paste to paste the screen into Paint, then click Yes to paste the large image if necessary. Click File on the menu bar, click Print, then click OK.)

FIGURE G-20

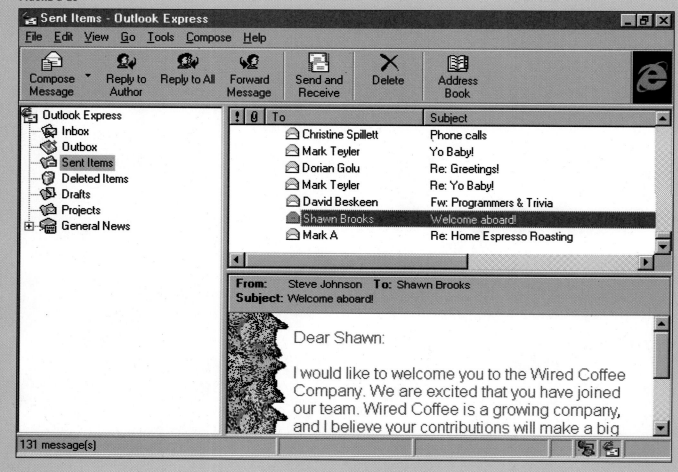

Managing

Shared Files Using Network Neighborhood

Objectives

- ► **Understand network services**
- ► **Open and view Network Neighborhood**
- ► **Examine network drive properties**
- ► **Create a shared folder**
- ► **Map a network drive**
- ► **Copy and move shared files**
- ► **Open and edit a shared file**
- ► **Disconnect a network drive**

Windows 98 includes Network Neighborhood, a powerful tool for managing files and folders across a network. A **network** is a system of two or more computers connected together to share resources. **Network Neighborhood** is integrated with Windows Explorer, allowing you to view the entire network and to share files and folders with people from other parts of the network. If you are not connected to a network, you will not be able to work the steps in this unit; however, you can read the lessons without completing the steps to learn what is possible in a network environment. ◆━━ In this unit John Casey will use Network Neighborhood to manage files and folders that will be used by multiple users on the Wired Coffee Company network.

Understanding Network Services

Windows 98 is a secure, reliable network operating system that allows people using many different computers to share programs, files, and folders that are stored on computers other than their own. A single computer, called a **server**, can be designated to store these resources. Other computers on the network, called **clients**, can access the resources on the server instead of having to store them. You can also share resources using two or more client computers. This sort of configuration is called peer-to-peer networking. Figure H-1 is an example of a typical network configuration. **File sharing** allows many people to work on the same files without the need for creating or storing multiple copies. In this unit you will integrate the essential Windows file management skills you have already acquired with the specific methods required to take full advantage of the Windows networking capabilities. John realizes there are many benefits to using the Wired Coffee network to manage files and folders.

Details

Share central resources through client/server networking

Windows 98 provides the option of using a setup called **client/server networking**. Under this arrangement, a single computer is designated as a server, allowing access to resources for any qualified user. Client/server networking provides all users on a network a central location for accessing shared files.

Share resources through peer-to-peer networking

The Windows 98 network operating system also offers a network configuration called peer-to-peer networking. **Peer-to-peer networking** enables two or more computers to link together without designating a central server. In this configuration, any computer user can access resources stored on any other computer, as long as those resources aren't restricted. Peer-to-peer networking allows individual computer users to share files and other resources, such as a printer, with other users on the network. Using peer-to-peer networking you can transfer files from one computer directly to another without having to access a server.

Grant permission to share designated files and folders on your machine with other users

Windows 98 provides support for security, so that even though your computer is connected to a network, you can designate which resources on your computer you want to share with others on the network. Before being able to take advantage of any resources on your computer, other users must be granted the required permission.

Map drives on your machine that let you share the resources of another client or server

If you have rights to share resources on another computer, Windows 98 includes a method for connecting automatically to the other computer. You can add a drive letter to your computer that is automatically linked to the shared folder on the other computer every time you log on.

FIGURE H-1: **A typical client/server network**

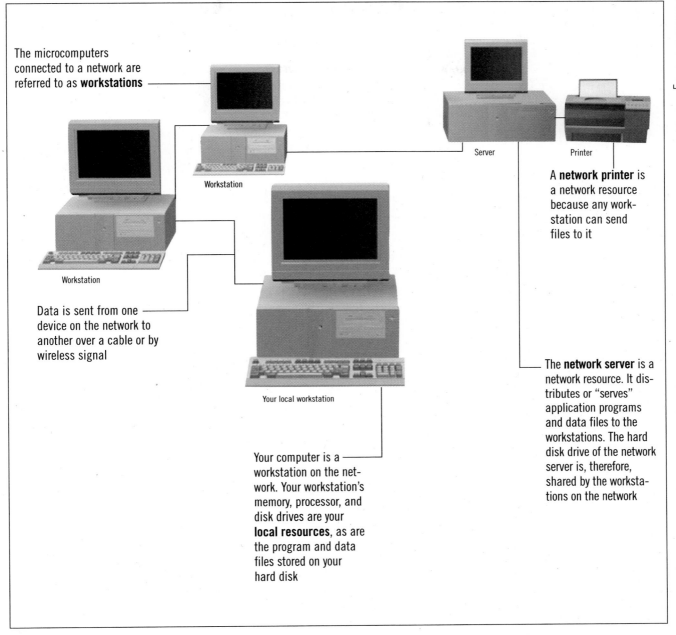

The microcomputers connected to a network are referred to as **workstations**

Workstation

Workstation

Data is sent from one device on the network to another over a cable or by wireless signal

Your local workstation

Your computer is a workstation on the network. Your workstation's memory, processor, and disk drives are your **local resources**, as are the program and data files stored on your hard disk

Server

Printer

A **network printer** is a network resource because any workstation can send files to it

The **network server** is a network resource. It distributes or "serves" application programs and data files to the workstations. The hard disk drive of the network server is, therefore, shared by the workstations on the network

File permission properties

Every file in the Windows 98 file system includes **permissions** for each user, or settings that designate what each user can and cannot do to each file. Two basic types of file permissions are available for users: read and full. **Read** permission allows the user to view the file, but not to make changes that can be saved to the file. **Full** permission allows the user to edit and save changes to the file (or "write") and execute programs on server or client computers. Qualified users or system administrators use file permissions to control who has access to any specific area of the network by using passwords. In this way, the network remains secure against unauthorized use.

Windows 98

Opening and Viewing Network Neighborhood

The key to managing files and folders in a network environment is understanding the structure of your particular network. Most networks are comprised of multiple types of computers and operating systems. Network Neighborhood lets you view the entire network or just your part of the network at a glance. ▰▰▰ John uses Network Neighborhood to see where his computer fits in with all the others on his network.

1. Double-click the Network Neighborhood icon on the desktop, then click the Maximize button in the Network Neighborhood window if necessary
The icon is usually located right below the My Computer icon on the desktop. Network Neighborhood opens, as shown in Figure H-2, and displays icons for all of the active computers in John's immediate network (including an icon for his own computer) and an icon for the Entire Network. John's immediate network, also known as the **neighborhood**, is currently running server and client computers.

2. Double-click the Entire Network icon 🌐 if available (if not, skip to Step 4)
Network Neighborhood displays the various segments and computers connected to John's network, as shown in Figure H-3. If you are on a large network, you might have other choices that will display more segments of the network.

3. Click the Back button ⬅ on the toolbar
The Network Neighborhood window again displays the active computers in John's immediate neighborhood. John decides to view the contents of a computer connected to his network.

4. Double-click a network computer icon 🖥 in your immediate network
The computer connected to your network opens and displays the contents of the drive or folder.

5. Click ⬅ on the toolbar
The Network Neighborhood window again displays the active computers in John's immediate neighborhood.

QuickTip

To check the status of your logon credentials and all current connections, right-click the Network Neighborhood icon, click Properties, then click the Identification tab.

CLUES TO USE

Setting up your computer for networking

Before you can use your computer on the network, you need to make sure the file and print sharing option is selected. To set up your computer for networking, right-click the Network Neighborhood icon, click Properties, click File and Print Sharing, click the I want to be able to give others access to my files checkbox, click OK (insert the Windows 98 installation CD if necessary and click Continue), then click OK. Now you can share files on your computer with other users on the network. If you are working in a lab, check with your administrator before setting up your computer for networking.

FIGURE H-2: Network Neighborhood window

Menu bar

Address bar

Your list of icons
might be different

Toolbar

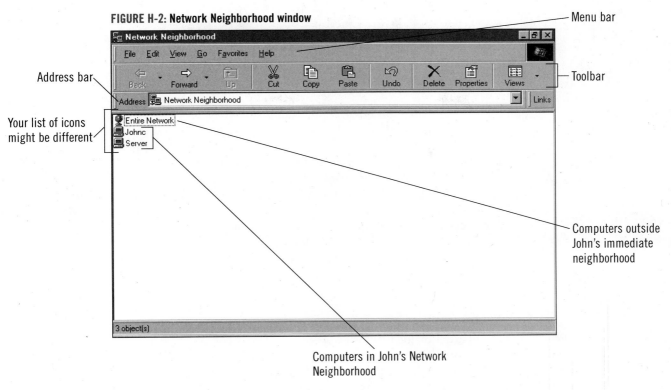

Computers outside
John's immediate
neighborhood

Computers in John's Network
Neighborhood

FIGURE H-3: Entire Network window

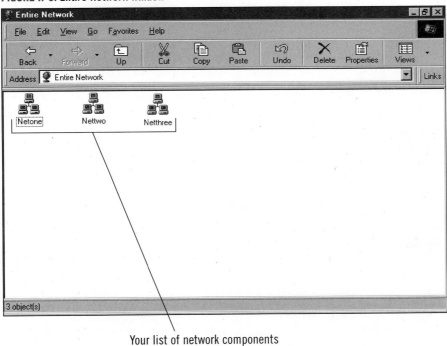

Your list of network components
might be different

Windows 98

Examining Network Drive Properties

Computers are identified on networks by names and workgroups. The computer's name refers to the individual machine. Individual machines are then organized into larger **workgroups**, which are specific computers that share a lot of information, also given a name. Workgroups are then organized into a larger group of related computer networks called a **domain**. In this way, computers anywhere in the network can be located easily through this naming hierarchy and can be addressed individually by name. You can find out the name, workgroup, and domain of a computer on the network by examining the network computer properties. ➤ John decides to check the properties of his network computer.

Steps

QuickTip

To identify your network computer name, double-click the Network icon in the Control Panel, then click the Identification tab.

1. **Right-click the icon for your network computer**
   John opens the networked computer called johnc. The icon representing the network computer is highlighted, and a pop-up menu opens.

2. **Click Properties on the pop-up menu**
   The Properties dialog box for the selected network computer opens with the General tab in front, as shown in Figure H-4. In Figure H-4, the network computer name appears at the top of the General tab. Below the network computer name appears a comment (generally the user name), the workgroup name, the name of the user logged on, and the name of the logon domain. In this case, the network computer name is Johnc; the workgroup and domain name is NETONE; and the user logged on is John Casey.

Trouble?

If a button to a utility program is grayed out, the utility is not installed on your computer. If necessary, see your instructor or technical support person for installation details.

3. **Click the Tools tab**
   The Tools tab appears, as shown in Figure H-5, displaying three utilities that can make working with networks easier: Net Watcher, System Monitor, and Administer. These tools are mostly used for monitoring and administering a network. Table H-1 describes the function of each utility.

4. **Click OK**
   The Properties dialog box closes.

CLUES TO USE

Viewing network properties

A computer that uses the Windows 98 network must be configured so that other machines on the network recognize it. On a small network, you might be responsible for configuring your computer or that responsibility might fall to the network administrator. You can view and modify some of the network settings for your computer using the Control Panel. In the Control Panel, double-click the Network icon to display the network settings. The Network dialog box opens displaying the Configuration tab. The network configuration consists of four components: client, adapter, protocol, and service. The client allows you to access resources such as files and printers that are available on computers on your network. The **adapter** is a device that connects your computer to the network. The **protocol** is the language that the computer uses to communicate with other computers on the network. The **service** allows you to share your computer resources, such as files and printers, with other networked computers. You can also click the Identification tab to change your network computer name, workgroup name, or computer description. This information is displayed over the network to identify your computer and appears in your network drive properties.

FIGURE H-4: Properties dialog box for a network computer

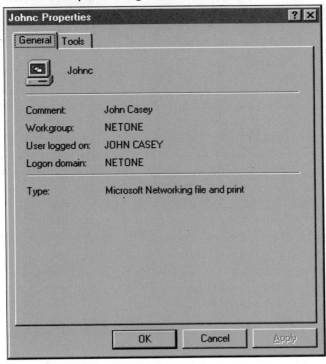

FIGURE H-5: Tools tab in the network computer Properties dialog box

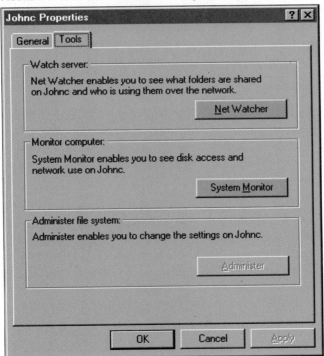

TABLE H-1: Network utilities

tool	function
Net Watcher	Allows you to see what folders are shared on the network computer and who is using them
System Monitor	Allows you to see disk access and network use on the network computer
Administer	Allows you to change the settings on the network computer

Creating a Shared Folder

To create a shared folder in Network Neighborhood, you use many of the file management skills you learned with Windows Explorer. You must first decide where you will put the new folder. If you are working at your own computer, you might create the shared folder in a subfolder within your My Documents folder. Otherwise, you may have to ask your instructor or technical support person for permission to create a folder in another location, or you can simply follow the steps without actually creating a folder. If you are not working in a network environment, you may not be able to complete these steps. In this case, simply read the steps without completing them. ◢◣◣ John has decided to create a shared folder called Sales on his computer that will allow employees from anywhere on the network to add information to Sales files.

Steps

1. **Click the Address list arrow on the Address bar**
   Network Neighborhood displays the desktop and drives of your computer. You can now work with the files and folders from your computer and still have the option of connecting to various other parts of the network.

2. **Click Hard Disk (C:) (or the name and drive letter assigned to your hard drive), then double-click the My Documents folder**
   Network Neighborhood displays the contents of the My Documents folder on your hard drive.

3. **Right-click anywhere in the Network Neighborhood window (except on a file or folder), point to New, then click Folder**
   A new folder, named New Folder, appears in the window.

4. **Type Sales, then press [Enter]**
   The folder is now named Sales.

5. **Click File on the menu bar, then click Sharing**
   The Sales Properties dialog box opens. The Sales Properties dialog box is where you adjust the settings to allow other users access to the files in your shared folder. The Sharing tab allows you to designate the kind of access you want other users to have for the folder you just created.

6. **Click the Shared As option button**
   The sharing information about the Sales folder is shown in Figure H-6. This tab includes a text box for entering the shared name of the folder. Unless you have a very good reason for naming it differently, it's best to make the shared name the same as the folder name. Keeping the names consistent will help to avoid confusion. By default, Windows automatically enters the name of the folder as the shared name and sets the file permission to Read-Only. John wants to give full access to other users with some password protection.

7. **Click the Full option button**
   John wants to add password protection to the Sales folder.

8. **Click the Full Access Password text box, then type Beans**

9. **Click OK to close the Sales Properties dialog box**
   The Password Confirmation dialog box opens, asking you to retype the password.

10. **Type Beans, then click OK**
    The Sales folder, shown in Figure H-7, is now accessible by anyone with the right password from anywhere on the network. The 🗀 icon, a folder with a hand underneath, indicates the folder is a shared folder.

Trouble?

If the Sharing command is not available, double-click the Network icon in the Control Panel, click File and Print Sharing, then click the I want to be able to give others access to my files check box.

FIGURE H-6: Sharing tab of Sales Properties dialog box

Click to designate Sales folder as shared

Enter name for shared Sales folder here

Click to set access type

Enter password for Sales folder here

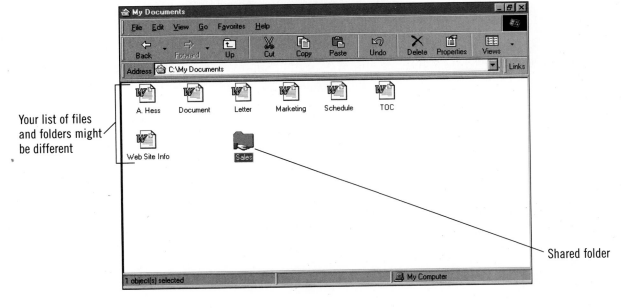

FIGURE H-7: Shared folder within the My Documents folder

Your list of files and folders might be different

Shared folder

Password protection

With Windows 98, you can use passwords to control access to your computer, the network, and specific files and folders. You can set different passwords and varying degrees of access for the different drives, folders, and files. You can also manage your files and printers from a remote computer and set password protection to limit access. To set or change password protection in

Windows 98, open the Control Panel and double-click the Passwords icon. You can also use the Power Management utility in the Control Panel to password protect your computer when it's in Sleep mode or use the Display utility to password protect files when in screen saver mode.

Mapping a Network Drive

Network Neighborhood enables you to connect your computer to other computers on the network quite easily. If you connect to a network location frequently, you might want to designate a drive letter on your computer as a direct connection to a shared drive or folder on another computer. Instead of spending unnecessary time opening Network Neighborhood and the shared drive or folder each time you want to access it, you can create a direct connection, called **mapping** a drive, to the network location for quick and easy access. ✐ At John's request, the network administrator created a shared folder called "wired coffee" on the computer named Server. Now John will use Network Neighborhood to map a drive letter from his computer to that folder so that he can easily move files to this central location for others to share. To complete these steps, you will need to map to a network computer and a folder specified by your instructor or technical support person.

Steps

Trouble?

Before beginning, ask your instructor which networked computer you can map onto your computer. If you do not have a networked computer available, read the steps without completing them.

1. Click the **Address list arrow**, then click **Network Neighborhood** (scroll down if necessary)

   Network Neighborhood shows all the active computers in your immediate neighborhood.

2. Double-click the **networked computer icon** supplied by your instructor or technical support person

   John opens the networked computer called Server. The window for the networked computer opens and displays the folders that are available for file sharing, as shown in Figure H-8. Your available folders might differ from those shown in Figure H-8.

QuickTip

If you already know the network path for the drive you want to map, right-click the Network Neighborhood icon, click Map Network Drive, enter the network path in the Path text box, then click OK.

3. Click the shared **wired coffee folder** (or the folder specified by your instructor or technical support person) to select it, click **File** on the menu bar, then click **Map Network Drive**

   The Map Network Drive dialog box opens, as shown in Figure H-9. By default the Map Network Drive dialog box highlights the next available drive letter. The network path is automatically entered by Network Neighborhood.

4. If you want to use a different drive letter, click the **Drive list arrow**, then click the **drive letter** you want to use

   John decides that the default choice is okay, but he would also like the drive to be reconnected every time he logs on.

Trouble?

If your mapped drives are not automatically reconnecting when you log on, make sure your user name and password are the same for all the networks to which you connect.

5. If not already checked, click the **Reconnect at logon** check box, then click **OK**

   The Map Network Drive dialog box closes, and Network Neighborhood maps a drive connecting your computer to the shared wired coffee folder (or to the shared folder specified by your instructor or technical support person). When the connection is complete, a window appears for the newly mapped drive, allowing you to view the files within the mapped drive, as shown in Figure H-10. John can now easily copy folders and files from his floppy disk into the shared folder.

6. Click the **Close button** in the mapped drive window

7. Click the **Back button list arrow** ⬅▾ on the toolbar, then click **Network Neighborhood**

   The Network Neighborhood window displays the active computers in your immediate neighborhood.

FIGURE H-8: **Server computer icon window**

Shared folder on networked computer

Your list of folders might be different

Networked computer

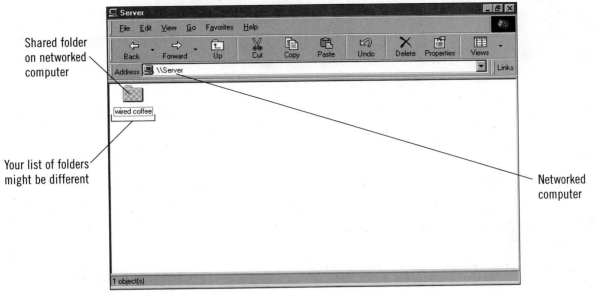

FIGURE H-9: **Map Network Drive dialog box**

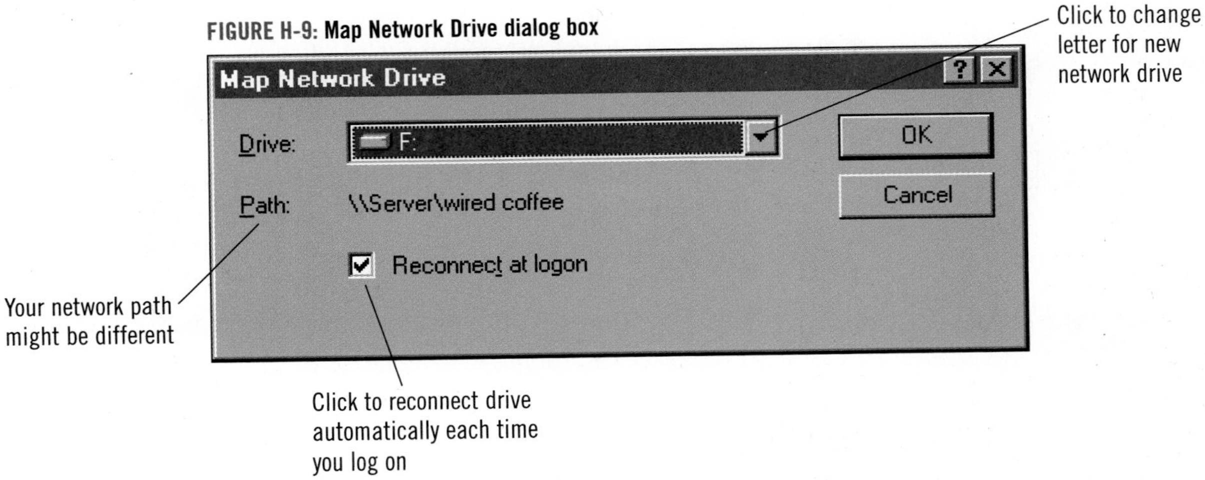

Click to change letter for new network drive

Your network path might be different

Click to reconnect drive automatically each time you log on

FIGURE H-10: **Wired coffee folder window**

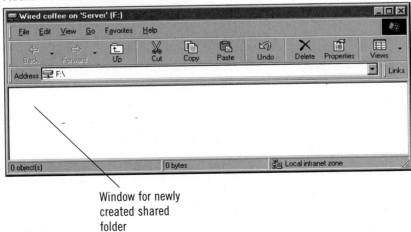

Window for newly created shared folder

Copying and Moving Shared Files

Windows 98

Once you have created shared folders and mapped your network drives, copying and moving shared files and folders in Windows is as easy as managing files on your own computer. The only difference is data transfer can take longer over a network than it does on your local computer. You can copy and move files using any of the Windows 98 file management tools: Network Neighborhood, My Computer, or Windows Explorer. Network Neighborhood works just like My Computer. ✎ John wants to copy files from his floppy disk into the shared Sales folder on his hard drive to make them accessible to the other users on his network. He also needs to move a file from the shared Sales folder to the wired coffee folder on the network drive (F:) to make it accessible to another department. Since he's copying files to several locations, John uses Windows Explorer to drag and drop the files.

Steps

1. Make sure your Student Disk is inserted in the appropriate disk drive

2. In the Network Neighborhood window, click the **Address list arrow**, then click **3½ Floppy (A:)** or **(B:)** (whichever drive holds your Student disk)
   Network Neighborhood displays the contents of the 3½ floppy drive.

3. Right-click the **Wired Coffee folder**, click **Explore**, then click the **Sales folder** in the Explorer Bar
   Windows Explorer opens, displaying the available folders and drives in the left pane, as shown in Figure H-11. You can now copy or move files easily from your computer to anywhere on the network. John will copy the files named Coffee Prices, Customer Profile, and Suppliers to the shared Sales folder he created on the (C:) hard drive.

Trouble?

If you click the shared Sales folder by mistake, click the Sales folder on the floppy disk then go to Step 5.

4. In the Explorer Bar, click the **+** next to the hard drive (C:) or the drive where you created your shared Sales folder, then click the **+** next to the My Documents folder to display the shared Sales folder (the one with a hand), as shown in Figure H-12, but *do not click the folder*

5. Click **Edit** on the menu bar, click **Select All**, then drag the files from the right pane to the shared **Sales folder** in the Explorer Bar
   The files are copied to the shared Sales folder on the hard drive. The employees who have access to John's computer can now share the files. Now John wants to move the Suppliers file to the network drive where the Supply Department can use it without any file permissions.

6. In the Explorer Bar, click the shared **Sales folder**, then click the **down scroll arrow** in the Explorer Bar until you can see the icon representing the mapped network folder
   See Figure H-12.

7. Right-click and drag the **Suppliers file** to the mapped networked folder in the Explorer Bar, then click **Move Here**
   The Suppliers file is moved to the networked folder.

8. Click the **mapped network folder** in the Explorer Bar to view the Suppliers file, then click the **Close buttons** in the Exploring and 3½ Floppy (A:) windows

FIGURE H-11: Exploring the Sales folder

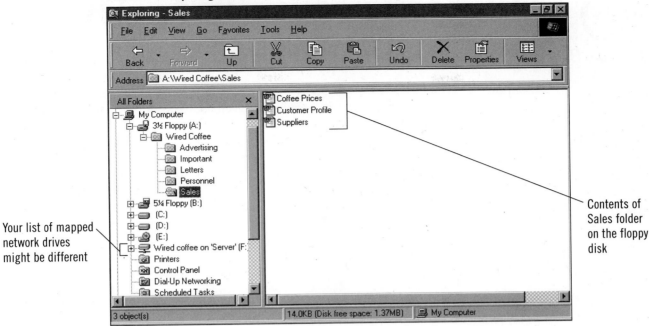

Your list of mapped
network drives
might be different

Contents of
Sales folder
on the floppy
disk

FIGURE H-12: Location of the wired coffee folder on the mapped network drive (F:)

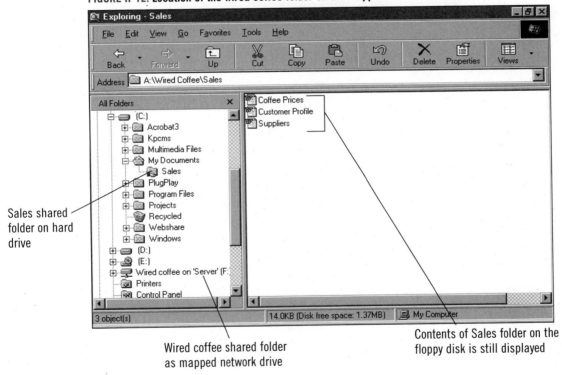

Sales shared
folder on hard
drive

Wired coffee shared folder
as mapped network drive

Contents of Sales folder on the
floppy disk is still displayed

CLUES TO USE

Network traffic

Large networks can serve hundreds of users simultaneously. Like water flowing through pipes, only a certain amount of data can pass through the wires connecting the individual computers at any given time. If the amount of network traffic is of sufficient volume, then the flow of data might slow considerably, causing file operations such as opening, saving, and copying to take longer to complete.

Windows 98

Opening and Editing a Shared File

Working with shared files on a network is a simple task with Windows. Once you have mapped all the necessary drives to your network folders, you can use network files in any program from your computer. For example, you can use WordPad to edit text files or Paint to create a graphic. You might also be able to use programs installed on the server specifically for the use of individual clients (ask your system administrator about available options). ✐ John will use WordPad to make corrections in the Suppliers file that he placed in the wired coffee folder on the Server.

Steps

1. **Click the** Start button **on the taskbar, point to** Programs, **point to** Accessories, **then click** WordPad
   The WordPad window opens.

2. **Click** File **on the menu bar, click** Open, **then click the** Look in list arrow
   The Open dialog box opens, as shown in Figure H-13, displaying the Look in list with local and networked drives. From here you can open files located on all drives and folders, including the drives mapped to the network.

3. **Click the** icon **for the mapped network drive to the wired coffee shared folder**
   A list of files stored in the networked folder appears in the Open dialog box, as shown in Figure H-14.

4. **Click** Suppliers, **then click** Open
   The file named Suppliers opens. John wants to add another supplier to the list.

5. **Click the bottom of the list, then type** Homegrown USA Coffee

6. **Click the** Save button 💾 **on the toolbar**
   WordPad saves the changes to the file Suppliers.

7. **Click the** Close button **in the WordPad window**

FIGURE H-13: **Open dialog box**

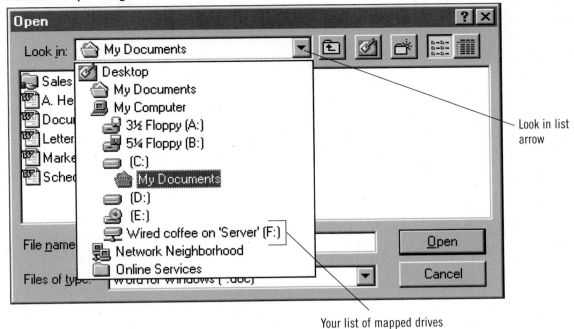

Look in list arrow

Your list of mapped drives might be different

FIGURE H-14: **Files in shared wired coffee folder**

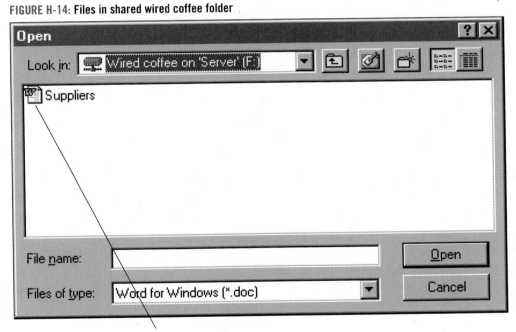

Contents of wired coffee on the 'Server' (F:) drive

CLUES TO USE

Opening read-only files

If you have read-only access to a folder, you can open a file from the folder, but you cannot make any changes to the file. When you open a read-only file, the words "Read Only" appear in the title bar. You can makes changes to the file, but an error message appears when you try to save it. However, if you like, you can save the file with a new name in a different location (one you have full access to).

Disconnecting a Network Drive

Usually, you map a network drive to automatically reconnect every time you log on. However, sometimes you might find it necessary to manually disconnect a mapped drive. Your system administrator might have added new hard drives to the server, or she might have reorganized the directory structure of the network, in which case the network path for the mapped drive might now be incorrect. Windows makes the process of disconnecting a mapped drive very easy in the case of such an event. John was informed by the system administrator of a network reorganization that will take place over the weekend. He will disconnect the drive mapped to (F:) until he finds out what changes have been made. Before disconnecting the mapped drive, John cleans up his hard drive and the mapped drive.

1. **Double-click the My Computer icon on the desktop, then double-click the mapped drive**
   The contents of the mapped drive appear. John wants to delete the Suppliers file.

2. **Right-click the Suppliers file, click Delete, then click Yes to confirm the deletion**

3. **Click the Back button ⬅ on the toolbar**

4. **Double-click the hard drive with the shared Sales folder, then double-click the My Documents folder**
   John wants to delete the shared folder.

5. **Right-click the shared Sales folder, then click Delete**
   The Confirm Folder Delete dialog box appears. John confirms the deletion.

6. **Click Yes, click Yes, then click the Close button in the My Documents window**
   After cleaning up his hard drive and the mapped drive, John disconnects the mapped drive.

7. **Right-click the Network Neighborhood icon on the desktop**
   A pop-up menu appears for Network Neighborhood, as shown in Figure H-15. This menu provides several options for working in a network environment. See Table H-2 for a description of the options available through this menu.

8. **Click Disconnect Network Drive on the pop-up menu**
   The Disconnect Network Drive dialog box appears, as shown in Figure H-16. The dialog box displays a list of all the network drives that you have mapped from your computer. You should check with your system administrator or instructor before actually disconnecting a drive. To quit without actually disconnecting a drive, click Cancel. John wants to disconnect the drive he mapped.

9. **To disconnect the drive you mapped, click the mapped drive with the wired coffee folder, click OK, then click Yes, if necessary, to the warning message**
   Windows disconnects the drive you have selected and closes the Disconnect Network Drive dialog box.

QuickTip

To disconnect a network drive in Windows Explorer, right-click the mapped network drive in the left pane, then click Disconnect.

Network paths

The path to a shared network directory is like the path to a file on a hard or floppy disk. For example, the path to the Suppliers file on your Student Disk is A:\Wired Coffee\Sales\Suppliers. Network paths replace the drive designation with the host computer name, as in \\Server\Wired Coffee. In either example, the path tells the computer where to go look for the files you need.

FIGURE H-15: Pop-up menu for Network Neighborhood

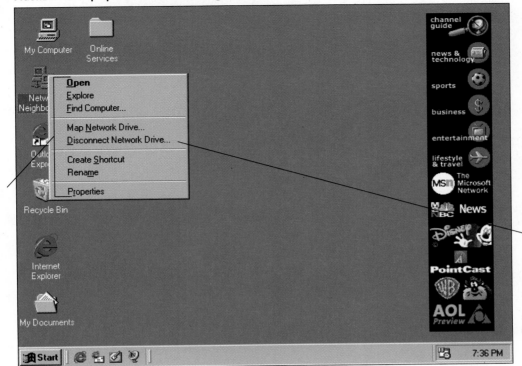

Pop-up menu
options

Click to
disconnect
network
drive

FIGURE H-16: Disconnect Network Drive dialog box

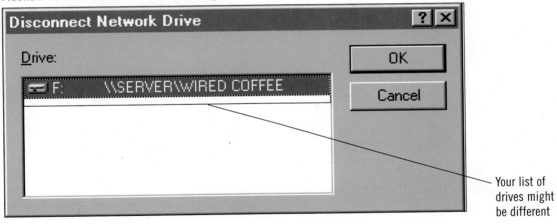

Your list of
drives might
be different

TABLE H-2: Pop-up menu commands for Network Neighborhood

option	function
Open	Starts Network Neighborhood
Explore	Opens Windows Explorer in order to copy and move files or folders from one folder to another, whether on your local computer or the network
Find Computer	Finds a computer whose name you know but not its location
Map Network Drive	Maps a drive from your computer to a shared directory on another computer
Disconnect Network Drive	Disconnects a drive on your computer from a shared directory on another computer
Create Shortcut	Creates a shortcut to Network Neighborhood
Rename	Renames the Network Neighborhood icon
Properties	Views the properties of your network

Practice

▶ Concepts Review

Label each of the elements of the screen shown in Figure H-17.

FIGURE H-17

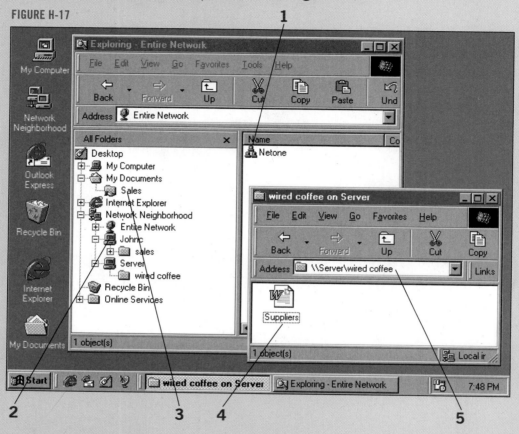

Match each of the terms with the statement that describes its function.

6. Shared folder
7. File permissions
8. Entire Network icon
9. Network path
10. Disconnect Network Drive command

a. Displays all workgroups and computers attached to a network
b. The address for an individual computer on a network
c. Determines who can read, write, or execute files
d. A location where multiple users can access the same files
e. Removes a mapped drive from the local computer

Select the best answer from the following list of choices.

11. The windows network management tool that allows you to inspect the configuration of your network is called
    a. Windows Explorer.
    b. My Computer.
    c. Network Neighborhood.
    d. File Manager.

12. **To disconnect a network drive**
    a. Double-click the drive letter in Network Neighborhood.
    b. Highlight the drive letter, click File on the menu bar, then click Delete.
    c. Click the drive letter, then drag it to the Recycle bin.
    d. Right-click the Network Neighborhood icon, then click Disconnect Network Drive.

13. **When you highlight a drive letter in Network Neighborhood, click File on the menu bar, then click Explore**
    a. My Computer starts allowing you to manage files and folders.
    b. Network Neighborhood displays the entire network.
    c. Windows Explorer starts allowing you to manage files and folders.
    d. File Manager starts allowing you to manage files and folders.

14. **When you map a networked drive**
    a. Network Neighborhood displays a graphic showing the entire structure of the network.
    b. You can use the shared files and folders of another computer on the network.
    c. The computer you are using is attached to the network.
    d. Network Neighborhood adds your computer to the network path.

15. **If the file permissions for a shared folder are set to read-only**
    a. No one can read the files in the folder.
    b. You can edit the file and save your changes.
    c. Everyone can read the files but not write to the files.
    d. Everyone can execute files but not write to the files.

► Skills Review

1. **Open and view Network Neighborhood.**
    a. Double-click the Network Neighborhood icon.
    b. Double-click the Entire Network icon.
    c. Click the Back button.
    d. Double-click the network icon in your immediate network.
    e. Click the Back button.

2. **Examine network drive properties.**
    a. Right-click your network computer icon.
    b. Click Properties.
    c. View the network properties.
    d. Click OK.

3. **Create a shared folder.**
    a. Click the Address list arrow, click your computer's hard drive, then double-click the My Documents folder.
    b. Right-click in the My Documents window, point to New, then click Folder.
    c. Name the new folder Memos, then press Enter.
    d. Click File on the menu bar, then click Sharing.
    e. Click the Shared As option button.
    f. Click OK.

4. Map a network drive.
  a. Click the Address list arrow, then click Network Neighborhood.
  b. Double-click the icon for the computer to which you want to map.
  c. Click the shared folder to which you want to map.
  d. Click File on the menu bar, then click Map Network Drive.
  e. Click the Reconnect at logon check box.
  f. Click OK.
  g. Click the Close button.

5. Copy shared files.
  a. Insert your Student Disk in the appropriate disk drive.
  b. Click the Address list arrow, then click 3½ Floppy (A:) or (B:).
  c. Click the Wired Coffee folder.
  d. Click File on the menu bar, then click Explore.
  e. Click the Letters folder in the Explorer Bar.
  f. Click the + next to the hard drive with the Memos folder.
  g. Click the + next to the My Documents folder.
  h. Click Edit on the menu bar, then click Select All.
  i. Drag all the files to the shared Memos folder you created on your hard drive.
  j. Click the Close buttons in the Explorer and 3½ Floppy (A:) windows.

6. Open and edit a shared file.
  a. Start WordPad.
  b. Open the IRS Letter file from the shared Memos folder on your hard drive.
  c. Change the month in the body of the letter from "July" to "August".
  d. Save the file, print it, then close the file and WordPad.

7. Disconnect a network drive.
  a. Double-click the My Computer icon.
  b. Double-click the hard drive with the shared Memos folder.
  c. Double-click the My Documents folder.
  d. Right-click the shared Memos folder, then click Delete.
  e. Click Yes, then click Yes again.
  f. Click the Close button.
  g. Right-click the Network Neighborhood icon.
  h. Click Disconnect Network Drive.
  i. Select the drive you mapped in Step 4.
  j. Click OK.

► Independent Challenges

1. As the new clerk at Holly (a craft store), you have been asked to create a list of suppliers' names. Your task is to enter the supplier information into a new file and place that file in two places for others to use. You must create a shared folder on your computer that will store the file, then map a drive to a network folder that will also contain the file. (Note: If you are not connected to a network, ask your instructor or technical support person for help in completing this independent challenge. If you are working in a lab environment, you may not be able to create a shared folder. If so, do not create a shared folder, and use the folder supplied by your instructor.)

To complete this independent challenge:

1. Open Network Neighborhood and select the icon for your computer.
2. Right-click your computer icon, then click Explorer.
3. Select a place on your hard drive to create a folder.
4. Create a shared folder called Suppliers.
5. Open WordPad and enter the following information in a new document:

Name	Address	City & State
Baskets & Things	101 Hopyard Road	Chicago, IL
Frames R Us	1934 Hummingbird Lane	Los Angeles, CA
Season's	125 34th Street	New York, NY

6. Save the file as "Supplier List" in the newly created Suppliers folder.
7. Print the Supplier List file.
8. Map a drive to a shared folder on another computer to which you have permission.
9. Create a US Suppliers folder on that drive.
10. Copy the Supplier List file from the Suppliers folder on the local computer to the US Suppliers folder on the mapped drive.
11. Print the Screen. (Press the Print Screen key to make a copy of the screen, open Paint, click Edit on the menu bar, click Paste to paste the screen into Paint, then click Yes to paste the large image if necessary. Click File on the menu bar, click Print, then click OK.)
12. Disconnect the network drive you mapped, and delete the shared folder you created.

2. As the president of your company, you have decided to increase the pay rates for two of your employees, Jessica Thielen and Debbie Cabral. You will use WordPad to write a memo that you can edit and use for both employees. After completing the memos, you will print the documents for the employees. You also want to copy the documents to the company server so they can be stored in their employee folders.

To complete this independent challenge:

1. Create a Memos folder on your Student Disk.
2. Open WordPad and type the following memo in a new document:
   Dear Jessica,
   Your service to this company is greatly appreciated. To show my appreciation to such an outstanding employee as yourself, I have decided to give you a 10% raise in salary. The raise will go into effect with the next pay period.
   Sincerely yours,
   [your name here]
3. Use the Save As command to name the document "Thielen Raise" and save it in the Memos folder, then print the document.
4. Change "Dear Jessica" to "Dear Debbie" in the Thielen Raise memo.
5. Save the file as "Cabral Raise" in the Memos folder and print the document.
6. Close the file and close WordPad.
7. Map a drive to a shared folder on another computer to which you have permission. Create a folder on that mapped drive called Thielen and copy the Thielen Raise file from your Student Disk into the Thielen folder.
8. Create a shared folder called Cabral on the mapped drive, and copy the Cabral Raise file into the Cabral folder.
9. Print the screen. (See Independent Challenge 1, Step 10 for screen printing instructions.)
10. Delete the Thielen and Cabral shared folders on the mapped drive.
11. Disconnect the network drive you mapped.

3. You are the system administrator for your company's computer network. During peak usage of the network, you want to monitor who is on the network. You will use the Properties command in the Network Neighborhood to find out who is connected to the network.

1. Using Network Neighborhood, display the properties of two or three mapped drives connected to your computer.
2. Print the screen. (See Independent Challenge 1, Step 10 for screen printing instructions.)

4. The system administrator for your network calls and informs you that he needs to make some changes to the directory structure. He advises you to move any files you have put on the server recently and to disconnect any mapped drives.

1. Map a drive to a shared folder on another computer to which you have permission, and copy two files from your Student Disk to this mapped drive.
2. Using Network Neighborhood, create a shared folder on your local hard disk called Network Files.
3. Move the files from the folder on the network drive to the shared Network Files folder on the local hard disk.
4. Print the screen. (See Independent Challenge 1, Step 10 for screen printing instructions.)
5. Disconnect the mapped drive from the network.
6. Delete the shared folder on your local hard drive.

▶ Visual Workshop

Re-create the screen shown in Figure H-18, which displays the Network Neighborhood. Print the screen. (See Independent Challenge 1, Step 10 for screen printing instructions.)

FIGURE H-18

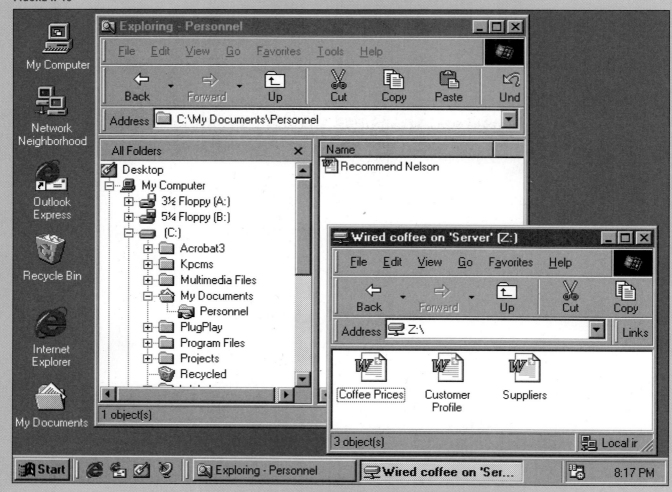

Creating
a Web Page with FrontPage Express

Objectives

- ► Open and save a new **Web page**
- ► Apply paragraph styles
- ► Format paragraphs
- ► Format text
- ► Insert and format a horizontal line
- ► Insert graphics
- ► Add a background pattern
- ► Create bookmarks and internal links
- ► Create links to Web pages

Windows 98 includes **FrontPage Express**, a program that you use to create Web pages. FrontPage Express allows you to create, edit, and format your Web page in a **WYSIWYG** environment ("what you see is what you get", pronounced "whiz-ee-wig") so that you see a preview of the document. When your page is complete, you can use the Web Publishing Wizard to **publish** the page by saving it on a **Web server**, a computer on the Internet. ◢— John Casey has agreed to help Marti Crawford create a simple Web page for the climbing school that she recently started.

Opening and Saving a New Web Page

Windows 98

When you create a Web page with FrontPage Express, you can either save it to a disk on your computer or you can publish it directly to the Web. In this unit, you will save a Web page as a file on your Student Disk. When you save a file in FrontPage Express, regardless of whether you save it to a Web server or to a disk on your computer, FrontPage Express gives you the opportunity to assign a page title. This title appears in the title bar of any browser that displays your page. John and Marti start FrontPage Express and begin creating her Web page. Her climbing school is named The Colorado Experience, so that is the title John will use.

1. Click the **Start button**, point to **Programs**, point to **Internet Explorer**, click **FrontPage Express**, then maximize the FrontPage Express window, if necessary

2. So that you have the necessary tools available, click **View** and check that your toolbar options match Figure I-1

   The Format toolbar helps you format your page, the Standard toolbar helps you compose your page, and the Forms toolbar helps you create a form on your page. Because The Colorado Experience Web page will not contain forms, you do not need the Forms toolbar in this unit.

3. Click **File**, then click **Save As**

   Even though your document is blank, by saving it first, you can assign it a title at the outset.

4. Type **The Colorado Experience** in the Page Title text box, as shown in Figure I-2, but do *not* click OK yet

   The Page Location text box in your Save As dialog box probably has a URL (a Web site address) that begins with http:// and that is followed by the name of your computer and the filename "colorado.htm." FrontPage Express assigns a URL as the page location because it assumes your page's destination is a Web server. Because you are not ready to publish your page, you can ignore whatever address is in the Page Location text box and follow Steps 5 through 8 to save the page as a file on your disk.

5. Click **As File**, as shown in Figure I-2

6. Click the **Save in list arrow**, then click the drive containing your Student Disk

7. Type **Colorado** in the File name text box

8. Click **Save**

Trouble?

If a message opens that says, "Unable to save the page via WebPost," you probably clicked OK after Step 4. Click OK to return to the FrontPage Express window, then start over at Step 3.

FIGURE I-1: **FrontPage Express**

Standard toolbar

Format toolbar

View menu options to select in Step 2

Document window will display the page as you create it

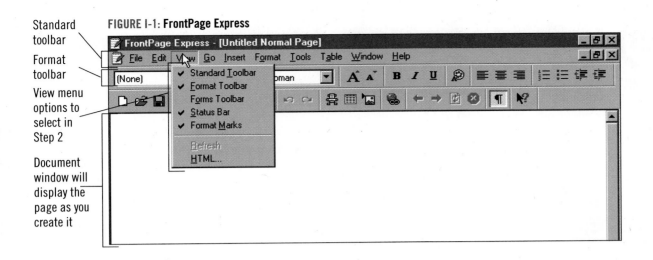

FIGURE I-2: **Saving a Web page**

This title will appear in browser title bar

Location displays path for your computer; yours wil be different

Clicking OK would start publishing the page on the Web

Click to save as a file on your Student Disk

CLUES TO USE

Understanding HTML

FrontPage Express works much like a word processor. There are, however, some important differences between a document created with a word processing program such as Microsoft Word and one created by FrontPage Express for use on the Web. When you create a document using FrontPage Express, you are actually creating a file that consists of HTML codes. **HTML**, which stands for Hypertext Markup Language, is the computer programming language in which a Web page is written. HTML uses special codes to describe how the page should appear on the screen. Figure I-3 shows a Web page as it appears on your computer screen, and behind the Web page, the underlying HTML code.

FIGURE I-3: **Web page and the HTML code it employs**

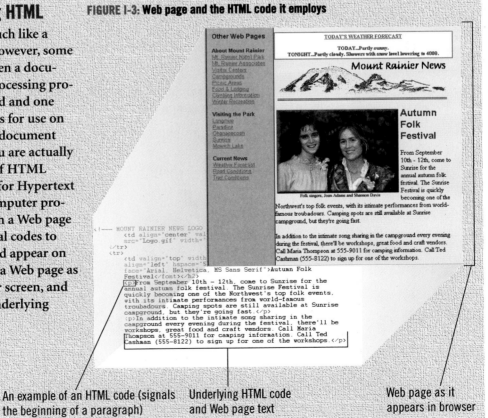

An example of an HTML code (signals the beginning of a paragraph)

Underlying HTML code and Web page text

Web page as it appears in browser

Applying Paragraph Styles

When you enter text into FrontPage Express, you can format it using the tools on the Format toolbar. With FrontPage Express, just as with a word processor, you can apply attributes such as centering or indenting to your paragraphs and attributes such as boldface or italics to individual phrases, words, or characters. In this lesson you will work with **paragraph styles**, formatting that applies to entire paragraphs, to set off the sections of your Web page. To assign a style, you click anywhere in the paragraph and select the style from the Change Style list. Like most word processors, FrontPage Express has several pre-assigned styles you can use. John suggests that they first insert Marti's text file and then format the file's section headings with the Heading 1 style.

Steps

1. Click **Insert** on the menu bar, then click **File**

2. Click the **Look in list arrow**, then click the drive containing your Student Disk, if necessary

3. Click the **Files of type list arrow**, then click **Text Files** (you might have to scroll to see it)

4. Click **Marti**, then click **Open**
   The Convert Text dialog box opens with options for formatting paragraphs.

5. Click the **Normal paragraphs option button**, then click **OK**
   By selecting the Normal paragraphs option, you ensure that your text will be assigned the Normal style, which is the text style that usually makes up the body of a Web page.

6. Scroll up the document, then click at the beginning of the line **Our Philosophy** (the fourth paragraph)
   Do not be confused when the term "paragraph" is applied to a single phrase such as "Our Philosophy." Every section of text that ends with a paragraph break (created by pressing [Enter]) is considered a paragraph when applying styles.

7. Click the **Change Style list arrow**, then click **Heading 1**, as shown in Figure I-4
   All of the text in the paragraph containing the insertion point is changed to the Heading 1 style. In this case, the paragraph is only two words long.

8. Scroll down to locate the phrase **Climbing Lessons**, then repeat Steps 6 and 7 for that paragraph
   Compare your Web page to Figure I-5.

9. Click the **Save button** 💾

FIGURE I-4: Applying a paragraph style

Change Style list arrow

Choose Heading 1

All the words in this paragraph will take on the Heading 1 style

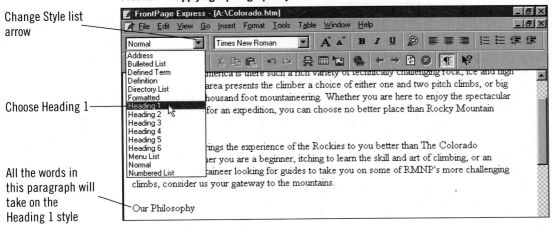

FIGURE I-5: Heading 1 style

Heading 1 style is selected

Paragraph in Heading 1 style

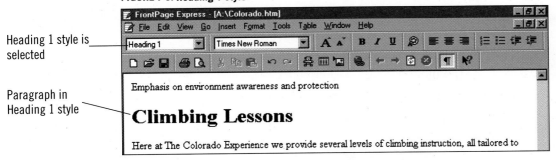

CLUES TO USE

Markup tags

When a browser opens a Web page, it retrieves and interprets the HTML code that created the page to determine how the Web page should appear on the screen. The appearance of each element in the page, such as a heading or a bulleted list, is indicated by a **markup tag**—a label in angle brackets that identifies the element to a browser. A tag with the label <H1>, for example, stands for "Heading 1" and indicates that the text that follows is a top-level heading in the document. To view the HTML tags that are automatically assigned to your Web page by FrontPage Express, click View, then click HTML. Markup tags are very generic so that many different kinds of browsers can read the document and determine how to display it. Because of the generic nature of the markup tags, different browsers display Web pages differently. Figure I-6 shows how two different browsers might interpret text formatted with a Heading 1 tag.

FIGURE I-6: Same tag as it appears in different browsers

Formatting Paragraphs

Windows 98

In addition to the styles FrontPage Express makes available for the paragraphs in your document, you can assign more specific attributes to your paragraphs by using the buttons on the Format toolbar, shown in Table I-1. You can click anywhere in the paragraph that you want to format, and the attribute that you select will format the entire paragraph. When you want to apply the attribute to more than one paragraph, you need to select the paragraphs. 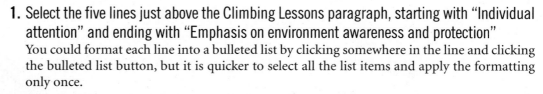 John wants to improve the appearance of the text by formatting a bulleted list, and Marti asks if he could add her company's address to the page.

1. **Select the five lines just above the Climbing Lessons paragraph, starting with "Individual attention" and ending with "Emphasis on environment awareness and protection"**
   You could format each line into a bulleted list by clicking somewhere in the line and clicking the bulleted list button, but it is quicker to select all the list items and apply the formatting only once.

2. **Click the Bulleted List button ▦ and then click a blank area of the Web page to deselect the bulleted list**
   Figure I-7 shows the five lines with the Bulleted List style applied.

3. **To move to the end of the page, where you will add the climbing school's address, press and hold down [Ctrl], then press [End]**
   The insertion point should be at a blank line at the end of the page.

4. **Type The Colorado Experience, then, while pressing and holding down [Shift], press [Enter]**
   Pressing [Enter] alone inserts a **paragraph break**, which tells FrontPage Express to create white space between the paragraphs. Pressing [Shift] while you press [Enter] (usually expressed as [Shift][Enter]) tells FrontPage Express to insert a **line break**, which creates a new line without the extra white space. In an address, you want to use line breaks rather than paragraph breaks.

5. **Type 2411 Agnes Avenue, then press [Shift] [Enter]**

6. **Type Vale Park, CO 80517, press [Enter], then type (970) 555-2341**
   By pressing [Enter] after the address, you've inserted a paragraph break rather than a line break, so the phone number is slightly separated from the address and easier for viewers to find.

7. **Select the last four lines (the address and phone number), click the Center button ▤, then click a blank area of the page to deselect the text**
   Your Web page should now look like Figure I-8.

QuickTip

You can change the appearance of the bulleted list by selecting the bulleted list, right-clicking it, then clicking List Properties. Click the Bullet tab, click the bullet style you want, then click OK.

Time To
✔ Save

Numbered and bulleted lists

Formatting information into a list helps people absorb related pieces of information more quickly. To display chronological information, like the steps needed to complete a task, use the Numbered List style. If the order of the items does not matter, use the Bulleted List style. The Numbered List and Bulleted List buttons on the Format toolbar are also available on the Change Style list because they are styles that correspond to HTML markup tags.

FIGURE I-7: Applying the Bulleted List style

Change Style box shows Bulleted List style (yours might show a different style depending on where you clicked in Step 2)

These paragraphs are formatted with the Bulleted List style

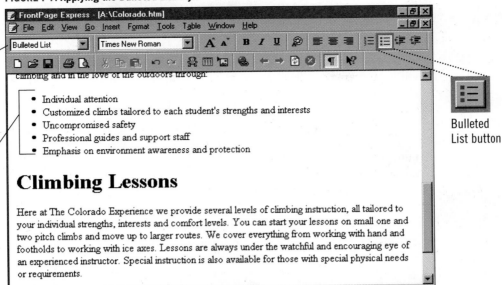

Bulleted List button

FIGURE I-8: Centered text

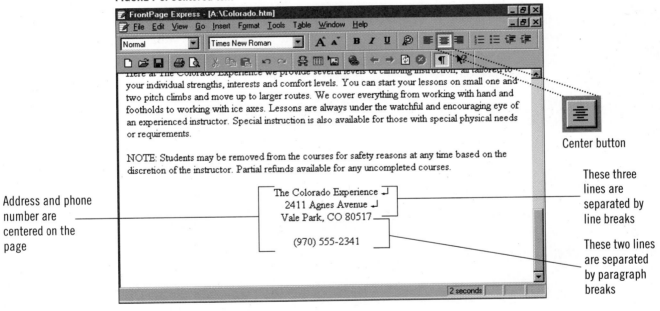

Center button

Address and phone number are centered on the page

These three lines are separated by line breaks

These two lines are separated by paragraph breaks

TABLE I-1: Paragraph formatting buttons

button	label	description
	Align Left	Aligns paragraph to the left page margin
	Center	Centers paragraph on the page
	Align Right	Aligns paragraph to the right page margin
	Numbered List	Indents and numbers paragraphs
	Bulleted List	Indents and applies a bullet symbol to paragraphs
	Decrease Indent	Moves paragraph to the left
	Increase Indent	Moves paragraph to the right

Formatting Text

Now that you've applied styles and special formatting to the paragraphs of your document, you are ready to apply formatting that will change the attributes, such as bold or italics, of individual words or characters. Because these are character formats, they will only format text you select, unlike the paragraph formats that alter an entire paragraph when it contains the insertion point. Table I-2 displays the toolbar buttons on the Format toolbar that you use to format characters. You can, of course, apply these attributes to entire paragraphs—you just have to select the whole paragraph rather than just click in it. John wants to draw attention to the company's name, so he formats it with bold and italics. He also wants to change the color of the heading paragraphs.

Steps

Trouble?

To remove formatting, select the text, then click the appropriate formatting button again.

1. Scroll up, then in the third paragraph, select the text The Colorado Experience

2. Click the Bold button **B**, then click the Italic button

3. Select the Our Philosophy paragraph

4. Click the Text Color button, as shown in Figure I-9

QuickTip

You can select additional colors by clicking the Define Custom Colors button in the Color dialog box.

5. Click the first color in the fourth row, as shown in Figure I-9, click OK, then click outside the text to deselect it
   The heading changes to brown.

6. Repeat Steps 3-5 for the Climbing Lessons heading

Time To

✔ Save

7. Select the address and phone number at the bottom of the page, click the Bold button **B**, then click outside the text to deselect it
   Your Web page should look like Figure I-10.

Accessing font properties

To view and change the character properties of any text in your document, select the text, right-click it, then click Font Properties from the pop-up menu. The Font Properties dialog box allows you to view all of the attributes, such as bold, italics, underline, font, font size, and text color, that are assigned to the selected text. You can alter as many of these properties as you want from within the Font Properties dialog box.

FIGURE I-9: Changing text color

Change heading text to this color

This heading should be selected

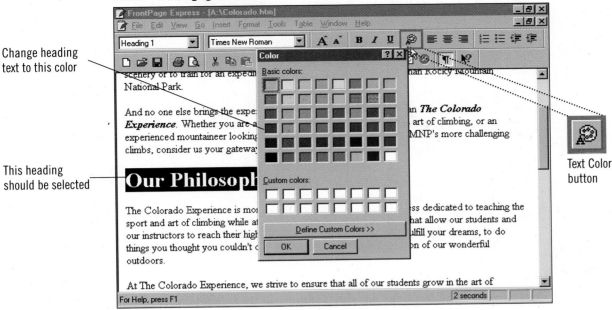

Text Color button

FIGURE I-10: Formatted text

New text color

Address and phone number are boldface

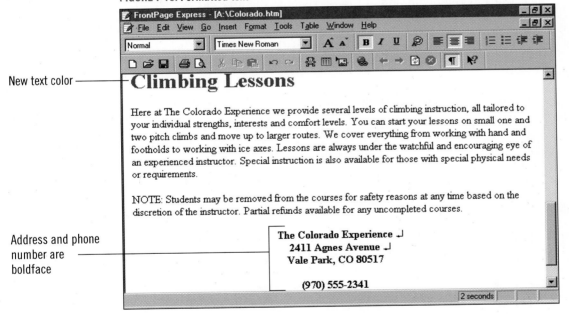

TABLE I-2: Character formatting buttons

button	label	description
▼	Change Font	Applies a different typeface to selected text
A˄	Increase Text Size	Increases font size of selected text in pre-determined increments
A˅	Decrease Text Size	Decreases font size of selected text in pre-determined increments
B	Bold	Applies boldface font to selected text
I	Italic	Applies italic font to selected text
U	Underline	Underlines selected text
🎨	Text Color	Opens the Color dialog box, from which you can choose a different font color

Inserting and Formatting a Horizontal Line

Part of the popularity of the Web is due to the ability of browsers like Internet Explorer to display graphic objects in Web pages. **Graphic objects**, such as lines, pictures, patterns, and logos, make Web pages more attractive and allow Web authors to share visual information. Horizontal lines divide your Web page into sections for easy viewing; you can add visual interest to the lines by formatting their width, height, alignment, color, and shadow. Because graphic objects require more time than normal text for a browser to access, you should decide whether the contribution an object makes to your page is significant enough to offset the time viewers will have to wait for your page to download. John and Marti decide to add two lines to the Web page, one before the address, and one at the top of the page.

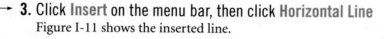

1. If necessary, scroll to the end of the page so you can see the address

2. Click at the beginning of the first line of the address, The Colorado Experience

Trouble?
If the line is inserted in the middle of your text, you probably did not click just to the left of the text. Click the Undo button, then repeat Steps 1-3.

3. Click Insert on the menu bar, then click Horizontal Line
   Figure I-11 shows the inserted line.

4. Right-click the line you inserted, then click Horizontal Line Properties
   The Horizontal Line Properties dialog box allows you to change the attributes of your horizontal line. See Figure I-12.

Trouble?
If the line height is already 5 pixels, click Cancel, then skip Step 6.

5. Click the up spin arrow button next to "Pixels" in the Height section to change the height of the line from 2 pixels to 5 pixels, as shown in Figure I-12

6. Click OK
   The line increases in size.

7. Scroll to the top of the page, click the beginning of the first paragraph (to the left of "Welcome"), then press [Enter]
   Now there will be space available at the top of the page for a graphic you will insert in a later lesson.

QuickTip
You can verify that the line height is 5 pixels by right-clicking the line and clicking Horizontal Line Properties. Adjust the line height, if necessary.

8. With the insertion point still just to the left of the word "Welcome," click Insert, then click Horizontal Line
   The line height is automatically set to 5 pixels, the value you chose for the earlier line.

9. Click the Save button

FIGURE I-11: Inserting a horizontal line

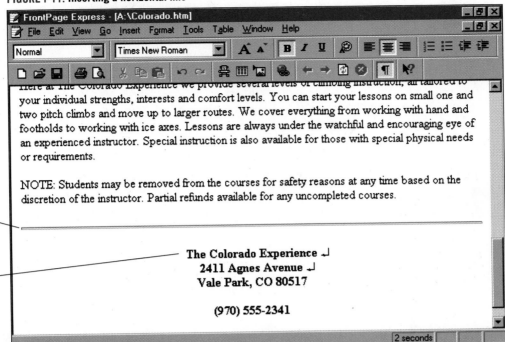

Horizontal line appears above insertion point

Click here to insert line

FIGURE I-12: Increasing line size

Up spin arrow

Centers line on page

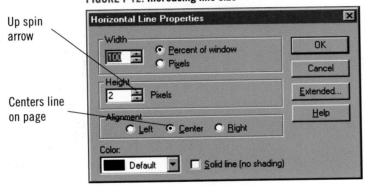

Formatting horizontal lines

As you've seen, the Horizontal Line Properties dialog box shown in Figure I-12 allows you to specify line height in pixels; a **pixel** is a single point on your monitor's screen. To specify line width, you have two choices: Percent of window or Pixels. Setting the line width to 100 Percent of window means the line will stretch the full width of the document window, regardless of screen resolution. If you want to define the line width so that it is the same for all browsers, you can specify a pixel number, but recognize that on monitors with higher screen resolution, a line specified with pixels will look shorter. Figure I-13 shows examples of lines formatted with a variety of properties from the Horizontal Line Properties dialog box.

FIGURE I-13: Examples of line styles

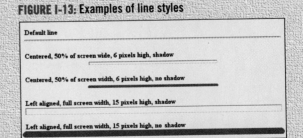

Windows 98

Inserting Graphics

In addition to horizontal lines, you can also insert graphic images or pictures into a Web page. Graphic images come from a variety of sources: you can create them in a graphics software package, you can scan paper images such as photos or drawings and save them as electronic files, or you can access them from graphic clip art collections that come with certain software packages or that are available on the Web. To use a graphic image on a Web page, the image must be saved in a graphics file format (such as GIF or JPEG) that browsers can display. You can use FrontPage Express to change an image's size, border, alignment, and the distance between the graphic and surrounding text. ✐ Marti has two graphics in JPEG format that she wants John to include on her Web page.

Steps

1. Press the [Up Arrow] on your keyboard twice to move the insertion point to the first blank line, then click the **Insert Image button** 🖼

2. On the Other Location tab, make sure the **From File option button** is selected, then click **Browse**

3. Click **Look in list arrow**, then click the drive that contains your Student Disk, if necessary

QuickTip

If you want to move an image once you've inserted it, you can select it, then drag it to where you want it.

4. Click **Logo**, click **Open**, then, if necessary, click anywhere on the page to deselect the image
   The Colorado Experience logo should look like Figure I-14.

5. Click the **Logo image** to select it, then click the **Center button** ≣ to center the image on the page

6. To insert the second graphic image, click to the left of "Welcome," click the **Insert Image button** 🖼, click **Browse**, click **Rappel**, click **Open**, then, if necessary, click anywhere in the document to deselect the image
   The Lessons graphic image is inserted into your Web page. Notice, however, that it moved all the text down, leaving a large white space to the right of the picture. You can fix this problem by aligning the image to the right of the page so that the text wraps to the left.

7. Right-click the **Rappel image**, click **Image Properties**, then click the **Appearance tab**

8. Click the **Alignment list arrow**, then click **right**, as shown in Figure I-15

9. Enter **5** into the **Horizontal Spacing box**, then click **OK**
   The spacing options allow you to leave space between the text and the picture. Your Web page should now look like Figure I-16.

Image formats

You can include graphic images on your page as inline images or as external images. An **inline image** is part of the Web page and appears directly on the Web page. An **external image** is not part of the page, but users can view it by clicking a link that will either open the image on a separate page or load software that will display the image on the original page. If you want to use an inline image, it should be in a file format, such as GIF or JPEG, that most browsers will be able to display. If your image is not in this format, you can use a separate graphics program to convert it, or you can insert it as an external image.

FIGURE I-14: **Inserting a graphic image**

Inserted graphic is currently left-aligned; you will center it

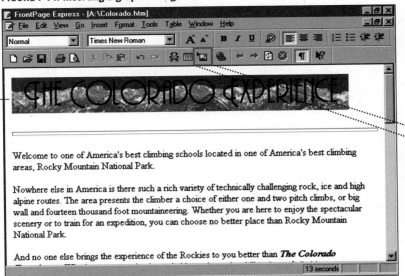

Insert Image button

FIGURE I-15: **Aligning a graphic image**

Select right from the image alignment options

Spacing options allow you to increase the distance between the image and the text

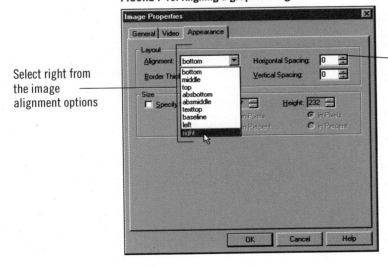

FIGURE I-16: **Aligned graphic image**

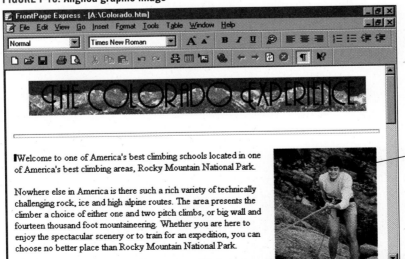

Graphic is now right-aligned and text wraps to the left

Windows 98

Adding a Background Pattern

FrontPage Express allows you to add color or patterns to your Web page as a background. Many Web pages employ interesting background images to great effect. Generally the file size of the graphic used to create the background should not exceed 30 kilobytes. If it is larger than 30 kilobytes, you will create a lengthy download time for viewers who might be too impatient to wait. You also want to avoid overpowering your text with the background image you choose. There are many sites on the Web that offer interesting background graphic files that you can download and use for free. ◢▬▬ Marti wants to use an earth-tone graphic as the background of The Colorado Experience page. She saved it as a JPEG file on the disk that she brought.

1. Click **Format** on the menu bar, then click **Background**
   The Page Properties dialog box opens with the Background tab showing.

2. Click **Background Image check box** to select it, as shown in Figure I-17

3. Click **Browse**

4. On the **Other Location tab**, make sure the **From File option button** is selected, then click **Browse**

5. Make sure that the Look in box displays the drive containing your Student Disk

6. Click **Earth**, then click **Open**

7. Click **OK** in the Page Properties dialog box
   The image appears as a background behind the text and pictures, as shown in Figure I-18.

8. Click the **Save button** 🖫

QuickTip

If you just want to change the color of your background, you do not have to use a background image. Instead, click Format, click Background, then select the color you want from the Background Color list box.

FIGURE I-17: Setting background properties

Settings that control background and text color

Click to choose a background graphic image from a file

Settings that control link color

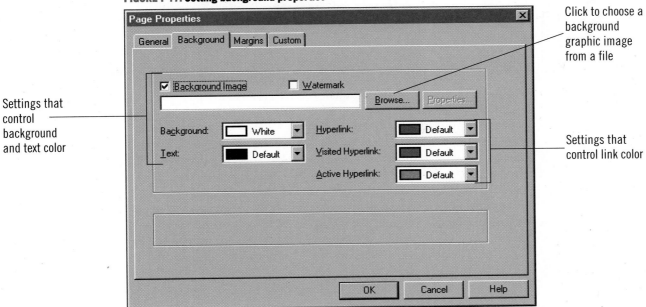

FIGURE I-18: Web page with a background

Background uses a textured graphics file

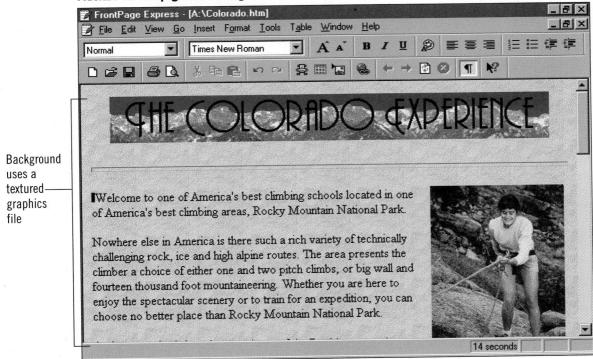

Choosing hyperlink colors

You can assign a color to your hyperlinks that is different from your normal text color in order to draw attention to the links on your page. You can also use color to distinguish hyperlinks that have already been visited from hyperlinks that have not: The hyperlink that is active can also have its own distinct color. The

Page Properties dialog box displays the current colors used for hyperlinks. You can change the default colors assigned to the three types of hyperlinks by clicking the list arrow for each. You might want to change them to complement changes that you make to other colors on your page.

Windows 98

Creating Bookmarks and Internal Links

Web pages generally contain links that you can select to jump to other Web pages. Some also contain **internal links**, which take you to other locations within the Web page. Internal links provide some important organizational benefits. For example, if you have a very long page, you can help users find information quickly by placing a table of contents at the top of the page, with each topic acting as an internal link to key parts of the page. To create these links, you must first place a **bookmark**, or reference point, at the spot to which you want your link to jump. Then, you create the link to jump to that bookmark. You cannot see the bookmark icon when you view the page in the browser, but FrontPage Express displays the bookmarks to make it easy for you to work with them. Because The Colorado Experience Web page is too long to fit on a computer screen, John thinks it would be helpful to create a link that takes viewers from the bottom back up to the top. The bookmark will go at the top of the page and the link will go at the bottom.

Trouble?

Don't delete the small black rectangle to the left of "Welcome." It is the image marker for the graphic file you inserted.

1. Click to the left of the word "Welcome"
This is where the bookmark will go.

2. Click Edit, then click Bookmark

3. Type **Top of page** in the Bookmark Name text box, as shown in Figure I-19
You should try to choose a name that describes your bookmark, using either its location on the page or a heading to which it corresponds; it will help you keep your bookmarks straight if you have a Web page with multiple bookmarks.

4. Click **OK**
The bookmark icon appears, as shown in Figure I-20. This is the location your link (which you will create next) will target.

5. Scroll to the bottom of the page, click the **blank line** below the phone number, then, if necessary, click the **Align Left button** [icon] to align this paragraph to the left
You can add an extra line, if necessary.

Trouble?

If your typing appears bold, select the text you typed, then click the Bold button [B] to remove the bold formatting.

6. Type **Return to the top**

7. Select **Return to the top** (the text you just typed), click the **Create or Edit Hyperlink button** [icon], then click the **Open Pages tab**, if necessary

8. Click the **Bookmark list arrow**, then click **Top of page**, as shown in Figure I-21
Note that "Return to the top" is the link, and "Top of page" is the bookmark; the link will jump to the bookmark.

Time To
✔ Save

9. Click **OK**, then click anywhere on the Web page to deselect the text
The link is underlined and in blue. Your page has to be displayed in a browser for the link to work.

FIGURE I-19: **Setting a bookmark**

Place bookmark here (black bar indicates place you have inserted graphic image)

If this Web page had other bookmarks, they would be listed here

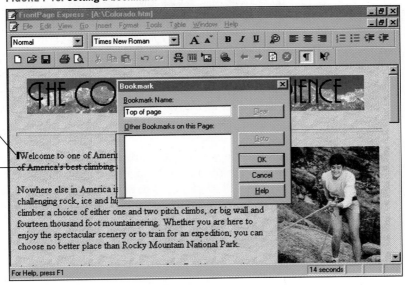

FIGURE I-20: **Bookmark icon**

Bookmark icon will be hidden in browser

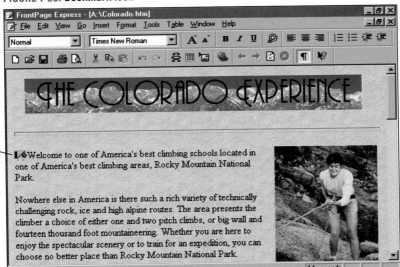

FIGURE I-21: **Linking to a bookmark**

Create or Edit Hyperlink button

Bookmarks on current page

Link you are creating

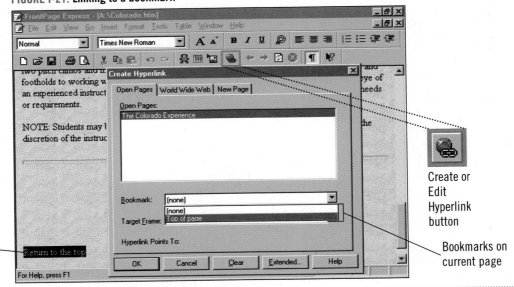

Creating Links to Web Pages

Creating links within your own document provides easy navigation for the viewers of your page, but you really start making use of the power of the Web when you link your document to other Web pages. If you are linking to a local page (one on the same server as your page), you must specify its filename. If the page is located on a different Web server, you must specify its URL. In both cases, when a viewer clicks the link, the browser connects to the URL targeted in the link and displays the new page. John isn't planning on charging Marti for creating her Web page, but he asks if he could add a link to her page that targets his Wired Coffee Company home page and gives it a little advertising. She thinks it's a great idea.

Steps

1. If necessary, add a blank line after the Return to the top link you added in the previous lesson

2. Type **After your climb, hang out at the chalet, where we feature Wired Coffee Company brews!**

3. Select **Wired Coffee Company** in the line you just typed
   See Figure I-22.

4. Click the **Create or Edit Hyperlink button** and, if necessary, click the **World Wide Web tab**

5. Type **http://www.course.com/illustrated/wired** in the URL box, as shown in Figure I-23, click **OK**, then click outside the link to deselect it
   Notice that both links are underlined and in blue.

6. Save your Web page, close FrontPage Express, then start Internet Explorer so you can test your links

7. To open your page in Internet Explorer, click **File**, click **Open**, click **Browse**, then in the Look in box select the drive containing your Student Disk

8. Make sure the Files of type box displays HTML Files, click **Colorado**, click **Open**, then click **OK**
   Your completed Web page, viewed in the Internet Explorer browser, should look like Figure I-24.

9. Scroll to the bottom of the page, click the **Return to the top link** (this should return you to the Welcome paragraph), scroll back down, click the **Wired Coffee Company link** (this should open the Wired Coffee Company Web page), then close Internet Explorer

Trouble?

To test your external link, you must be connected to the Internet. If you can't connect to the Internet, you can still look at the Web page in Internet Explorer and test the internal link.

Trouble?

If a link does not jump to the correct destination, click Edit, then click Page in the Internet Explorer browser. When FrontPage Express opens your document, right-click the link to open the Link Properties dialog box. Make any necessary corrections, then repeat Steps 6 through 9.

FIGURE I-22: Linking to a Web page

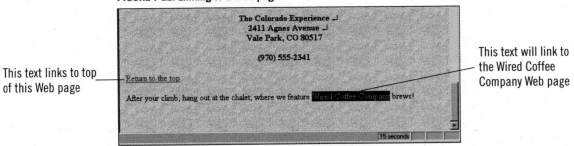

The Colorado Experience ↵
2411 Agnes Avenue ↵
Vale Park, CO 80517

(970) 555-2341

Return to the top

After your climb, hang out at the chalet, where we feature Wired Coffee Company brews!

15 seconds

This text links to top of this Web page

This text will link to the Wired Coffee Company Web page

FIGURE I-23: Entering a URL

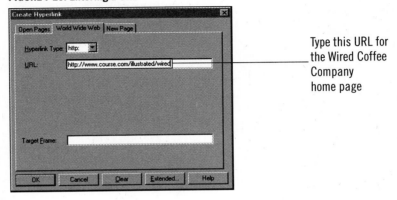

Create Hyperlink

Open Pages | World Wide Web | New Page |

Hyperlink Type: http:

URL: http://www.course.com/illustrated/wired

Target Frame:

OK   Cancel   Clear   Extended...   Help

Type this URL for the Wired Coffee Company home page

FIGURE I-24: Viewing completed page in the browser

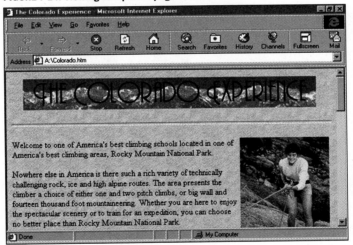

The Colorado Experience - Microsoft Internet Explorer

File Edit View Go Favorites Help

Back Forward Stop Refresh Home Search Favorites History Channels Fullscreen Mail

Address A:\Colorado.htm

THE COLORADO EXPERIENCE

Welcome to one of America's best climbing schools located in one of America's best climbing areas, Rocky Mountain National Park.

Nowhere else in America is there such a rich variety of technically challenging rock, ice and high alpine routes. The area presents the climber a choice of either one and two pitch climbs, or big wall and fourteen thousand foot mountaineering. Whether you are here to enjoy the spectacular scenery or to train for an expedition, you can choose no better place than Rocky Mountain National Park.

Done   My Computer

Publishing a Web page

To publish a page on the Web so the general public can access it, you must first have space on a Web server. Your Internet Service Provider (ISP) usually has server space available for your use. Once you have worked with your ISP to acquire and register the name of your Web page, you can use the Windows 98 Web Publishing Wizard to publish your document. To do this, start Windows Explorer, select the file you want to publish, right-click it, click Send To, then click Web Publishing Wizard. Read the information on the opening screen, click Next, select your Web server when prompted, then click Finish. If you are prompted for your user name and password, provide the information, then click OK when you are informed that the files have been properly transferred. You should connect to your page on the Web to make sure that all of the graphics appear correctly and that all of the links work.

Practice

► Concepts Review

Label each of the elements of the screen shown in Figure I-25.

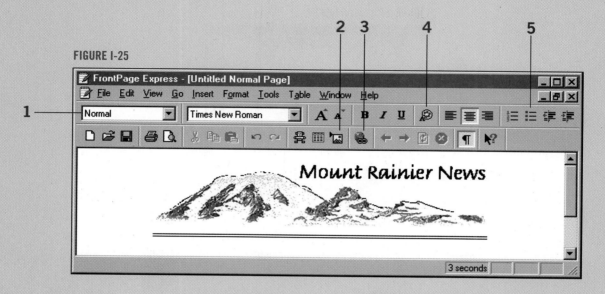

FIGURE I-25

Match each of the terms with the statement that best describes it.

6. **FrontPage Express**
7. **HTML**
8. **Bulleted List**
9. **Pixel**
10. **JPEG**
11. **Inline image**
12. **Bookmark**
13. **Link**

a. The paragraph style you apply to ordered information
b. An image that appears directly on a Web page
c. The language in which Web pages are written
d. When clicked in an HTML document, this will take you to the targeted bookmark or URL
e. A graphics file format that most browsers can display
f. The Internet Explorer component of Windows 98 that allows you to edit and create Web pages
g. A designated place in a Web page that a link targets
h. A single point on your monitor's screen

Select the best answer from the following list of choices.

14. **Which of the following is an option for text formatting in FrontPage Express?**
   a. Bolding   c. Underlining
   b. Italicizing   d. All of the above

15. **An HTML document that you create is available to World Wide Web users:**
   a. anytime your computer is on.   c. if you put it on a Web server.
   b. anytime you are online.   d. none of the above.

16. **If you wanted to put a link to a Web page created by someone else in your own Web page, you would:**
   a. get permission to put a bookmark in his or her page.
   b. open his or her Web page in FrontPage Express and copy it.
   c. specify that page's URL in the Link Properties dialog box.
   d. publish your Web page on the Web server that they are using.

17. **Which of the following is a paragraph style that you can apply to your HTML document in FrontPage Express?**
   a. Heading 1   c. Font size
   b. Font   d. Bold

 # Skills Review

1. **Save a new Web page.**
   a. Start FrontPage Express and open the file "Colorado" from your Student Disk.
   b. Save the page title as "Colorado Climbing School."
   c. Save the file as "Colorado Climbing School" on your Student Disk.
2. **Apply styles.**
   a. Click at the beginning of "Our Philosophy," click the Change Style list arrow, then click Heading 2.
   b. Click the beginning of "Climbing Lessons," then click the Change Style list arrow, then click Heading 2.
3. **Format paragraphs.**
   a. Select the five lines from "Individual Attention" to "Emphasis on environment awareness and protection."
   b. Apply the square bullet option to this text.
   c. Click "Our Philosophy," then click the Center button.
   d. Click "Climbing Lessons," click the Center button, then save the page.
4. **Format text.**
   a. Select "Our Philosophy."
   b. Click the Text Color button, click the fifth color in the third row, then click OK.
   c. Repeat Steps b and c for "Climbing Lessons."
   d. Italicize the text from "NOTE:" to "…for any uncompleted courses," then save the page.
5. **Insert and format a horizontal line.**
   a. Right-click the horizontal line at the top of the page, then click Horizontal Line Properties.
   b. Change the height of the line to 10 pixels and the color of the line to Blue.
   c. Right-click the horizontal line above the address and phone number of The Colorado Experience.
   d. Repeat Steps b and c, then save the page.
6. **Insert graphics.**
   a. Place insertion point to the left of the words "At the Colorado Experience…" in the Our Philosophy section.
   b. Click Insert, click Image, then click Browse.
   c. Click the Look in list arrow, and click the drive containing your Student Disk.
   d. Click Climb, click Open, then click the image on the Web page.
   e. Click the Align Right button, then save the Web page.
7. **Add a background pattern.**
   a. Click Format, then click Background.
   b. Make sure a check appears in the Background Image check box, then click Browse.
   c. On the Other Location tab, make sure the From File option button is selected, then click Browse.
   d. Click the Look in list arrow to locate the drive containing your Student Disk.
   e. Click Sky, click Open, click OK in the Page Properties dialog box, then save the page.
8. **Create bookmarks and internal links.**
   a. Place the insertion point to the left of the first line of the address ("The Colorado Experience").
   b. Click Edit, click Bookmark, type "Address" in the Bookmark Name box, then click OK.

   c. Place the insertion point at the end of the third paragraph.

   d. Type "Click here to find out where you can call or write to schedule your date with the Rockies!"

   e. Select the word "here," then click the Create or Edit Hyperlink button.

   f. Click Open Pages tab, then click the Bookmark list arrow.

   g. Click Address, click OK, then save the Web page.

9. Create links to Web pages.

   a. Start Internet Explorer, connect to the Internet, then go to http://www.nps.gov/romo/.

   b. With the Rocky Mountain National Park page open in your browser, select the page's URL in the Address box.

   c. Right-click the URL and then click Copy.

   d. Close your browser and disconnect from the Internet, then maximize FrontPage Express.

   e. Select the text "Rocky Mountain National Park" in the second paragraph of your Web page.

   f. Click the Create or Edit Hyperlink button, then click the World Wide Web tab, if necessary.

   g. Right-click the URL text box, click Paste, then click OK.

   h. Save your document (leave FrontPage Express open).

   i. Start Internet Explorer, then open the file Colorado Climbing School from your Student Disk.

   j. Test the links you added, then close Internet Explorer.

   k. Print the page, then close FrontPage Express.

► Independent Challenges

1. You're writing your dissertation on Robert Frost. A friend of yours owns Muse's Brew, a local coffee shop and bookstore, and has asked if you would create next month's Feature Poet Web page on his Web site. Using FrontPage Express, create a document using the files you find in the IC1 folder on your Student Disk.

1. Start FrontPage Express, open the file Robert from the IC1 folder, save it with the title "Feature Poet: Robert Frost" and the filename Frost in the IC1 folder.

2. Make the following formatting changes:
- Italicize "A Further Place" in the third paragraph.
- Center and apply the Heading 2 style to the poem title "Devotion" (the fourth paragraph).
- Center the poem.

3. Insert a horizontal line at the top of the page (click to the left of the first paragraph), then format it with an 8 pixel height, the Default color, and shading (remove the check mark from the Solid line check box).

4. Insert and right-align at the top of the page the graphic image Logo from your Student Disk.

5. Create a background for your page using the file Green from your Student Disk.

6. Save and then print your document.

2. You work at the Lincoln Museum of Natural History as director of community outreach. You feel that developing a child-friendly Web page would be great for families. In FrontPage Express, create a document using all of the pieces you find in the IC2 folder on your Student Disk.

1. Start FrontPage Express, then open the file Lincoln from the IC2 folder. Save the file with the title "The Lincoln Museum of Natural History" and with the filename Lincoln Museum in the IC2 folder.

2. Insert and align the following graphic images as directed. The text will wrap incorrectly around the graphic unless you place the graphics properly. If the text seems to disappear as you enter a graphic, click the Save button.
- At the top of the page (the blank line) insert and center the graphic LMNHHead.
- Click to the left of the first paragraph, then insert and right-align the graphic Dino.
- Click between the marker for the Dino graphic and the word "Located", insert the LMNH1 graphic, then press [Shift][Enter].
- Click to the left of the second paragraph (before the word "If"), insert the LMNH2 graphic, then press [Shift][Enter].
- Click to the left of the third paragraph (before the word "As"), insert the LMNH3 graphic, then press [Shift][Enter].
- Click to the left of the fourth paragraph (before the word "We"), insert the LMNH4 graphic, then press [Shift][Enter].
- Click to the left of the third paragraph (before the word "As"), then insert and left-align the Dino2 graphic.

3. At the bottom of the page in the blank line (create one if necessary), type "Hours", type a space, type "Contact", type a space, type "Location", then center the entire line.
4. Place bookmarks before the hours of operation listed in the third paragraph, the phone number in the third paragraph, and the address in the first paragraph.
5. Link the words "Hours," "Contact," and "Location," to the bookmarks you created (match the links appropriately).
6. Start Internet Explorer to test your links (you do not need to connect to the Internet to test internal links).
7. Save, then print the Web page in FrontPage Express.

3. You have been hired as advertising coordinator for the 1999 American Juggler Association Convention. Your first task is to put together a Web page about the convention. Use the files in the IC3 folder on your Student Disk to create this page.
1. Start FrontPage Express, then open the text file Text from the IC3 folder. Choose the Normal paragraphs option. Save the new document with the title "Juggler Association Convention 1999" and the filename Convention in the IC3 folder.
2. Insert the following graphic files as directed (add blank lines wherever necessary to improve layout).
   - Insert a blank line at the top of the page, then insert and center the Logo graphic in the blank line.
   - Insert and center the HLine graphic on its own line between the Logo graphic and the first paragraph.
   - Insert and left-align the Welcome graphic above the first paragraph, below the new horizontal line.
   - Insert and left-align the Workshop graphic on its own line above the second paragraph.
   - Insert and center the HLine2 graphic on its own line below the last paragraph.
3. Save your Web page.
4. Start Internet Explorer, search for Web pages on juggling, and insert at the bottom of your Web page (below the horizontal line) links from two of the pages. (*Hint*: Keep your Web page open in FrontPage Express. When you find a Web page in Internet Explorer, copy the URL, leave Explorer open, go to FrontPage Express, type a phrase for the link, click the Create or Edit Hyperlink button, then paste the URL in the URL text box on the World Wide Web tab.)
5. Save your Web page, then close FrontPage Express.
6. Use Internet Explorer to test your links.
7. Reopen, then print your page.

4. An online resume allows you to advertise your skills when you enter the job market. Create a resume in FrontPage Express that lists your job objective, your educational background, and any job experience you have.

Use headings such as "Job Objective," "Education," "Experience," and so on. Format the text and the headings appropriately. Insert horizontal lines, a background color, and an image or two. Include links at the top of the page that will take viewers to the important parts of your page. Include links to Web pages for your university or for places you've worked in the past. Open your page in Internet Explorer to test the links, then print the page.

► Visual Workshop

Recreate the following Web page for Mayer Photography using FrontPage Express and the files you find in the Visual folder on your Student Disk. Save your page as a file with the title "Mayer Photography" and the filename Photography in the Visual folder.

FIGURE I- 26

Who Are We?

Mayer Photography is a family-owned business of professional photographers, providing our customers with the highest-quality images and services. We specialize in portraits, senior class photos, and weddings. If your special day is approaching, pay us a visit and we'll show you how Mayer Photography can help you preserve your memories forever.

A Family Business

Ted and Jane Mayer started Mayer Photography in 1972 after graduating from the New England School of Photography. Their work has won numerous awards in competitions across the country. Joining the business in 1992, their sons, Jason and Andrew, uphold the family tradition of excellence in photography.

Contact us at:

Mayer Photography
8911 Bronte Avenue
Elmridge, NH 79112
603-555-8121

Creating
a Docucentric Desktop

Objectives

- ► **Create a document object**
- ► **Create a Start menu group**
- ► **Create a desktop object**
- ► **Send documents**
- ► **Send documents to programs**
- ► **Use scraps**
- ► **Create a printer shortcut**
- ► **Remove desktop elements**

Document is another word for **file**, which is the electronic data (such as a resume or spreadsheet) that you create with a program. The Windows 98 interface is **docucentric** because the emphasis is on documents rather than on programs. This is an important distinction. With older operating systems, if you wanted to edit a resume, you would first locate and start your word processor, then you would locate and open your resume file. In a docucentric environment, you open your file without worrying about its exact location on your hard disk or even the program that created it. The operating system locates the file and starts the program you need. ◂━ John Casey is going to modify his desktop to get better access to the documents that he uses most often. If you are in a restricted network environment, you might not be able to complete all of the lessons in this unit.

Windows 98

Creating a Document Object

One of the documents that John Casey uses on a regular basis is a memo in which he jots down notes as the work day progresses (things he has to do, calls he has to make, meetings he has to attend, errands he has to run, and so on). This memo has to be easy to create and access. With Windows 98, John can create a document right from his desktop, and he can also place an icon on the desktop to quickly access that document in the future. He creates such a document to record his daily notes. If your network is restricted so you can't place objects on the desktop, you won't be able to do the steps in this unit, but you can read them to familiarize yourself with the concepts. If you are in a lab that does allow you to place icons on the desktop, be sure to restore your desktop to its original appearance when you finish your work. Your first step in this lesson is to check two settings on your computer that will make completing this unit easier.

Steps

1. Close any open programs so you can see the Windows 98 desktop

2. Double-click the **My Computer icon**, click **View**, click **Folder Options**, then click the **View tab**

3. Be sure the **Hide file extensions for known file types check box** is selected (click it if it is not), click **OK**, then close My Computer
   By hiding the file extensions, you don't have to worry about including them when you type the names of your files.

4. Right-click an empty area of your desktop, point to **Active Desktop**, then click **Customize my Desktop** from the pop-up menu

5. Click the **box** in front of Internet Explorer Channel Bar to deselect it if necessary, then click **OK**
   Having the Channel Bar closed will make it easier for you to work with the desktop.

6. Right-click the desktop, point to **New**, then click **Text Document** as shown in Figure J-1
   An icon for a document is placed on your desktop, ready for you to name.

7. Type **Daily Memo** to name the text document you just created, then press **[Enter]**
   The icon on the desktop is a **document icon**. You can distinguish an icon that represents a short-cut from an icon that represents a document by the small arrow 🔗 in the lower-left corner of a shortcut icon. You can delete a shortcut icon from the desktop without removing the object it represents, but if you delete a document icon from the desktop, the document itself is deleted.

8. Double-click the **Daily Memo icon** to open the file
   Windows 98 knows that this is a text document, so it automatically starts Notepad, a program that comes with Windows 98. Notepad is useful when you want to enter text without graphics or extensive formatting.

Trouble?
If your Notepad window scrolls to the right as you type, click Edit, then click Word Wrap so it is checked.

9. Type the text shown in Figure J-2, click the **Close button** to close Notepad, then click **Yes** when prompted to save changes
   Notepad closes. The Daily Memo icon remains on John's desktop, so he can open the memo by simply double-clicking the icon. He does not have to start Notepad first, nor does he have to search for the document on the hard drive.

FIGURE J-1: **Creating a new text document on the desktop**

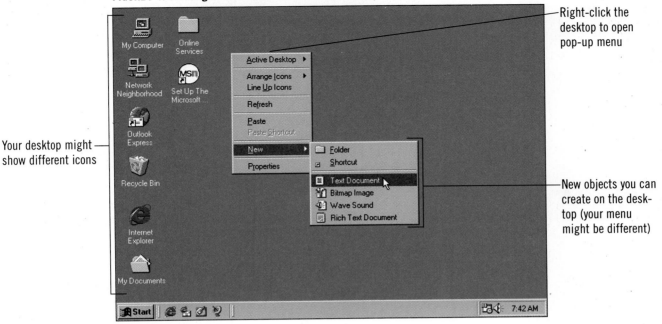

Your desktop might show different icons

Right-click the desktop to open pop-up menu

New objects you can create on the desktop (your menu might be different)

FIGURE J-2: **Daily Memo document on the desktop**

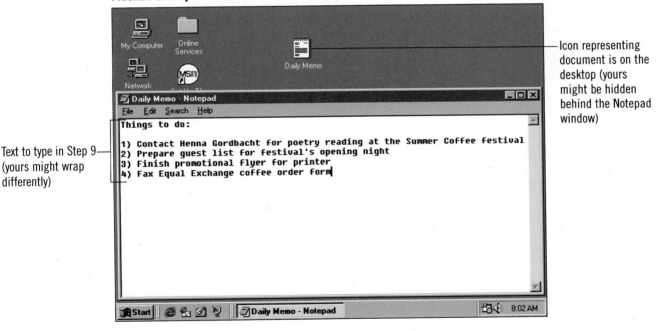

Icon representing document is on the desktop (yours might be hidden behind the Notepad window)

Text to type in Step 9 (yours might wrap differently)

Creating shortcut icons on the desktop

In this lesson, you placed a document on the desktop. You can place a shortcut to any document on your desktop if you want to leave the file in its original location but still have access to it on the desktop. Right-click the desktop, point to New, then click Shortcut on the pop-up menu. Locate the document using the Browse button, click Next, use the name provided or type a name for the shortcut in the dialog box, then click Finish.

Creating a Start Menu Group

A docucentric environment offers many ways for you to access your documents. You can, for example, modify your Start menu so that it lists your documents in addition to the programs you have installed on your computer. The Start menu is organized into different groups, such as the Programs group and the Settings group. You can create your own groups to better organize the tasks you perform and the documents with which you work. ✎ John would like to be able to access his Daily Memo document and other similar documents directly from the Start menu. He decides to add a new group called "Memos" to his Start menu. Then he'll create a shortcut to the Daily Memo on the desktop, and finally, he'll add that shortcut to the new Memos group on his Start menu.

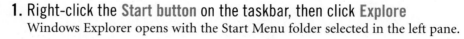

Steps 1 2 3 4

Trouble?

If your right pane displays the icons differently than in Figure J-3, click View, then click Large Icons.

1. **Right-click the Start button on the taskbar, then click Explore**
   Windows Explorer opens with the Start Menu folder selected in the left pane.

2. **If necessary, move or resize the Windows Explorer window so you can see both it and the Daily Memo icon, as shown in Figure J-3**

3. **Click File on the Windows Explorer menu bar, point to New, then click Folder**
   A new folder is placed in the right pane, ready for you to name.

4. **Type Memos, then press [Enter]**
   This folder represents the new Memos group on the Start menu.

5. **On the desktop, right-click the Daily Memo icon, then click Create Shortcut**
   The shortcut is placed on the desktop.

6. **Drag the Shortcut to Daily Memo icon to the Memos folder as shown in Figure J-4 (you might have to move the Windows Explorer window)**

7. **Click the Close button to close Windows Explorer**

8. **Click the Start button on the taskbar, then point to Memos**
   The new Memos group with the Daily Memo shortcut appears on the Start menu, as shown in Figure J-5.

9. **Click outside the Start menu to close it**

FIGURE J-3: **Preparing to add a group to the Start menu**

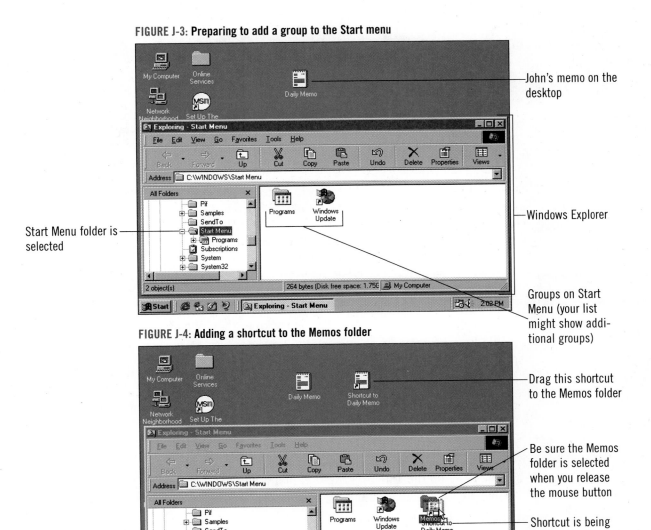

Start Menu folder is selected

John's memo on the desktop

Windows Explorer

Groups on Start Menu (your list might show additional groups)

FIGURE J-4: **Adding a shortcut to the Memos folder**

Drag this shortcut to the Memos folder

Be sure the Memos folder is selected when you release the mouse button

Shortcut is being dragged to the Memos folder

FIGURE J-5: **Start menu with Memos group and shortcut to Daily Memo**

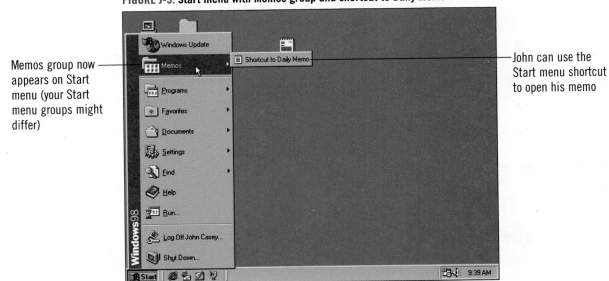

Memos group now appears on Start menu (your Start menu groups might differ)

John can use the Start menu shortcut to open his memo

Creating a Desktop Object

When you added the new Memos group to the Start menu in the last lesson, you opened Windows Explorer, which is used to manage folders on a computer or network. Accessing Windows Explorer was no accident; the contents of the Start menu are determined by the Start Menu folder on your computer. Likewise, the contents of the desktop are determined by the Desktop folder on your computer. To customize your desktop, you must start Windows Explorer, locate and open the Desktop folder, then add or change objects in the Desktop folder. Any changes you make in the Desktop folder are reflected on the desktop itself. Table J-1 shows a list of other common Windows 98 desktop objects and their corresponding folders. 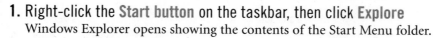 John wants to add a new memo to his desktop. This memo will be the start of a letter he is writing to The Beanery regarding an overdue shipment.

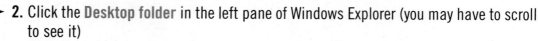

1. **Right-click the Start button on the taskbar, then click Explore**
   Windows Explorer opens showing the contents of the Start Menu folder.

2. **Click the Desktop folder in the left pane of Windows Explorer (you may have to scroll to see it)**
   The Desktop folder on the computer shown in Figure J-6 is located in the Windows folder, which is located on the C drive. The Desktop folder shows the contents of the desktop, with the exception of objects that are part of the desktop, such as My Computer and the Recycle Bin. Notice that the Desktop folder contains the Daily Memo file you created earlier.

3. **Click File on the Windows Explorer menu bar, point to New, then click Text Document**
   An icon for a new document is placed in the Desktop folder, ready to be named.

4. **Type Beanery Memo, then press [Enter]**

5. **Double-click the Beanery Memo icon, then enter the text shown in Figure J-7**

6. **Click the Close button to close Notepad, then click Yes when prompted to save changes**
   The Beanery Memo file is saved and Notepad closes.

7. **Click the Windows Explorer Close button**
   Figure J-8 shows the icon for the new Beanery Memo file that you placed on your desktop from the Desktop folder in Windows Explorer.

Trouble?

If you can't find the Desktop folder, ask your instructor or technical support person for assistance. On some systems, this folder is hidden, so to view it, you must click View, click Folder Options, click the View tab, click the Show all files button, then click OK.

Trouble?

Your Beanery Memo file might appear in a different location on the desktop.

TABLE J-1: Desktop objects and their folders

desktop object	folder
Windows 98 desktop	C:\Windows\Desktop
Most recently opened documents in the Start menu	C:\Windows\Recent
Entries in the Start menu	C:\Windows\Start Menu

FIGURE J-6: Viewing the Desktop folder in Windows Explorer

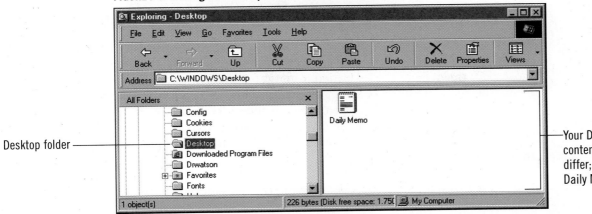

Desktop folder

Your Desktop folder contents might differ; look for the Daily Memo file

FIGURE J-7: Notepad window with John's new memo

Click Edit, then click Word Wrap if text doesn't move to the next line

Enter this text

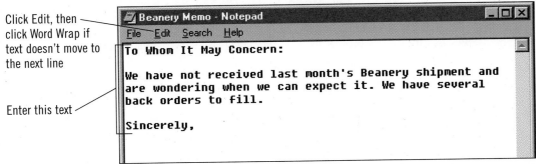

FIGURE J-8: Document you created from Windows Explorer's Desktop folder

Documents in the Desktop folder

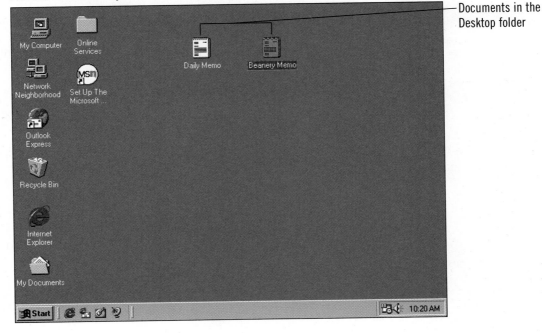

Sending Documents

The Windows 98 **Send To command** provides another way to manage your documents efficiently. Located on the pop-up menu of any desktop object, the Send To command lets you move a document to a new destination. You right-click the document, click Send To, then click the destination you want, like a floppy drive, a printer, or a different folder. If the location you want isn't available in the Send To list, you can add it to the SendTo folder. Then the next time you use the Send To command, the new location will be listed. ◢━━ John would like to be able to send a desktop memo to the Memos group on the Start menu, so he adds this option to the SendTo folder.

1. Right-click the **Start button** on the taskbar, then click **Explore**
   Windows Explorer opens showing the contents of the Start Menu folder.

2. Click the **Memos folder** in the left pane

3. Click **Edit**, then click **Copy**
   The Memos group is copied to the Clipboard so that you can paste it into the SendTo folder.

Trouble?

You might have to scroll to see the SendTo folder. If you can't locate it, see your instructor or technical support person for assistance.

4. Click the **SendTo folder**, click **Edit**, then click **Paste Shortcut**
   A shortcut for the Memos group appears in the SendTo folder, as shown in Figure J-9.

5. Right-click the new **shortcut**, click **Rename**, type **Memos**, then press **[Enter]**
   Renaming the shortcut will allow you to see "Memos" rather than "Shortcut to Memos Group" when you click the Send To command.

6. Click the **Close button** to close Windows Explorer
   Now when John creates a new memo on his desktop, he can easily send it to the Memos group, which will allow him to open the memo from the Start menu in the future. John decides to send his Beanery Memo to the Memos group on the Start menu.

QuickTip

The Send To command moves files if the destination is the same disk, but if the destination is a different disk, Send To copies the file instead.

7. Right-click the **Beanery Memo** on the desktop, point to **Send To**, then click **Memos**, as shown in Figure J-10
   The icon for the Beanery Memo disappears from the desktop. John verifies that it has been placed on his Start menu.

8. Click the **Start button**, then point to **Memos**
   John's Beanery Memo has been placed in the Memos group of the Start menu. See Figure J-11.

9. Click a blank area of the desktop to close the Start menu

FIGURE J-9: **Adding an option to the SendTo folder**

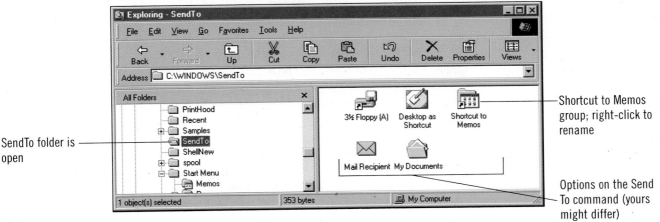

SendTo folder is open

Shortcut to Memos group; right-click to rename

Options on the Send To command (yours might differ)

FIGURE J-10: **Memos group appears on the Send To menu**

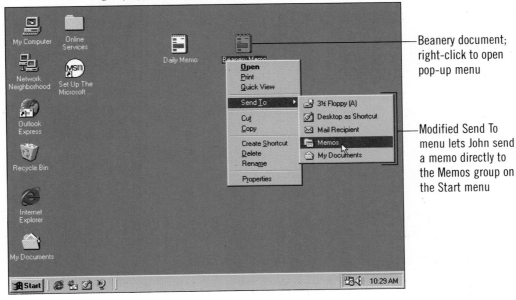

Beanery document; right-click to open pop-up menu

Modified Send To menu lets John send a memo directly to the Memos group on the Start menu

FIGURE J-11: **Document in Memos group**

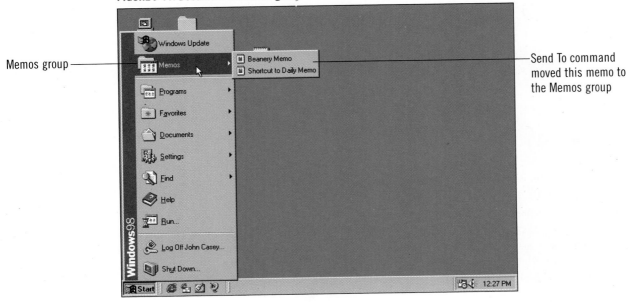

Memos group

Send To command moved this memo to the Memos group

Windows 98

Sending Documents to Programs

Most documents on your desktop are associated with a specific program. For example, if you double-click a document whose filename ends with the three-letter extension ".txt," Windows 98 automatically opens the document with Notepad, a text editor. There are situations, however, when you need to open a document with a program other than the one Windows 98 chooses. For example, you might want to open a text document in WordPad rather than in Notepad so you can add special fonts and graphics. You can add WordPad to the Send To command so you can right-click a document, then select the program in the Send To menu. ✐ John would like to have the option of opening his text memos with WordPad for the times he needs to add special fonts and graphics. To allow for this option, he places a shortcut to WordPad in his SendTo folder.

1. Right-click the Start button on the taskbar, then click Explore
   Windows Explorer opens showing the contents of the Start Menu folder.

2. In the left pane, click the plus box to the left of the Programs folder to display its subfolders, then click the Accessories folder
   The contents of the Accessories folder are displayed in the right pane.

3. In the right pane, right-click the WordPad shortcut icon, then click Copy
   Scroll down the right pane if you don't see the WordPad shortcut icon.

Trouble?

If you are asked if you want to replace a file called WordPad, click No.

4. Locate and right-click the SendTo folder in the left pane, click Paste, then click the SendTo folder in the left pane, if necessary
   The SendTo folder now contains a shortcut to WordPad, so the SendTo command will include the option to send a document to WordPad. See Figure J-13.

5. In the left pane, click the Memos folder in the Start Menu folder
   John opens the Memos folder because he wants to access the Beanery Memo, which was moved in the previous lesson.

Trouble?

If the text in the WordPad window doesn't wrap, click View on the menu bar, click Options, click the Wrap to window option button, then click OK.

6. Right-click the Beanery Memo file, click Send To, then click WordPad
   WordPad opens with the contents of the Beanery Memo, as shown in Figure J-14.

7. Close Windows Explorer but leave WordPad open

File extensions

The program that Windows 98 uses to open a document depends on the extension to the document's filename, called a **file extension.** You will not see a document's file extension if your system is set up to hide it. The file extension for many text files is ".txt" (pronounced "dot t-x-t"), while many graphics files have the extension ".bmp" (pronounced "dot b-m-p"). This means that the full name for your Daily

Memo file is Daily Memo.txt. If you want to change the program that Windows 98 automatically starts with a given file extension, open My Computer, click View, then click Folder Options. Click the File Types tab to see the list of the file extensions that Windows 98 recognizes and the programs that are associated with each of the extensions and make changes as appropriate.

FIGURE J-12: **Locating the WordPad shortcut to add it to the Send To menu**

Programs folder

Accessories folder

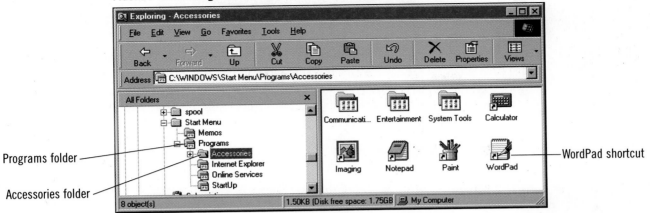

WordPad shortcut

FIGURE J-13: **Option for sending a document to WordPad**

SendTo folder

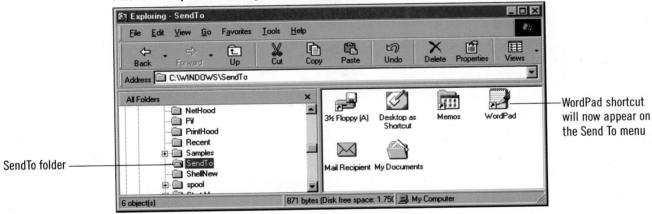

WordPad shortcut will now appear on the Send To menu

FIGURE J-14: **Beanery Memo in WordPad**

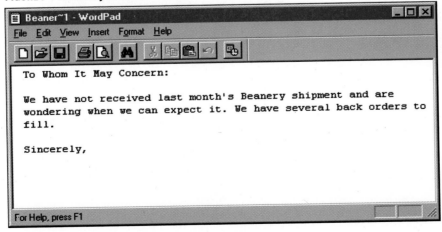

Windows 98

Using Scraps

There are certain text or graphic items, such as your return mailing address, signature, or company logo that you include in almost every document you create. Windows 98 allows you to save such items in special documents called **scraps** that you can easily insert into your documents. John includes his mailing address in many of the notes he writes. He decides to create a scrap containing his address and to place it on his desktop so he can easily drag it into a document whenever he needs it.

Steps

1. With the WordPad document you created in the previous lesson still open, type the new lines shown in Figure J-15 at the start of the memo

2. Select the lines you just typed including the blank line
   You should be able to see the WordPad window and a blank area of the desktop.

QuickTip

If you want to create a document scrap without leaving the selected text or graphic in the original document, press and hold [Shift] while you drag your selection to the desktop.

3. Drag the selected text to the desktop
   The selected text is placed as a document scrap on the desktop, as shown in Figure J-16. You might have to move the WordPad window to see the scrap. Now John can use this scrap in any of his WordPad documents.

4. Click the **Close button** to close the WordPad window, then click **Yes** when prompted to save changes
   John would now like to test the document scrap he just created.

5. Click the **Start button** on the taskbar, point to **Programs**, point to **Accessories**, click **WordPad**, then resize the WordPad window as necessary so that you can see the document scrap on the desktop
   A new document opens in WordPad, which John will use to test the scrap.

6. Drag the **document scrap** into the WordPad window, as shown in Figure J-17
   The contents of the document scrap are placed at the beginning of the new WordPad document. In dropping the scrap into your document, you did not remove it from the desktop; thus, you can use it again.

QuickTip

You can create document scraps for many Windows 98 programs besides WordPad, such as a Paint scrap containing a company logo.

7. Click the **Close button** to close WordPad, then click **No** when prompted to save your changes
   John doesn't need to save this document since he was just using it to test his scrap.

FIGURE J-15: John's revised memo in WordPad

Make sure to include a blank line at the end of the address

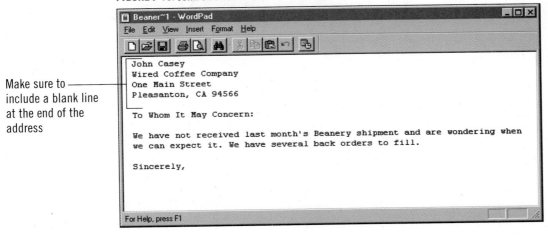

FIGURE J-16: John's memo and the document scrap

Document scrap contains John's address

Drag this selected text to desktop

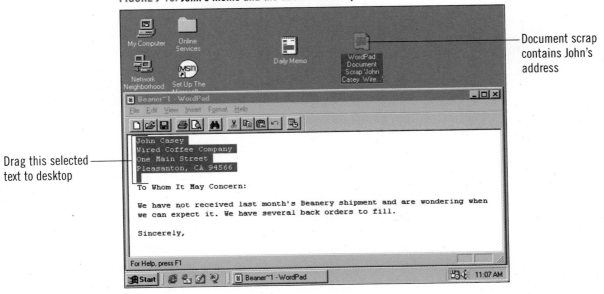

FIGURE J-17: Inserting a document scrap into a document

Document scrap on the desktop

Mouse pointer as you drag scrap into new WordPad document

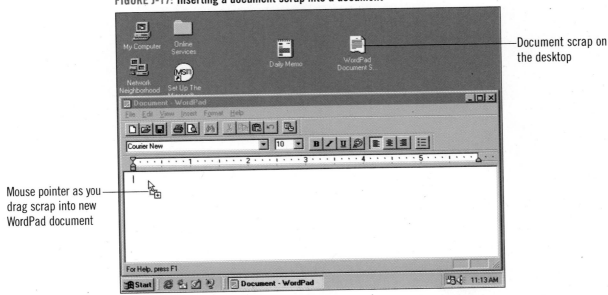

Windows 98

Creating a Printer Shortcut

In addition to placing documents and shortcuts to documents on the desktop, you can also place shortcuts on the desktop to resources, such as drives or printers, on your computer. Once such a shortcut is on your desktop, you can access that resource almost instantaneously. For example, if you regularly use your floppy drive, you might want to create a shortcut to it on the desktop. Then, you don't have to go through My Computer to view its contents; you can simply double-click the shortcut. To add a shortcut to a device on your computer, you use the right mouse button to drag its icon from the My Computer (or Printers) window to the desktop, then click Create Shortcut(s) Here. John decides to place a shortcut to his printer on his desktop. He can then print any document by dragging its icon to the printer shortcut icon. He'll experiment with this by printing his Daily Memo document.

1. Click the **Start button** on the taskbar, point to **Settings**, then click **Printers**
   The Printers window opens.

2. Point to the printer you use, then press and hold the right mouse button

3. Drag the printer icon to the desktop using the right mouse button, then release the right mouse button, as shown in Figure J-18
   A pop-up menu opens.

4. Click **Create Shortcut(s) Here**
   A shortcut to your printer appears on the desktop, as shown in Figure J-19. Your shortcut icon might look different, depending on the printer you are using.

5. Click the **Close button** in the Printers window

6. Drag the **Daily Memo icon** to the printer shortcut icon, as shown in Figure J-20
   Windows 98 opens the Daily Memo document briefly in Notepad, prints it, and then closes the document again so quickly that you might not notice it unless you are watching carefully. John is pleased that he can print his documents without even opening them.

Trouble?

If you receive an error message, you might have created a shortcut to a non-default printer. Printing with a printer shortcut works only with the default printer. See your instructor or technical support person for assistance.

FIGURE J-18: Creating a printer shortcut on the desktop

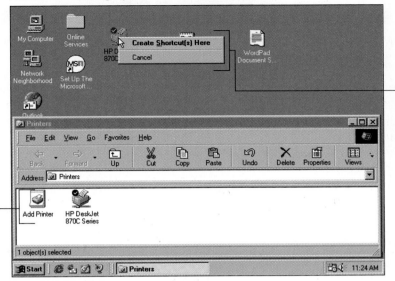

Dragging the printer icon with right mouse button opens this menu

Your list of printers may differ

FIGURE J-19: Printer shortcut

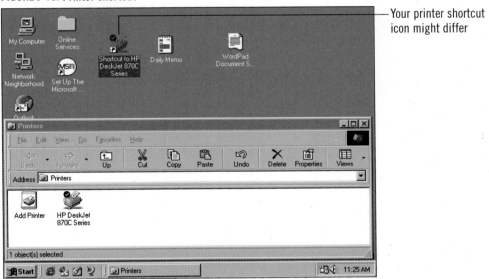

Your printer shortcut icon might differ

FIGURE J-20: Printing a document using the printer shortcut icon

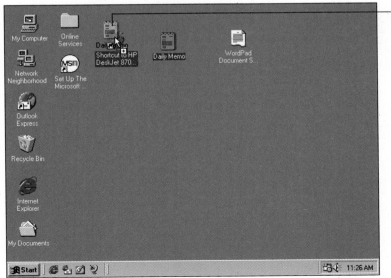

Drag a document icon to the printer shortcut icon to print the document

Removing Desktop Elements

Windows Explorer is an excellent tool for creating and removing parts of your desktop and menus. Rather than using different tools to delete the items you created in this unit, you can use one tool, Windows Explorer, to remove all of the items and return your desktop to its original state. Remove all the modifications you made to the desktop so the next user has a clean desktop.

Steps

1. **Right-click** the **Start button** on the taskbar, then click **Explore**
   Windows Explorer opens showing the contents of the Start Menu folder.

2. **Right-click** the **Memos folder** in the left pane, click **Delete** as shown in Figure J-21, then click **Yes** when prompted to move the selected items to the Recycle Bin

3. Click the **SendTo folder** in the left pane
   The right pane now shows the contents of the SendTo folder. The two shortcuts you created, Memos and WordPad, should be visible.

   > **Trouble?**
   > If your Start Menu, Desktop, and SendTo folders are in different locations, see your instructor or technical support person for assistance.

4. Click the **Memos shortcut**, press and hold down **[Ctrl]**, click the **WordPad shortcut**, then release **[Ctrl]**
   See Figure J-22. The Memos group and the WordPad shortcuts are selected.

5. Click the **Delete button** ⊠ on the toolbar, then click **Yes** to confirm the deletion
   The two shortcuts you created are removed from the SendTo folder.

   > **QuickTip**
   > To select a contiguous group of files you can press and hold [Shift], click the first file, then click the last file in the list; the two files you clicked and all files in between should be selected.

6. Click the **Desktop folder** in the left pane, click the **Daily Memo document** in the right pane, press and hold **[Ctrl]**, click the **document scrap**, click the **shortcut to the printer**, then release **[Ctrl]**
   All three items are selected.

7. Click ⊠, then click **Yes** to confirm deletion
   The two shortcuts and the document scrap you created are removed from the Desktop folder.

8. Close Windows Explorer
   The desktop should now look as it did when you started this unit.

FIGURE J-21: **Deleting the Memos folder from the Start Menu folder**

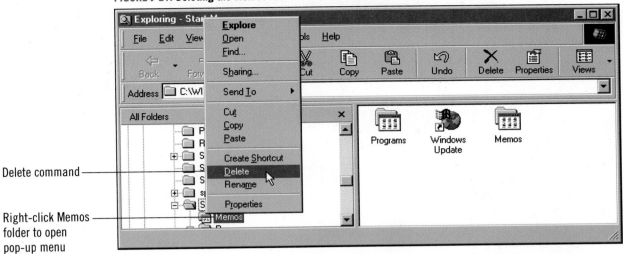

Delete command

Right-click Memos folder to open pop-up menu

FIGURE J-22: **Selected shortcuts that you will delete**

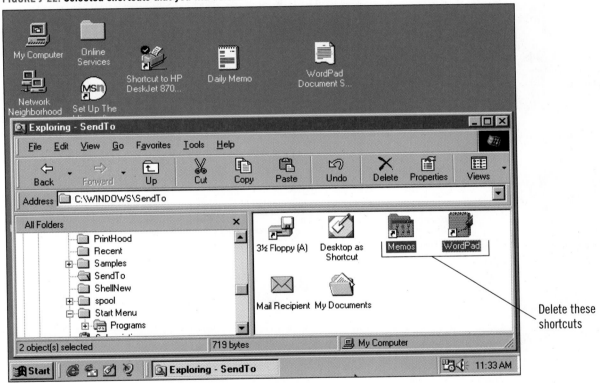

Delete these shortcuts

Using Undo in Windows Explorer

Windows 98 keeps track of all the changes you've made to your folders and documents from the start of your computer session. You can use Windows Explorer to undo all of your work quickly and to restore the folders to their original state. Windows 98 keeps track of the actions you did even when Windows Explorer was not running. To take advantage of this feature, click Edit on the Windows Explorer menu bar, then click Undo (this option may be different depending on the task you are doing). By repeating this command, you will eventually undo every document and folder action that you took in a computer session.

Practice

► Concepts Review

Label each of the elements of the screen shown in Figure J-23.

FIGURE J-23

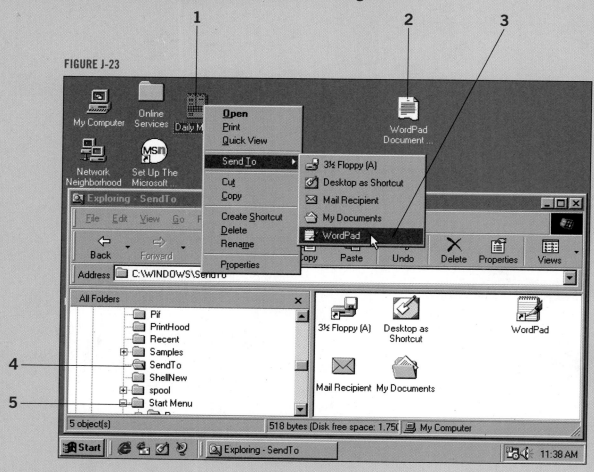

Match each of the terms with the statement that describes its function.

6. Emphasis on documents rather than software
7. A command that redirects a document to a drive, printer, folder, or program
8. A program that you can use to modify both the desktop and the Start menu
9. A piece of a document
10. Program that Windows 98 uses to open text documents
11. Icons on the desktop that target objects stored in different locations on your computer
12. Icons on the desktop that represent actual documents or objects located on the desktop
13. Part of a filename that indicates the program associated with the file

a. Scrap
b. Docucentric
c. Notepad
d. File extension
e. Windows Explorer
f. Send To
g. Icon with a small arrow
h. Icon without a small arrow

Select the best answer from the list of choices.

14. Which of the following is NOT an aspect of a docucentric interface?
    a. Creating documents without starting programs
    b. Accessing documents from several locations
    c. Creating documents from the desktop
    d. Creating documents only from within programs

15. To create a text document on your desktop, you should
    a. right-click the desktop, then click Insert Text.
    b. right-click the desktop, point to New, then click Text Document.
    c. click the Start button, then click Text Document.
    d. open Windows Explorer, click File, click New, then click Text Document.

16. If you set it up properly, you can use the Send To command to send documents to a:
    a. floppy drive.
    b. program.
    c. printer.
    d. all of the above.

17. To quickly open a text document with WordPad, you can use:
    a. a document scrap.
    b. the Send To command.
    c. the Start menu.
    d. the Desktop folder.

18. To create a document scrap on the desktop for selected text in a WordPad document:
    a. right-click the selection, click New, then click Scrap.
    b. right-click the selection, click Send To, then click Scrap.
    c. drag the selection to the desktop.
    d. drag the selection to the scraps folder in Windows Explorer.

19. The part of the filename that indicates the default program for the document is called the:
    a. title bar.
    b. file extension.
    c. document attribute.
    d. all of the above.

Skills Review

For the Skills Review exercises, you will need to make a hard copy of your computer screen. Press [Print Screen] to make a copy of the screen, start Paint, click Edit on the menu bar, click Paste to paste the screen into Paint, then click Yes to paste the large image, if necessary. Click File on the menu bar, click Print, click OK, then close Paint and click No when asked to save changes.

1. **Create a text object on the desktop.**
   a. Right-click an open area on the desktop.
   b. Point to New.
   c. Click Text Document from the pop-up menu.
   d. Type "My Address" for the document name.
   e. Press [Enter].
   f. Double-click the document icon to open it in Notepad.
   g. Type your name, address, and phone number in the document.
   h. Resize the Notepad window so you can see the text you typed and the icon for the document on the desktop, then create a hard copy of your text document on the desktop using the steps listed above.
   i. Click the Close button to exit Notepad.
   j. Click Yes when prompted to save the document.

2. **Add a group titled "Work Documents" to the Start menu.**
   a. Right-click the Start button on the taskbar.
   b. Click Explore.
   c. Click File, point to New, then click Folder from the Windows Explorer menu bar.
   d. Type "Work Documents", then press [Enter].
   e. Create a hard copy of your Windows Explorer window using the steps listed above.
   f. Click the Close button.
   g. Click the Start button on the taskbar and verify that the Work Documents group has been added to the Start menu.

3. **Add a folder object to the desktop.**
   a. Right-click the Start button on the taskbar.
   b. Click Explore from the pop-up menu.
   c. In the left pane, click the Desktop folder.
   d. Click File, point to New, then click Folder.
   e. Type "Important Memos" as the folder name.
   f. Press [Enter].
   g. Resize the Windows Explorer window so you can see the new folder on the desktop and in Windows Explorer, then create a hard copy of your screen using the steps listed before the steps of the Skills Review.
   h. Close Windows Explorer.

4. Modify and use the Send To command.
   a. Right-click the Start button on your taskbar, then click Explore from the pop-up menu.
   b. Click the Work Documents folder in the right pane, click Edit on the menu bar, then click Copy.
   c. Click the SendTo folder in the left pane.
   d. Click Edit on the menu bar, then click Paste Shortcut.
   e. Click the Shortcut to Work Documents icon, click File, then click Rename.
   f. Type "Work Documents", then press [Enter].
   g. Create a hard copy of your screen using the steps listed above.
   h. Click the Close button.
   i. On the desktop, right-click the Important Memos folder, point to Send To on the pop-up menu, then click Work Documents.
   j. Click the Start button on the taskbar, then point to the Work Documents folder to verify that the Important Memos folder has been placed on the Start menu.

5. Send a text document to WordPad.
   a. Right-click the Start button, then click Explore.
   b. Double-click the Programs folder in the left pane, then click the Accessories folder in the left pane.
   c. Click the WordPad icon in the right pane, click Edit on the menu bar, then click Copy.
   d. Click the SendTo folder in the left pane, click Edit, then click Paste Shortcut.
   e. Rename the shortcut to WordPad icon as "WordPad", if necessary.
   f. Print your screen.
   g. Close Windows Explorer, then right-click the My Address text document on your desktop to display the pop-up menu.
   h. Point to Send To, then click WordPad.
   i. Click File, then click Print to open the Print dialog box. Click OK to print the document.

6. Create a document scrap on the desktop.
   a. Type your school's address into the WordPad document. Select the text you just typed, and drag it to the desktop.
   b. Print a hard copy of your screen showing both the WordPad window and the scrap icon on the desktop using the steps listed before the steps of the Skills Review.
   c. Click the Close button to exit WordPad. Do not save the document.
   d. Create a new WordPad document, then drag the scrap into the document.
   e. Print the document from WordPad.
   f. Close WordPad without saving the document.
   g. Click the scrap icon on the desktop, then press [Delete] and Yes to remove it from the desktop, then click Yes, if necessary.

7. Create a printer shortcut.
   a. Click the Start button, point to Settings, then click Printers.
   b. Using the left mouse button, drag the printer icon to the desktop, then click Create Shortcuts Here.
   c. Close the Printers window.
   d. Drag the My Address document, which should still be on the desktop, over the printer icon you created.
   e. Create a hard copy of your window showing both the My Address document icon and the printer icon on the desktop using the steps listed before the steps of the Skills Review.
   f. Right-click the printer icon, click Delete on the pop-up menu, then click Yes to confirm the deletion.

8. Remove objects from the Start menu, Send To command, and Desktop.

   a. Right-click the Start button.
   b. Click Explore from the pop-up menu.
   c. Click the Work Documents folder in the right pane.
   d. Click File on the menu bar, click Delete, then click Yes if necessary.
   e. Click the SendTo folder in the left pane.
   f. Select the Work Documents and WordPad shortcut icons in the right pane.
   g. Click File, click Delete, then click Yes to confirm the deletion.
   h. Click the Desktop folder in the left pane.
   i. Select the My Address and the New WordPad Document text documents, click File, click Delete, then click Yes to confirm the deletion.
   j. Close Windows Explorer.

► Independent Challenges

1. You are a graphic artist at MJ & G Associates. You want to create quick and easy Paint documents to record the ideas that occur to you throughout the day. You decide to take advantage of the ability of Windows 98 to create such objects directly on the desktop.
   To complete this independent challenge:

   1. Right-click the desktop, point to New, then click Bitmap Image.
   2. Name the new Paint file "Idea Sketches."
   3. Double-click the Paint file to open it. If Paint does not open, you might need to configure Windows 98 so that it associates a bitmap image with Paint. See your instructor or technical support person for assistance.
   4. Draw a simple sketch and save it.
   5. Close Paint.
   6. Create a hard copy of your desktop using the steps listed before the steps of the Skills Review.
   7. Remove any changes you made to the desktop.

2. You work as a receptionist in a church office. You want to make it easier to print the documents that you've placed on your desktop. You decide to use drag and drop techniques to create shortcuts on your desktop to your printer.
   To complete this independent challenge:

   1. Double-click the My Computer icon on your desktop.
   2. Double-click the Printers folder in the My Computer window.
   3. Right-click your default printer from the list of printers and while holding down the right mouse button, drag it to an empty space on your desktop.
   4. Click Create Shortcut(s) Here. An icon representing the shortcut to your printer appears on the desktop.
   5. Create a hard copy of your desktop using the steps listed before the steps of the Skills Review.
   6. Test the shortcut to your printer by creating a text document on your desktop and dragging the text document icon to the printer icon.
   7. Remove any changes you made to the desktop.

3. You have been diagnosed with carpal tunnel syndrome and are trying to find ways to minimize your wrist movements. You like the idea of placing objects on your computer's desktop, but you need to avoid too much dragging action with the mouse. You decide to add the Desktop folder to the Send To command so you can easily move documents to the desktop.

To complete this independent challenge:

1. Open Windows Explorer.
2. Copy the Desktop folder to the Clipboard.
3. Paste a shortcut to the Desktop folder in the SendTo folder.
4. Create a hard copy of Windows Explorer using the steps listed before the steps of the Skills Review.
5. Close Windows Explorer.
6. Right-click an object on the desktop to verify that the Send To command has been changed.
7. Create a hard copy of your desktop using the steps listed before the steps of the Skills Review.
8. Remove any changes you made to the desktop.

4. You're the owner of a small bookstore that is being expanded to make room for a coffee bar for your customers. You like the Wired Coffee Company and decide to feature only their blends of coffee. Because you will be visiting the company's Web site frequently to place orders and get updates, you decide to add a shortcut icon to your desktop for the Wired Coffee Company Web site.

To complete this independent challenge:

1. First, create a new shortcut on the desktop.
2. In the Command line box, type the Wired Coffee Company URL, which is http://www.course.com/illustrated/wired/, then press [Enter].
3. Name your shortcut "Wired".
4. Create a hard copy of your desktop with the new Wired shortcut, using the steps listed before the Skills Review.
5. Connect to the Wired Coffee Company Web site using the shortcut icon.
6. Print the first page of the Web site.
7. Remove the Wired shortcut from your desktop.

▶ Visual Workshop

Recreate the screen shown in Figure J-24. It displays three desktop objects: a text document named Phone Numbers, a bitmap image object named Company Logo, and finally, a printer shortcut named My Printer. When you have duplicated this desktop, create a hard copy of your screen using the steps listed before the steps of the Skills Review, then delete the icons from the desktop. (*Hint:* To delete icons from the desktop, you can select them and press [Delete]. You can select multiple desktop objects that are grouped together by dragging a selection box around them. Try this technique to delete the three icons you created for this visual workshop.)

FIGURE J-24

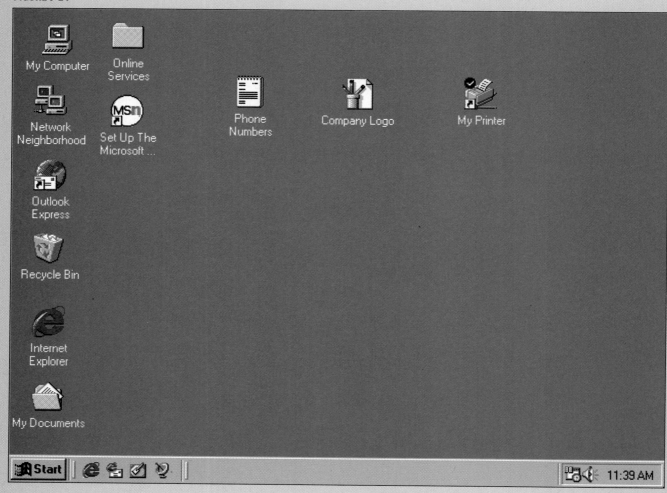

Sharing
Information between Programs

- ► Understand object linking and embedding
- ► Embed a new object
- ► Embed an existing file
- ► Edit an embedded object
- ► Embed a video clip
- ► Modify a video clip
- ► Link an object
- ► Update a link

When you are preparing a document, you can supplement text with pictures and other visuals to make your document more interesting. Charts, tables, and pictures, when combined with succinct text, can convey your message much more effectively than text alone. Windows 98 makes it easy to insert a file (or part of a file) that was created in one program into a file that was created in a different program. The ability to share files and information between different programs is called **object linking and embedding** (**OLE**, pronounced "oh-lay"). With OLE, you can work with a document in WordPad and at the same time, take advantage of the specialized tools in an application like Paint or Microsoft Excel. In this unit, John Casey uses OLE to place a picture of his signature and a picture of his company logo into a sales promotion document. He also uses OLE to insert a video clip into a promotional document and to link a picture to a flier.

Understanding Object Linking and Embedding

Object linking and embedding (OLE) involves sharing information between two programs. This information, often referred to as an **object**, can be a picture from a graphics program, a chart from a spreadsheet program, a video clip, text, or almost anything else you can create on a computer. The program that creates the object is called the **source program**; the program that created the file where you want to insert the object is called the **destination program**. Likewise, the file that originally contains the object is called the **source file**, and the file where you want to insert the object is called the **destination file**. Both embedding and linking involve inserting an object into a destination file; however, they differ in where their respective objects are stored. With **embedding**, a copy of the object becomes part of the destination file. If you want to edit the object, you make changes in that destination file. With **linking**, the object is displayed in the destination file, but it is stored in the source file. There are not two copies of the same object; rather, the object exists in the source file and a representation of the object exists in the destination file. If you want to edit the object, you make changes in the source file, and the changes will be reflected in the destination file. Figure K-1 shows a diagram of embedding an object into a document, and Figure K-2 shows a diagram of linking an object to a document. Table K-1 can help you decide whether to embed or link an object. John wants to explore the benefits of sharing information between programs.

By using OLE, John will be able to do the following:

Access features from other programs

With OLE, John can put information from one program into another. For example, he can insert a picture into WordPad (a word processing program) by using Paint (a drawing program).

Edit data easily

When John embeds or links an object, he can edit the object directly in the embedded program. For example, if John embeds or links a Paint drawing into a WordPad document, he can edit the drawing from WordPad while using Paint tools.

Update to the latest information

John sometimes inserts objects from source files that are accessed by many users. If he inserts the object with a link, Windows 98 will update the object automatically if a user changes the object. For example, John can link a Paint drawing to his WordPad document. If someone changes the Paint drawing, John's WordPad document is updated with the changes the next time he opens the document in WordPad.

Save space

When John links an object to his document, a representation of the object, which takes up less disk space than the object itself, appears in the document. The actual object is stored in the source file; and the destination file stays small. Embedding, on the other hand, can require more disk space because the object is actually copied to the destination file.

FIGURE K-1: **Embedding an object**

Destination program
(WordPad)

Embedded object

Program (Paint) with
open source file

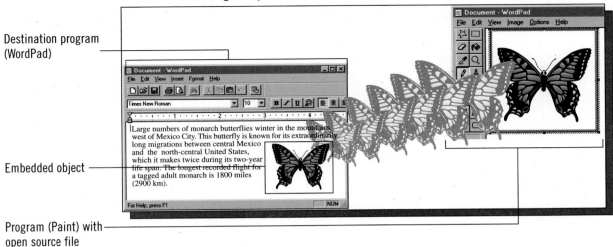

FIGURE K-2: **Linking an object**

Destination program
(WordPad)

Representation of the
object

Linked object

Any changes are
reflected in both files

Source program
(Paint) with open
source file

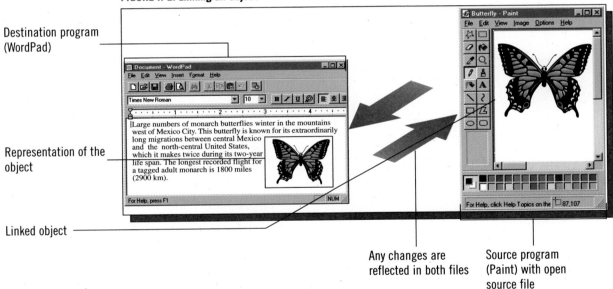

TABLE K-1: **Embedding vs. linking**

situation	action
You are the only user of an object and you want it to be part of your document	Embed
You want to access the object in its source program, even if the original file is not available	Embed
You want to update the object manually while working in the destination program	Embed
You always want an updated object	Link
The object's source file is on a network where others can change or access it	Link
You want to keep your document file size small	Link

Embedding a New Object

Windows 98

Sometimes, an application isn't designed to handle the data you need to display. For example, if you wanted to include a picture in your WordPad document, which is not designed for drawing, you could leave WordPad, start Paint, create a picture in Paint, copy it, return to WordPad, and paste the picture into your document. With Windows 98, however, you don't have to leave WordPad and start Paint. When you embed a Paint object into your WordPad document, Paint automatically opens in WordPad so you can create and edit the drawing without leaving WordPad. Embedding can be done with the Insert Object command and, in some situations, the Copy and Paste commands. ⬥ In this lesson, John will use the Insert Object command to place a picture of his signature at the bottom of a sales document.

Steps

1. Click the **Start button** on the taskbar, point to **Programs**, point to **Accessories**, then click **WordPad**

2. Open the file **WIN K-1** from your Student Disk, then save it as **Sales Promotion** on your Student Disk

3. Maximize the WordPad window (if necessary), scroll to the bottom of the document, then click below the phrase Sincerely yours,

4. Click **Insert** on the menu bar, then click **Object**
   The Insert Object dialog box, shown in Figure K-3, lets you select an object type and specify whether to create a new object or to insert an object from a file that already exists. To draw his signature, John needs to create a new Paint picture.

5. Make sure the **Create New option button** is selected

6. In the Object Type list box, scroll to and click **Paintbrush Picture**, then click **OK**
   An empty Paint canvas appears inside a selection box (gray slanted lines) in the WordPad document, and Paint's menus and tools are available. Though it appears that you have switched to Paint (the source program), the title bar confirms that you are still in WordPad. As long as the Paint object is selected, however, you can use the Paint tools as if you were in the stand-alone Paint program.

7. In the Paint object, drag the **Pencil tool** to draw the name **John**, as shown in Figure K-4
   If you don't like how a line appears, use the Undo command on the Edit menu.

QuickTip

To delete an object in the destination program, click the object, then press [Delete].

8. Click outside of the drawing area to exit Paint, then click to the right of the embedded object in WordPad
   When you click outside the embedded object, you exit the embedded program and return to the destination program. The embedded Paint object becomes part of your document.

9. Click the **Save button** 🖫 on the toolbar
   Compare your screen to Figure K-5.

FIGURE K-3: Insert Object dialog box

Insert Object options

List of objects you can insert (your list might be different)

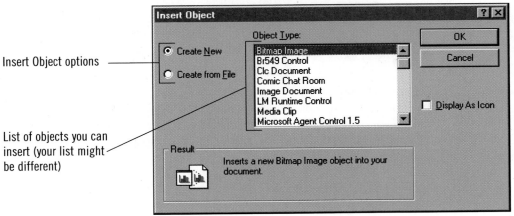

FIGURE K-4: Embedded Paint program

Title bar shows you are still in WordPad

Paint menu bar

Paint Tool Box

Pencil tool

Embedded Paint object

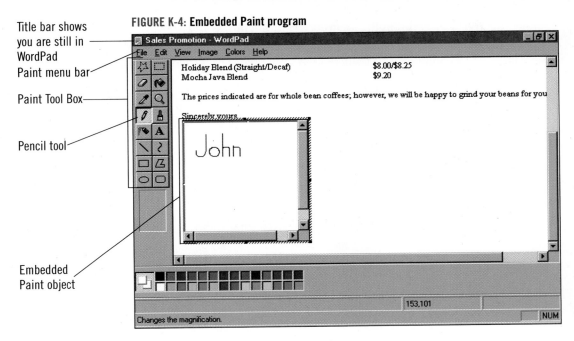

FIGURE K-5: WordPad document with Paint object

Paint object (not currently selected)

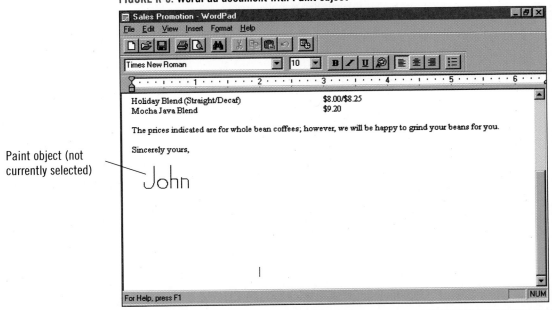

Embedding an Existing File

Windows 98

In addition to creating and embedding an object from scratch, you can also embed an existing file. When you embed an existing file into a document, a copy of the file is stored in the destination document as an object. The original file remains unchanged, and the object becomes part of the document. ➤ John wants to embed the company logo into his sales document.

Steps

1. **In the WordPad document, click above the title "Wired Coffee Company" (scroll if necessary)**
   The insertion point is placed where John wants the company logo to appear.

2. **Click Insert on the menu bar, then click Object**
   The Insert Object dialog box opens.

3. **Click the Create from File option button**
   The Object Type list box changes to the File text box.

4. **Click Browse, click the Look in list arrow, locate the drive that contains your Student Disk, click Wired Coffee Logo, then click Insert**
   As shown in Figure K-6, the full path name appears in the File text box. The object type for Wired Coffee Logo is a bitmap image. A **bitmap image (BMP)** is a common file format for pictures that are used by drawing programs.

5. **Click OK**
   The embedded object is inserted into the WordPad document. Compare your screen to Figure K-7. Sizing handles appear around the embedded object. In WordPad, the sizing handles are used to change the shape and size of the embedded object.

6. **Click the Save button 🖫 on the toolbar**

QuickTip

When you insert an existing file into a document, the source program for the embedded object is not opened. You can open the source program by double-clicking the object.

FIGURE K-6: Insert Object dialog box

Full path name of
your file appears
here

Click to find file

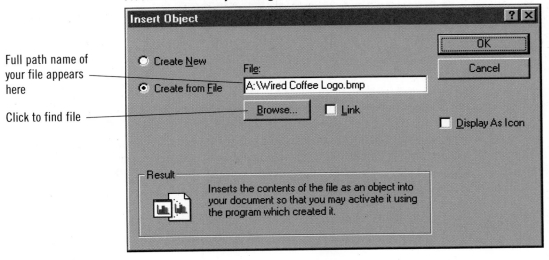

FIGURE K-7: WordPad document with embedded object file

Embedded
object

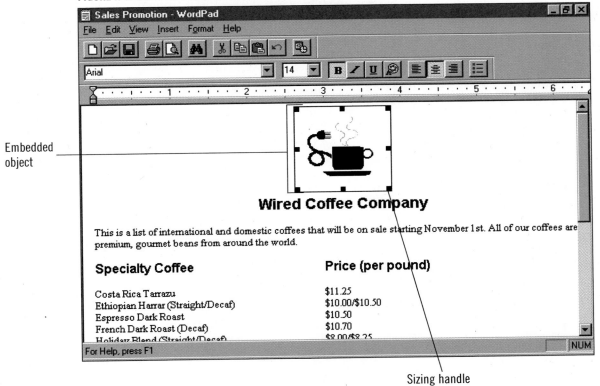

Sizing handle

CLUES TO USE

Viewing object properties

You can click Object Properties on the Edit menu to examine an object's properties, such as type, size, and location. The General tab appears with the object information, including the object's type and original location. You can also change the appearance of an object with the View tab in the Object Properties dialog box.

An embedded object can appear as editable information, such as a picture or chart, or as an icon. By default, an object is displayed as editable information, but you can change an object to appear as an icon in order to save space.

Windows 98

Editing an Embedded Object

To edit or change the information in an embedded object, you can double-click the object in the destination file. Windows 98 locates the object's source program and opens the program in the destination file. You don't have to leave the program in which you are working. Once the source program is open, you edit the information as you normally would. When you're done, you click outside the object and Windows 98 returns you to the destination program (in this case, WordPad). ✏️ John wants to enlarge and add color to the Wired Coffee Logo in the sales document.

Steps 1234

1. **Double-click the Wired Coffee Logo**
   The source program (Paint) opens from within the WordPad document. If you can't see the entire object in WordPad, scroll bars will appear around the logo, so you might need to resize the object to fit in WordPad.

2. **If necessary, position the ↖ pointer over the lower-right sizing handle of the embedded object, then drag the sizing handle to match Figure K-8**
   Sizing handles are the small black boxes around the edge of a selected object. As you drag the sizing handles of an embedded object, the border size of the object changes.

3. **Click the Fill With Color button 🔲 on the Paint Tool Box**
   The pointer changes to 🪣 when you move it in the Paint object.

4. **Click the third color cell (from the left) in the second row of the Paint Color Box**
   The Foreground color in the Paint Color Box changes to red, as shown in Figure K-9. John wants the coffee cup to be red.

5. **Click the tip of 🪣 inside the coffee cup**
   The Fill With Color tool fills only the area inside the lines. If you fill the wrong area, use the Undo command to reverse the action and try again.

6. **Click the seventh color cell in the second row of the Paint Color Box, then click the tip of 🪣 inside the saucer below the cup**
   The saucer is filled with blue.

7. **Click outside the object to exit Paint, then click to the right of the embedded object**
   The embedded Paint program closes and you return to WordPad. Compare your screen to Figure K-10. The changes you made to the embedded object appear only in this document. If you opened the Wired Coffee Logo in Paint, you would see that it is still black and white.

8. **Click the Save button 🔲 on the toolbar**

FIGURE K-8: **Editing an embedded object in Paint**

Sizing handle for embedded object

Drag this sizing handle

Foreground color preview box

FIGURE K-9: **Paint Color Box**

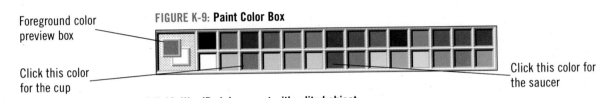

Click this color for the cup

Click this color for the saucer

FIGURE K-10: **WordPad document with edited object**

Paint object changes appear here, but not in original logo file

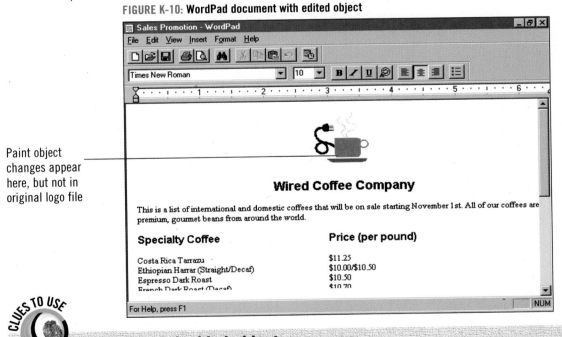

CLUES TO USE

Saving an embedded object

If you have changed an embedded object and you decide to save the object not only in the destination program but also in a separate file, you can save a copy of the embedded object. For example, to save a copy of the color logo in a separate file, select the image, click Edit on the WordPad menu bar, point to Bitmap Image Object, then click Open. The Paint program opens with the company logo in a separate Paint window that is in front of the WordPad window. Click File on the menu bar, click Save Copy As, then save the file. To exit Paint and return to WordPad, click File on the menu bar, then click Exit & Return to Sales Promotion.

Embedding a Video Clip

Windows 98

With Windows 98 you can transform a simple document into a multimedia document by adding a video or sound clip. You can play back the clip with **Media Player**, an accessory program that comes with Windows 98 that plays audio, video, or animation files, and controls the settings for multimedia hardware devices. See Table K-2 for a description of the Media Player media types. To play a video clip that has audio, you need to have a sound card. You can still play a video without a sound card, but you won't get any sound. To insert a video clip into a document, you use the Object command on the Insert menu. ◢ John wants to insert a video clip into a WordPad document in order to promote international coffee.

Steps 1 2 3 4

1. **In WordPad, open the file WIN K-2 from your Student Disk, then save it as Global Coffee on your Student Disk**
   WordPad closes the Sales Promotion document and opens the new document.

2. **In the Global Coffee document, click two lines below the title "Wired Coffee Company"**
   The insertion point is placed where John wants the video to appear.

3. **Click Insert on the menu bar, then click Object**
   The Insert Object dialog box opens.

4. **Click the Create from File option button**
   The Object Type list box changes to the File text box.

5. **Click Browse, click the Look in list arrow, locate the drive that contains your Student Disk, click Globe, then click Insert**
   The full path name of the video clip appears in the File text box. The file's object type, Video Clip, appears above the File text box. John is ready to embed the video clip into the WordPad document.

6. **Click OK**
   The video clip is embedded in the WordPad document. Sizing handles appear around the embedded object. Compare your screen to Figure K-11. John wants to play the video clip.

7. **Double-click the video clip to play it, then quickly click the Pause button ❚❚ on the Control Bar**
   The video clip plays until you pause it, as shown in Figure K-12, or until it reaches the end of the video clip. When you play a video clip, a Control Bar appears with playback buttons, such as Play, Stop, and Pause, that are similar to those on a VCR.

8. **Click the Play button ▶ on the Control Bar**
   The video plays until the end, then stops.

Trouble?

If the video clip ends before you click the Pause button, you will see that the Pause button changes back to the Play button. Double-click the globe or press the Play button to start the video clip again, then press the Pause button.

Inserting a sound

You can insert a new or existing sound into a document in the same fashion that you insert a video clip. To insert a sound, click Insert, click Object, then click the Wave Sound object type or browse to select a sound in the Object dialog box. The Sound Recorder embedded program opens. Sound Recorder allows you to adjust volume and speed, add echo, play in reverse, and mix sound elements to create the effect you want. When you exit Sound Recorder, a small speaker icon appears in your document. Before you can play a sound, you need to install a sound card and speakers.

FIGURE K-11: WordPad document with video clip

Double-click globe to play the video clip

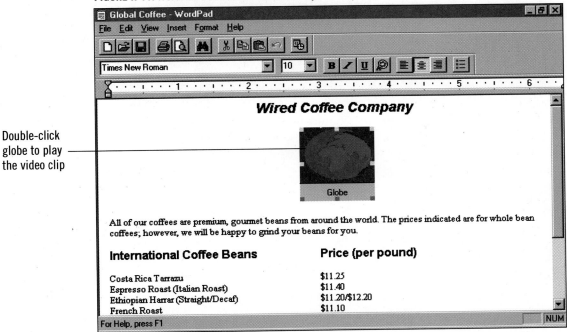

FIGURE K-12: Embedded video clip with Control Bar

Click to play video

Control Bar

Click to stop video

Drag to rewind or forward video

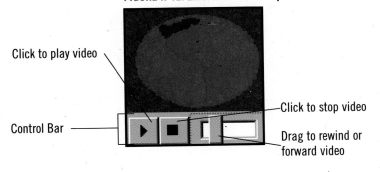

TABLE K-2: Media Player media types

media type	media format	hardware	description
Video	Video for Windows or ActiveMovie	None	Continuous digital video
Animation	Video for Windows	None	A series of graphic images
Audio	CD Audio	Sound card and speakers	A series of sound waves
Musical Instrument Device Interface (MIDI)	MIDI Sequencer	Sound card and speakers	Electronic instructions to play sheet music

Windows 98

Modifying a Video Clip

After you insert a video clip, you can edit it or modify its playback options. Media Player offers basic editing capabilities to select, cut, copy, and paste segments of a video clip. Media Player also allows you to set the video clip to automatically repeat or rewind, to display the Control Bar, and to set display and playback options. You can buy specialized software for advanced editing, recording, or compressing of video clips. ✎ John wants to modify the playback options of the Globe video clip so that it repeats and so the Control Bar is not displayed.

1. **Right-click the Globe video Clip Object, point to Video Clip Object, then click Edit**
   The Media Player menus and toolbar appear, as shown in Figure K-13. John changes the playback options of the Globe video clip for a better look in the document.

2. **Click Edit on the menu bar, then click Options**
   The Options dialog box opens, as shown in Figure K-14.

3. **If necessary, click the Control Bar On Playback check box to deselect it**
   The Control Bar On Playback option appears deselected and the Control Bar will not appear when you play the video clip.

4. **If necessary, click the Auto Repeat check box to select it**
   The Auto Repeat option appears checked and the video will repeat when it is done playing.

5. **Click OK**
   The video clip appears without the Control Bar.

6. **Click the Play button ▶ on the Media Player toolbar**
   The video clip plays without the Control Bar and automatically repeats until you click the Stop button.

7. **Click the Stop button ■ on the Media Player toolbar**
   Compare your screen to Figure K-15. Because the settings you specified will apply to all files played using the Media Player, you should restore the original settings.

8. **Click Edit on the menu bar, click Options, click the Auto Repeat check box to deselect it, click the Control Bar On Playback check box to select it, type Globe in the Caption text box, then click OK**

9. **Click a blank area of the WordPad window to exit Media Player, click the Save button 🖫 on the WordPad toolbar, then click the Close button in the WordPad window**

QuickTip
To start Media Player separately, click Start, point to Programs, point to Accessories, point to Multimedia, then click Media Player.

FIGURE K-13: Embedded Media Player program in WordPad

Media Player
menu bar

Media Player
toolbar

Embedded
video clip

Control Bar

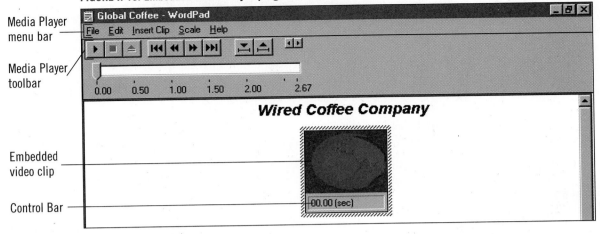

FIGURE K-14: Options dialog box

Click to select Auto
Repeat

Click to deselect
the Control Bar

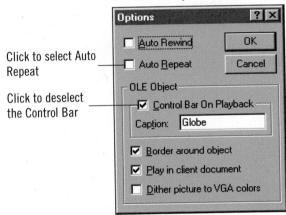

FIGURE K-15: Video clip with new settings

Embedded
video clip
(Control Bar
no longer
showing)

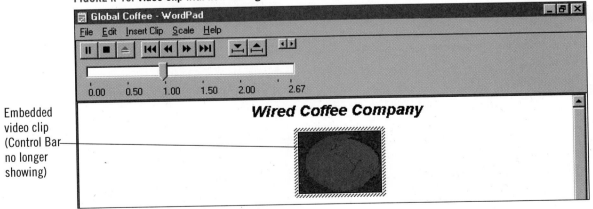

Linking an Object

When you want to keep source and destination files in synch with each other, you can link the source file that created the object with the destination file that displays the object. Unlike an embedded object, which is stored directly in the destination file, a linked object remains stored in its source file. Only a representation of the object appears in the destination file. You can edit the object itself in the source file, or you can edit its representation in the destination file—either way, changes you make will be updated in the other file the next time you open the other file. John wants to link a picture of a coffee cup to an informational flier he is creating, so that if he decides to change the picture, it will be changed in the flier as well.

Steps

1. Start **Paint**, open the file **Coffee Cup** from your Student Disk, save it as **Coffee Cup Image** on your Student Disk, then close Paint
   Saving the file with a new name will keep the original file intact.

2. Start **WordPad**, open the document **WIN K-3** from your Student Disk, then save it as **Roasting Flier** on your Student Disk

3. In the WordPad document, click two lines below the title "Wired Coffee Company"

4. Click **Insert** on the menu bar, click **Object**, then click the **Create from File option button**
   The Insert Object dialog box opens.

5. Click **Browse**, click the **Look in list arrow**, locate the drive that contains your Student Disk, click **Coffee Cup Image**, then click **Insert**
   So far you have done the same steps that you would do for embedding; however, John wants to link the two files so when he changes the coffee cup image in Paint or in the destination file, the revisions are seen in all of the documents linked to the source file.

6. Click the **Link check box**, as shown in Figure K-16, then click **OK**
   The linked object appears on the WordPad page, as shown in Figure K-17. The linked object looks just like an embedded object; the difference is that any changes you make will affect both files. You can check or change the status of a linked file with the Links commands. John checks the link status of the coffee roast link image.

7. Click **Edit** on the menu bar, then click **Links**
   The Links dialog box appears, as shown in Figure K-18. For supported programs, you can automatically update a linked object when the associated file is revised and saved. For more control, you can manually update the revised file. Since the image is located on a removable disk, it is a good idea to change the update status of the link from automatic to manual. John changes the update status.

8. Click the **Manual option button**, click **Close**, then click the **Save button** on the WordPad toolbar

Linking objects using Paste Special

You can link files by copying and pasting. For example, if you want to link a chart from a Microsoft Excel file to a Word document, you open the Excel file, select the chart, then click Copy. Open the Word document, click Edit on the menu bar, click Paste Special, click the Paste Link option button, then click OK.

FIGURE K-16: Insert Object dialog box

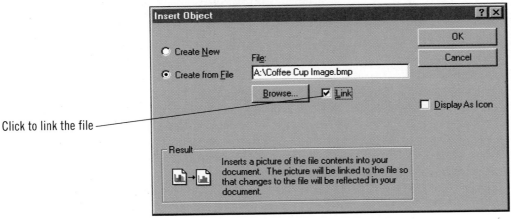

Click to link the file

FIGURE K-17: WordPad document with linked object

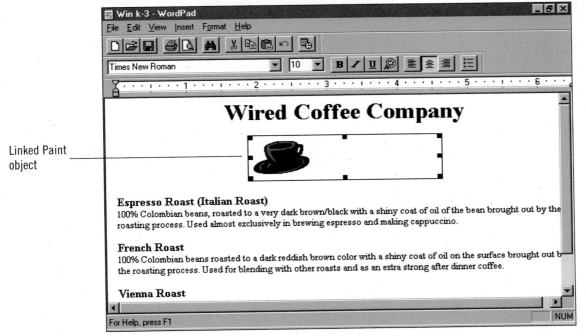

Linked Paint object

FIGURE K-18: Links dialog box

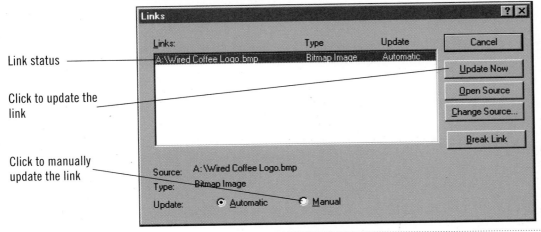

Link status

Click to update the link

Click to manually update the link

Windows 98

Updating a Link

When you want to edit a linked object, you can double-click it in the destination file, just as you do with embedded objects, or you can start the source program, open the source file, and make and save your changes. When you double-click a linked object in the destination file, the source program and source file open in a separate window from the destination file. Remember that the object is only represented in the destination file, so any changes you want to make to the object are done in the source file, whether you access it by double-clicking the object in the destination file or by opening it in the source program. John wants to add some text to the coffee cup image. He'll open the linked Paint object, add some information, then update the linked object in WordPad.

Steps

QuickTip

To open a linked object, the object's source program and source file must be available on your computer or network.

Trouble?

If you can't see the Fonts toolbar, click View, then click Text Toolbar.

1. **Click the Start button, point to Programs, point to Accessories, click Paint, then open the file Coffee Cup Image from your Student Disk**
   Paint opens, displaying the linked file.

2. **Click the Text button A on the Paint Tool Box, then drag to create a text box, as shown in Figure K-19**
   The text box appears with an insertion point and the Fonts toolbar.

3. **Click the Font list arrow on the Fonts toolbar, click Arial Narrow (Western) or a similar font, click the Font Size list arrow, , then click 14**

4. **Click the text box, then type A great cup of coffee is all in the roasting!**
   The text automatically wraps inside the text box. When the text box initially appears, you can edit the text. Press [Backspace] to correct any mistakes.

5. **Click a blank area outside the text box**
   When you deselect the text box, the text becomes part of the image. Compare your screen to Figure K-20. John is satisfied with the changes, so he exits Paint.

6. **Click the Close button in the Paint window, then click Yes to save the changes**
   Paint closes and the WordPad window appears.

7. **Click the linked object to select it, click Edit on the menu bar, then click Links**
   The Links dialog box opens. The Links dialog box allows you to open the source file, change the source file, or break the link. You can also change the way linked objects are updated; the default setting is automatic.

8. **Click the Update Now button, then click Close**
   Compare your screen to Figure K-21. Notice that the linked object shows the changes you made in Paint.

9. **Click the Close button in the WordPad window, then click Yes to save the changes**

FIGURE K-19: **Paint object with text box**

Fonts toolbar

Drag from here to create text box

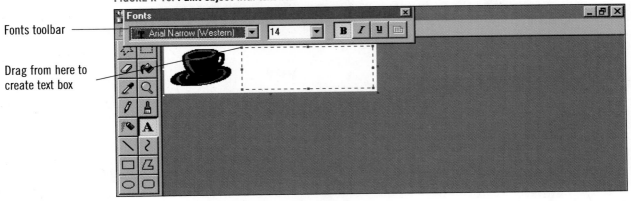

FIGURE K-20: **Paint object with new text**

Text becomes part of the object

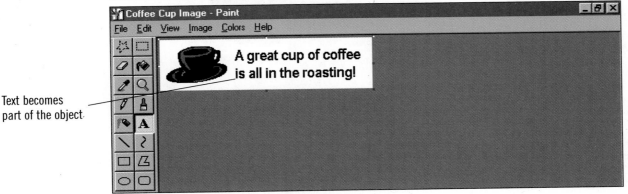

FIGURE K-21: **WordPad document with updated object**

Updated paint object

CLUES TO USE

Finding and changing a linked object

Instead of opening a linked object from the source file to make changes, you can open a linked object from the destination file using the Open Source button in the Links dialog box. The Open Source button finds the source file containing the linked object and opens that file. After making changes, you exit and return to the destination file. The Links dialog box keeps track of the source file location. You can change the linked source to a different file by using the Change Source command, or you can disregard a link by using the Break Link command.

Practice

► Concepts Review

Label each of the elements of the screen shown in Figure K-22.

FIGURE K-22

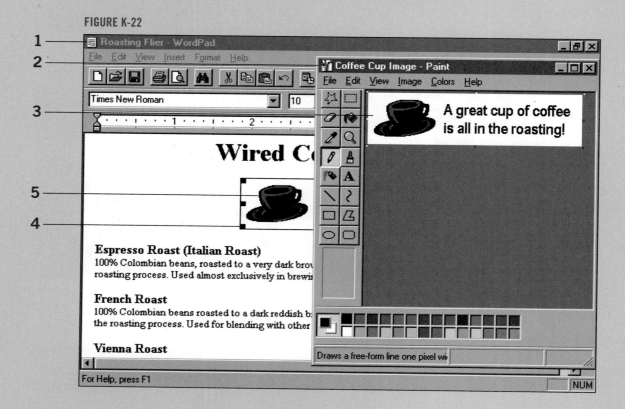

Match each of the terms with the statement that describes its function.

6. An object created in one program and stored in another   a. Object
7. The place where an embedded object is stored   b. Embedded object
8. The WordPad menu command to embed a file   c. Links
9. WordPad menu command to check the status of a document's links   d. Link
10. The place where a linked object is stored   e. Destination file
11. The connection between an object from a source file and the   f. Source file
respective destination file

Select the best answer from the list of choices.

12. Which of the following objects can be embedded into WordPad?
   a. Video clip
   b. Picture
   c. Microsoft Excel chart
   d. All of the above

13. **Which type of object is stored only in its source file?**
   a. A linked object
   b. An embedded object
   c. A text placeholder
   d. None of the above

14. **Which program would you most likely use to create an embedded object that resembles a drawing?**
   a. Media Player
   b. Microsoft Word
   c. Microsoft Paint
   d. Microsoft Excel

15. **Each of the following is true about embedded objects, *except*:**
   a. Embedded objects are editable from the destination file.
   b. Embedded objects are stored in the destination file.
   c. Embedded objects are displayed in the destination file.
   d. Embedded objects are stored in the source file.

16. **Each of the following is false about linked objects, *except*:**
   a. To edit a linked object, you must open its source file.
   b. A linked object is an independent object embedded directly in a document.
   c. You can access a linked object even when the source file is not available.
   d. A linked object substantially increases your destination file size.

17. **Which of the following is NOT true about updating a link?**
   a. You can manually update a link.
   b. You can update a linked object even when the link is broken.
   c. When you link an object, the default setting for updating is "automatic."
   d. An automatic link updates when the source file is saved.

▶ Skills Review

1. **Embed a new object.**
   a. Start WordPad.
   b. Open the file "WIN K-4" from your Student Disk.
   c. Save the document as "Company Memo" on your Student Disk.
   d. Click below the phrase "Sincerely yours."
   e. Click Insert, then click Object.
   f. Click the Paintbrush Picture object type, then click OK.
   g. Draw John's signature in the embedded object.
   h. Click outside the object to exit Paint.
   i. Save the WordPad document.

2. **Embed an object file.**
   a. Click the blank line above the title at the top of the WordPad document.
   b. Click Insert, then click Object.
   c. Click the Create from File option button, click Browse, then locate the drive containing your Student Disk.
   d. Click the file "Wired Coffee Company Logo."
   e. Click Insert, then click OK.

    f. Click outside the object to exit Paint.

    g. Save the WordPad document.

3. **Edit an object.**

    a. Double-click the Wired Coffee Company Logo at the top of the WordPad document.

    b. Click the Fill With Color tool, choose a color, then click the cup to change it to a different color.

    c. Click outside the object to exit Paint.

    d. Save the WordPad document.

4. **Insert a video clip.**

    a. Click the blank line below the title in the WordPad document.

    b. Click Insert, click Object, click the Create from File option button, then click Browse.

    c. Locate the drive with your Student Disk, then click the Globe video clip file.

    d. Click Insert, then click OK.

    e. Play the video clip.

    f. Save the WordPad document.

5. **Modify a video clip.**

    a. Right-click the video clip, point to Video Clip Object, then click Edit.

    b. Click Edit, then click Options.

    c. Click the Control Bar On Playback check box to deselect it.

    d. Click the Auto Repeat check box to select it, then click OK.

    e. Play the video clip, then stop it.

    f. Click Edit on the menu bar, then click Options.

    g. Click the Control Bar On Playback check box to select it.

    h. Type "Globe" in the Caption text box.

    i. Click the Auto Repeat check box to deselect it.

    j. Click OK.

    k. Click outside the object to exit Media Player.

    l. Save the WordPad document.

    m. Exit WordPad.

6. **Link an object.**

    a. Start Paint.

    b. Open the file "Burst Sign" from your Student Disk.

    c. Save the file as "Burst Sign Image" on your Student Disk.

    d. Exit Paint.

    e. Start WordPad.

    f. Open the file "WIN K-5" from your Student Disk.

    g. Save the document as "Holiday Sale" on your Student Disk.

    h. Click the second blank line below the title of the WordPad document.

    i. Click Insert, Click Object, click the Create from File option button, then click Browse.

    j. Locate the drive containing your Student Disk, click the file "Burst Sign Image," then click Insert.

    k. Click the Link check box to select it, then click OK.

    l. Click Edit, click Links, click the Manual option button, then click Close.

    m. Save the document.

7. Update a link.
  a. Start Paint.
  b. Open the file "Burst Sign Image" from your Student Disk.
  c. Click the Text tool, then drag to create a text box inside the burst sign.
  d. Type "Sale"(do not click outside the text box yet).
  e. Click the Font Size list arrow on the Fonts toolbar, then click a font size that matches the text in the burst.
  f. Click outside the text box.
  g. Save your changes to the file, then close Paint.
  h. Make sure the burst image is selected in the WordPad document, click Edit, then click Links.
  i. Click Update Now, then click Close.
  j. Save and print the document.
  k. Close WordPad.

► Independent Challenges

Note: Do not use your Student Disk for the Independent Challenges in this unit. Instead, label a blank, formatted disk "IC Disk". Use the IC Disk for the Independent Challenges in this unit. If you work through all the Independent Challenges and Visual Workshop, you might need a second IC Disk.

1. You opened a small arts and craft store called Stamp By Me. You want to create a flier that contains sales and promotional information for the next three months.
To complete this independent challenge:

1. Start Paint, then create a Sales Logo. You can create your own or use the Text tool and the Rectangle tool to place the name of the store inside a rectangle.
2. Save the image as "Sales Logo" on your IC Disk, then close Paint.
3. Start WordPad.
4. Enter store information, including the name, address, city, state, zip, phone number and store hours of the arts and craft store.
5. Enter store specials. They can include "buy one, get one of equal or lesser value at 50% discount," "25% off," or anything else.
6. Create a calendar with dates such as the following: "January 5, Introduction to Stamping," "March 2, Introduction to Stamping," and "March 19, Masking, Reverse Images, and Other Tricks."
7. Format the information in the document.
8. Above the name of the arts and craft store, embed the Sales Logo image from your IC Disk.
9. Embed a new bitmap image of your signature at the bottom of the document.
10. Close Paint and return to WordPad.
11. Proofread your flier and correct any errors.
12. Print the flier.
13. Save the flier as "Stamp By Me" to your IC Disk.
14. Close WordPad.

2. You are the owner of Hiezer Bakery. In an attempt to increase sales to businesses, you want to create a new catering menu with pastries and desserts. Using WordPad, enter and format text, then embed and edit a drawing to make the menu appealing.

To complete this independent challenge:

1. Start Paint, then create a rectangular frame using the Rectangle tool. Add appropriate text using the Text tool.
2. Save the image as "Menu Sign" to your IC Disk, then close Paint.
3. Start WordPad.
4. Create a menu with descriptions of at least 5 items.
5. Format the menu information to make it readable and attractive.
6. Embed the file "Menu Sign" from your IC Disk at the top of your menu.
7. Edit the embedded object from WordPad so that it contains the text "Now offering catering!" inside a circle.
8. Proofread your document and correct any errors.
9. Save the document as "Hiezer Menu" to your IC Disk.
10. Print the document.
11. Close WordPad.
12. Open Paint, then open and print the Menu Graphic file.
13. Close Paint.

3. You are the director of sales at Classified Collectibles, a large distributor of stamps, pins, coins, and other rare items. You are seeking rights to distribute Olympic memorabilia to retail stores across the country. Write a letter to persuade the United States Olympic Committee to grant you the exclusive rights. Assume the following facts:

- The company currently distributes United States collectible stamps and coins.
- The company currently distributes 15,000 items through 25 distribution centers in the United States.
- There are four direct-sales centers with toll-free numbers.

To complete this independent challenge:

1. Start Paint.
2. Create the Olympic logo rings using the Ellipse tool. (To make perfect circles, press [Shift] while you drag the Ellipse tool.) Add color to the rings.
3. Save the image as "Olympic Rings" to your IC Disk, then close Paint.
4. Start WordPad.
5. Write a letter to convince the Olympic Committee to award you the contract, and format the letter as needed.
6. Save the WordPad file as "Olympic Letter" to your IC disk.
7. Link the file "Olympic Rings" on your IC Disk to your document.
8. Start Paint and open the file "Olympic Rings."
9. Add the text "Classified Collectibles" to the logo, then exit Paint.
10. Update the linked file in your WordPad document.
11. Print the document.
12. Save the file, then close WordPad.

4. You are the president of Garfield Graffiti Removal, Inc., a company that specializes in the removal of graffiti. The company's patented RemoveX system removes paint from all types of surfaces. After removing the paint, GGRI restores surfaces with PreventX, a special clear coating that makes graffiti easier to clean up in the future. Write a letter to persuade the Los Angeles city council to award GGRI the contract to remove graffiti from city property.

To complete this independent challenge:

1. Start Paint.
2. Create a logo for GGRI.
3. Save the logo as "GGRI Logo" to your IC Disk, then close Paint.
4. Start WordPad.
5. Write a letter to convince the city council to award GGRI the contract, and format the letter as needed.
6. Save the document as "LA Graffiti" to your IC Disk.
7. Link the file GGRI Logo on your IC Disk to your letter.
8. Start Paint and open the GGRI Logo.
9. Add graffiti to the GGRI Logo using the Airbrush tool (the fifth tool down in the left column), then close Paint.
10. Update the linked file in your document.
11. Print the document.
12. Save the file, then close WordPad.

▶ Visual Workshop

Create a document that looks like the example in Figure K-23. Use WordPad as the destination program and Paint as the source program; use linking to save disk space. Save the document as "Accident Report" to your IC Disk. Print the document.

FIGURE K-23

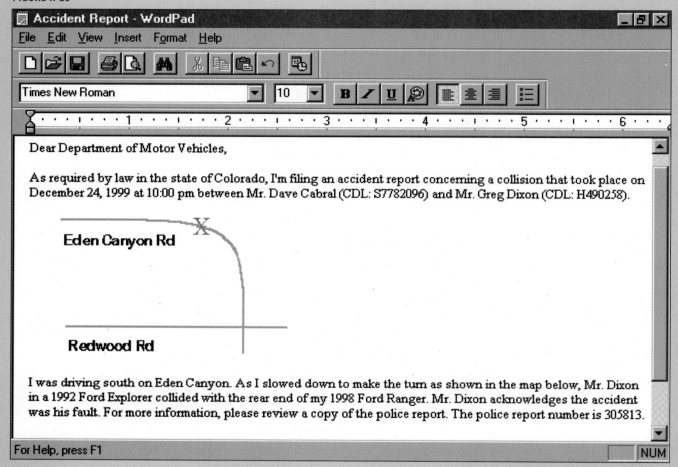

Maintaining
Your Computer

Objectives

► **Make an emergency startup disk**
► **Format a disk**
► **Copy a disk**
► **Find and repair disk errors**
► **Defragment a disk**
► **Install a program**
► **Compress a disk to maximize space**
► **Uncompress a disk to access files**
► **Remove a program**

Windows 98 offers a number of useful tools for managing routine tasks like installing and removing programs, and formatting, copying, and compressing disks. Windows 98 also provides the tools to fix disk problems, speed up disk access, and maximize disk space. By periodically finding and repairing disk errors, you can keep your files in good working condition, prevent disk problems that might cause you to lose your work, compress a disk to free up more space for other files, and uncompress a disk when you need quicker access to its files. In this unit, John Casey creates an emergency startup disk (in case he has major disk problems), installs DriveSpace (a disk compression tool), and performs several routine disk management tasks.

Making an Emergency Startup Disk

An **emergency startup disk** contains tools that help you troubleshoot your computer when a problem with your hard disk prevents you from starting your computer. You can start your computer from the emergency startup disk, then use the disk to run diagnostic programs and fix any problems. You can use the Add/Remove programs option in the Control Panel to make an emergency startup disk. For this lesson, you'll need a blank disk or one that does not contain files you want to keep because creating an emergency disk removes all existing files on that disk. John did not create a startup disk when he installed Windows 98. Now, he wants to create one.

1. Click the Start button on the taskbar, point to Settings, then click Control Panel
   The Control Panel opens, displaying Windows tools and accessories, as shown in Figure L-1.

2. Double-click the Add/Remove Programs icon
   The Add/Remove Programs Properties dialog box opens. Table L-1 describes the options available in each of the tabs in this dialog box.

3. Click the Startup Disk tab
   The Startup Disk tab appears with information about creating an emergency startup disk, as shown in Figure L-2.

4. Click Create Disk
   A progress meter appears, displaying status. If a dialog box opens saying you need an installation disk, insert the disk if you have it, or see your instructor or technical support person for assistance. When the progress meter reaches 100%, the startup disk is complete.

5. Label a blank floppy disk (or one that has files you do not need) with "Windows 98 Startup Disk", insert the disk into the appropriate drive on your computer, then click OK

6. Remove the startup disk
   You should store your startup disk in a safe place. Then, if your computer is having trouble starting, turn it off, insert the startup disk into the floppy drive, then turn the computer back on. The computer will start from the startup disk, not the hard drive.

7. Click OK, then click the Close button in the Control Panel

Trouble?

This process will remove any files on your disk, so do not use your Student Disk or any disk that has files you want to keep.

FIGURE L-1: **Control Panel**

Double-click to access the Startup Disk command

FIGURE L-2: **Add/Remove Programs Properties dialog box**

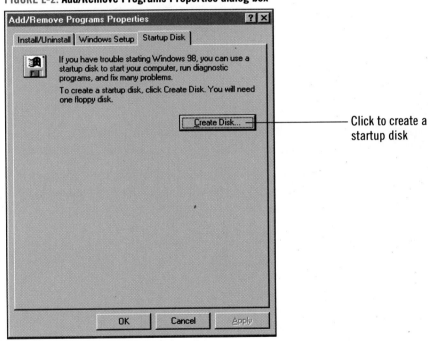

Click to create a startup disk

TABLE L-1: **Add/Remove Programs dialog box**

properties tab	description
Install/Uninstall	Allows you to install or uninstall a new program from a floppy disk or a CD-ROM drive
Windows Setup	Allows you to add or remove Windows 98 components
Startup Disk	Allows you to create a Windows 98 emergency startup disk

Windows 98

Formatting a Disk

Formatting a disk prepares it so that you can store information on it. Formatting removes all information from the disk, so you should never format a disk that has files you want to keep. Disks are now usually formatted before you buy them, so you no longer need to format a new disk before you can use it; however, formatting is still a quick way to erase old files from a floppy disk and to scan a disk for errors. Do not use your Student Disk for this lesson; use a disk that does not contain files you want to keep. ✒ John wants to make a copy of the Student Disk for safe keeping, but first he needs to format the disk to which he will copy.

Steps 1234

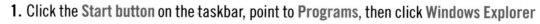

1. **Click the Start button on the taskbar, point to Programs, then click Windows Explorer**

2. **Insert a 3½" floppy disk into the appropriate drive**
   Make sure the disk you are using does not contain any files you want to keep.

Trouble?

Formatting removes all the files on your disk, so do not use your Student Disk or any disk that has files you want to keep.

3. **Locate and then right-click the drive containing your blank disk in the left pane of Windows Explorer**
   The icon representing the 3½" disk drive is highlighted and the drive's pop-up menu opens.

4. **Click Format on the pop-up menu**
   The Format dialog box opens, as shown in Figure L-3.

5. **In the Format type area, click the Full option button**
   The Full format type formats a floppy disk and scans it for errors. See Table L-2 for information about the other formatting options.

Trouble?

If the Format Results dialog box doesn't open, you might not have selected the Display summary when finished check box. This is okay.

6. **Click Start**
   A progress meter appears at the bottom of the dialog box. After a few moments, the Format Results dialog box opens.

7. **Read the results, then click Close twice**
   The Format Results dialog box and the Format dialog box close.

8. **Remove your blank formatted disk from the floppy drive**
   Now you can use the formatted disk in the next lesson to make a copy of your Student Disk.

FIGURE L-3: **Format dialog box**

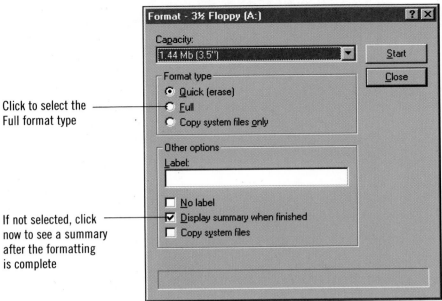

Click to select the Full format type

If not selected, click now to see a summary after the formatting is complete

TABLE L-2: **Format types**

option	description
Capacity	Use to specify the amount of information your disk is made to hold; for a high-density disk, choose 1.44 Mb, for double-density disks, choose 720Kb
Quick (erase)	Use for an already-formatted disk that contains files that you want to erase; it takes less time than the Full option
Full	Use for a new, unformatted disk; This option initializes the disk, which prepares it to receive data; it takes more time than the Quick option
Copy system files only	Use to make an already-formatted disk bootable, meaning you will be able to start your computer with it
Label	Use to give your disk a name to make it easier to identify later
Display summary when finished	Use to see information, such as how much space is available on the disk, about the disk after formatting is finished
Copy system files	Use to format the disk and then make it bootable after formatting by copying system files to it

Using Drive Converter (FAT32) or DriveSpace 3

All disks are formatted with a **file system**, which makes the disk compatible with the operating system in storing, managing, and accessing data. One of the most common file systems is FAT (for File Allocation Table), which is on most Windows 98 computers. A **file allocation table** is a list maintained by the operating system of the status of the various sections of a disk. A major enhancement of Windows 98 is that it can handle the FAT32 file system in addition to the previous FAT16 file system. You can use Drive Converter (a program that comes with Windows 98) to convert your drive from FAT16 to FAT32. The FAT32 file system is a very efficient system for storing files on large disk drives (over 512 MB). FAT32 stores data more efficiently, creating up to several hundred MB of extra disk space on the drive. In addition, programs load up to 50% faster and your computer uses fewer system resources with FAT32. Once you convert your hard drive to FAT32 format using Drive Converter, you cannot return to using the FAT16 format unless you repartition and reformat the FAT32 drive. To convert a drive to FAT32, click the Start button, point to Programs, point to Accessories, point to System Tools, click Drive Converter, then follow the Drive Converter wizard step-by-step instructions.

Windows 98

Copying a Disk

One way to protect the information on your disks from possible problems is to regularly place copies of the information onto other disks. Then, if information goes bad on a disk, you still have the copied information. You can use one disk drive to copy information from one disk to another. Windows 98 manages the process for you. 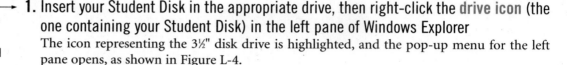 John wants to make a copy of the information he has compiled on his floppy disk. He'll use the disk he formatted in the previous lesson.

Steps

Trouble?

If your student files are stored on a network or hard drive, subsitute any disk which has files on it.

Trouble?

When you copy disks, the disks must be the same type (3½" or 5¼") and size (1.44 MB or 1.2 MB).

1. Insert your Student Disk in the appropriate drive, then right-click the drive icon (the one containing your Student Disk) in the left pane of Windows Explorer
The icon representing the 3½" disk drive is highlighted, and the pop-up menu for the left pane opens, as shown in Figure L-4.

2. Click Copy Disk on the pop-up menu
The Copy Disk dialog box opens, as shown in Figure L-5. On the left side of the dialog box, you select the **source disk** from which you want to copy. This source disk is your Student Disk. On the right side, you select the **destination disk** to which you want to copy. This destination disk is the disk you formatted in the previous lesson. The 3½ Floppy (A:) or (B:) icons on both sides of the dialog box are selected by default.

3. Click Start
A progress meter appears with the status message "Reading source disk." After reading the source disk, a Copy Disk message dialog box opens, asking you to insert a destination disk.

4. Remove your Student Disk, then insert a blank formatted disk in the same drive

5. Click OK
The progress meter continues with the status message "Writing to destination disk." Upon completion, the status message "Copy completed successfully" appears.

6. Click Close

7. Click the Close button to close Windows Explorer

8. Remove the disk, then label it "Copy of Student Disk"
Now that he has a copy of his disk, John can perform maintenance operations on his disk without worrying about losing any information.

FIGURE L-4: Windows Explorer with pop-up menu for floppy disk drive

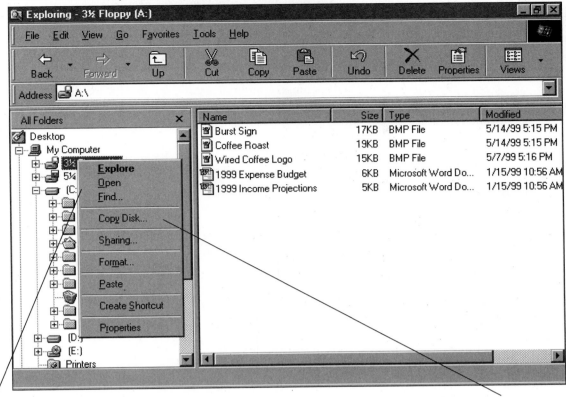

Menu options may vary

Click to copy a disk

FIGURE L-5: Copy Disk dialog box

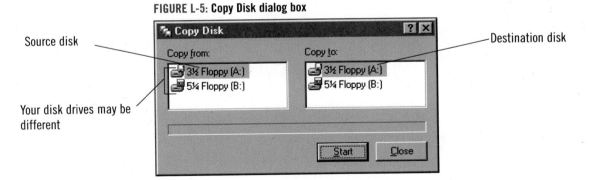

Source disk

Your disk drives may be different

Destination disk

Synchronizing files between computers

If you want to work on files that are copied onto two different computers (such as your work computer and your home computer), you can use **Briefcase** to keep the various copies updated between computers. To use Briefcase, drag the files you want to copy to your other computer from Windows Explorer to the My Briefcase icon. The My Briefcase icon appears on the desktop if you chose the Portable option during Windows Setup. Then, drag the My Briefcase icon to

the icon for the floppy drive, and remove the floppy disk. You can now insert the floppy disk into a different computer. If you edit the files, you will need to synchronize them when you return to your main computer: reinsert the floppy disk, double-click the My Briefcase icon, then click Update All on the Briefcase menu. This will copy the new versions of your files from the floppy disk to the hard disk.

Windows 98

Finding and Repairing Disk Errors

Sometimes an unexpected power loss or program error can create inaccessible file segments that take up space on your disk. The **ScanDisk** program that comes with Windows 98 helps you find and repair damaged sections of a disk. To keep your floppy or hard disk working properly, you should run ScanDisk from time to time. Table L-3 provides information on customizing ScanDisk functions. John wants to make sure his disk has no problems, so he runs ScanDisk. For this lesson, use the copy of your Student Disk that you made in the last lesson.

1. Click the **Start button** on the taskbar, point to **Programs**, point to **Accessories**, point to **System Tools**, then click **ScanDisk**
   The ScanDisk dialog box opens, as shown in Figure L-6.

2. Insert the "Copy of Student Disk" disk in the appropriate drive, then click **the drive that contains the disk** (you might have to scroll to see it)
   John wants to check files, folders, and the disk surface for errors, so he selects the Thorough option.

3. In the Type of test area, click the **Thorough option button**

4. If not already selected, click the **Automatically fix errors check box**
   With this option checked, ScanDisk repairs most errors automatically using predetermined settings.

5. Click **Start**
   A progress meter appears, displaying scanning status. After a few moments, the ScanDisk Results dialog box opens, as shown in Figure L-7.

6. Click **Close** to close the ScanDisk Results dialog box, then click **Close** to exit ScanDisk
   Leave the "Copy of Student Disk" disk in the floppy drive for the next lesson.

QuickTip

For Help on an item in the ScanDisk dialog box, right-click the item, then click the What's This? command.

FIGURE L-6: ScanDisk dialog box

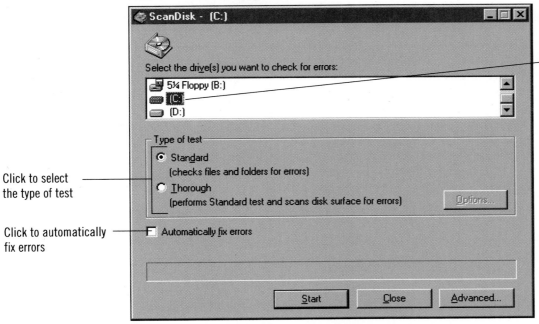

Scroll to locate and click to select a drive to scan

Click to select the type of test

Click to automatically fix errors

FIGURE L-7: ScanDisk Results dialog box

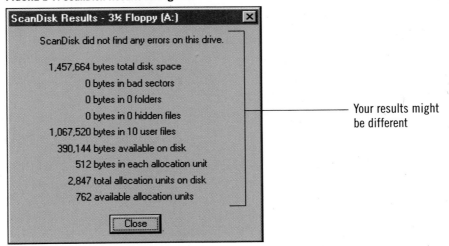

Your results might be different

CLUES TO USE

Scheduling disk maintenance

With the **Maintenance Wizard** that comes with Windows 98, you can schedule your computer to automatically perform ScanDisk and other disk maintenance tasks at designated times. The Maintenance Wizard helps you speed up your most frequently used programs, check your hard disk for errors, and delete unnecessary files from your hard disk. To schedule disk maintenance tasks, click the Start button on the taskbar, point to Programs, point to Accessories, point to System Tools, click Maintenance Wizard, then follow the step-by-step instructions.

TABLE L-3: Other ScanDisk settings

button/option	description
Options	Changes how ScanDisk checks the disk's surface
Advanced	Changes how ScanDisk checks files and folders
Automatically fix errors	Deselect if you want to specify how ScanDisk repairs any errors it finds

Windows 98

Defragmenting a Disk

When you delete files from a disk, the empty space that is created might be fragmented over different areas of the disk. When you create a new file on a fragmented disk, parts of the file are stored in these empty spaces; thus, a single file might be broken into many parts. A file that is broken up in this way is called a fragmented file. To retrieve a fragmented file, the computer must search many areas on the disk, which lengthens retrieval time. You can use the Disk Defragmenter program to place all of the parts of a file in one location. This procedure, which efficiently arranges all of the files and unused space, is called optimization. Optimization makes your programs run faster and your files open more quickly. For best results, run ScanDisk to check for errors on your disk before you start the disk defragmentation process. *John uses Disk Defragmenter to optimize his floppy disk.*

QuickTip

While Disk Defragmenter works, you can use your computer to carry out other tasks; however, your computer will operate more slowly. To temporarily stop Disk Defragmenter so you can run other programs at full speed, click Pause.

Trouble?

If a message appears saying that the defragmentation is complete before you get a chance to do Step 4, click Yes, then continue to the next lesson.

1. **Click the Start button on the taskbar, point to Programs, point to Accessories, point to System Tools, then click Disk Defragmenter**
   The Select Drive dialog box opens.

2. **Click the drive list arrow, then click the drive that contains the "Copy of Student Disk" disk (you might have to scroll to see it)**
   The drive appears in the list, as shown in Figure L-8.

3. **Click OK**
   The Defragmenting Drive A dialog box opens, as shown in Figure L-9. The defragmentation process can take several minutes or more, depending on the extent of the fragmentation on your disk. You can monitor the process with the progress meter.

4. **If available, click Show Details, then click Legend (if necessary, drag the Legend dialog box title bar to the lower-right corner to see details)**
   As shown in Figure L-10, this gives you a better picture of the disk defragmentation process. The Defragmenting Drive A dialog box has expanded to show the defragmentation process. Different colored squares appear on your screen. To find out what the different colored squares mean, you can use the legend. The Defrag Legend dialog box has small boxes, each representing a disk section known as a cluster. The different patterns tell you the status of each cluster, and the legend explains how to interpret the patterns. When your disk is defragmented, a message box opens.

5. **Click Yes to close Disk Defragmenter**
   Your disk is now optimized. Leave the "Copy of Student Disk" disk in the floppy drive and continue to the next lesson.

Cleaning up your disk

You can run a Windows 98 program called **Disk Cleanup** to help free up space on your hard drive. Disk Cleanup searches your drive, then lists temporary files, Internet cache files, and unnecessary program files that you can safely delete. To use Disk Cleanup, start Disk Cleanup, select the disk or drive you want to clean up, click OK, select the files you want to delete, then click OK. Before you select and delete files, make sure you will not need them in the future. You can start Disk Cleanup by clicking the Start button, pointing to Programs, pointing to Accessories, pointing to System Tools, then clicking Disk Cleanup.

FIGURE L-8: **Select Drive dialog box**

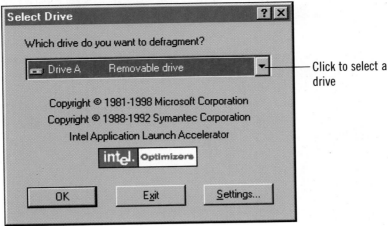

Click to select a drive

FIGURE L-9: **Defragmenting Drive A dialog box**

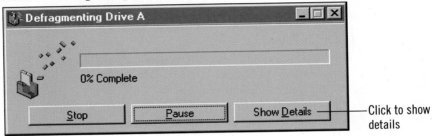

Click to show details

FIGURE L-10: **Defragmenting Drive A dialog box**

Defragmentation process

Your screen might look different

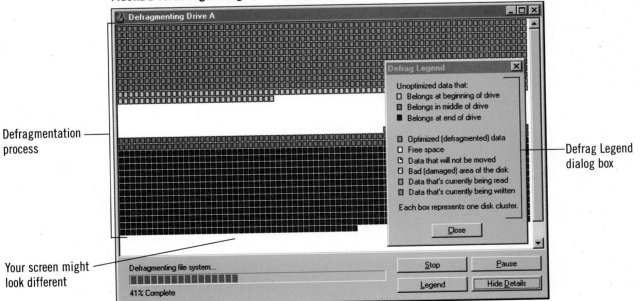

Defrag Legend dialog box

Installing a Program

Not every user needs all the programs that come with Windows 98, and programs take up space on your hard drive. Windows 98 only installs the most common programs, leaving it to you to install or remove others as needed. Windows 98 includes a program called **DriveSpace**, which might not be installed on your computer, that helps you free up space on your disks. With Add/Remove Programs in the Control Panel, you can add DriveSpace and other Windows 98 features that might not be installed on your computer. To free up more space on a disk, John decides to install DriveSpace.

Steps

1. Click the Start button on the taskbar, point to Settings, then click Control Panel
The Control Panel opens.

2. Double-click Add/Remove Programs
The Add/Remove Programs Properties dialog box opens.

3. Click the Windows Setup tab
The Windows Setup dialog box opens. At the same time, the Setup program searches for components installed on your computer (this may take a few moments). The Components list shows all of the components of Windows 98, as shown in Figure L-11. Each component contains one or more parts that you can install or remove. A blank box means that none of the parts of that component are installed, a shaded box means that only some of the parts of the component are installed, and a white box with a check means that all of the parts of that component are installed. To display what is included in a component, click the component name (not the check box), then click Details.

4. Click the down scroll arrow to locate "System Tools," click System Tools (not the check box), then click Details
The System Tools dialog box opens listing the parts of this component. The check boxes indicate which parts are currently installed on your computer.

Trouble?
If Disk compression tools doesn't appear, skip Step 5 and continue. DriveSpace is installed.

5. Click the check box next to Disk compression tools
See Figure L-12. The DriveSpace program is one of the disk compression tools. You'll learn about disk compression in the next lesson. Make sure that you make no changes other than the ones in these steps.

6. Click OK twice
A status bar appears, indicating progress.

Trouble?
See your instructor or technical support person if you do not have the Windows 98 installation disk or CD-COM.

7. If necessary, insert the Windows 98 installation disk or CD-ROM in the appropriate drive, then click OK
The files are copied from the installation disk or CD-ROM onto your hard drive.

8. When the installation is complete, remove the installation disk or CD-ROM if necessary, then click the Close button in the Control Panel

FIGURE L-11: **Add/Remove Programs Properties dialog box with Windows Setup tab**

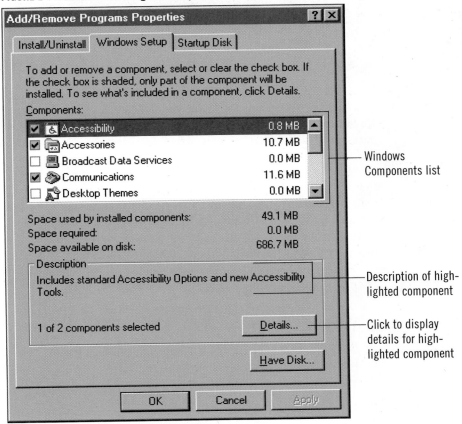

Windows Components list

Description of high-lighted component

Click to display details for high-lighted component

FIGURE L-12: **System Tools dialog box**

Click to install disk compression tools

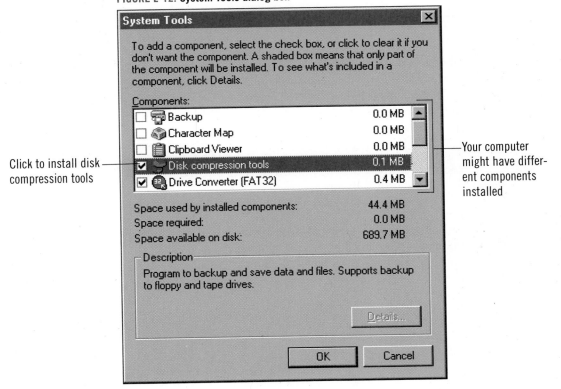

Your computer might have different components installed

Compressing a Disk to Maximize Space

If you need more room on your floppy disk or hard disk, you can use DriveSpace to compress the disk and free up more space. When you **compress** a disk, all of the folders and files become a single file called the **compressed volume file (CVF)**. The CVF is then stored on an uncompressed part of the disk, called the **host drive**. For example, suppose you want to compress the floppy disk in drive A. DriveSpace first assigns a different drive letter, such as H, to your disk. Drive H is the host for drive A. DriveSpace then compresses the contents of your floppy disk into a CVF that is stored on drive H. To Windows and your programs, the CVF on drive H appears to be your original drive A with more free space than it originally had. The disadvantage of compressing a disk is that it takes Windows 98 longer to access your files. John wants to compress files on his floppy disk to make more room. You will use your "Copy of Student Disk" disk in this lesson in order to keep your Student Disk in its original condition.

1. Close all open programs

For DriveSpace to function properly, all of the programs on your computer (except Windows 98) should be closed.

2. Click the Start button on the taskbar, point to Programs, point to Accessories, point to System Tools, then click DriveSpace

The DriveSpace 3 window opens, as shown in Figure L-13.

3. In the Drives on this computer list, click the drive with your "Copy of Student Disk" disk

Make sure that the correct drive is selected so you do not accidentally compress your computer's hard drive.

4. Click Drive on the menu bar, then click Compress

The Compress a Drive dialog box opens, as shown in Figure L-14.

5. Click Start

The Are You Sure? dialog box opens, explaining the compression process. Before you compress the floppy disk, make sure that all of the other open programs are closed. If you do not, you are putting the data on your disk at risk.

6. Click Compress Now

A progress meter appears, displaying status. This procedure can take several minutes. Upon completion, the Compress a Drive dialog box reopens explaining the results of the compression process on your disk.

7. Click Close

The DriveSpace window now displays the host drive for the drive you compressed, as shown in Figure L-15, which is often drive letter H.

FIGURE L-13: DriveSpace window

Click to select the floppy disk to compress

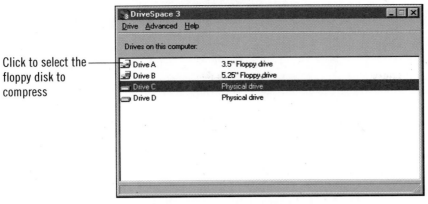

FIGURE L-14: Compress a Drive dialog box

Current disk capacity

Estimated compressed disk capacity

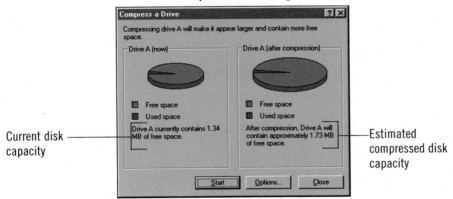

FIGURE L-15: DriveSpace window

Host drive for compressed drive A

Your screen might look different

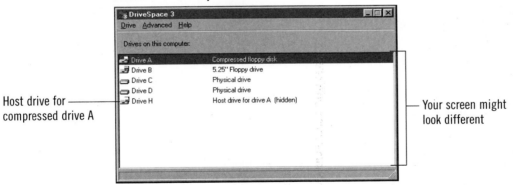

CLUES TO USE

Using Compression Agent

When you install disk compression tools, DriveSpace is not the only program that is added. A Windows 98 program called **Compression Agent** is also installed. With Compression Agent, you can recompress your files and improve performance by changing the level of compression. While files on your drive are being recompressed, Compression Agent updates information in a table to reflect how your disk space changes as files are moved from one compression method to another. You can use Compression Agent to compress files only on drives compressed using DriveSpace. To use Compression Agent, compress the disk using DriveSpace, start Compression Agent (click the Start button, point to Programs, point to Accessories, point to System Tools, then click Compression Agent), then select the files and specify the settings you want to use.

Windows 98

Uncompressing a Disk to Access Files

When you browse a computer that has a compressed disk in one of its drives, you see two icons for the compressed disk: the original icon and a new icon for the host drive (often letter H). You can access a compressed disk as you would a noncompressed disk. For example, if you want to open one of the files on your compressed disk, you open it as usual (you can ignore the host drive) and Windows 98 automatically uncompresses the file. Access to the compressed disk, however, is slower because Windows 98 has to uncompress the file before you can use it. If your disk does not have a space problem, it is better to uncompress it. To uncompress a floppy disk, click the drive icon in the DriveSpace window (do not click the host drive icon), then click Uncompress on the Drive menu. Uncompressing the disk drive reduces its free space. Files on the host drive are copied to drive A or B. ▶ John uncompresses the compressed floppy disk.

1. Click **Compressed floppy disk** in the Drives on this computer box for the drive containing your "Copy of Student Disk" disk, as shown in Figure L-16

2. Click **Drive** on the menu bar, then click **Uncompress**

   The Uncompress a Drive dialog box opens, as shown in Figure L-17. Uncompressing the disk drive will reduce its free space and copy the files from the host drive back to your floppy disk.

3. Click **Start**

   The Are You Sure? dialog box opens, explaining the uncompression process. During the uncompression, you are unable to use your computer.

Trouble?

If your computer can't read the compressed floppy disk, a ReadThis icon, which explains the problem and offers solutions, appears.

4. Click **Uncompress Now**

   A progress meter appears, displaying status. The Remove Compression? dialog box opens, asking if you want to remove the compression driver from memory. DriveSpace uses the compression driver to communicate disk operations to Windows 98. You should keep the compression driver for future use.

5. Click **No**

   The progress meter continues displaying status. Upon completion, the Uncompress a Drive dialog box reopens with the uncompression results.

6. Click **Close**

   The DriveSpace window now displays the drive without compression.

7. Click **Drive** on the menu bar, click **Exit**, then remove your uncompressed "Copy of Student Disk" disk

FIGURE L-16: DriveSpace 3 window

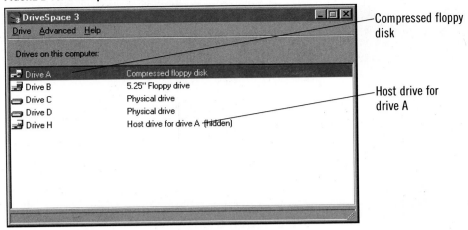

Compressed floppy disk

Host drive for drive A

FIGURE L-17: Uncompress a Drive dialog box before compression

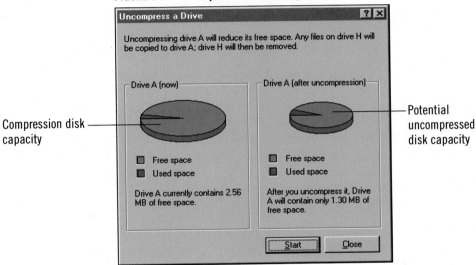

Compression disk capacity

Potential uncompressed disk capacity

CLUES TO USE

Mounting a compressed disk

To use a compressed disk that wasn't present when you turned on your computer during a given computing session, you need to mount it. When you **mount** a compressed disk, you identify the compressed disk to Windows 98 so it can access the files on the disk. For example, if you take your compressed Student Disk to a different computer, you need to make sure that Windows 98 knows it is a compressed disk. It is possible that Windows 98 is set to automatically identify compressed disks. You can verify this by opening DriveSpace, clicking Settings on the Advanced menu, then checking whether the Automatically mount new compressed drives check box is selected, as shown in Figure L-18. If you select this option, Windows 98 will mount a compressed disk automatically. You can also mount a compressed disk manually. In the DriveSpace window, select the compressed drive, click Advance on the menu bar, then click Mount.

FIGURE L-18: Disk Compression Settings dialog box

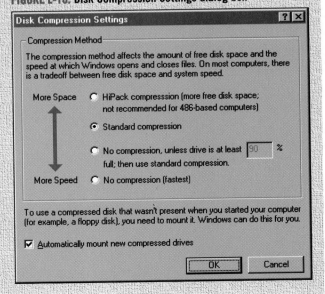

Windows 98

Removing a Program

The ability to add and remove Windows components gives you the flexibility to use the programs you need, when you need them, and maximize the free space on your hard drive. If you do not use a program very often and want to free up some space on your hard drive, you can remove the program. You can always reinstall it if you need it again. ◣▬▬ John needs more space on his hard drive, so he decides to remove the DriveSpace program.

Steps

1. Click the **Start button** on the taskbar, point to **Settings**, then click **Control Panel**

2. Double-click **Add/Remove Programs**, click the **Windows Setup tab**, click the **down scroll arrow**, then click the name **System Tools** in the Components area
   The Add/Remove Programs Properties dialog box appears with the Windows Setup tab format, as shown in Figure L-19.

3. Click **Details**
   The System Tools dialog box opens, listing the parts of this component.

Trouble?

If Disk compression tools does not appear in the System Tools list, skip Step 4 and continue.

4. Click the **down scroll arrow** until the Disk compression tools component appears in the list box, then click the **Disk compression tools check box** to deselect it
   The Disk compression tools check box clears, as shown in Figure L-20. When you clear a check box, Windows 98 will remove the component. Make sure that you do not change any other settings.

5. Click **OK**, then click **OK** again
   Windows 98 removes the program.

6. When the installation is complete, remove the installation disk or CD-ROM, then click the **Close button** in the Control Panel

FIGURE L-19: **Add/Remove Programs Properties dialog box with Windows Setup tab**

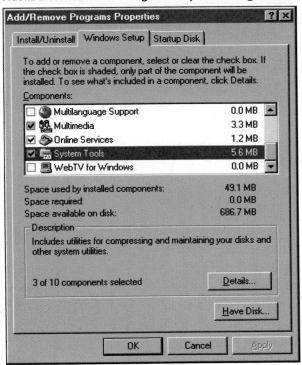

FIGURE L-20: **System Tools dialog box**

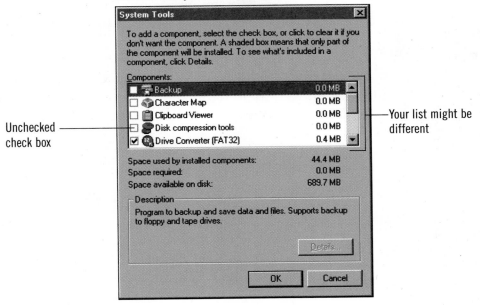

Unchecked check box

Your list might be different

Adding and removing programs

You can use Windows 98 to install or uninstall programs that are not included on the Windows 98 installation disks. You should avoid using Windows Explorer to remove a program because program files and other information could be located in unexpected places and you might not find everything. Instead, use the Install/Uninstall feature to make sure all of the program files are removed. Click the Install/Uninstall tab in the Add/Remove Programs Properties dialog box. To install a program, click the Install button. To remove or change an installed program, click the program in the list box and then click the Add/Remove button. In both cases, you will need the program installation disk or disks.

Practice

▶ Concepts Review

Label each of the elements of the screen shown in Figure L-21.

FIGURE L-21

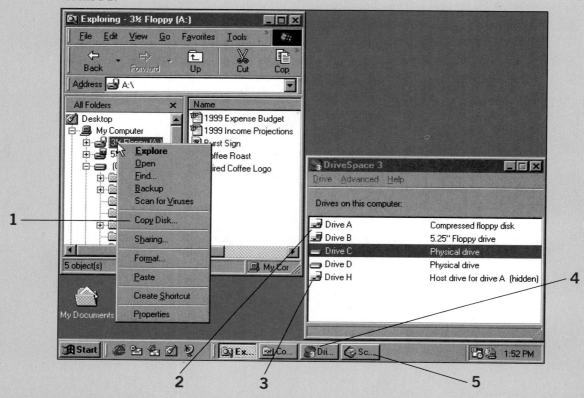

Match each of the terms with the statement that describes its function.

6. Starts your computer after disk problems
7. Optimizes disk access
8. Compresses a disk
9. Stores files
10. Finds and repairs disk errors

    a. DriveSpace
    b. ScanDisk
    c. Disk Defragmenter
    d. Startup disk
    e. Formatted disk

Select the best answer from the following list of choices.

11. Which of the following is NOT a format type?
    a. Quick
    b. Copy system files only
    c. Copy data files only
    d. Full

12. When copying a floppy disk, the disks that you use do NOT need to be:
    a. Formatted.
    b. The same size.
    c. The same type.
    d. Nonwrite-protected.

13. When installing a Windows 98 component, which icon do you double-click in the Control Panel?
    a. System icon
    b. Install/Uninstall icon
    c. Add/Remove Programs icon
    d. Add New Hardware icon

14. **Which scan test checks the disk surface for errors?**
    a. Standard
    b. Surface
    c. Thorough
    d. Professional
15. **Disk defragmentation arranges:**
    a. Data files.
    b. Unused space.
    c. System files.
    d. All of the above.
16. **Compressed files are stored in:**
    a. A single file on an uncompressed drive.
    b. A single file on a compressed drive.
    c. Individual files on an uncompressed drive.
    d. Individual files on a compressed drive.

► Skills Review

1. **Make an emergency startup disk.**
    a. Click Start, point to Settings, then click Control Panel.
    b. Double-click Add/Remove Programs, then click the Startup Disk tab.
    c. Click Create Disk, then insert your Windows 98 installation disk or CD-ROM, if requested. See your instructor or technical support person for assistance.
    d. Insert a blank disk into the same drive (you can reuse the startup disk from the unit, but not your Student Disk), then click OK.
    e. Close the Control Panel, then remove the startup disk from the drive.

2. **Format a disk.**
    a. Click Start, point to Programs, then click Windows Explorer.
    b. Insert a blank disk in the floppy drive (you can reuse "Copy of Student Disk" that you created in this unit).
    c. Right-click the floppy disk drive, then click Format.
    d. Click the Full option button, click Start, then click Close twice.
    e. Close the Control Panel, then remove the formatted disk from the drive.

3. **Copy a disk.**
    a. Insert your Student Disk in the floppy drive.
    b. Right-click the floppy disk drive, then click Copy Disk.
    c. Click the drive containing your Student Disk, then click Start, then remove the floppy disk.
    d. Insert the blank disk you just formatted (not your Student Disk) into the floppy drive.
    e. Click OK, click Close, then close Windows Explorer.
    f. Remove, then label the disk "Copy 2 of Student Disk".

4. **Scan a disk for errors.**
    a. Click Start, point to Programs, point to Accessories, point to System Tools, then click ScanDisk.
    b. Insert "Copy 2 of Student Disk" in the floppy drive.
    c. Click the drive containing your Student Disk, click Start, then click Close twice.

5. **Defragment a disk.**
    a. Click Start, point to Programs, point to Accessories, point to System Tools, then click Disk Defragmenter.
    b. Click the Drive list arrow, then click the drive containing your "Copy 2 of Student Disk".
    c. Click OK, then click Yes.

6. **Install disk compression tools.**
   a. Click Start, point to Settings, then click Control Panel.
   b. Double-click Add/Remove Programs, then click the Windows Setup tab.
   c. Click System Tools (scroll to see it if necessary), then click Details.
   d. Click Disk compression tools, then click OK twice.
   e. Insert a Windows 98 installation disk or CD-ROM when prompted, click OK, then click the Close button.
7. **Compress a disk.**
   a. Click Start, point to Programs, point to Accessories, point to System Tools, then click DriveSpace.
   b. Click the drive containing "Copy 2 of Student Disk".
   c. Click Compress on the Drive menu, click Start, then click Compress Now.
   d. Click Close, then click Exit on the Drive menu.
8. **Uncompress a disk.**
   a. Click Start, point to Programs, point to Accessories, point to System Tools, then click DriveSpace.
   b. Click the drive containing your compressed "Copy 2 of Student Disk".
   c. Click Uncompress on the Drive menu, click Start, then click Uncompress Now.
   d. Click No, click Close, then click Exit on the Drive menu.
9. **Remove the disk compression tools you installed earlier.**
   a. Click Start, point to Settings, then click Control Panel.
   b. Double-click Add/Remove Programs, then click the Windows Setup tab.
   c. Click System Tools (scroll to see it if necessary), then click Details.
   d. If available, click the Disk compression tools check box to deselect it.
   e. Click OK twice, then click the Close button.

▶ Independent Challenges

1. You are the network administrator at Franklin International Group, a family of insurance companies and services. Recently, employees have been reporting serious disk problems. To ensure that they will be able to start Windows 98 in the event of a problem, you want to create emergency startup disks for them to use. You decide to create one emergency startup disk and then make copies.
   To complete this independent challenge:

1. Format a blank floppy disk (or one that does not have any files that you want to keep) using the Full Format type and the label "Startup". You can use the startup disk you created in this unit. Do not use your Student Disk.
2. Using Add/Remove Programs, create an emergency startup disk.
3. Make a disk copy of the emergency startup disk. You can use the disk from this unit if you want, but not your Student Disk.
4. Label both disks for easy identification.

2. As the network administrator at Franklin International Group, you want employees to monitor their computer systems to make sure recent problems are corrected. You decide to install a Windows 98 program called System Resource Meter on your own computer in order to evaluate whether the program meets the employees' needs. After you evaluate it, you will uninstall it from your computer and decide whether all employees should install it.
   To complete this independent challenge:

1. Using Add/Remove Programs, install System Resource Meter from the System Tools area (use the Windows 98 installation CD-ROM or disk when prompted).

2. Start Resource Meter (click Start, point to Programs, point to Accessories, point to System Tools, click Resource Meter, then click OK). A small meter appears on the right side of the taskbar and displays the percent of resources being used on your computer. As the computer uses more resources, the level of the meter decreases, and vice versa. If the meter decreases below 30%, your open programs might not function properly.

3. To display a quick status of your computer resources at any time, you can point to the meter on the taskbar. A small box appears telling you the current percentage of resource usage.

4. For more information, right-click the meter on the taskbar, then click Details.

5. Right-click the meter on the taskbar, then click Exit.

6. Uninstall the System Resource Meter program.

3. You own Wilkenson & Associates, a public relations firm that specializes in overseas travel. With the major problems caused by software viruses, you want to protect important company data from possibly being destroyed. You need to format a disk, make a disk copy of the company documents, then scan the disk for errors.
To complete this independent challenge:

1. Format a blank floppy disk using the Full Format type and the label "Backup". You can use the disk from the unit if you want, but not your Student Disk.

2. Copy the files "1999 Income Properties" and "1999 Expense Budget" from your Student Disk to a blank-formatted disk

3. Scan the floppy disk for errors.

4. Label the disk for easy identification.

4. You are a course developer at EZSoft Inc., a computer training company that specializes in training beginner to expert level software users. You are developing a new course on maintaining a computer. You are currently working on a lesson to teach students how to speed up disks by using the Windows 98 system tool Disk Defragmenter. To complete the lesson, write down the steps to use Disk Defragmenter and take screen shots for the production staff. Create a WordPad document on a floppy disk with steps that explain how to defragment a disk, compress a floppy disk to maximize space, and uncompress files.
To complete this independent challenge:

1. Insert a blank floppy disk in the appropriate drive. You can use one of the disks from the unit, but not your Student Disk.

2. Open WordPad, then create a document called "Disk Defrag" on the floppy disk that instructs students on how to use the Disk Defragmenter system tool. Print the document, then close WordPad.

3. Follow the steps in the WordPad document to defragment the floppy disk (make sure you defragment the floppy disk and not a hard disk), and take screen shots of the Defragmenting Drive A dialog box (with Show Details) as you go through the material. To take a screen shot of the currently displayed dialog box, press [ALT][Print Screen], which copies the image to the Clipboard, open Paint, paste the image, then save the image on the floppy disk with a name that includes the step number in your lesson.

4. Compress the files on the floppy disk.

5. Uncompress the files for the production staff.

Visual Workshop

Recreate the screen shown in Figure L-22, which displays the results from a scan of drive C. If drive C is not available, choose a different hard drive. Your results will differ from the ones shown here. The scan can take 5 or 10 minutes. Use [Print Screen] to make a copy of the screen, then print it from Paint. (Press [ALT][Print Screen], open Paint, click Edit on the menu bar, click Paste to paste the screen into Paint, then click Yes to paste the large image, if necessary. Click File on the menu bar, click Print, click OK, then close Paint.)

FIGURE L-22

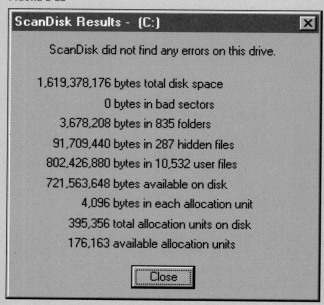

Windows 98

Managing

Hardware

Objectives

- ► **Understand plug-and-play hardware**
- ► **View printer properties**
- ► **Install a printer**
- ► **Manage printers and print jobs**
- ► **Install hardware devices**
- ► **View system hardware**
- ► **View hardware settings**
- ► **Remove hardware devices**

A **hardware device** is any physical object that you plug into your computer. This device can be, for example, a network card or a sound card that you install inside your computer, or it can be a printer or a scanner that you plug into the outside of the computer. Windows 98 makes it easy to manage your hardware. In this unit, you learn how to install hardware automatically with Windows 98 plug-and-play, install a printer using the Add Printer Wizard, manage printers and print jobs with a print manager, view hardware properties with the Device Manager, and remove hardware from the computer quickly and easily. John Casey uses Windows 98 to install, manage, and remove different computer hardware devices and to learn about plug-and-play hardware in the process.

Understanding Plug-and-Play Hardware

Support for plug-and-play devices is one of the most important features of Windows 98. Historically, adding a new device to your computer was confusing and frustrating. After opening your computer case and physically inserting the device, you had to make sure the new device did not conflict with existing devices. Often, this was a difficult and detailed task. With **plug-and-play** support, you can add a new device to your computer as easily as you can plug a game into a videogame player or hook a pair of speakers to a stereo system. You simply plug the device in, and Windows 98 handles the previously arduous task of setting the device to work with your existing hardware and resolving any system conflicts. ◢━━━ John wants to install a new printer, so he decides to learn about plug-and-play devices. Plug-and-play supports only those devices that indicate that they are plug-and-play compatible, as shown in Figure M-1.

To install a plug-and-play device, complete the following steps

 Turn off your computer.

 Gather your original Windows 98 floppy disks or CD-ROM, the hardware device that you want to install, and the disks that come with the device

 Follow the manufacturer's instructions to plug the new device into your computer

 Turn on your computer

 Windows 98 detects the new device and might ask you to insert into the appropriate drive a Windows 98 disk or the disk that comes with the device. If Windows 98 doesn't recognize a hardware change as your computer turns on, the hardware might not be plug-and-play compatible.

 Follow the instructions on the screen until a message indicates that you are finished. Windows 98 automatically notifies all other devices of the new device so there are no conflicts.

FIGURE M-1: **Computer with attached printer**

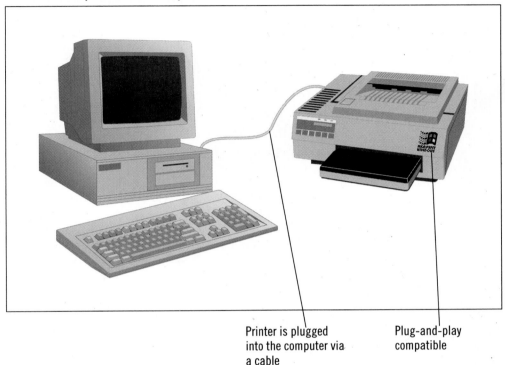

Printer is plugged into the computer via a cable

Plug-and-play compatible

CLUES TO USE

Using System Monitor

Windows 98 comes with System Monitor, which is a program that helps you assess the speed of various components. Technicians and network administrators can use System Monitor to analyze hardware performance. System Monitor charts the amount of time used by a component or process. To start System Monitor, click the Start button, point to Programs, point to Accessories, point to System Tools, then click System Monitor. If System Monitor is not available, use Add/Remove Programs in the Control Panel to install it.

Viewing Printer Properties

A new printer is one of the most common hardware devices that computer users install. Before you install a new printer, it is a good idea to view printer properties of currently installed printers, so you can install the new printer with the appropriate settings. Viewing printer properties gives you information about a printer's computer connection or network location, related software, paper options, graphics settings, and installed fonts. ◄━━━ John views the printer properties of a currently installed printer.

Steps

Trouble?

If you do not have a printer installed on your computer, install a printer by following the steps in the next lesson, then complete the steps in this lesson.

1. **Click the Start button on the taskbar, point to Settings, then click Printers**
   The Printers window opens, as shown in Figure M-2. To match the view in the figure, click View on the menu bar, then click Large Icons. Every installed printer on your computer is represented by an icon in the Printers window. Your Printers window will have different printers than the ones in Figure M-2. When a printer icon in the window appears with a cable, the printer is connected to your computer over a network and is known as a **network printer**. When a printer icon appears without a cable, the printer is directly connected to your computer and is known as a **local printer**. When a printer icon appears with a hand, the printer directly connected to your computer is shared with other network users and is known as a **shared printer**.

Trouble?

If you don't see the Properties by then, click the Maximize button.

2. **In the Printers window, click a printer icon, then click the Properties button 🖅 on the toolbar**
   The Printer Properties dialog box opens with the General tab showing. Table M-1 describes the Printer Properties tabs in the dialog box; your tabs might differ. To make sure a printer is working properly, you can print a test page.

3. **Click Print Test Page**
   A dialog box opens, asking if the test page printed correctly. John retrieves a test page off the printer. The test page looks fine.

4. **Click Yes**
   When you install a hardware device, Windows 98 installs related software known as a **driver** that allows the hardware to communicate with Windows 98 and other software applications. To maximize hardware performance, it is important to use the driver that matches the printer.

QuickTip

To install an updated driver for the selected printer, click New Driver, click Yes, click Have Disk, then double-click the new driver.

5. **Click the Details tab**
   The Details tab, shown in Figure M-3, shows a printer's local or network connection and its current driver. Your screen might look different, depending on your printer's settings. The Printer Properties dialog box also gives you specific printer paper options from which you can choose.

6. **Click OK**
   You return to the Printers window.

FIGURE M-2: **Printers window**

Printer connected directly to the computer

Printer connected over a network

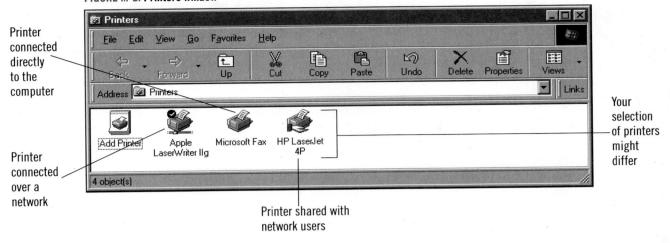

Your selection of printers might differ

Printer shared with network users

FIGURE M-3: **Printer Properties dialog box with the Details tab**

Selected printer

Place where the printer cable is connected to the computer

Printer driver

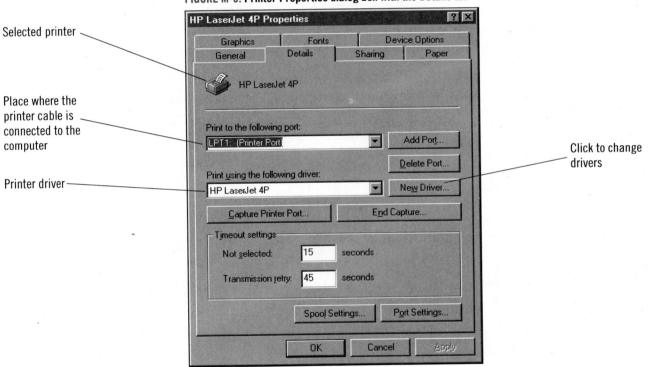

Click to change drivers

TABLE M-1: **Printer Properties dialog box**

tab	description
General	Lists general information about the printer and allows you to print a test page
Details	Lists the printer's connection port and software drivers
Sharing	Allows you to share the printer over a network
Paper	Lists available paper options that you can use with the printer
Graphics	Lists available graphics printing options
Fonts	Lists font-handling options available with the printer
Device Options	Allows you to change printer memory and related settings

Installing a Printer

Windows 98

Windows 98 makes installing a printer quick and easy with the Add Printer Wizard. The Add Printer Wizard asks you a series of questions to help you install either a network or local printer, establish a connection, and print a test page to make sure that the printer works properly. If the printer does not work properly, Windows 98 starts an automated troubleshooter to help you fix the problem. ✎ John purchased a new HP OfficeJet printer and wants to install it. You can complete this lesson even if you are not actually installing a printer.

Steps

QuickTip

To install a printer, you can also double-click the Add/Remove Hardware icon in the Control Panel.

Trouble?

If an HP OfficeJet printer is already installed on your computer, select another printer.

Trouble?

If LPT1 or LPT2 is already in use, click COM1 or COM2.

Trouble?

If the Windows 98 installation disk or CD-ROM is not available, click Cancel, then click OK in Step 8 to cancel the operation. For the remaining lessons, you will need to use a different printer.

1. Double-click the Add Printer icon, as shown in Figure M-4, then click Next

The wizard asks you to select a local or network printer. A local printer is directly connected to your computer, and a network printer is connected to a network to which you have access. The local printer option is already selected.

2. Click Next

The wizard asks you to select a printer.

3. Press [H], click HP in the Manufacturers list (if necessary), then click HP OfficeJet in the Printers list (if necessary), as shown in Figure M-5

4. Click Next

The wizard asks which port you want to use with this printer. A **port** is the location on the back of your computer where you connect the printer cable. You can connect the cable to either a printer port, which is labeled LPT1 or LPT2, or to a communications port, which is labeled COM1 or COM2.

5. Click LPT1 or LPT2, then click Next

For this lesson, it does not matter whether the port is actually in use. The wizard asks you to type a name for the printer and whether you want the printer to be the default printer. HP OfficeJet appears as the printer name, and the No option button is selected. If you have access to several printers, the **default printer** is the printer that you use most often. When you start a print job without specifying a particular printer, the job is sent to the default printer. Next to the default printer's icon is a black dot with a check mark, as shown in Figure M-4.

6. Click Next

The wizard asks if you want to print a test page. Since you are just practicing and are not actually installing a printer, you do not need a test page. Normally, printing a test page is important to make sure the printer is working properly.

7. Click the No option button, then click Finish

8. If necessary, insert the Windows 98 installation disk or CD-ROM into the appropriate drive, then click OK

Windows 98 needs to install the appropriate printer driver from the CD-ROM to complete the printer installation and to test the printer. If necessary, click the Close button in the Windows 98 CD-ROM window. Upon completion, the HP OfficeJet printer icon appears in the Printers window, as shown in Figure M-6.

FIGURE M-4: Printers window

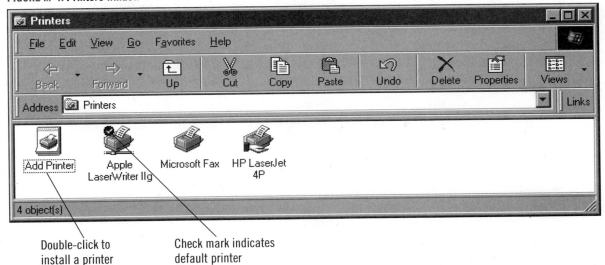

Double-click to
install a printer

Check mark indicates
default printer

FIGURE M-5: Add Printer Wizard dialog box

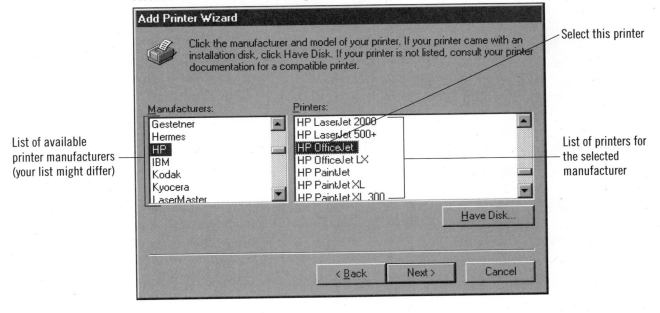

Select this printer

List of available
printer manufacturers
(your list might differ)

List of printers for
the selected
manufacturer

FIGURE M-6: Printers window with new printer

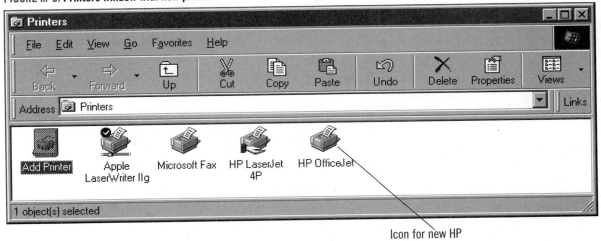

Icon for new HP
OfficeJet printer

Windows 98

Managing Printers and Print Jobs

When you want to check the status of a printer or manage print jobs, double-click the appropriate printer icon in the Printers window. A window opens showing the **print queue**, which is the list of documents to be printed. You can use this window to cancel print jobs, temporarily pause print jobs, view printer properties, and so on. In this lesson, since you are not actually printing to a real printer, you will use deferred printing. With **deferred printing**, you can send a job to be printed even if your computer is not connected to a printer. To do this, you pause printing, and the document waits in the print queue until you hook a printer to the computer and turn off pause printing. 📝 John wants to learn how to manage the printer and print jobs.

1. Be sure your Student Disk is in the floppy drive, then, in the Printers window, right-click the HP OfficeJet icon
   Since this printer is not connected to your computer, you should first pause the printer.

2. Click Pause Printing, or for a network printer, click Use Printer Offline
   Not all printers have an offline mode. When a printer is offline, the printer's icon dims.

3. Double-click the My Computer icon, double-click the icon for the drive containing your Student Disk, then drag the open windows so you can see both the floppy drive window and the HP OfficeJet icon in the Printers window
   Compare your screen to Figure M-7.

4. Click Edit on the menu bar of your floppy drive window, click Select All, drag the files to the HP OfficeJet icon in the Printers window, then click Yes to confirm multiple print jobs.
   When you drag the documents over the printer icon, a plus sign (+) appears indicating that it is safe to release the mouse button. When a printer is not paused, a printer icon 🖨 appears on the taskbar next to the clock, indicating that a job has been sent to be printed. Since you do not actually have this printer attached to your computer (and the printer has been paused anyway), nothing will print; the job simply waits in the print queue until you either delete the job or connect a printer to your computer.

5. Double-click the HP OfficeJet icon
   The HP OfficeJet window opens. The HP OfficeJet window displays the printer status in the title bar and the print jobs currently in the queue. The documents are listed in the order in which they will be printed.

6. In the HP OfficeJet window, drag Coffee Roast above Burst Sign, then click a blank area in the window
   The "Coffee Roast" document moves up in the print queue, as shown in Figure M-8, so it will be printed first.

7. Click Printer on the menu bar, then click Purge Print Documents
   This deletes all of the print jobs from the queue.

8. Close all open windows

QuickTip

To view jobs that have been sent to a network printer, you need to go to the computer that is physically connected to the printer and double-click the printer's icon.

QuickTip

You can delete a single document from the print queue by selecting the document, clicking Document on the menu bar, then clicking Cancel Printing.

FIGURE M-7: **Preparing to drag files to print**

Select these files to print

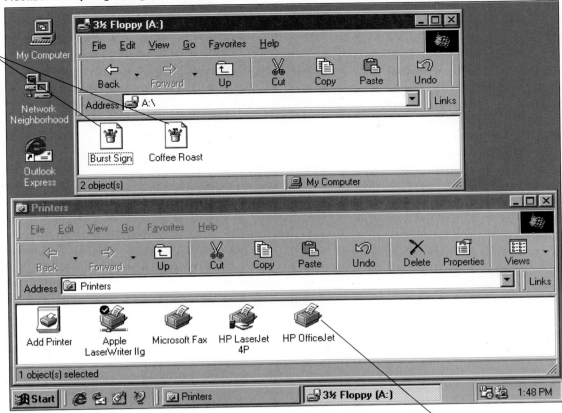

Drag files here to print them

FIGURE M-8: **HP OfficeJet window**

Printer is currently paused

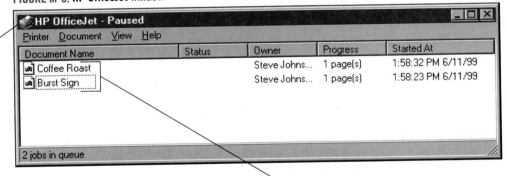

Files in the print queue

CLUES TO USE

Adding a separator page to print jobs

When you work in a network environment in which many different users are printing to the same printer, adding a separator page to your documents can be helpful. A **separator (or banner) page** lists the name, author, date, and time of the print job. You can set up separator pages only to a printer attached directly to your computer; in a network, the network administrator would make the change. To add a separator page to print jobs, right-click the printer icon, click Properties, click the Separator page list arrow, then click Full or Simple. Both settings print the same information, but each uses a different font and size. If you want to use a custom separator page, click Browse, then select the file that you want to use.

Windows 98

Installing Hardware Devices

Windows 98 makes installing hardware devices easy with the Add New Hardware Wizard, which asks you a series of questions to help you set up the software that is necessary for the new hardware device to work properly on your computer. In this lesson you won't actually install a new hardware device, but you'll go through the wizard to learn how it installs the appropriate software for the hardware device. Normally you would turn off your computer, physically connect your hardware to your computer, then turn your computer back on. In most cases, Windows automatically detects your new hardware device and starts the wizard. If Windows doesn't detect the new hardware, you can also start the Add New Hardware Wizard in the Control Panel and select the new hardware device to install it. John uses the Add New Hardware Wizard to install support software for a hardware device (a global positioning device) he just connected to his computer.

1. Click the Start button on the taskbar, point to Settings, then click Control Panel

Trouble?

Before you continue, make sure that you close all open programs.

2. Double-click Add New Hardware, then click Next

The wizard asks for permission to search for any new plug-and-play devices that are on your system.

3. Click Next

Wait while Windows 98 searches your computer for new plug-and-play devices. The wizard asks for permission to search for any hardware that is not plug-and-play compatible, or it asks you to select a hardware device from a list, as shown in Figure M-9.

4. If necessary, click the No, the device isn't in the list option button, then click Next

5. Click the No, I want to select the hardware from a list option button, then click Next

The wizard asks you to select the type of hardware for which you want to install the support software, as shown in Figure M-10.

6. Click Global positioning devices, then click Next

The wizard asks you to select a make and model for the new hardware. The default manufacturer is Rockwell, and the default model is Rockwell NavCard (Binary) Revision A.

7. Click Next, then click Next to install the software

Trouble?

If the Windows 98 installation disk or CD-ROM is not available, click OK, then click Cancel.

8. If necessary, insert the required Windows 98 installation disk or CD-ROM into the appropriate drive, then click OK

Windows 98 needs to install the appropriate driver to complete the installation. If necessary, click the Close button in the Windows 98 CD-ROM window.

9. Click Cancel

Since you are not actually installing a global positioning device, you should cancel the wizard.

FIGURE M-9: **Add New Hardware Wizard dialog box**

Click this option if the device is not in the list

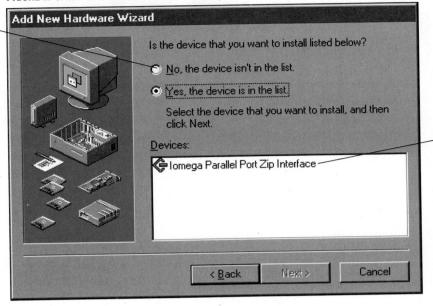

The device you are installing is not on the list

FIGURE M-10: **Add New Hardware Wizard dialog box**

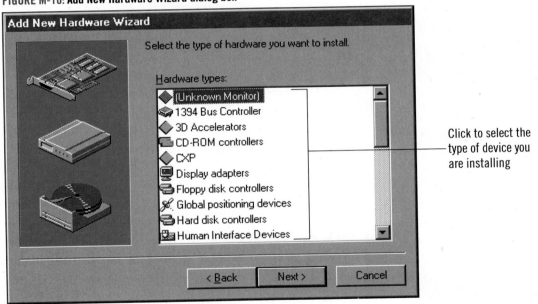

Click to select the type of device you are installing

CLUES TO USE

Updating drivers using the Add New Hardware Wizard

Manufacturers of computer hardware devices are constantly updating the software that is used to run the devices. You can locate the updated driver on the Drivers folder of the Windows 98 CD-ROM, on the hardware manufacturer's Web site, or on the Microsoft Web site. When you have downloaded the driver to your hard drive, double-click Add New Hardware in the Control Panel, then follow the instructions on your screen. When you are asked if you want Windows to search for your new hardware, click No, click the hardware type for the driver you are installing, click Have Disk, enter the location of the driver file, then follow the step-by-step instructions on your screen.

Windows 98

Viewing System Hardware

When you install a new operating system, such as Windows 98, it is important to make sure that you are using the latest software drivers with your system hardware. If you are not using the latest software drivers, your hardware devices might not work to full capacity. You can view your system hardware using a Windows 98 utility called the **Device Manager**. With the Device Manager, you can determine the software driver versions that are being used with your system hardware. After viewing your software driver version numbers, you can call the manufacturer to determine the latest versions. ◢▬▬ John wants to make sure that he is using the latest software driver version numbers.

Steps 1 2 3 4

Trouble?

If a specific device is conflicting with some other device, its icon is marked by an exclamation point within a yellow circle, as shown in Figure M-11.

1. **In the Control Panel, double-click the System icon (you might have to scroll to see it), then click the Device Manager tab**

   The System Properties dialog box opens with the Device Manager tab in front, as shown in Figure M-11. The Device Manager provides you with a list of the hardware types, also known as **hardware classes**, that are attached to your computer. To see the specific devices within a hardware type, you click the plus sign (+) next to the hardware device type. Once you select a specific device within a hardware device type, you can investigate the properties of the hardware device. On his computer, John uses an older **display adapter**, a hardware device that allows a computer to communicate with its monitor, so he decides to learn its properties.

2. **Click + next to the Display adapters icon**

   The display expands to show the name of the display adapter attached to your computer.

3. **Click the display adapter type that is connected to your computer, then click Properties at the bottom of the dialog box**

   The Display Adapter Properties dialog box opens with the General tab showing identification and status information about the display adapter. Table M-2 describes the options available in each of the tabs.

4. **Click the Driver tab**

   As shown in Figure M-12, you can click Driver File Details to learn the current version of the software driver, or you can click Update Driver to install the latest driver for the display adapter that is connected to your computer.

5. **Click Driver File Details**

   After calling the manufacturer of the display adapter, John discovers that he is using the latest version, so he closes the Properties dialog box.

QuickTip

To view hardware devices by what they are connected to, click the View devices by connection option button in the Device Manager tab.

6. **Click OK, then click OK**

   John restores the display before he examines other computer properties.

7. **Click + next to the Display adapters icon**

   Leave the Device Manager open.

FIGURE M-11: System Properties dialog box with Device Manager tab

Click to display a specific device

Hardware device conflict

Hardware types attached to your computer (your list might differ)

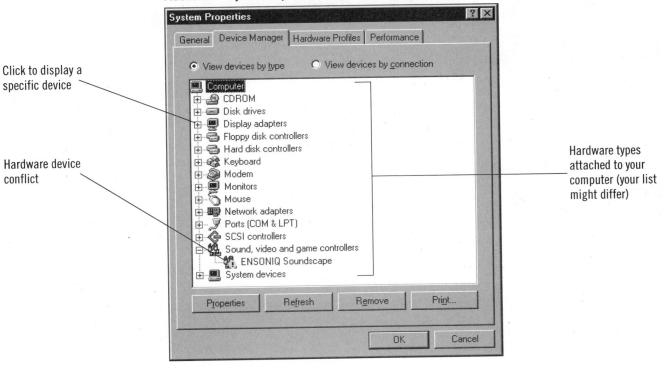

FIGURE M-12: Display Adapter Properties dialog box

Selected display adapter

Click to view driver details

Click to update driver

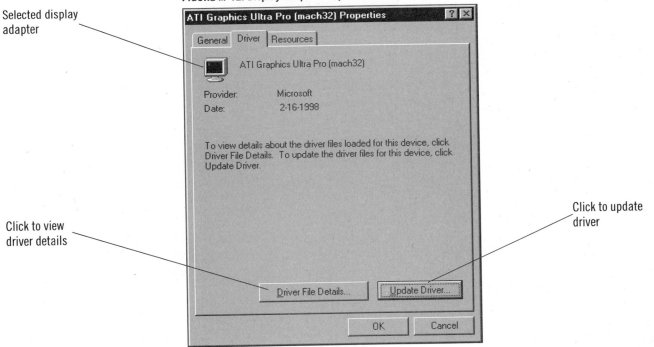

TABLE M-2: Display Adapter Properties dialog box

properties tab	description
General	Lists general status and usage information about the hardware device
Driver	Lists the software drivers related to the hardware device
Resources	Lists the memory settings related to the hardware device

Viewing Hardware Settings

Legacy hardware is any device that is not designed for Windows plug-and-play. If you have a hardware device that is not designed for plug-and-play, then it is important to find out current hardware settings to avoid conflicts during installation. Before you actually place a legacy hardware device into your computer, you should browse through the devices currently attached to your computer system, and ensure that you have enough hardware space. ➤ John wants to examine current computer properties.

Steps

1. **Click the Computer icon in the Device Manager**

2. **Click Properties**

   The Computer Properties dialog box opens with the View Resources tab, as shown in Figure M-13. The View Resources tab displays the resource values currently in use and the hardware that is using each resource. Each installed device requires a communication line called an **interrupt request line (IRQ)**, which allows the hardware device to communicate with your computer's software. Each device must have its own IRQ. If two devices attempt to share an IRQ, you will have an IRQ conflict, and neither device will work properly.

3. **Drag the scroll bar to the bottom of the dialog box**

   Take note of the available IRQs on your computer. When you install a legacy hardware device, the device's instructions might ask you to provide an IRQ setting. When prompted by the device instructions, provide an IRQ that is not already in use.

4. **Click OK**

   The Computer Properties dialog box closes. Instead of writing down your computer resource information on paper, you can print a system summary report.

5. **Click Print**

   The Print dialog box opens, as shown in Figure M-14. Table M-3 describes the report options available in the Print dialog box. Before you print, make sure that an available printer is selected.

6. **Click OK**

   If you are having trouble installing a hardware device, a technical support person might ask you questions that this summary report will help you answer. Figure M-15 shows the first part of the summary report. You don't have to understand what is there; you just need to know how to get this information so you can get help if you have to do so.

7. **Click OK, then click the Close button in the Control Panel**

Using the hardware troubleshooter

One kind of hardware conflict that can occur is when two or more devices try to use the same IRQ. In many cases, one of the devices will not work. If you have a conflict, you can use the hardware troubleshooter. To use the troubleshooter, click Help on the Start menu, click the Contents tab, click the Troubleshooting book, click Windows 98 Troubleshooters book, click the Hardware Conflict icon in the list, then follow the instructions and suggestions listed in the right pane of the Help window.

FIGURE M-13: Computer Properties dialog box with the View Resources tab

FIGURE M-14: Print dialog box

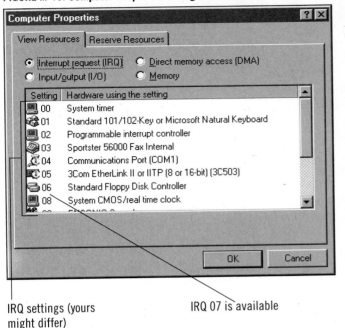

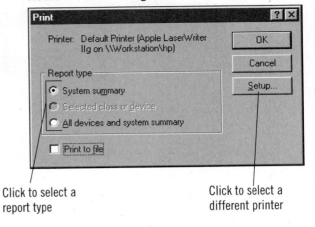

Click to select a report type

Click to select a different printer

IRQ settings (yours might differ)

IRQ 07 is available

FIGURE M-15: Summary Report

Take note of the system summary information

Take note of the IRQ usage summary information

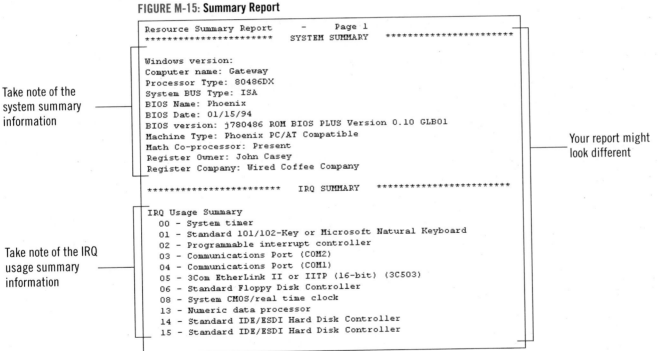

Your report might look different

TABLE M-3: Print dialog box report types

report types	description
System summary	Prints general system, IRQ, port, memory, and DMA channel usage information about your computer
Selected class or device	Prints device type, resource, and driver information
All devices and system summary	Prints general system, IRQ, port, memory, DMA channel usage, and driver information for all devices on your computer

Removing Hardware Devices

If you no longer use a hardware device or you have an older hardware device that you want to upgrade, you need to remove the hardware device drivers and related software before you remove the physical hardware device from your computer. Windows 98 makes it easy to remove device drivers. Just as Windows 98 uses different methods to install a printer than it uses to install other hardware, it uses different methods to remove a printer than it uses to remove other hardware. In this lesson, you will learn how to remove the printer driver that you installed earlier. To delete a different hardware device, select the device that you want to remove in the System Properties dialog box, which you access from the Control Panel, then click Remove. To delete a printer, you select the printer that you want to remove in the Printers window, which you access with the Settings command on the Start menu, then click the Delete button. ✏ John wants to delete a printer that he is not using.

1. **Click the Start button, point to Settings, then click Printers**
   The Printers window opens as shown in Figure M-16.

2. **Click the HP OfficeJet icon**
   The HP OfficeJet icon appears highlighted in the Printers window.

Trouble?

If a printer contains a print job, Windows 98 ignores the Delete command. You need to purge all print jobs before you can delete a printer.

3. **Click File on the menu bar, then click Delete**
   The Printers dialog box appears, asking if you want to delete the printer.

4. **Click Yes to confirm the delete**
   The HP OfficeJet dialog box appears, asking if you want to delete HP printer-specific files. These driver-related files are used only by the HP OfficeJet printer, so they are no longer needed.

5. **Click Yes to delete printer-specific files (if necessary)**
   The HP OfficeJet icon is removed from the Printers window.

6. **Click the Close button in the Printers window**

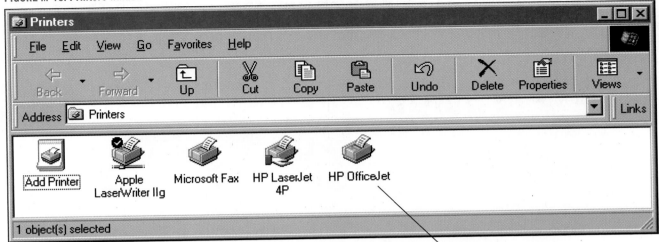

Click to select the
printer for deletion

CLUES TO USE

Deleting a hardware device

To delete a hardware device other than a printer, use the Device Manager tab in the System Properties dialog box, which you access from the Control Panel. Before you remove a device, it is a good idea to print the device settings in case you need to reinstall the device later. To print the settings, click Print at the bottom of the Device Manager tab. To delete a hardware device, click + next to the hardware type that contains the device you want to remove, select the device, then click Remove, as shown in Figure M-17.

FIGURE M-17: **System Properties dialog box**

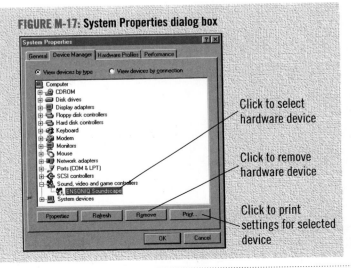

Click to select
hardware device

Click to remove
hardware device

Click to print
settings for selected
device

Practice

▶ Concepts Review

Label each of the elements of the screen shown in Figure M-18.

FIGURE M-18

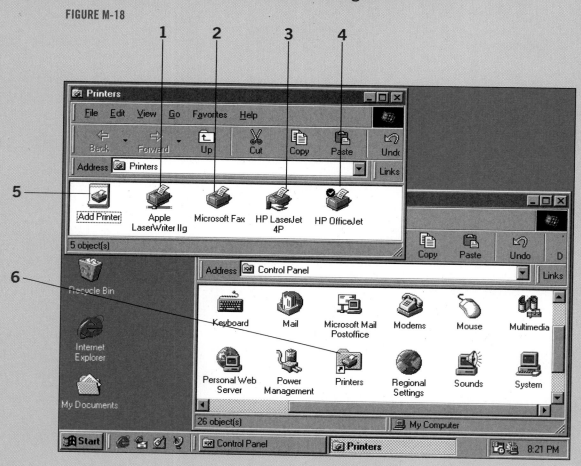

Match each of the terms with the statement that describes its function.

7. Where you connect a cable to a computer
8. Where you find device drivers
9. Hardware designed for Windows 95 or 98
10. Where you find printer drivers
11. How a device communicates
12. Hardware designed for pre-Windows 95

a. Details tab
b. Plug-and-play device
c. Port
d. Drivers tab
e. Legacy device
f. IRQ

Select the best answer from the list of choices.

13. **Which of the following is a way to print a document?**
    a. Select the Print command from a program
    b. Right-click a document, then click Print
    c. Drag a document to the printer icon
    d. All of the above

14. **When right-clicking a printer icon, which of the following can you NOT do?**
    a. Open the printer's window
    b. Set the printer as the default printer
    c. Delete the printer
    d. Close the printer's window

15. **Which tab in the Printer Properties dialog box do you click to check which port a printer is using?**
    a. the General tab
    b. the Device Options tab
    c. the Paper tab
    d. the Details tab

16. **To check computer properties in the System window of the Control Panel, click the:**
    a. General tab.
    b. Device Manager tab.
    c. Hardware Profiles tab.
    d. Performance tab.

17. **Which of the following commands is NOT a way to stop a print job that is currently in progress?**
    a. Purge Print Jobs
    b. Pause Printing
    c. Cancel Printing
    d. Stop Printing

18. **Which of the following is NOT a system report?**
    a. System summary
    b. All device and system summary
    c. Class or device summary
    d. Selected class or device

▶ Skills Review

1. View printer properties.
 a. Click Start, point to Settings, then click Printers.
 b. Click a printer icon.
 c. Click the Properties button on the toolbar.
 d. Click Print Test Page, then click Yes.
 e. Click the Details tab.
 f. Click OK.

2. Install a printer.
 a. Double-click the Add Printer icon.
 b. Click Next.
 c. Click Next.
 d. Click HP as the manufacturer.
 e. Click "HP DeskJet" as the model.
 f. Click Next.
 g. Click an open port (COM or LPT).
 h. Click Next.
 i. Click Next.
 j. Click the No option button.
 k. Click Finish.
 l. If necessary, insert a Windows 98 disk or CD-ROM into the appropriate drive, then click OK.
 m. If necessary, close the Windows 98 CD-ROM window.

3. Manage printers and print jobs.
 a. Right-click the HP DeskJet 1600C icon.
 b. Click Pause Printing.
 c. Open My Computer.
 d. Insert your Student Disk.
 e. Double-click the drive containing your Student Disk.
 f. Click the down scroll arrow if necessary.
 g. Click the "Burst Sign" document.
 h. Hold down [Shift], then click the "Coffee Roast" document.
 i. Drag the files to the HP DeskJet 1600C icon in the Printers window (you might have to drag the windows to see the documents and the icon at the same time).
 j. Double-click the HP DeskJet 1600C icon, then click Yes.
 k. Move the "Coffee Roast" document above the "Burst Sign" document.
 l. Click Purge Print Documents on the Printer menu.
 m. Click Close on the Printer menu.
 n. Click the Close button in all of the open windows.

4. **Install a hardware device.**
   a. Click Start, point to Settings, then click Control Panel.
   b. Double-click Add New Hardware, then click Next.
   c. Click Next.
   d. If necessary, click No, then click Next.
   e. Click No, then click Next.
   f. Click Global positioning devices, then click Next.
   g. Click Next, then click Next.
   h. If necessary, insert a Windows 98 disk or CD-ROM, then click OK.
   i. If necessary, close the Windows 98 CD-ROM window.
   j. Click Cancel since you are not actually installing a global positioning device.

5. **View system hardware.**
   a. Double-click the System icon in the Control Panel (you might have to scroll to see it).
   b. Click the Device Manager tab.
   c. Click + next to the Display adapters icon.
   d. Click a display adapter.
   e. Click Properties.
   f. Click the Driver tab.
   g. Click Cancel.
   h. Click - next to the Display adapters icon.

6. **View hardware settings.**
   a. Click the Computer icon in the Device Manager tab.
   b. Click Properties.
   c. Drag the scroll bar to the bottom.
   d. Click OK.
   e. Click Print.
   f. Click OK.
   g. Click Cancel.
   h. Click the Close button in the Control Panel.

7. **Remove hardware devices.**
   a. Click Start.
   b. Point to Settings.
   c. Click Printers.
   d. Click the HP DeskJet 1600C icon.
   e. Click the Delete button.
   f. Click Yes, then click Yes.
   g. Click the Close button in the Printers window.

► Independent Challenges

1. You are an administrator at the U.S. Geological Survey and are in charge of creating earthquake reports on seismic activity in California. Your boss recently approved the purchase of a new color printer to help you create better reports. You want to install the color printer on your computer.

To complete this independent challenge:

1. Install a printer using the Add Printer Wizard.
2. Assume the following about the installation: local printer, manufacturer is Tektronix, and printer model is Tektronix Phaser IIPX.
3. Choose an open port (LPT or COM).
4. Do not set the printer as default.
5. Do not print a test page.
6. Check the printer properties.
7. Use [Print Screen] to print the Printer Properties screen. (Press [Print Screen], start Paint, click Edit on the menu bar, click Paste to paste the screen into Paint, then click Yes to paste the large image, if necessary. Click File on the menu bar, click Print, then click OK. Close Paint.)
8. If you are working in a lab, delete the printer you just added.

2. You are the director of a youth center called Hosanna Homes for troubled teens. Half of your funding comes from the state and the other half comes from donations. At the end of the month, you need to send a report to the state indicating the status of each teen at the home. You also send a report to donors to let them know what happened during the month. For this challenge, create several reports, print the documents, and manage the print jobs.

To complete this independent challenge:

1. Use a real, working printer that is attached to your computer.
2. Pause printing or work offline. Get permission from your instructor or technical support person to do this.
3. Assume the following information about the youth center:
   Hosanna Homes   ID: 251523
   35 Live Oak Ranch Road
   Livermore, TX 82510
4. Using WordPad, create a file named "June 99 State" on your Student Disk, then enter the following information:
   State of Texas Protective Services

Name	Age	Level	Number of Days
Maura Colligan	16	4	30
Brian Hubbard	17	5	30
Jill Meyer	16	3	30
David Smith	17	4	30
Earl Todd	15	1	16
5. Print the file to the chosen printer.

6. Open a new WordPad window and create a file named "June 99 Donor" on your Student Disk, then enter the following information:
    Dear Donor,
    During the month, Hosanna Homes received a new teenager at the ranch. His name is Earl Todd. He is 15 years old. His hobbies are playing football and basketball, and drawing sports pictures.
    Hosanna Homes is in need of sports and recreational equipment. If you or anyone you know has any equipment to donate, please contact me at the main office.
    Thank you for all your support.
    Your name, Director
7. Print the file to the chosen printer.
8. Cancel the print job "June 99 State".
9. Choose the Pause Printing command to turn off Pause Printing and print the job "June 99 Donor".
10. Check the status of the printer.
11. Open the file "June 99 State" in the WordPad window, change the number of days for Earl Todd from 16 to 18, then save the file.
12. Print the file.

3. You are the owner of Lasting Impressions, a photography studio that specializes in wedding and location photography. To increase revenues, you want to add the ability to create wedding videos for your photography clients. To edit the videos, you want to connect a VCR to your computer. Before you invest in the hardware and software needed to make computer connections with your VCR, you decide to check your computer's multimedia properties.
    To complete this independent challenge:

1. Open the Control Panel.
2. Double-click the Multimedia icon.
3. Click the Devices tab.
4. Display the list of Media Control Devices.
5. Select the VISCA VCR Device (Media Control) device.
6. Display the properties for this device.
7. Display the settings for this device.
8. Use [Print Screen] to print the screen showing all of the open windows, following the directions shown in Independent Challenge 1.
9. Close open windows.

4. You are an engineer at Denson Engineering, a company that specializes in technical drawings. You want to install a special hardware device to create 35mm slides for a technical presentation that you have developed with some of your drawings. During the installation of the legacy hardware, you encountered some problems. When you called technical support, the representative asked you to print a resource summary report to help diagnose the problem.
    To complete this independent challenge:

1. Open the Control Panel.
2. Open System.
3. Display the Device Manager tab.
4. Select the computer.
5. Check properties.
6. View the IRQ resources.
7. Cancel resources.
8. Print a resource summary report.
9. Cancel the System properties.
10. Close open windows.

▶ Visual Workshop

Recreate the screen shown in Figure M-19, which displays information about a network adapter. Your results will differ from the ones shown here. Use [Print Screen] to print the screen, following the directions shown in Independent Challenge 1.

FIGURE M-19

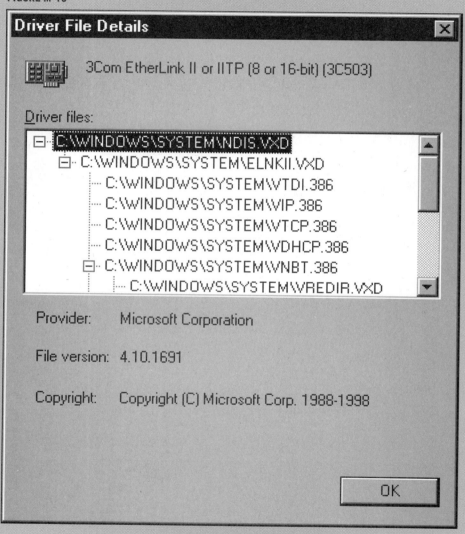

Backing
Up Your Disk

Objectives

- ▶ **Develop a backup strategy**
- ▶ **Copy files to a hard drive**
- ▶ **Start Backup**
- ▶ **Select files for a backup**
- ▶ **Perform a normal backup**
- ▶ **View and print a report**
- ▶ **Perform an incremental backup**
- ▶ **Restore a backed up file**
- ▶ **Delete a backup job**

You should make backup copies of your files. The term **back up** usually refers to the process of using a special software program designed to read your data quickly, compress it into a small, efficient space, then store it on a medium, such as a set of disks or a tape cartridge. Windows 98 includes a backup program called **Backup**. Using Backup has several advantages over simply copying files to a floppy disk, such as compressing files as it copies them so you can fit more onto a floppy disk. It can also split a large file across two or more floppies, something you cannot do with the Copy command. Also, in an emergency, Backup offers several data-recovery aids to help you locate and restore important files quickly. ✐ John uses Backup to back up important files on a floppy disk.

Windows 98

Developing a Backup Strategy

The **backup medium** that you use to store backed up files from a hard drive is usually a set of floppy disks or a tape cartridge designed to store computer data. A tape cartridge requires special hardware on your computer, including a tape drive, but it is worth the expense if you depend on your computer for business. With Microsoft Backup, you can back up files from a local or network hard drive to a floppy disk, a network drive, or a tape drive that is attached to your computer, as shown in Figure N-1. This unit assumes you are using a floppy disk as your backup medium and focuses primarily on backup strategies using floppies. Before you back up files, it is a good idea to develop a backup strategy. A **backup strategy** is a method for regularly backing up your work that balances tradeoffs between safety, time, and media space. For example, if safety was your only concern, you could back up your entire hard drive every hour. But you would not have any time to work, and you would spend a fortune on backup tapes. If spending minimal time and money on backups was your only concern, you might back up only a few crucial files once a month. The best choice is a balance between the two extremes. ✎ John wants to explore the different methods of backing up files in order to develop a backup strategy. See Table N-1 for a description of a weekly backup strategy.

Details

These are some of the different methods for backing up files with Microsoft Backup:

 A **normal backup** copies all selected files to the backup medium, regardless of when the files were last changed, and clears the archive attribute for each file in order to mark the file as backed up. An **archive attribute** is a Windows marker indicating whether a file needs to be backed up.

 An **incremental backup** copies only the files that have changed since your most recent normal or incremental backup. It also clears the archive attribute for each file that is backed up. Therefore, the first incremental backup after a normal backup copies all files that have changed since the normal backup, and the second incremental backup copies only those files that have changed since the first incremental backup, and so on.

 A **differential backup** copies only the selected files that have changed since your most recent normal or incremental backup. Unlike incremental backups, however, the archive attribute is not cleared during a differential backup. Therefore, successive differential backups copy all the files that have changed since the last normal or incremental backup, not just the ones that have changed since the last differential backup. Differential backups take longer than incremental backups and require more disk or tape space.

FIGURE N-1: **Computer with a tape drive**

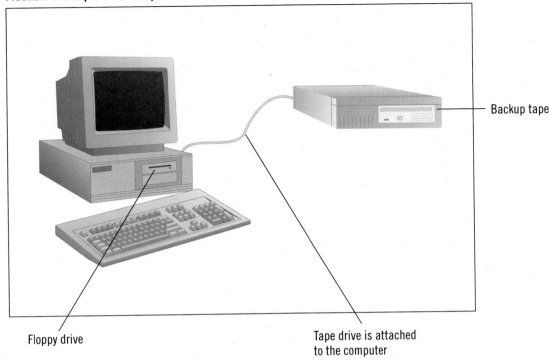

Backup tape

Floppy drive

Tape drive is attached
to the computer

TABLE N-1: **Example of a weekly backup strategy**

day	tasks to do
Monday, Week 1	Label your media (floppy disk or tape); if your backup requires more than one medium, label and number all the media in advance so you can recognize them easily; insert your first medium into the backup device and perform a normal backup with the All Selected File option
Tuesday, Week 1	Reinsert the medium you used for the normal backup and perform an incremental backup; the incremental backup is automatically appended to the normal backup
Wednesday through Friday, Week 1	Perform incremental backups; each subsequent incremental backup is appended to the previous backup; if you need more than one medium, you will be prompted to insert another one; after your Thursday backup, you will have a complete rotation set
Monday through Friday, Week 2	Repeat the cycle with a second set of media
Monday through Friday, Week 3	Repeat the cycle with the first set of media; continue rotating in this fashion

CLUES TO USE

Rotating your backups

For extra security, it is a good idea to rotate backup tapes or disks. For example, if you do a complete normal backup once a week and incremental backups on the intervening days, you might want to keep one week's worth of backup on one tape or set of disks and then use a different tape or set of disks the following week. If your original storage medium and your backup tape or set of disks are both damaged, you will still be able to restore files from the previous time period's backup. The file you restore probably will not be the most current versions, but you will be better off than if you had to re-create everything from scratch. If possible, store your backup tape or disks away from your computers. That way, if you experience a fire or theft, you will not necessarily lose both your originals and your backups.

Windows 98

Copying Files to a Hard Drive

Microsoft Backup is designed to back up the contents of a hard drive (or several hard drives) onto a backup medium. It is unable to back up files from one floppy disk to another. So that you have some files to back up, this unit begins by having you copy the files from your Student Disk to a hard disk. As you proceed through the lessons, you will back up the files you copied onto the hard disk to a different blank floppy disk. If you do not have access to a hard drive, you might not be able to complete this unit, although you could check with your instructor about backing up different files that are already on a network drive. 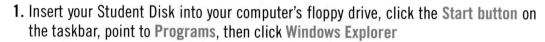 In this lesson, you will copy the files on your Student Disk to the C drive so in the next lesson, you can begin to back them up.

1. Insert your Student Disk into your computer's floppy drive, click the Start button on the taskbar, point to Programs, then click Windows Explorer

2. In the left pane of Windows Explorer, scroll until you locate the hard drive icon (usually C:) onto which you will copy your student files, then, if a + (plus sign) appears next to the icon, click the +; if a – (minus sign) is next to the icon, the drive is already expanded

3. In the left pane of Windows Explorer, click the hard drive (C:) icon, click File on the menu bar, point to New, click Folder, type John's Backup, then press [Enter]
   The new John's Backup folder appears in the list of folders and files on the hard drive. You will use this folder to store your Student Disk files temporarily. If you make a mistake typing, you can select the folder name and then retype your text.

4. In the left pane of Windows Explorer, scroll until you locate the floppy drive containing your Student Disk, then click the floppy drive icon
   Windows Explorer displays the contents of the floppy disk in the right pane, as shown in Figure N-2.

5. Click Edit on the menu bar, click Select All, then click the Copy button 📄 on the Windows Explorer toolbar

6. In the left pane of Windows Explorer, scroll until you locate the John's Backup folder you just created, click the John's Backup folder, then click the Paste button 📋 on the Windows Explorer toolbar
   Windows Explorer copies the files to the John's Backup folder on your hard drive and displays the files in the right pane, as shown in Figure N-3. You are now ready to use Microsoft Backup.

7. Click the Close button in the Windows Explorer window, then remove your Student Disk from the floppy drive

QuickTip

This unit assumes you are using the C drive as your hard drive. If you are not, substitute the correct letter for your hard drive each time the steps refer to the C drive.

QuickTip

To copy files quickly from one disk to another, such as from a floppy disk to a hard disk, you can drag the selected files from the right pane of Windows Explorer to a folder or disk in the left pane.

FIGURE N-2: Windows Explorer

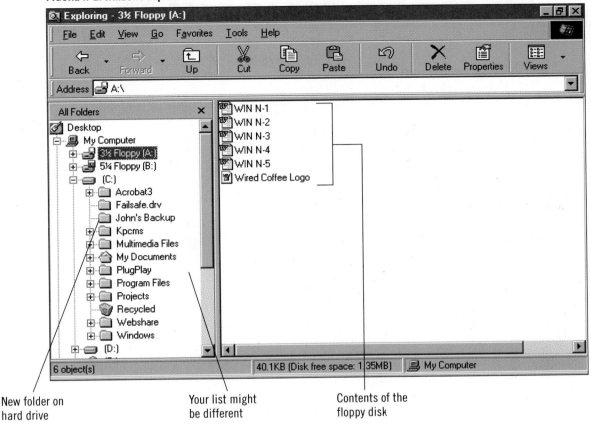

New folder on hard drive

Your list might be different

Contents of the floppy disk

FIGURE N-3: Windows Explorer with John's Backup folder

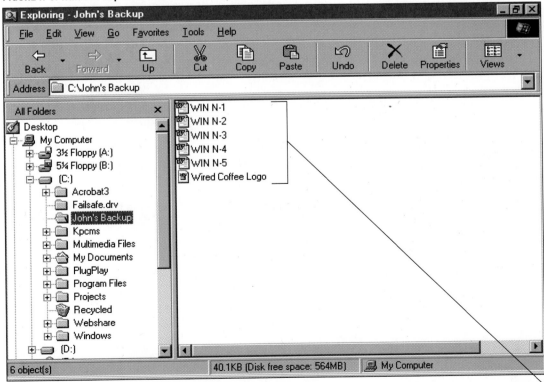

Contents of the newly created John's Backup folder

Windows 98

Starting Backup

Now that you have files on the hard drive to back up, you can use Microsoft Backup. Because backups take time, you should not back up all of the files on your computer every time you perform a backup. For example, since you can easily reinstall your program files from their original program disks, you do not need to back them up as often as your document files. An effective backup strategy begins with a complete normal backup, which backs up all files on your system, and continues with incremental backups, which back up only the files that have changed since your last backup. Ask yourself how much work can you afford to lose. If you can afford to lose the work accomplished in one day, back up once a day. If your work does not change much during the week, back up once a week. ➤ John starts Backup to do a normal backup of his important files on the hard drive.

 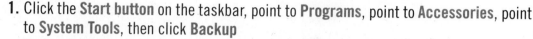

Trouble?

If Backup does not appear on your System Tools menu, use Add/Remove Programs in the Control Panel to install it. You will need your Windows 98 installation disks or CD-ROM.

QuickTip

To bypass the Backup Wizard and display the Microsoft Backup window, click Close.

1. Click the **Start button** on the taskbar, point to **Programs**, point to **Accessories**, point to **System Tools**, then click **Backup**

Backup initializes program settings and checks to determine if a backup device is connected to your computer. If you do not have a tape drive or removable disk connected to your computer (or if the tape drive or removable disk is turned off), a message appears, as shown in Figure N-4. Since John is backing up files to a floppy disk, a tape or removable drive is not required.

2. If necessary, click **No** to close the message box

The Microsoft Backup dialog box opens (if a previous user has not disabled it), as shown in Figure N-5, with options to create a new backup, open an existing backup, or restore backed up files.

3. If necessary, click the **Create a new backup job option button**

When you select the Create a new backup job option button or the Open an existing backup job option button, Backup starts the Backup Wizard to walk you through the process. If you had selected the Restore backed up files option, Backup would start the Restore Wizard.

4. Click **OK**

The Backup Wizard dialog box opens. The Backup Wizard walks you through the process of backing up files on your computer.

5. Click the **Back up selected files, folders and drives (Click Next to select files, folders and drives) option button**

The Backup Wizard dialog box appears as shown in Figure N-6.

6. Click **Next**

Leave the Backup Wizard dialog box open and continue to the next lesson, where you will select the files to back up.

FIGURE N-4: Microsoft Backup dialog box

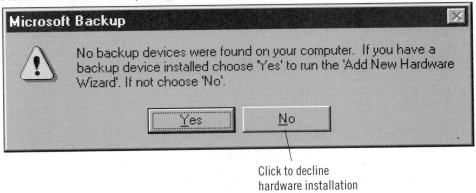

Click to decline
hardware installation

FIGURE N-5: Microsoft Backup Welcome dialog box

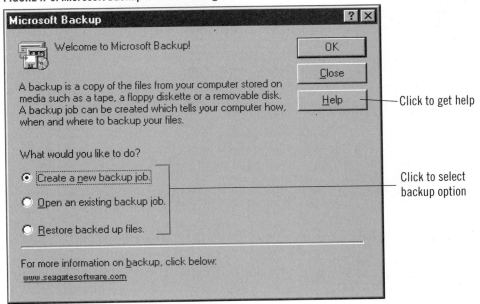

Click to get help

Click to select
backup option

FIGURE N-6: Backup Wizard dialog box

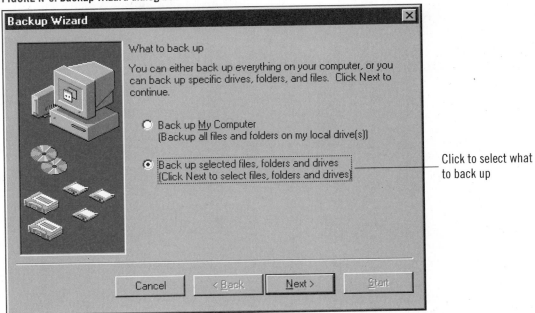

Click to select what
to back up

Selecting Files for a Backup

Once you have started Backup, you need to display and then select the folders and files that you want to back up. The Microsoft Backup window works like Windows Explorer. To display or hide the folders located on your hard drive, click + or − to the left of the drive or folder icon. In addition to the + and −, there is a check box to the left of each storage device, folder, or file on your computer. After using + and − to display and hide the appropriate files, you click this check box to select the folders and files you want to back up. Once you have made your selection, Backup allows you to save the selection settings in a **file set**, so you do not need to reselect them next time you perform a backup. ▰▰▰ John begins by selecting the files he wants to back up. He then saves his selection to a file set.

Steps 1 2 3 4

1. **In the What to back up list, click + to the left of the hard drive (C:) icon, then, if necessary, drag the vertical scroll bar to view the John's Backup folder icon**
   The hard drive (C:) icon expands to display all the folders and files it contains. See Table N-2 for information concerning the display of drives and folders.

2. **In the What to back up list, click the John's Backup folder icon**
   The folders and files stored in the John's Backup folder are displayed in the right pane. To back up all the files in a folder, click the check box next to the folder in the left pane. To back up a specific file, click the check box next to the file in the right pane.

3. **In the What to back up list, click the John's Backup folder check box**
   The folders and files in the John's Backup folder appear checked, as shown in Figure N-7; all of the files in the John's Backup folder will be backed up. The shaded check box beside the hard drive (C:) icon indicates that only some of the folders and files in that drive are selected.

4. **Click Next**
   The Backup Wizard asks you to specify whether to back up all of the files you have selected, or only the files that are new or have changed since the previous back up.

5. **Make sure the All selected files option button is selected, then click Next**
   The Backup Wizard asks you to select a backup destination (the place where you will store your backed up files).

6. **Insert a blank, formatted floppy disk in the floppy drive, then click the Where to back up button ▣**
   The Where to back up dialog box opens.

7. **Click the Look in list arrow, click 3½ Floppy (A:) or (B:) (scroll to see it if necessary), then click Open**
   The Backup Wizard dialog box appears as shown in Figure N-8. John uses the default name "MyBackup.qic" (QIC is the extension for all backup files) as the backup file name. In the next lesson, you will actually perform the backup.

FIGURE N-7: **Backup Wizard dialog box**

Click to display
folder contents

Click to select
folder contents for
backing up

Your list might
be different

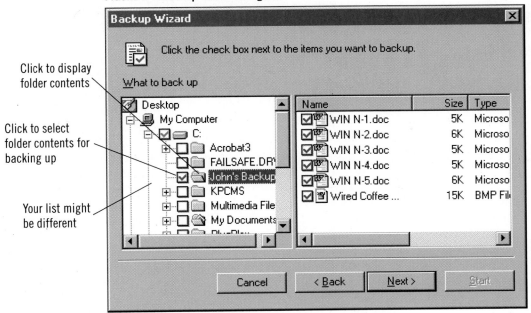

FIGURE N-8: **Backup Wizard dialog box**

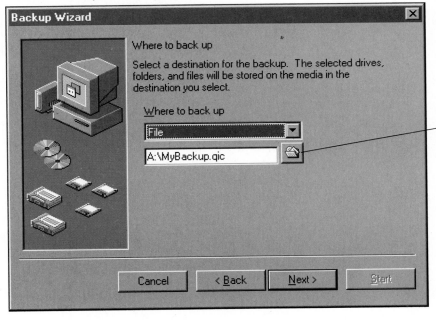

Click to select the
backup location
and filename

TABLE N-2: **Displaying drive and folder contents**

folder selection	item	function
+	A + to the left of a drive or folder	All the folders it contains are hidden
−	A − to the left of a drive or folder	All the folders it contains are displayed
	No sign to the left of a drive or folder	The folder does not contain any folders, although it may contain files
☑	A blue checked box to the left of a drive or folder	All the folders and files it contains are selected for backup
☑	A gray checked box to the left of a drive or folder	Only some of the folders and files it contains are selected for backup
☐	An unchecked box to the left of a drive or folder	None of the folders and files it contains are selected for backup

Performing a Normal Backup

Once you have selected the files that you want to back up and the destination where you want to store them, you are ready to perform the backup. During the backup, Backup compresses the files you selected and copies them to the floppy. When a file does not fit on a floppy, Backup splits the file, fitting what it can on the current floppy and then prompting you to enter the next floppy. Depending on the number and size of your files and the backup device you are using, the backup can take a few minutes to a few hours to complete. If you are planning to back up large amounts of information, such as your hard drive, it is best to start the backup at the end of the day and use a tape drive if possible so you do not have to swap multiple floppy disks. John selects backup options, enters a name for the backup job, then starts the backup of the files he just selected.

1. **Click Next**

   The Backup Wizard asks you to select options that will compare original and backup files after the backup. This is done to verify that the data was successfully backed up and to compress the backed up data to save space. Both options are selected by default.

2. **Click Next**

   The Backup Wizard asks you to enter a name for the back up job. When you perform a backup, Backup creates a **backup job**, also known as a backup set, which contains the compressed copies of the files you backed up. The backup job is stored in the backup file you specified in the previous lesson (in this case, MyBackup.qic on the floppy drive). You can store more than one backup job in a specified backup file.

3. **Type 22 July 1999**

   To make it easier to later identify the backup, John uses the current date to name the backup, as shown in Figure N-9.

4. **Click Start**

   The Backup Progress dialog box opens with a progress meter that indicates the current backup status. If the backup requires more than one floppy disk, a dialog box appears asking you to insert another disk. Upon completion, a message dialog box appears, indicating that the operation is complete.

5. **Click OK**

   The Backup Progress dialog box appears, as shown in Figure N-10.

6. **Click OK, then click the Maximize button in the Microsoft Backup window if necessary**

   The Microsoft Backup window appears, as shown in Figure N-11.

7. **Remove the floppy disk from drive A or B, label the disk Disk 1 22 July 1999 Backup, then reinsert the disk in drive A or B**

FIGURE N-9: Backup Wizard dialog box

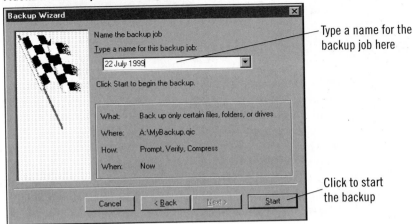

Type a name for the backup job here

Click to start the backup

FIGURE N-10: Backup Progress dialog box

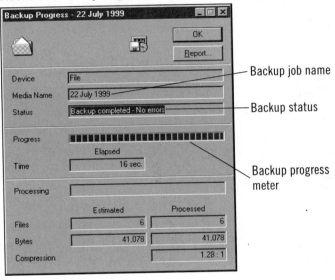

Backup job name

Backup status

Backup progress meter

FIGURE N-11: Microsoft Backup window

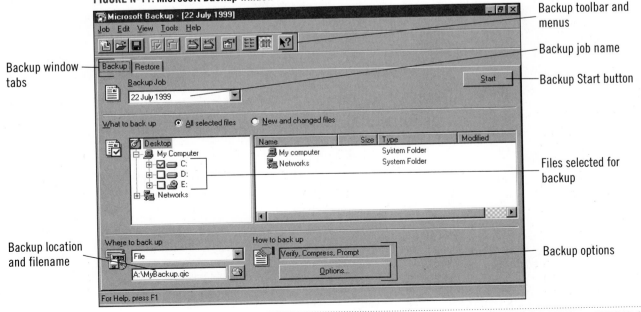

Backup toolbar and menus

Backup job name

Backup Start button

Backup window tabs

Files selected for backup

Backup location and filename

Backup options

Windows 98

Viewing and Printing a Report

After performing a backup, Backup creates a report with status information about the backup. The backup report is created in Notepad (a text program that comes with Windows 98) and saved in the Backup program folder on your hard drive. Each time you perform a backup, the report information is added to the beginning of the backup report file in order to create a backup history. To make it easier to manage your backup jobs, it is important to view and print a backup report after each backup. To customize your report, you can use the Report tab in the Backup Job Options dialog box to specify the items you want to include in your backup report. John views the backup report, changes a report option, then prints a copy. After printing the report, you will change a file so that you can perform an incremental backup (on changed files) in the next lesson.

Steps

1. **Click Tools on the Microsoft Backup menu bar, point to Report, then click View**
   Notepad opens, as shown in Figure N-12. The report displays the backup job start time, end time, date, the number of processed files, the amount of compression, and the comparison results.

2. **Click File on the Notepad menu bar, then click Print**
   Notepad prints the backup report. Notice that the report does not include the file names that were backed up. You can change an option so the file names are displayed in future reports.

3. **Click the Close button in the Notepad window to close Notepad**
   The Microsoft Backup window remains open.

4. **Click Options, then click the Report tab**
   The Backup Job Options dialog box opens with the Report tab, as shown in Figure N-13. See Table N-3 for a description of the Backup Job Options dialog box tabs.

5. **Click the List all files that were backed up check box to select the option, then click OK**
   Now when you perform the incremental backup in the next lesson, the report will list the files that were backed up.

6. **Leave the Microsoft Backup window open, click the Start button on the taskbar, point to Programs, point to Accessories, click WordPad, then open the document WIN N-1 from the John's Backup folder on your hard drive**
   Make sure you open the document from the correct location (the John's Backup folder on the hard drive, not your Student Disk). The WordPad window appears with the WIN N-1 document. This is the file you will change for the backup in the next lesson.

7. **In the first paragraph, select the word November, then type October**

8. **Click the Save button** 💾 **on the toolbar, then click the Close button**
   Leave Microsoft Backup open, then continue to the next lesson.

FIGURE N-12: Backup report in Notepad

Your information
might be different

Backup report
information

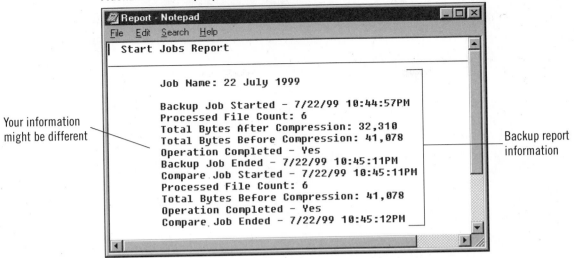

FIGURE N-13: Backup Job Options dialog box

Click to include
backed up files
in the report

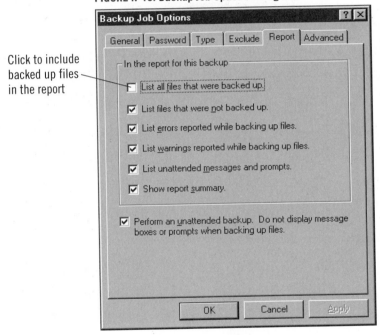

TABLE N-3: Backup Job Options dialog box tabs

tab	description
General	Allows you to verify that data is successfully backed up, select a compression setting, and specify how to handle media that already contain backups
Password	Allows you to set a password to protect your backup job
Type	Allows you to specify the new and changed files backup type to run as a differential or incremental backup, or to specify the all selected file backup type to back up all the files you have selected
Exclude	Allows you to add or remove files of a specified type to or from a backup
Report	Allows you to specify the items you want to include in your backup report and to set your unattended backup option
Advanced	Allows you to specify whether the Windows registry will be backed up

Performing an Incremental Backup

John's backup job contains compressed copies of all his files, but it does not have the current version of the file he just changed. Rather than having to redo the entire backup, you can use an incremental backup to save only the files that have changed since the last backup. Files created after the date of the incremental file set and files that have been renamed are not included in the incremental backup unless you update the backup job. John performs an incremental backup to include the change he just made to the WIN N-1 file.

Steps

1. **If necessary, click the Backup Job list arrow, then click 22 July 1999**
   The backup settings for the 22 July 1999 backup appear in the Microsoft Backup window.

2. **Next to the What to back up list, click the New and changed files option button**
   This is the option you use for an incremental backup.

3. **Click the Where to back up button 🖾, type MyBackup2, then click Open**

4. **Click Job on the menu bar, click Save As, type 29 July 1999, then click Save**
   This new job name, as shown in Figure N-14, will distinguish this backup from the complete backup you performed earlier. Now that you have opened a backup file, you are ready to start the incremental backup.

5. **Click Start**
   The Backup Progress dialog box opens with a progress meter indicating current backup status. The file that changed since the last backup is backed up. Upon completion, a message dialog box appears indicating that the operation is finished.

6. **Click OK, then click Report in the Backup Progress dialog box**
   Notepad opens with the backup report, as shown in Figure N-15. The name of the changed file appears in the backup report.

7. **Click the Notepad Close button, then click OK to close the Backup Progress dialog box**

8. **Click Options, click the Report tab, click the List of all files that were backed up check box to deselect the option, then click OK**
   This restores the report options to the original settings.

FIGURE N-14: Microsoft Backup window with incremental backup settings

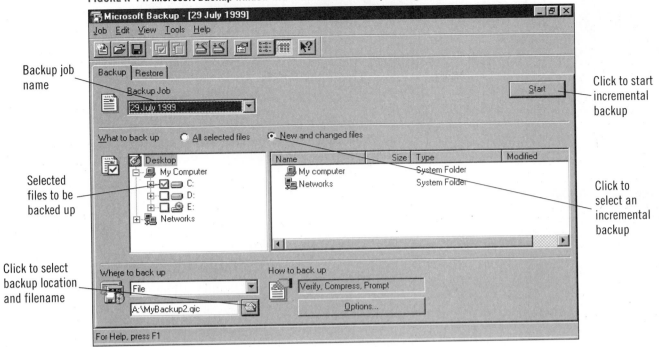

Backup job name

Selected files to be backed up

Click to select backup location and filename

Click to start incremental backup

Click to select an incremental backup

FIGURE N-15: Backup report in Notepad

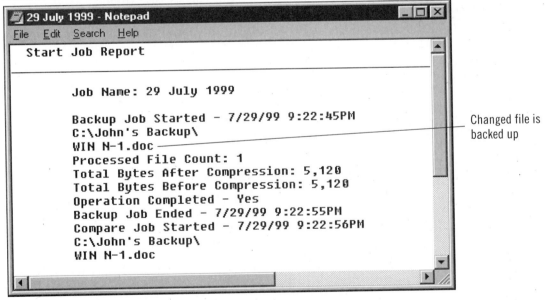

Changed file is backed up

Using a tape drive to back up files

Using a tape drive can make backing up large amounts of information, such as an entire hard drive, fast and easy. Before you use a tape drive with Microsoft Backup, make sure the tape drive is compatible with Microsoft Backup, which works only with QIC-compatible tape drives. For a complete list of compatible tape drives,

click Help Topics on the Help menu in the Microsoft Backup window. After connecting the tape drive to your computer and cleaning the tape drive head, you can use the Tools menu to detect the tape drive and to format or erase a tape cartridge to back up your files.

Windows 98

Restoring a Backed Up File

The real value in backing up your files becomes apparent if you lose or damage some files or need information from a document that has changed a great deal over time. You can restore a single file, several files, or an entire hard drive. Using the Restore Wizard, you can specify which files you want to restore and where you want them to be placed. ✍ A co-worker at Wired Coffee needs the original WIN N-1 file, so he asks John to restore that file onto the hard drive.

Steps 1 2 3 4

1. Click the **Restore tab** (below the toolbar), then click **NO** to refresh the view (if necessary)

2. Click the **Restore Wizard button** 🔲 on the Backup toolbar, click the **Where to back up button** 🔲, select the **floppy drive** containing your backup files, then double-click **MyBackup**

   The Restore Wizard asks you to choose from where to restore files. The Restore Wizard dialog box appears, as shown in Figure N-16.

3. Click **Next**, then click **Yes** to refresh the view (if necessary)

   The Select Backup Sets dialog box opens with a list of backup jobs in the MyBackup.qic file, as shown in Figure N-17.

4. Click **OK**

   After a moment, the Restore Wizard dialog box returns, asking you to click the items you want to restore.

5. In the What to restore list, click **+** to the left of the hard drive (C:) icon, click the **John's Backup folder**, then click the **WIN N-1 file check box** in the Contents list (scroll to see it, if necessary)

   The selected file appears checked, as shown in Figure N-18. John starts the restoration.

6. Click **Next**, then click **Next** to restore the file in its original location

7. Click the **Always replace the file on my computer option button**

8. Click **Start**, then click **OK** to confirm the required media

   The Restore Progress dialog box opens with a progress meter indicating current status. Upon completion, a message dialog box appears indicating that the operation is finished.

9. Click **OK**, then click **OK** to return to the Microsoft Backup window

   John opens the restored file and sees that the file is restored properly (you could also check this by opening the restored file in WordPad).

FIGURE N-16: Restore Wizard dialog box

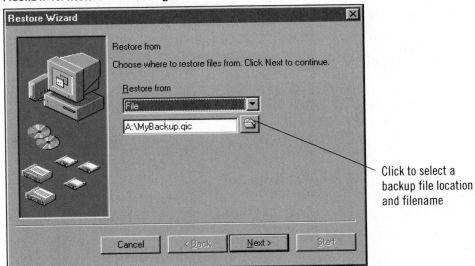

Click to select a backup file location and filename

FIGURE N-17: Select Backup Sets dialog box

Click to select a backup set

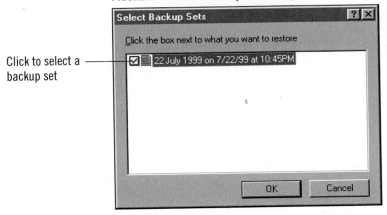

FIGURE N-18: Restore Wizard dialog box

Click here to select the file you want to restore

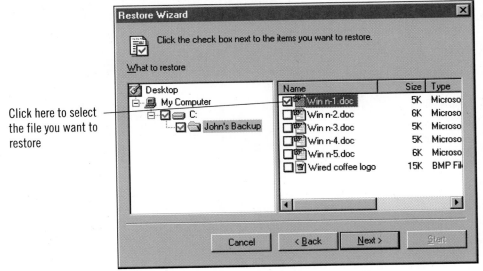

Windows 98

Delete a Backup Job

After backing up files for awhile, you might find a number of unneeded backup jobs accumulating in Backup. You can delete these jobs quickly and easily from within Backup. When you delete a backup job, such as 22 July 1999, only the backup job is deleted, while the backup file, such as MyBackup.qic, remains in the backup location. If you want to delete the backup file, drag the file icon into the Recycle Bin as you would any other Windows file. ▰▰▰ John deletes old backup jobs from Backup.

Steps

1. Click the **Backup tab**

2. Click **Job** on the menu bar, then click **Delete**
   The Delete Backup Job dialog box opens, as shown in Figure N-19.

3. Click **22 July 1999**, click **Delete**, then click **Yes**
   The backup job is deleted.

4. Click **Job** on the menu bar, then click **Delete**

5. Click **29 July 1999**, click **Delete**, then click **Yes**
   The Microsoft Backup window appears without any backup jobs, as shown in Figure N-20.

6. Click the **Close button** in the Microsoft Backup window to exit the program

7. Click the **Start button** on the taskbar, point to **Programs**, then click **Windows Explorer**
   You can use Windows Explorer to delete the John's Backup folder and backup files in order to restore your drives to their original state.

8. Click the **John's Backup folder** on your hard drive, press **[Delete]**, then click **Yes** in the Confirm Folder Delete dialog box

9. Locate the **floppy drive** containing the backup jobs, then click the **floppy drive icon**
   Windows Explorer displays the contents of the floppy disk in the right pane.

10. Click **Edit** on the menu bar, click **Select All**, press **[Delete]**, then click **Yes** to confirm the deletion

11. Click the **Close button** in the Windows Explorer window, then remove the **floppy disk** from the drive
    Now the backup jobs and John's Backup folder are deleted.

FIGURE N-19: Delete Backup Job dialog box

Click to select a
backup job to delete

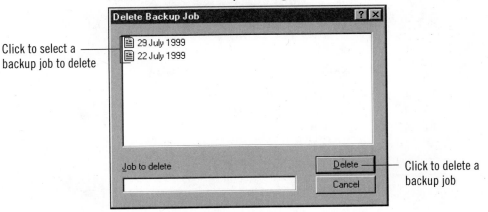

Click to delete a
backup job

FIGURE N-20: Microsoft Backup window

No backup jobs

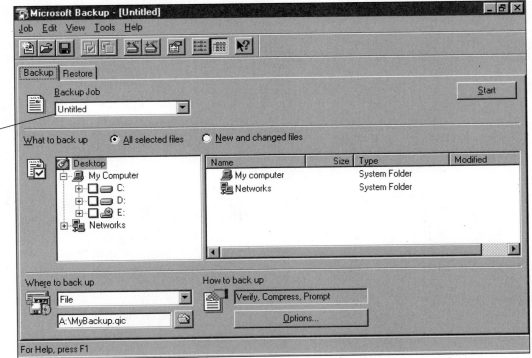

Practice

▶ Concepts Review

Label each of the elements of the screen shown in Figure N-21.

FIGURE N-21

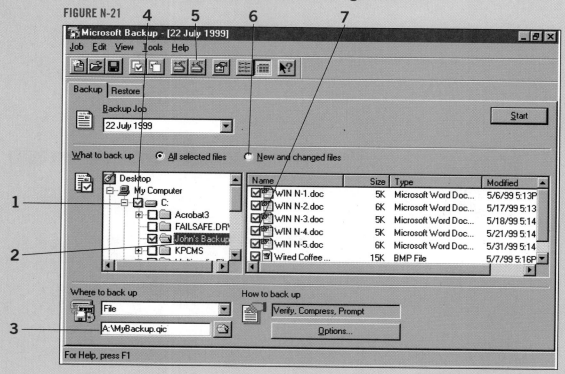

Match each of the terms with the statement that describes its function.

8. **Backs up files**
9. **Retrieves files**
10. **Archived attribute is cleared in this backup type**
11. **Saves backup jobs**
12. **Verifies a backup**
13. **Archived attribute is not cleared in this backup type**

a. A backup option
b. Backup Wizard
c. Normal backup
d. Restore Wizard
e. A backup job
f. Differential backup

Select the best answer from the list of choices.

14. **Which of the following is not an advantage of Microsoft Backup?**
    a. Compresses files as it copies them
    b. Backs up floppy to floppy
    c. Splits large files across two or more floppies
    d. Automatically detects tape drives
15. **Which of the following is something you CANNOT do with Microsoft Backup?**
    a. Back up files
    b. Compare files
    c. Modify files
    d. Restore files
16. **The gray checkmark indicates that:**
    a. All of the folders and files are selected.
    b. Some of the files are selected.
    c. Some of the folders and files are selected.
    d. All of the files are selected.

17. Which backup type copies only files that have changed since the last backup?
  a. System
  b. Compare
  d. Full
  c. Incremental

▶ Skills Review

1. Copy files to the hard drive.
  a. Insert your Student Disk in drive A or B, click Start, point to Programs, then click Windows Explorer.
  b. Click the hard drive (C:) icon, click File, point to New, click Folder.
  c. Type "Backup Files", then press [Enter].
  d. Locate the floppy disk drive containing your Student Disk, then click the floppy drive icon.
  e. Click Edit, click Select All, then copy the files from your Student Disk to the Backup Files folder.
  f. Close Windows Explorer, then remove your Student Disk from the disk drive.

2. Start Microsoft Backup.
  a. Click Start, point to Programs, point to Accessories, point to System Tools, then click Backup.
  b. Click the Create a new backup job option button, then click OK.
  c. Click the Backup selected files, folder and drives (click Next to select files, folders and drivers) option button, then click Next.

3. Select files for a backup.
  a. Click + to the left of the hard drive (C:) icon, then click the Backup Files folder check box.
  b. Click Next, then click Next.
  c. Insert a blank disk in the appropriate drive on your computer.
  d. Click the Where to back up button, click the Look in list arrow, click 3 1/2 Floppy (A:) or (B:), then click Open.

4. Perform a normal backup.
  a. Click Next, click Next, type "23 September 1999", then click Start.
  b. Click OK, click OK, then click Maximize, if necessary.
  c. Remove the floppy disk, label the disk, then insert it into the appropriate drive on your computer.

5. View and print a report.
  a. Click Tools, point to Report, then click View.
  b. In Notepad, click File, click Print, then click the Close button.
  c. Click the Options button, then click the Report tab.
  d. Click the List of all files that were backed up check box, then click OK.
  e. Click Start, point to Programs, point to Accessories, then click Paint.
  f. Open the file "Wired Coffee Logo" from the Backup Files folder.
  g. Add text to the image, save the file, then exit Paint.

6. Perform an incremental backup.
  a. Click the Backup Job list arrow, then click "23 September 1999", if necessary.
  b. Click the New and changed files option button.
  c. Click the Where to back up button, type "MyBackup2", then click Open.
  d. Click Job, click Save As, type "30 September 1999", then click Save.
  e. Click Start, click OK, then click Report.
  f. In Notepad, click the Close button, then click OK.
  g. Click Options, click the Report tab, click the List of all files that were backed up check box, then click OK.

7. Restore files.
  a. Click the Restore tab, click No (if necessary), then click the Restore Wizard button on the Backup toolbar.
  b. Click the Where to backup button, then double-click "A:\MyBackup.qic".

    c. Click Next, click Yes to refresh the view (if necessary), then click OK.

    d. Click + to the left of the hard drive (C:) icon, click the Backup Files folder icon, then click the Wired Coffee Logo file check box.

    e. Click Next, click Next, then click the Always replace the file on my computer option button.

    f. Click Start, click OK, click OK, then click OK again.

8. Delete backup jobs.

    a. Click the Backup tab, click Job, then click Delete.

    b. Click "23 September 1999", click Delete, click Yes, click Job, then click Delete.

    c. Click "30 September 1999", click Delete, click Yes, then click the Close button.

    d. Click Start, point to Programs, then click Windows Explorer.

    e. Click John's Backup folder, press [Delete], click Yes.

    f. Click the floppy drive icon, click Edit, click Select All, press [Delete], then click Yes.

    g. Click the Close button, then remove the floppy disk.

▶ Independent Challenges

1. You are the owner of Buds and Petals, Inc., a company that specializes in freeze-dried flowers. To grow your business, you attend craft fairs to sell arrangements and build a mailing list. After each fair, you send letters to those who purchased arrangements, and information to those who request it. For this independent challenge, create a thank-you letter, an arrangement and pricing information document, and several samples of the letters, then back up the files on a floppy disk.

    To complete this independent challenge:

1. Using Windows Explorer, create a folder named Customers on your hard drive.
2. Using WordPad, create the following documents in the Customers folder.
   a. A thank-you letter
   b. Sample thank-you letters with name and address information
   c. An arrangement and pricing information sheet
3. Start Microsoft Backup, then insert a blank floppy disk in the floppy drive.
4. Start the backup and create a new backup job.
5. Select the files that you created in WordPad, then back up the files to your floppy as "Buds and Petals".
6. Save the backup job as "Fair 1999", perform a normal backup, then print a report.
7. Delete the backup jobs, then using Windows Explorer, delete the Customers folder.

2. You are an associate at Andersen, Williams & Barnes law firm. You are currently helping two partners create a California corporation. To create a new corporation, you need to fill out corporation forms for the state, create by-laws, and hold board meetings. For this independent challenge, create the documents necessary to create a corporation, and then back up the documents on a floppy disk.

    In this challenge, you will create your own information. Assume the following facts about the corporation:

- Corporation name: IntSoft, Inc.
- Corporation date: 3/5/99
- Business: Develop testing tools for Windows software developers
- Ownership: Dorian Golu, 6,000 shares (60%); and John Yokela, 4,000 shares (40%)
- Address: 722 Main Street, Suite 100, Silicon Valley, CA 90028

To complete this independent challenge:

1. Using Windows Explorer, create a folder named IntSoft 99 on your hard drive.

2. Using WordPad, create the following documents in the IntSoft 99 folder.
   a. A document stating the above information called INTAOI
   b. Board meeting minutes stating all the steps taken to create the corporation called INT BM 001
   c. A bill for services called INT Bill 001
3. Start Microsoft Backup, then insert a blank floppy disk into the appropriate drive on your computer.
4. Start the backup, create a new backup job, then back up the selected files that you created in WordPad.
5. Back up the files to your floppy as "Important", then save the backup job as "INT Dec 1999".
6. Select the files that you created with WordPad, then perform the normal backup and print a report.
7. Add billing information to INT Bill 001, save the document, then perform an incremental backup.
8. Save the backup job as "INT Jan 2000", then restore the changed file and verify that the incremental backup stored the latest version.
9. Delete the backup jobs, then using Windows Explorer, delete the IntSoft 99 folder.

3. You are a graphic artist for Zero Gravity Designs, Inc., a company that specializes in logos. A real estate developer asks you to create a logo for his company, called Syntec, Inc. For this independent challenge, create several different logos in Paint, then back up the documents. After getting comments on the designs, make changes, then back up the documents. After making so many changes, compare your backups with your current files.

To complete this independent challenge:

1. Using Windows Explorer, create a folder named Syntec on your hard drive.
2. Using Paint, create several Paint documents with different logo designs, then save them in the Syntec folder.
3. Start Microsoft Backup, then insert a blank floppy disk in the appropriate drive on your computer.
4. Start the backup, create a new backup job, then back up the selected files that you created in WordPad.
5. Back up the files to your floppy as "Syntec Files", then save the backup job as "SYN Oct 10 1999".
6. Select the files that you created with Paint, then perform the normal backup.
7. Revise several designs, save the documents, then perform an incremental backup.
8. Save the backup job as "SYN Oct 17 1999", print a report, then delete the backup jobs.
9. Using Windows Explorer, delete the Syntec folder.

4. After retiring from the police force, you decide to start a company, called Safety One, Inc., that specializes in gun safety training programs for police academies and the general public. To get the company started, you need to create an introductory gun safety class. For this independent challenge, create a class outline and a letter, then back up the documents. After getting comments on the outline, make changes, then back up the documents. After saving your changes, restore the original document.

To complete this independent challenge:

1. Using Windows Explorer, create a folder named Safety 1 on your hard drive.
2. Using WordPad, create the following documents in the Safety 1 folder.
   a. An outline, called "GS 101 Outline", for the Gun Safety 101 class
   b. A letter, called "GS Comments", to friends at the police department asking for comments on the outline
3. Start Microsoft Backup, then insert a blank floppy disk in the appropriate drive.
4. Start the backup, create a new backup job, then back up the selected files that you created in WordPad.
5. Back up the files to your floppy as "Safety One", then save the backup job as "SO 062299".
6. Select the files that you created with WordPad, then perform the normal backup and print a report.
7. Revise "GS 101 Outline", then save the document.
8. Perform a differential backup. (Hint: Use the Options button and the Type tab.)
9. Save the backup job as "SO 072099".
10. Restore "GS 101 Outline" from the "SO 062296" backup job, print a report, then delete the backup jobs.
11. Using Windows Explorer, delete the Safety 1 folder.

▶ Visual Workshop

Recreate the screen shown in Figure N-22, which displays the Microsoft Backup window with settings to back up your entire hard drive. Your hard drive folders might be different. Use [Print Screen] to print the screen from Paint. (Press [Print Screen], start Paint, click Edit on the menu bar, click Paste to paste the screen into Paint, then click Yes to paste the large image, if necessary. Click File on the menu bar, click Print, then click OK.)

FIGURE N-22

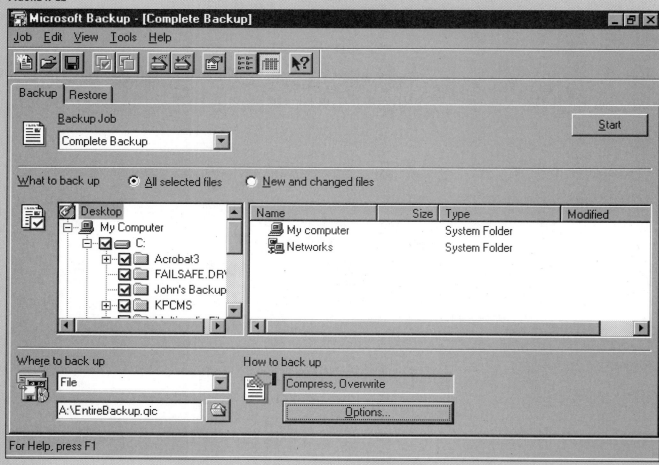

Exploring

Windows 98 Communication Features

Objectives

- ► **Understand Windows 98 communication features**
- ► **Set up a dial-up networking connection**
- ► **Use Connection Wizard advanced settings**
- ► **Connect to a dial-up service**
- ► **Install the MSN online service**
- ► **Dial over a modem with Phone Dialer**
- ► **Manage phone numbers**
- ► **Set up NetMeeting**
- ► **Call others over the Internet**

Windows 98 makes communicating over computers easier than ever. It provides accessories that allow you to connect to other computers and to the Internet, to dial phone numbers automatically, to chat with users on other computers, and to collaborate with others during online conferences. If you are already connected to the Internet, you can just read the second and third lessons in this unit that deal with setting up an Internet connection. This unit shows you how to use Windows 98 communication features such as Phone Dialer and NetMeeting, both of which are useful for home and business. ✐ John Casey recently purchased a computer so he can work from home. He wants to connect to the Internet so he can take advantage of Windows 98 communication features for his business.

Windows 98

Understanding Windows 98 Communication Features

Computers at universities or large companies are likely connected to the Internet via expensive, high-speed wiring that transmits data very quickly. Home computer owners, however, usually can't afford to run similar cables and wires to their homes, and instead must rely on phone lines that are already in place, as shown in Figure O-1. When a modem uses an ordinary voice phone line, which uses analog signals, it converts the modem's digital signals to analog. The receiving computer converts the analog signal back to digital. Data usually travels much more slowly over phone wires than over the networking infrastructure that makes up the Internet, and if there are any problems with the phone connection, data can be lost. But regular phone lines are often the only practical choice for homes and small businesses. In some areas, **ISDN lines**, which are wires that provide a completely digital path from one computer to another, are dropping in price so that some small businesses and homeowners can afford them. Figure O-2 contrasts an analog phoneline connection to a digital ISDN connection. Whether you use a regular phone line or a faster ISDN line, Windows 98 can help you establish a connection between your home or office computer and the Internet. To do so you will need to select an **Internet Service Provider (ISP)**, which is a company that sets up an **Internet account** for you that provides Internet access. ISPs maintain servers that are directly connected to the Internet 24-hours-a-day. You dial over your phone line into your ISP's server in order to use its Internet connection. You pay a fee for this service. Sometimes the fee is by the hour, but more often, it is a flat monthly rate.

Windows 98 includes the following tools to help you connect to the Internet:

 Dial-Up Networking

Some computer users have one Internet account for home use and a different account for business use. The Dial-Up Networking accessory helps you manage the accounts that you use to connect to the Internet. You can have just one or several accounts listed in the Dial-Up Networking folder, which you can access through My Computer.

 Connection Wizard

The Connection Wizard, available on the Internet Explorer menu, makes it easy for you to create an Internet account for the first time by prompting you for the needed information through a series of dialog boxes.

 Online Services folder

The Online Services folder helps you install software for some of the major online services, such as America Online or CompuServe, all of which provide Internet service. If the online service you want to use is not listed in this folder, you can receive software from the online service, or you can set up your account using the Connection Wizard.

FIGURE O-1: Phone line connection to the Internet

Computers and
networks on the
Internet

Your online service
maintains a server
directly connected
to the Internet

Modem inside your
computer

Phone jack on the
wall

Phone lines connect your
computer to your online
service's server

FIGURE O-2: Data traveling over a phone line

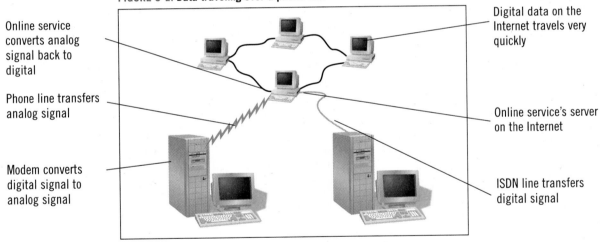

Online service
converts analog
signal back to
digital

Phone line transfers
analog signal

Modem converts
digital signal to
analog signal

Digital data on the
Internet travels very
quickly

Online service's server
on the Internet

ISDN line transfers
digital signal

CLUES TO USE

Online services

ISPs are sometimes referred to as **online services**, and vice versa. There used to be several differences between the two kinds of companies, but today they provide such similar services that the two terms are almost interchangeable. Online services include Internet access, e-mail, and much more. For example, **chat rooms** and **forums** allow users who share common interests to come together electronically and exchange messages on a specific topic in "real time." Many online services also offer newsgroup support.

Newsgroups, similar to forums, bring people together who share common interests in order to exchange messages through e-mail, rather than in real time. Some online services offer specialized Internet services, such as tools for searching the Internet, space for storing Web pages, and information services. When you are choosing your online service, make sure you consider your needs and compare the services you want with the price you pay.

Windows 98

Setting Up a Dial-Up Networking Connection

If you want to be able to connect to the Internet and other compatible networks using your home computer, you can set up a dial-up networking connection using the Internet Connection Wizard. If your ISP has provided you with an installation program that sets up the connection for you, install and run that program rather than using the Windows 98 Internet Connection Wizard, then skip this lesson and the next lesson. If you don't yet have an ISP, see the lesson "Installing the MSN Online Service" to select MSN or a different ISP. John has signed up with an ISP and has received the necessary information for his account. He will use the Internet Connection Wizard to set up the service.

1. Click the **Start button** on the taskbar, point to **Programs**, then point to **Internet Explorer**

2. Click **Connection Wizard**

3. Click the **I have an existing Internet account option button**, then click **Next**
John chooses this option because he has an account with an ISP but is not yet connected to it. The first option connects you to a referral service that helps you select an ISP, but you only use that option if you have not already bought an account with an ISP.

4. Click the **...Internet service provider option button** (the first one), click **Next**, click the **Connect using my phone line option button**, then click **Next**
John chooses this option, shown in Figure O-3, because he is not on a local area network.

5. If necessary, click the **Create a new dial-up connection option button**, then click **Next**

6. Type the area code and telephone number of your ISP in the appropriate boxes, then click **Next**
Your ISP documentation will provide you with the phone number you should use. John uses the one shown in Figure O-4; yours will be different.

7. Type your user name in the User name box, then press **[Tab]**
Your ISP documentation will provide you with the user name and password you should use.

8. Type your password into the Password box
You should keep your password secret so unauthorized users cannot access your account. As you type the password, asterisks appear instead of the letters you type, as shown in Figure O-5. This protects your password from the eyes of people who might be walking by your computer.

9. Click **Next**
You will continue working with the wizard in the next lesson.

Trouble?
If you have no other dial-up connections established on your computer, skip Step 4.

Trouble?
If you can not find your user name in your documentation, it might be called "User ID", "Member ID", "Login Name", or something similar.

FIGURE O-3: **Connection options**

Use if you have an
ISP account and
want to use your
modem and phone
line

Use if you are on a
network that has a
direct Internet
connection or a
server whose pur-
pose is to connect
to the Internet

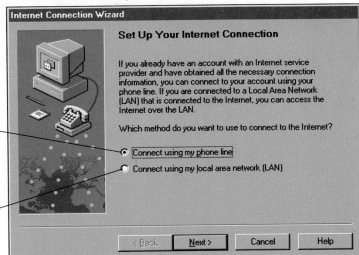

FIGURE O-4: **Entering ISP phone information**

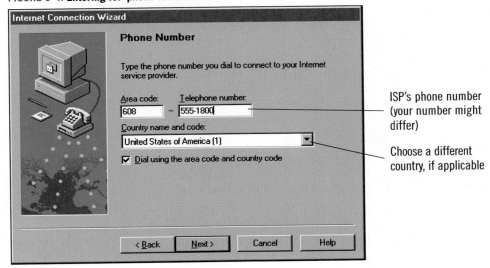

ISP's phone number
(your number might
differ)

Choose a different
country, if applicable

FIGURE O-5: **Entering a user name and password**

Asterisks appear
to protect your
password

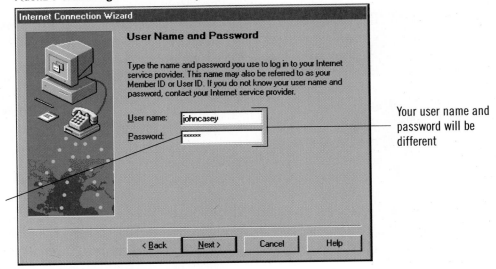

Your user name and
password will be
different

Using Connection Wizard Advanced Settings

When you are using the Internet Connection Wizard to set up an Internet connection, you can choose either to keep the default advanced settings or to change them. If you click No when asked about advanced settings, your connection will use the Windows 98 defaults. If you click Yes, you must provide the settings from your ISP documentation. John uses the advanced settings option because he wants to ensure that his connection is using the settings provided by his ISP.

1. Click the Yes option button when asked if you want to change advanced settings, then click Next

2. Click the PPP or SLIP option button, depending on what your ISP's documentation specifies

   A **connection type** is the kind of connection between your computer and your ISP's server. Windows 98 offers two connection types: PPP and SLIP. The preferred and more common connection type today is **Point to Point Protocol (PPP)**, which provides error-checking and better coping with noisy phone lines than SLIP. **Serial-Line Internet Protocol (SLIP)**, is a basic connection type that runs well on most systems but has no error checking or security features. Most ISPs use a PPP connection, but some require SLIP; check your ISP documentation to see which one to use.

3. Click Next

4. Click the appropriate Logon Procedure option button

   Some ISPs require you to log on before you can use the service. In some cases, you must log on manually by providing the information required by your ISP when you attempt to connect. In other cases, you can use a **logon script**, which is a program that runs on your computer and automatically logs you on to the service.

5. If you need to use a logon script, click Browse, locate and select the logon script specified by your documentation, then click Open

   By default, Windows 98 stores logon scripts in the C:\Program Files\Accessories folder. Your ISP's documentation will tell you which logon script to use, or it will provide you with a different one. John's is shown in Figure O-6.

6. Click Next, click the appropriate IP address option button, then, if you selected the second option, type the IP address

   An **Internet Protocol (IP) address**, is a unique address that identifies a server on the Internet. Usually your ISP automatically assigns you an IP when you log on because you are only using the address for the period of time that you are logged in.

7. Click Next, choose the appropriate DNS Server address option button, then, if you selected the second option, type the DNS numbers

   The **Domain Name System (DNS)**, is a database service that helps computers look up the names of other computers and locate their corresponding IP addresses. If your ISP documentation provides you with a primary and secondary DNS server address, enter them here, as John does in Figure O-7.

8. Click Next, type a name for your connection (such as your ISP's name), then click Next

9. Since you are only trying to set up your dial-up networking connection not your mail and news options, click No, click Next, click Next, then click Finish

   The Internet Connection Wizard closes and you return to the desktop.

Trouble?

If you are sure you can proceed using the default settings, click the No option button, then read through the rest of this lesson without performing the steps.

Trouble?

If you do not need to use a logon script, skip Step 5.

FIGURE O-6: **Choosing a logon procedure**

Option you choose
depends on your ISP

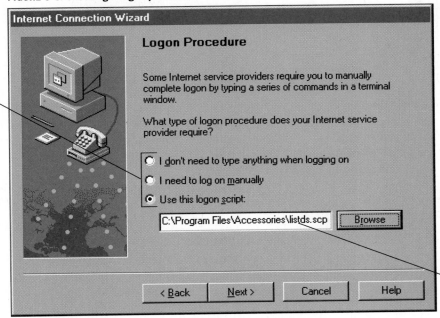

John's ISP uses the
listds.scp logon
script (yours might
differ)

FIGURE O-7: **Entering DNS server information**

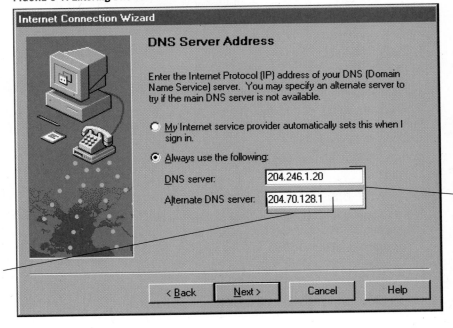

Your ISP might
not require this
information

DNS addresses
come in four sets of
1-3 digit numbers
that are separarted
by dots

Changing Dial-Up Networking settings

If you choose not to change advanced settings, you might encounter problems with your connection if the Windows 98 default settings do not match those of your ISP. You can change the way your dial-up networking connection is **configured**, or set up, from the Dial-Up Networking window. Open the Dial-Up Networking window as directed in the next lesson, right-click the connection you want to modify, then click Properties. Click the tabs to locate the settings that you want to change.

Windows 98

Connecting to a Dial-Up Service

Once you have established a dial-up networking connection, you are ready to use it to connect to the Internet or to another network or computer. You can have more than one dial-up networking service, in which case multiple icons appear in the Dial-Up Networking window. One connection might provide your business Internet service, another might be for home or family use, and another might access a university or institutional account. ✐ John decides to test the connection he just set up.

QuickTip

To open the Dial-Up Networking window using the Start menu: click the Start button, point to Programs, point to Accessories, then point to Communications.

1. Open My Computer, then double-click Dial-Up Networking

The Dial-Up Networking window, shown in Figure O-8, displays icons for each dial-up networking connection you have.

2. Double-click the connection you just created (it will have the same name that you entered in Step 8 of the last lesson)

Trouble?

If your user name and password are not correct, type them in the appropriate boxes before you proceed to Step 4.

3. Make sure your user name and password are correct in the Connect To dialog box

John's Connect To dialog box is shown in Figure O-9; yours will reflect the information you entered in the wizard.

4. Click Connect

Trouble?

If a Pre-Dial Terminal Screen dialog box opens after you click Connect, click Continue.

5. Wait as your modem connects

The Connecting dialog box appears and identifies the steps of establishing a connection. First it uses your modem to dial the number, then it verifies your user name and password, and finally, it establishes a connection. A Connection Established dialog box (or something similar) may open indicating that you are connected to your ISP.

6. Close the Dial-Up Networking window

An icon appears on your taskbar, indicating that you are connected. You can now start your Internet browser to view Web pages, check your e-mail, or use any of the other Windows 98 communication features.

Trouble?

If your pop-up menu does not have Disconnect as an option, you right-clicked the wrong icon. Click outside the pop-up menu to close it, then repeat Steps 7 and 8.

7. Right-click the connection icon 🖳 on the taskbar

A pop-up menu appears, as shown in Figure O-10.

8. Click Disconnect

Now that you have tested your dial-up networking connection, you can continue with the next lesson.

FIGURE O-8: **Dial-Up Networking window**

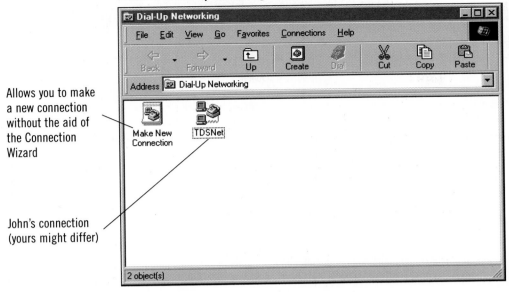

Allows you to make a new connection without the aid of the Connection Wizard

John's connection (yours might differ)

FIGURE O-9: **Connecting to the Internet**

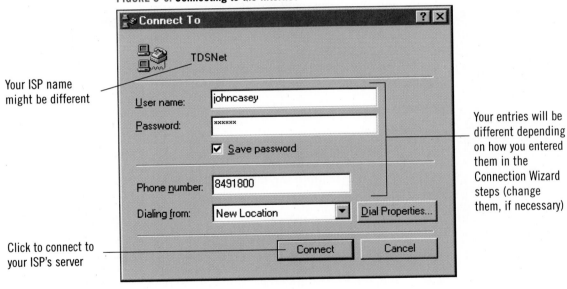

Your ISP name might be different

Your entries will be different depending on how you entered them in the Connection Wizard steps (change them, if necessary)

Click to connect to your ISP's server

FIGURE O-10: **Disconnecting from your ISP**

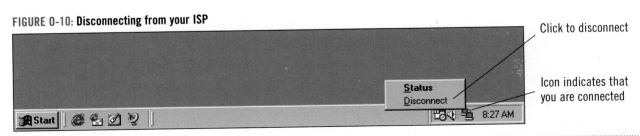

Click to disconnect

Icon indicates that you are connected

Windows 98

Installing the MSN Online Service

Windows 98 comes with installation procedures for five popular services that offer a variety of communications features, such as e-mail, newsgroups, Internet service, chat groups and forums, and other individualized features. When you select one of these services, the installation routine guides you through the setting up of an account with that service. In setting up an account, you will also have to set up payment options. This lesson shows you how to begin the installation; if you choose to go with the service, you can complete the installation by following the prompts on the screen. John wants to try the **Microsoft Network**, commonly called **MSN**.

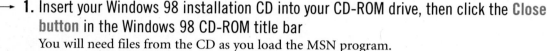

Steps

Trouble?

See your instructor or technical support person for access to the installation CD.

1. Insert your Windows 98 installation CD into your CD-ROM drive, then click the **Close button** in the Windows 98 CD-ROM title bar
You will need files from the CD as you load the MSN program.

2. Click the **Start button**, point to **Programs**, then point to **Online Services**
The Online Services menu, shown in Figure O-11, shows the services available through Windows 98.

QuickTip

If you select a different service, you will go through a setup procedure that is different from the procedure in these steps.

3. Click **The Microsoft Network**, then click **OK**

4. Read the two opening screens and click **Next** on each screen
If your computer doesn't find the files it needs, click the Browse button, select the MSN Setup file in the OLS folder on the installation CD, then click OK. These screens inform you of the service to which you are subscribing and warn you to close any programs that are running that might interfere with the MSN Setup.

5. If necessary, select your country from the country list, then click **Next**

6. Read the MSN Member Agreement, then click **I Agree**
By clicking "I Agree," you accept the terms Microsoft has outlined in the member agreement.

7. Click **Next** to start installing the Microsoft Network
The installation files are copied from the CD to the hard drive.

8. When the installation is finished, answer the questions shown in Figure O-12
John requests a new MSN account but wants to use his existing Internet connection, the one he set up when he went through the Dial-Up Networking procedures.

9. Click **Next**, then complete the procedure as directed on the screen
The service guides you through the setting up of an account. Each screen provides you with instructions; read them carefully before you proceed. When you are finished, your service is set up. You should test your service once it is set up. If it has a problem, contact your ISP for assistance. Icons to start the service are installed on your desktop. In John's case, he will use TDSNet to connect to the Internet, but he will also receive the benefits of the MSN online service.

FIGURE O-11: **Online services**

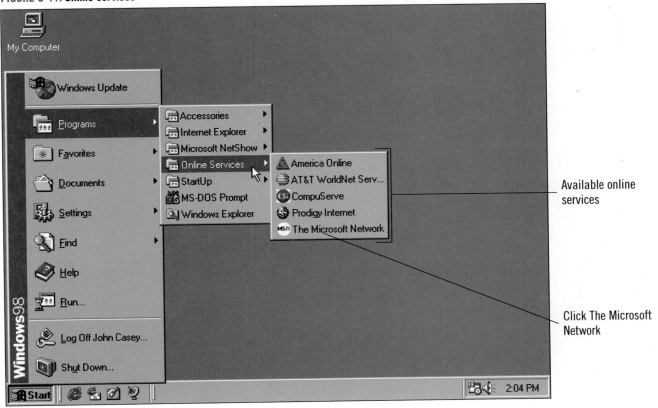

Available online services

Click The Microsoft Network

FIGURE O-12: **Completing the MSN installation routine**

Click to obtain a new MSN account

Click to use an existing account

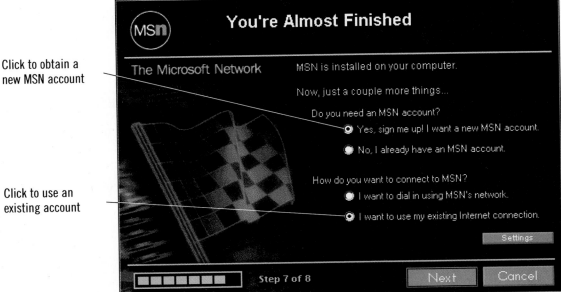

Windows 98

Dialing Over a Modem with Phone Dialer

Phone Dialer allows you to dial regular phones using your modem. Once the modem connects with the number you are dialing, called the **remote party**, you can pick up your phone and talk. This feature is useful for people who spend long periods of time near their computers because it allows them to place calls without first having to dial numbers on a phone. When you use Phone Dialer, it is helpful to have your modem's speakers on so you can hear what is actually going on with the connection. ✎ John decides to use Phone Dialer to place a call. First, he checks his modem settings.

Steps

1. Click the **Start button**, point to **Programs**, point to **Accessories**, then point to **Communications**

2. Click **Phone Dialer**

Trouble?

If the Speaker volume slider is not available, your modem does not allow you to adjust the volume.

3. To check your modem speaker's settings, click **Tools** on the menu bar, click **Connect Using**, click **Line Properties**, if necessary drag the **Speaker volume slider** up, click **OK**, then click **OK**

   Once you have placed a call and have heard how loud your modem is, you can re-adjust Speaker volume as necessary.

4. Type a number into the Number to dial text box

   John decides to use an automated number, such as a local Time and Temperature number, so he can experiment with the Phone Dialer feature without inconveniencing anyone. See Figure O-13. You can also use the mouse to click the numbers you want to dial on the numeric keypad.

5. Click **Dial**

   You will hear dialing, then ringing.

6. Once the remote party picks up the line, lift the receiver of your own phone

   If you have a multi-line phone and one line is dedicated to your modem, press the line button for your *modem*, not the line button for your normal voice calls.

Trouble?

If you do not see the Call Status dialog box, click Call Status in the taskbar, or skip Step 7.

7. Click **Talk** in the Call Status dialog box

   You are now connected to the remote party, and you can communicate over the phone as you normally would. See Figure O-14. When you use Phone Dialer, make sure you are quick to act as soon as the Call Status dialog box indicates that you can pick up the receiver. If you allow a long pause to occur after the remote party has answered, the remote party will not realize that there is someone on the other line. However, do not pick up the receiver too quickly, because if you do so before a connection is established, Phone Dialer aborts its dialing attempt.

8. When you are finished with the phone call, hang up your phone, then click **Hang Up**

FIGURE O-13: **Phone Dialer dialog box**

Enter an automated
number such as
Time and
Temperature (yours
might differ)

Dials number you
entered

FIGURE O-14: **Call Status dialog box**

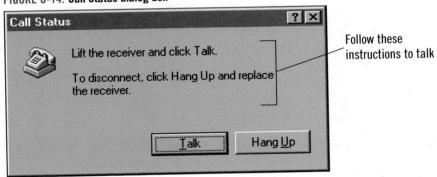

Follow these
instructions to talk

Windows 98

Managing Phone Numbers

Most phones have speed dial buttons that you can press to dial numbers that you have previously stored. With Phone Dialer you can store up to eight Speed dial numbers. Another handy feature of Phone Dialer is that you can log your phone calls. This is especially useful for businesses who need to track long-distance calls by client or project. ✒ John communicates with one of the Wired Coffee stockholders, Patrick Carey, on a regular basis. He decides to add Patrick's name and number to one of the Speed dial buttons. He also decides to log his calls to Patrick. You can use the automated number you used in the last lesson or the number of someone with whom you have made prior arrangements.

Steps 123 4

1. **Click the first Speed dial button, labeled 1**
   The Program Speed Dial dialog box, in which you enter a name and phone number for the remote party whose number you want to save, opens.

2. **Type a name (such as "Time and Temp") in the Name text box, then press Tab**
   John types the name "Patrick Carey," but you should type a name that you will find useful.

3. **Type the corresponding phone number in the Number to dial text box**
   Figure O-15 shows the name and number John entered. Although you do not have to type hyphens between the area code and the groups of numbers that make up a phone number, you can if you are used to viewing phone numbers that way.

4. **Click Save**
   You can also click the Save and Dial button to save your entry and dial at the same time. The name you entered appears on the Speed dial button.

5. **Click the first Speed dial button, now labeled with the name you specified in Step 2**

Trouble?

If you do not see a Talk button, skip Step 6.

6. **When you are connected, click Talk**
   The Active call dialog box opens.

7. **In the Name to place in call log text box, type Testing log feature, then click Hang Up**
   Figure O-16 shows the entry John typed for testing his log while calling Patrick Carey. This entry will appear in his log.

8. **Click Tools on the menu bar, then click Show Log**
   Figure O-17 shows the log.

9. **Close the Call Log window, then close Phone Dialer**

CLUES TO USE

Dialing contacts from an address book

If you have stored addresses and phone numbers in an address book such as the one provided with Microsoft Outlook (a communications program that comes with Microsoft Office), you might be able to use phone dialing technology with the contacts you have entered there. In your contacts list, right-click a contact, then look for an option, such as "AutoDialer" or "Dial," on the pop-up menu. Click that option, start the call by clicking the appropriate button, then pick up the handset as directed in this lesson.

FIGURE O-15: **Entering a Speed dial number**

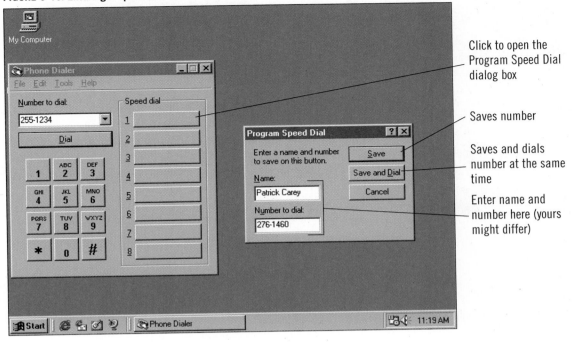

Click to open the
Program Speed Dial
dialog box

Saves number

Saves and dials
number at the same
time

Enter name and
number here (yours
might differ)

FIGURE O-16: **Logging a call**

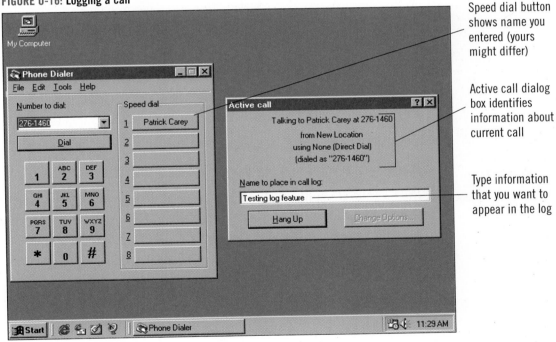

Speed dial button
shows name you
entered (yours
might differ)

Active call dialog
box identifies
information about
current call

Type information
that you want to
appear in the log

FIGURE O-17: **Viewing the log**

Information you
entered in the
log appears
here

Date, time, and
duration of call

Windows 98

Setting Up NetMeeting

Microsoft NetMeeting provides state-of-the-art computer communication features. With NetMeeting, you can talk to others over the Internet just as you do on a regular phone, and you can use video to see others and let others see you as you converse. In addition, you can share programs and files with others, collaborate on documents and even share a whiteboard (a drawing canvas), and you can send messages using Chat. The first time you use NetMeeting, you need to set up the NetMeeting service. John would like to be able to use NetMeeting to communicate with his business contacts.

Steps

1. Click the **Start button**, point to **Programs**, point to **Internet Explorer**, then click **Microsoft NetMeeting**

2. Click **Next**

Trouble?
If NetMeeting starts without opening the setup wizard, this is not the first time NetMeeting has been used on your machine. Read through this lesson without performing the steps.

3. Click the **directory server list arrow**, shown in Figure O-18, then click **ils.business.four11.com** or whatever directory server you want to use
   A **directory server** lists the people you can call using NetMeeting. When you log onto a directory server, your name appears in the list, and others who are also logged on to that server can communicate with you. John chooses the directory server shown in Figure O-18.

4. Click **Next**, then enter the requested information using your real name and email address
   John enters the information shown in Figure O-19. You do not have to enter anything in the Comments text box if you do not want to do so.

5. Click **Next**, click the **For business use option button**, then click **Next**

6. Click the **option button** corresponding to your modem speed, then click **Next**

Trouble?
If you have no video capture device, skip Step 7.

7. If you have a video capture device, select it from the list, then click **Next**

8. If you have a sound card, click **Next** (if directed, close any programs that play or record sound, then click **Next**), adjust the Volume slider as necessary, click **Next**, read the requested text into your microphone to test it, then click **Next**
   If you need to tune your audio settings again later, click Tools on the NetMeeting menu bar, click Audio Tuning Wizard, then follow the steps.

9. Click **Finish**
   Continue to the next lesson as NetMeeting starts.

FIGURE O-18: **Selecting a directory server**

If this check box is selected, you will log on automatically to the selected directory server when you start NetMeeting

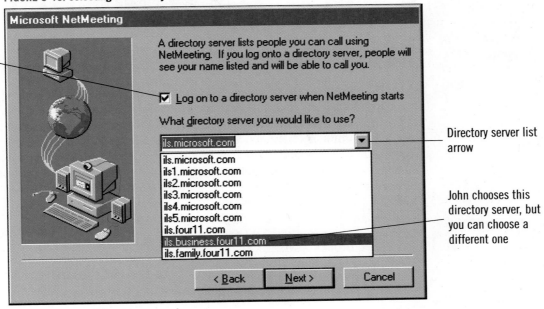

Directory server list arrow

John chooses this directory server, but you can choose a different one

FIGURE O-19: **Entering contact information**

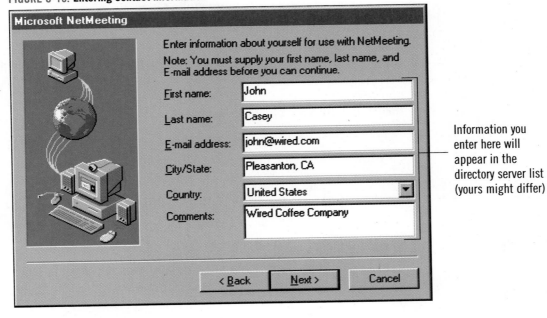

Information you enter here will appear in the directory server list (yours might differ)

Calling Others Over the Internet

Windows 98

Once NetMeeting is set up on your computer, you can use it to talk over the Internet. You have two communication choices: Chat, or Audio and Visual. In Chat, you type messages back and forth. In Audio and Visual, you speak into a microphone and hear the other person's response over your computer's speakers. If you have a video capture device, you can send video to others so they can receive images as well as sound. John wants to confer about a stockholders meeting with Patrick Carey, who lives in Madison, Wisconsin, and who is one of the Wired Coffee Company stockholders. Before attempting this lesson, you should make arrangements with someone else who has a Windows 98 computer with an Internet connection, a sound card, speakers, and a microphone. That person should start NetMeeting and be logged on to the same directory you chose in the last lesson when you start this lesson.

Steps

QuickTip

To call a person on the Speed dial directory, skip Steps 2 and 3. To call someone not on the Speed dial directory, click the Directory button.

Trouble?

If you do not see your name, click the Refresh button again.

1. If necessary, start NetMeeting and make sure you are connected to the Internet, then maximize the NetMeeting window

2. View the NetMeeting status bar at the bottom of the screen, as shown in Figure O-20, if it says "Logged on," skip this step, but if it does not, click Call on the menu bar, click Log On to [name of your directory], then wait for the directory to display a list of the people currently logged on

3. Click the Last Name header button, as shown in Figure O-20, to organize the list by last name, then scroll to find your name; if you do not see it, click the Refresh button 🔁, then wait for the new list to appear

4. Locate the name of the person with whom you want to confer
   The person with whom you want to confer must be logged on to the same directory. See Figure O-20, which shows that both John Casey and Patrick Carey are logged on. If you can not find the person's name, click the Refresh button; if that doesn't work, have the person follow the steps in this lesson to make sure he or she is logged on properly.

5. Right-click the person's name, then click Call in the pop-up menu
   On the computer of the person you are calling, the Microsoft NetMeeting dialog box appears saying "Incoming call from [your name]." The recipient must click Accept to begin the conference. The conference begins.

6. Click the Chat button 💬, type a message, press [Enter], wait for a response (this may take a few moments), then continue to converse in this manner
   Figure O-21 shows an exchange between John Casey and Patrick Carey.

QuickTip

To save the contents of the Chat window as a text file, click Yes when you close the Chat window.

7. Close the Chat window (it's entitled "Untitled – Chat"), then click No when asked if you want to save the conversation

8. To communicate using Audio and Video, speak clearly into your microphone, wait for a response (there might be a short delay), then continue to converse
   Figure O-22 shows Patrick Carey's image appearing on video.

9. When you are finished with the call, click the Hang Up button 📞, then click the Close button to close the Microsoft NetMeeting window and exit the program

FIGURE O-20: **List of those logged on to the directory server**

Click to display list
of those logged on
to the current
directory server

Current directory
list (yours might
differ)

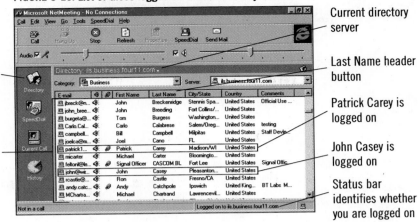

Current directory
server

Last Name header
button

Patrick Carey is
logged on

John Casey is
logged on

Status bar
identifies whether
you are logged on

FIGURE O-21: **Chatting with NetMeeting**

List of those
participating in
the current call

Chat window shows
exchange between
John and Patrick
(yours might differ)

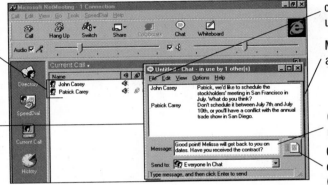

You can save the
conversation by
using the File menu

Messages that have
already been sent

Current message,
not yet sent

Click to send
current message
(or press [Enter])

FIGURE O-22: **Audio and Video connection**

Click to hang up and
end the conference

Click to switch
between Chat and
Audio and Video

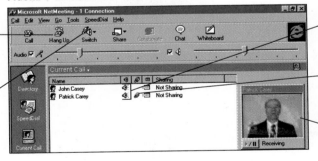

Both John and
Patrick have audio
available

Only Patrick has
video available

John's computer
screen shows a
video of Patrick

CLUES TO USE

Sharing documents during a conference

To share your programs and documents with others in the conference, open the document you want to share in its application window, click the Share button 🖳 on the NetMeeting toolbar, then click the name of the program displaying the document. Others will be able to see your document and the program on their computer screens, but cannot work with the document until you give access to it by clicking the Collaborate button 🖾 on the toolbar. Click

OK to acknowledge the security message. Remote users are told to click the application window to start collaborating. The user who clicks the application window "takes control" of the document, and all other users see "In Control" next to that user's name in the list of participants in the call. To discontinue sharing, click the Share button again, then click the application you want to stop sharing.

Practice

► Concepts Review

Label each of the elements of the screen shown in Figure O-23.

FIGURE O-23

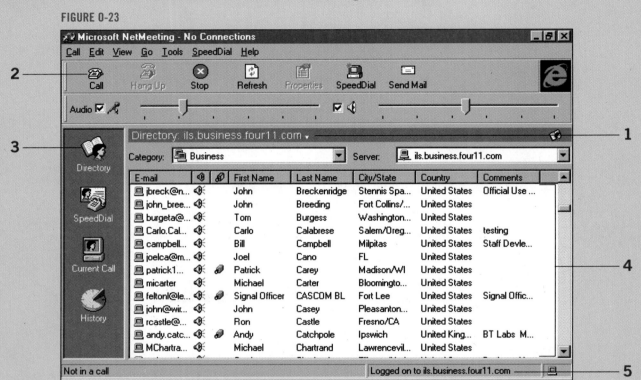

Match each of the terms with the statement that describes its function.

6. Provides a completely digital path from one computer to another

7. Accessory that allows you to dial phone numbers from your computer

8. Service that allows users who share common interests to come together electronically and to exchange messages on a specific topic

9. Common server connection type that you use to connect to an Internet server

10. Online service available through the Online Services folder

11. Allows you to talk to others over the Internet

12. Program that runs on your computer and that automatically logs you on to an Internet service

a. Microsoft NetMeeting
b. ISDN
c. Forum
d. PPP
e. Logon script
f. MSN
g. Phone Dialer

Select the best answer from the list of choices.

13. Under what circumstances will you likely need to establish a dial-up networking connection?
a. On a university computer
b. On a home computer
c. On a computer at IBM headquarters
d. On a computer at the Library of Congress

14. What connection possibilities are likely to exist for a home computer?
a. ISDN line
b. High-speed satellite connection
c. Phone line
d. Both a and c

15. With NetMeeting you can:
a. Talk with others over the Internet.
b. Share a document.
c. Save a text file of a conversation.
d. All of the above.

16. If you need to keep track of calls you make to clients, which accessory should you use?
a. NetMeeting
b. Chat
c. Connection Wizard
d. Phone Dialer

► Skills Review

To print a hard copy of your computer screen, press [Print Screen] to make a copy of the screen, start Paint, click Edit on the menu bar, click Paste to paste the screen into Paint, then click Yes to paste the large image, if necessary. Click File on the menu bar, click Print, then click OK.

1. Set up Dial-Up Networking.
a. Start the Internet Connection Wizard.
b. Assume you have an existing Internet service and that you are using a phone line.
c. Enter your ISP's phone number and your user name and password.

2. Set up advanced settings.
a. Click Yes to change advanced settings, then select PPP or SLIP, depending on your ISP.
b. Choose the appropriate logon procedure, then enter the required IP and DNS address information.
c. Finish the Connection Wizard by following the prompts.

3. Connect to a dial-up service.

   a. Open Dial-Up Networking, then double-click the connection you want to use.

   b. Verify your user name and password, click OK, then click Connect.

   c. Print an image of your screen with the Dial-Up Networking window open and the connection icon on the taskbar.

   d. Disconnect from your service and close any open windows.

4. Connect to an online service.

   a. Open the Online Services window from the Start menu or the desktop, then select an online service.

   b. Proceed through the setup procedure of the online service you selected.

   c. Once you have installed the service, run it, then print an image of your screen with the service running (you will be able to do this only if you have paid for the service).

5. Dial over a modem with Phone Dialer.

   a. Click the Start button, click Phone Dialer, dial the number of your local Time and Temperature recording, then pick up the receiver.

   b. Print an image of your screen, hang up the phone, then click Hang Up.

6. Manage phone numbers.

   a. Click a blank Speed dial button, enter the name and number of someone you call frequently, then click Save.

   b. Repeat Step a for another number you call frequently.

   c. Click one of the Speed dial buttons you just programmed, hang up the phone, then click Hang Up.

   d. Click Tools, click Show Log, then arrange the windows so you can see them all.

   e. Print your screen showing the phone log and the programmed Speed dial buttons, then close all open windows.

7. Set up NetMeeting.

   a. Start NetMeeting, then if prompted, proceed through the setup procedure.

8. Call others with NetMeeting.

   a. Click the Directory button, if necessary, to display the directory of the server you are using.

   b. Click Call on the menu bar, then click Log on if the status bar indicates that you are not logged on.

   c. Scroll to locate your name; if you don't see it, click the Refresh button on the toolbar.

   d. Right-click the name of the person you want to call, then click the Call button on the toolbar.

   e. Click the Chat button on the toolbar, type a message, click the Send button, then wait for a response.

   f. Close the Chat window, then click Yes to save the contents as a text file.

   g. Click the Hang up button on the toolbar, then close NetMeeting.

   h. Print the contents of your Chat window using the method described before the Skills Review.

▶ Independent Challenges

1. You run a small office machines repair business called Tech-One. You would like to establish a connection to the Internet from your office, but you are not sure what service you should use. You want e-mail and Internet service, and later on you might need the capability to publish your own Web page. You decide to research some of the local ISPs for the best service.

1. Using the local Yellow Pages, look up "Internet Service Provider," or "Internet On-Line Service Provider." Select three ISPs that might meet your needs.
2. Call each ISP and ask about the services they provide, their rates, and their technical support availability.
3. Write a one-page report that compares the three ISPs you chose, and indicate which ISP you would choose and why.

2. You work at a small pet shop supply company called PetWorld, and because you have some experience with computers and the Internet, your manager has asked that you establish an Internet connection for the company.

1. Use the Connection Wizard to establish a new Internet connection with an ISP. Call this connection "PetWorld".
2. Open the Dial-Up Networking window and use the connection you just created to dial in to your service.
3. Print an image of your screen by following the directions listed before the Skills Review, with the Dial-Up Networking window open. Draw a circle around the connection icon in the taskbar to show you are connected.

3. You are a financial service advisor for Point Financial Services, but you work from a home office. You place frequent calls to your company's headquarters, and you would like to be able to use your computer to dial the number.

1. Start Phone Dialer and enter a number into one of the Speed dial buttons (use a number, such as Time and Temperature, that will not inconvenience anyone with the label "Point FS".
2. Call this number and log the call as "Point FS stock quotes".
3. Print an image of your screen by following the directions listed at the beginning of the Skills Review, showing the log and the Speed dial button.

4. You are a student at Midwest University, and you will be collaborating with another student on a project this semester. Because you commute to the university from a distance, you want to be able to work on the project at your home computer while communicating efficiently with your partner.

1. Select someone you know who has access to a Windows 98 computer with an Internet connection.
2. Choose a directory server and a time for conferencing.
3. At the appointed time, start NetMeeting, call your partner over the Internet, then use Chat to talk about your project.
4. Open one of your software programs, create a document for your project, then share the document with your partner.
5. Print an image of the screen by following the directions listed at the beginning of the Skills Review, showing the shared document in the NetMeeting window.
6. Save and print your Chat conversation.

► Visual Workshop

Recreate the screen shown in Figure O-24, which displays a NetMeeting conference. You will not be able to duplicate the exact window because you have a different user name than that shown in the figure. Observe these guidelines in creating the window:

- You will need to arrange a time to call a recipient who has NetMeeting.

- Your name and the name of the recipient will be different.

- Your directory server might be different.

- Duplicate the messages.

When you have duplicated this window, print a copy of your screen using the steps listed at the beginning of the Skills Review.

FIGURE O-24

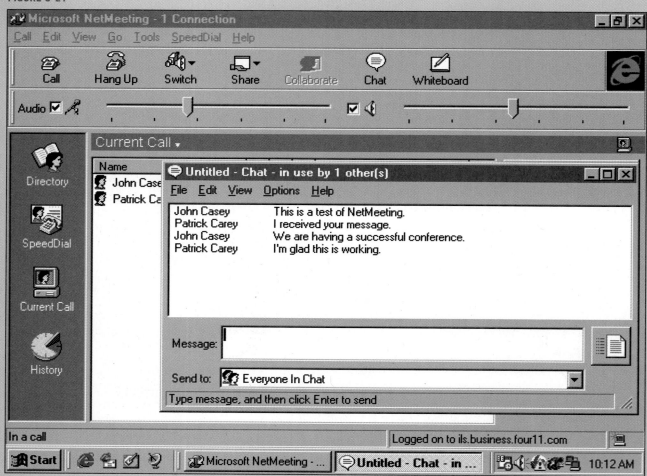

Glossary

Accessories Built-in programs that come with Windows 98 that you can use for day-to-day tasks.

Active channel A specialized Web page that delivers Internet content from a specific channel, such as Disney, MSNBC, or The Microsoft Network.

Active Desktop The desktop that allows you to access the Internet and view Internet content (Active Desktop items) directly from it.

Active Desktop item An element you can place on the desktop to access or display information from the Internet.

Active program The program that is currently running.

Active window A window that you are currently using; if a window is active, its title bar changes color to differentiate it from other windows, and its program button on the taskbar appears pressed in.

ActiveMovie Control A new media program for Windows 98 that delivers high-quality continuous video playback.

Adapter The device that connects a computer to a network.

Address Book An electronic book where you can store detailed information about a person or company.

Alias A filename created by Windows 98 for each file on the system, designed to conform to the DOS 8.3 filename restriction.

Article A newsgroup message.

Auto Hide A feature that helps you automatically hide the taskbar.

Autoexec.bat The file of DOS commands that runs when DOS is started, it defines several properties of the DOS environment.

Background The surface of your desktop on which icons and windows appear; you can customize its appearance using the Display Properties dialog box.

Backup The process you perform to read your data quickly and compress it into a small space on a set of disks or a tape cartridge.

Backup set A file that Backup creates when you perform a back up.

Backup strategy The process in which you select a backup method by evaluating tradeoffs between safety, time, and media space.

Banner page The printed page that reports the name, owner, date, and time of a print job.

Bitmap Image A file format for pictures commonly used by drawing applications.

Bitmapped character A character that consists of small dots organized to form a letter.

Bookmark A reference point in a document to which you want to create a link.

Briefcase Windows 98 accessory that synchronizes files between two different computers.

Browser A program, such as Microsoft Internet Explorer, designed to access the Internet. *See also* Web browser.

Bullet mark An indicator that shows an option is enabled.

Bulletin Board Systems Telecommunications services you can access to read and post messages and download and upload software.

Cascading menu A list of commands from a menu item with an arrow next to it. Pointing to the arrow displays a submenu from which you can choose additional commands.

Center A Display properties option that positions the wallpaper picture or pattern in the center of the desktop screen.

Channel Bar The bar on the right side of the desktop that displays the buttons you can use to access the Internet and view Web pages known as active channels, like those on television.

Chat rooms Services that allow users who share common interests to come together electronically and exchange messages on a specific topic.

Check box A square box in a dialog box that you click to turn an option off or on.

Check mark An indicator that shows a feature is enabled.

Click To press and release the left mouse button once.

Client A computer that accesses shared resources on a server.

Client/server network A network setup that provides all users on a network a central location for accessing shared files.

Clipboard Temporary storage space on a hard drive that contains information that has been cut or copied.

Close To exit a program or remove a window from the desktop. The Close button usually appears in the upper-right corner of a window.

Cluster A section of a disk.

Command Directive that provides access to a program's features.

Command button In a dialog box, a button that carries out an action. A command button usually has a label that describes its action, such as Cancel or Help. If the label is followed by an ellipsis (. . .), clicking the button displays another dialog box.

Command prompt A character like > or $ that appears at the beginning of a line and that signals the user to enter commands.

Command Prompt Only mode A Windows 98 operating environment in which Windows 98 and all the start-up files, but not the graphical user interface, are loaded.

Command-line interface An interface in which you perform operations by typing commands at a command prompt.

Compressed Volume File (CVF) A single file where DriveSpace compresses folders and files.

Compression Agent Windows 98 accessory that recompresses files to improve performance.

Config.sys The file that defines how DOS handles memory and various devices on a computer system.

Configured The way a program or device on a computer is set up.

Connection type The type of connection between a computer and an ISP's server. Windows 98 offers two connection types: PPP and SLIP.

Contact A person or company with whom you communicate.

Contact group A group of contacts that you can organize together.

Context-sensitive help Help that relates to the task on which you are currently working.

Control Panel A Windows utility for changing computer settings.

Conventional memory The first 640 kilobytes of memory that DOS uses to run applications.

Copy To copy data onto the Clipboard, and from the Clipboard to another location, while leaving it in the original location.

Cut To remove data and place it on the Clipboard to be pasted in another location.

Cut and paste To move information from one place to another using the Clipboard as the temporary storage area.

Default printer The printer that you use most often.

Defragment A feature that allows you to rewrite the files on your disk to contiguous blocks rather than in random blocks.

Delete To remove a file or folder that is placed in the Recycle Bin, then removed from the disk.

Desktop An on-screen version of a desk that provides a workspace for different computing tasks.

Destination application Application where you store an embedded object.

Destination disk The disk to which you want to copy.

Destination file The file where you store a representation of a linked object.

Dialog box A window that requests information. Many dialog boxes have options you must choose before Windows or a program can carry out a command.

Differential backup A Backup type that copies only selected files that have changed since the most recent normal or incremental backup.

Directory server Computer that maintains a list of people logged on to the NetMeeting service.

Disk Cleanup Windows 98 accessory that deletes temporary, Internet cache, and unnecessary program files.

Disk Defragmenter Windows 98 accessory that restores fragmented files in one location.

Disk label Name that you assign to a disk by using the Properties dialog box.

Display adapter A hardware device that allows a computer to communicate with its monitor.

Display pane The bottom pane of Outlook Express that displays the e-mail message selected in the preview pane. *See also* Preview pane.

Distribution list A single name or address that represents the e-mail addresses of several users.

Docucentric interface An interface in which the emphasis is on the documents rather than on the software applications.

Document A file that a program, such as WordPad, creates.

Document window The part of a program window that displays the current document.

Domain Name System (DNS) A database service that helps computers look up the names of other computers and locate their corresponding IP addresses.

DOS Short for Disk Operating System, the standard operating system for PCs for over ten years prior to Microsoft Windows.

Double-click To press and release the left mouse button twice quickly.

Download The process by which you access and display a Web page from the Internet.

Drag To move an item or text to a new location using the mouse button.

Drive mapping The process by which you assign drive letters to network folders, making them appear as extra drives.

Drivers Software that allows a hardware device (e.g., printer) to communicate with Windows and other software applications.

DriveSpace A Windows 98 accessory that compresses folders and files on a disk to free up more space.

Edit To change the contents of a file without having to re-create it.

Electronic mail (e-mail) A system used to send and receive messages electronically.

Embedding Inserting an object created in one application into a document created in another application.

Emergency startup disk Disk that contains a set of utilities and tools that help start a computer in an emergency.

Explorer Bar The pane on the left side of the screen in Windows Explorer that displays all objects available to the computer.

External image Users can view it by clicking a link that will open the image on a separate page or load software that will display the image on the original page.

Favorite A shortcut to a Web address.

File An electronic collection of information that has a unique name, distinguishing it from other files.

File allocation table A list of information about the status of the various sections of a disk that is maintained by the operating system.

File extension Extension to a filename that an operating system uses to determine the file type.

File hierarchy A logical structure for folders and files that mimics how you would organize files and folders in a filing cabinet.

File management The process of organizing and keeping track of files and folders.

File permission A user setting, such as Read or Full, that designates what a user can and cannot do to a file. Read permission allows the user to view the file but not to make changes. Full permission allows the user to edit and save changes to the file.

File set A file that specifies which folders and files you want to back up.

File system A format applied to a disk to make it compatible with the operating system in storing, managing, and accessing data.

Filter The process of retrieving newsgroup messages from a particular person, about a specific subject, of a certain length, or older than a number of days.

Floppy disk A disk that you insert into the disk drive of your computer and on which you can save files.

Folder A collection of files and/or other folders that helps you organize your disks.

Font The design of a set of characters. For example, Times New Roman.

Format To change the appearance, but not the actual content, of information.

Forums Services that allow users who share common interests to come together electronically, and exchange messages on a specific topic.

Fragmented file A file that is broken up and stored on different parts of a disk.

FrontPage Express An Internet Explorer program that you use to create Web pages.

Full System Backup A backup option that backs up all files on your system.

Graphical user interface (GUI) An environment made up of meaningful symbols, words, and windows that controls the basic operation of a computer and the programs that run on it.

Hard disk A disk (usually drive C) that is built into the computer and on which you store programs and files.

Help button A button in a Help window that when clicked, jumps to a dialog box or opens a program to answer your question.

Highlight When an item is shaded differently, indicating that it is selected. *See also* Select.

Home page The first Web page that appears when you open a Web browser.

Horizontal scroll bar Moves your view from right to left through a window.

Host A device on a network.

Host Drive The uncompressed drive where the Compressed Volume File (CVF) is located.

Host name The name that identifies a computer on a network.

Hyperlink Highlighted words, phrases, and graphics that open other Web pages. *See also* Link.

HyperTerminal A telecommunications accessory provided by Windows 98.

Hypertext Markup Language (HTML) Language used to write Web pages.

Icon Graphical representation of a file or another screen element.

Incremental backup A backup option that backs up only the files that have changed since your last backup.

Inline image Graphic image that appears directly on a Web page.

Insertion point The blinking vertical line in a document window, such as WordPad, that indicates where text will appear when you type.

Internal links Hyperlinks that take you to another location on the same Web page.

Internet A collection of networks that connects computers all over the world using phone lines, coaxial cables, fiber-optic cables, satellites, and other telecommunications media. *See also* Network.

Internet account Allows you to access the features of the Internet.

Internet service provider (ISP) A company that provides access to the Internet. *See also* Online services.

Interrupt Request Line (IRQ) A software setting that allows a hardware device to communicate with your computer's software.

ISDN lines Wires that provide a completely digital path from one computer to another.

Keyboard shortcut A keyboard alternative for executing a menu command, for example, [Ctrl][X] for Cut.

Keyword A word you submit to a search engine that is compared with words found on various Web sites on the Internet. *See also* Search engine.

Landscape orientation Print option where the page is wider than it is tall.

Legacy hardware Any hardware device that is not designed for Windows 95 Plug-and-Play.

Legacy programs A program that pre-dates Windows 95; Windows 98 accommodates legacy programs because people are reluctant to abandon familiar programs for new untested and unfamiliar versions.

Line break Creates a new line in FrontPage Express without leaving white space.

Link An element in a hypertext document that moves you to another place in the document. *See also* Hyperlink.

Linking When you connect an object in one application to a document in a second application without actually removing the object from its original location.

List box A box in a dialog box containing a list of items. To choose an item, click the list arrow then click the item you want.

Local folder A file folder located on the computer on which you are currently working.

Local printer A printer connected directly to a computer.

Logon script A program that runs on your computer automatically to log you on to a dial-up networking service.

Mail client A program that queries the mail server and requests new messages for a particular user.

Mail profile The set of characteristics that describes how a user's mail service is set up.

Mail server The network host that stores mail messages sent by users on the system.

Maintenance wizard Windows 98 accessory that schedules your computer to automatically perform ScanDisk and other disk maintenance tasks at designated times.

Margin The extra space around the edge of a document.

Markup tag Used in HTML, a label in angle brackets that identifies the element to a browser.

Maximize To enlarge a window so it fills the entire screen. Usually, the Maximize button is located in the upper-right corner of a window.

Media Player A Windows accessory that plays video, sound, or animation files.

Menu A list of available commands in a program.

Menu bar A bar at the top of the program window that organizes commands into groups of related operations.

Message flag An icon associated with an e-mail message that helps you determine the status or priority of the message.

Microsoft Backup A Windows 98 accessory, also known as Backup, for backing up files.

Microsoft Network, The An online service provided by Windows 98.

Minimize To reduce the size of a window. The Minimize button is usually located in the upper-right corner of a window. Clicking the Minimize button shrinks the window to a button on the taskbar.

Mount The procedure to identify a compressed disk so that it can access the compressed files.

Mouse A hand-held input device that you roll on your desk to position the mouse pointer on the Windows desktop. *See also* Mouse pointer.

Mouse buttons The buttons (right and left) on the mouse that you use to make selections and issue commands.

Mouse pointer The arrow-shaped cursor on the screen that follows the movement of the mouse as you roll the mouse on your desk and which you can use to select items, choose commands, and start programs. The shape of the mouse pointer changes depending on the program and the task being executed.

MS-DOS mode A Windows 98 operating environment in which only DOS is loaded.

Multitasking The ability to run several programs at once and easily switch among them.

My Computer Window that displays the devices and folders available on your computer.

Navigate To reposition the insertion point in a document.

Network Two or more computers connected together in order to exchange and share data, programs, and hardware.

Network folder A folder on a network that is made available to other computers on the network.

Network Neighborhood An icon on the Windows 98 desktop that lists the computers on the network.

Network operating system The software that creates, maintains, and controls the operations of the network.

Network printer A printer made available to other computers on a network.

News server A computer located on the Internet where articles on different topics are stored.

Newsgroup Online discussion groups about a particular topic, usually in an e-mail format.

Normal backup A Backup type that backs up all selected files, regardless of when the files were last changed.

Normal mode A Windows 98 operating environment in which Windows 98 and all the usual startup files are loaded.

Object Linking and Embedding (OLE) The ability to place and work with the same objects in different programs.

Offline When the connection to the Internet is disconnected.

Online services Companies that sell communications services such as e-mail, Internet access, Web page storage space, and newsgroup access. *See also* Internet service provider.

Operating system A program that controls the basic operation of your computer and the programs you run on it.

Optimization The procedure to rearrange fragmented files into one location on a disk.

Option button A small circle in a dialog box that you click to select an option.

Outlook Express Start Page A page that displays tools you can use to read e-mail, compose e-mail messages, download the latest newsgroup messages, read newsgroup messages, enter and edit Address Book information, and find people on the Internet.

Pane Part of a window that divides the window into two or more sections.

Paragraph break Creates a white space between paragraphs in FrontPage Express.

Paragraph styles Formatting that applies to entire paragraphs.

Pattern A design that will display as your desktop background.

Peer-to-peer network A network setup that enables two or more computers to link together without designating a central server.

Phone Dialer Allows you to dial regular phones using your modem.

Pixel A single point on your monitor's screen.

Plug-and-Play Hardware device designed for quick and easy installation with Windows 98.

Point To move the mouse pointer to position it over an item on the desktop.

Point to Point Protocol (PPP) Common dial-up networking connection type that provides error-checking and the ability to cope with noisy phone lines.

Pointer trail A mouse setting that adds a shadow to the mouse pointer.

Pop-up menu The menu that appears when you right-click an item.

Portrait orientation Print option where the page is taller than it is wide.

Post office The network host that stores mail messages sent by users on the system.

Preview pane The top pane of Outlook Express that displays a list of all of the messages in your Inbox.

Print Preview A feature that shows the layout and for-matting of a document before you print it.

Printout A document that you printed on paper.

Program Task-oriented software, such as Microsoft Access, Corel WordPerfect, and Microsoft Word, that you use for a particular kind of work, such as word processing or database management.

Program button The button that appears on the taskbar that represents a program that is minimized but still running.

Properties The characteristics of a specific element (such as the mouse, keyboard, or desktop display) that you can customize.

Protocol A language that the computer uses to com-municate with other computers on the network.

Proxy server An Internet connection option that provides a secure barrier between your network and the Internet.

Publish To save a file on a Web server, making the file available to the World Wide Web.

Queue The order in which a printer prints documents.

Quick Launch toolbar A toolbar located next to the Start button on the taskbar that contains buttons to quickly start Internet-related programs and show the desktop.

Quick View A Windows 98 accessory that helps you quickly view the contents of a document without starting or even requiring the program that created it.

Random access memory (RAM) The memory that programs use to perform necessary tasks while the computer is on, and when you turn the computer off, all information in RAM is lost.

Recycle Bin An icon that appears on the desktop and which represents a temporary storage area on your hard drive for deleted files. Files remain in the Recycle Bin until you empty it or you restore the file(s).

Remote party Recipient of a call you place with Phone Dialer or NetMeeting.

Reserved memory Memory, other than conventional memory, that DOS uses to run devices and system operations.

Restore To reduce the window to its previous size before it was maximized. The Restore button usually is located in the upper-right corner of a window.

Right-click To press and release the right mouse button once quickly.

Run To operate a program.

Safe mode A Windows 98 operating environment in which Windows 98 and some of the startup files are loaded; used to troubleshoot problems with Windows 98.

ScanDisk A Windows 98 accessory that checks for and then marks or repairs damaged sections of a disk.

Scheme A combination of color, fonts, or character designs for window elements.

Scraps Sections of documents you can save, place on your desktop, and paste into other documents.

Screen saver A moving pattern that fills your screen after your computer has not been used for a specified amount of time.

ScreenTip A description of a toolbar button that appears on your screen when you position the mouse pointer over the button.

Scroll bar A bar that appears at the bottom and/or right edge of a window whose contents are not entirely visible and which contains a scroll box and two scroll arrows.

Scroll box A box located in the vertical and horizontal scroll bars that indicates your relative position in a window. *See also* Horizontal scroll bar and Vertical scroll bar.

Search engine A program on the Web that allows you to search through a collection of information found on the Internet. *See also* Keyword.

Select To click and highlight an item in order to perform some action on it. *See also* Highlight.

Send To command Lets you send a document to a new location.

Serial-Line Internet Protocol (SLIP) A basic dial-up connection type that runs well on most systems but has no error checking or security features.

Server A computer that stores and shares resources, such as programs, files, and folders, with other users on a network.

Service The network component that allows you to share resources on your computer, such as files and printers, with other networked computers.

Shared printer A printer made available to computers on a network.

Shortcut A link that you can place in any location that gives you instant access to a particular file, folder, or program on your hard disk or on a network.

Shut down The action you perform when you are finished working with Windows and after which it is safe to turn off your computer.

Source application The application where you create or insert an object.

Source disk The disk from which you want to copy.

Source file The file where you store a linked object.

Start button A button on the taskbar that you use to start programs, find and open files, access Windows Help, and more.

Stretch A Display properties option that displays the wallpaper picture or pattern enlarged across the desktop screen.

Syntax A set of rules that you follow to write a command.

Tab A section at the top of the dialog box that separates options into related categories.

Task Scheduler A tool that enables you to schedule tasks to run at specific times.

Taskbar A bar at the bottom of the screen that contains the Start button and the Quick Launch toolbar, and shows which programs are running.

Template A preformatted page that you can use as a model when creating a new page.

Text box A box in a dialog box in which you type text.

Thread A collection of newsgroup messages that consists of the original message on a particular topic along with any responses.

Tile A Display properties option that displays the wallpaper picture or pattern consecutively across the desktop screen.

Title bar The area along the top of the window that contains the filename and the program used to create it.

Toggle A button that acts as an on/off switch.

Toolbar A bar that contains buttons that allow you to activate a command quickly.

Triple-click In some programs, this action causes an entire line to be selected.

TrueType character A character that is based on a mathematical equation so the curves are smooth and the corners are sharp.

Uniform Resource Locator (URL) Another name for a Web address. *See also* Web address.

Vertical scroll bar Moves your view up and down through a window.

Virtual DOS machine (VDM) The environment that Windows 98 creates to run DOS programs.

Wallpaper An image that you display as your desktop background.

Web address A unique address on the Internet where you can locate a Web page. *See also* Uniform Resource Locator.

Web browser A program that retrieves and displays Web pages. *See also* Browser.

Web page A document that contains highlighted words, phrases, and graphics that link the document to other documents on the Internet.

Web server A computer on the Internet that hosts Web sites, making them available to the World Wide Web.

Web site A computer on the Internet that contains Web pages.

Window A rectangular frame on a screen that might contain icons, the contents of a file, or other usable data.

Windows Explorer A Windows 98 program that lets you manage files, folders, and shortcuts; more powerful than My Computer and allows you to work with more than one computer, folder, or file at a time.

Windows Help A book stored on your computer, complete with an index and a table of contents, that provides information on the features and tasks associated with a Windows program.

Wizard A series of dialog boxes that guides you through steps to complete a task and prompts you for information.

Wordwrap When text that will not fit on one line is automatically placed onto the next line.

Workgroup A group of computers within a network that shares resources, such as files and printers.

World Wide Web (Web, or WWW) Part of the Internet that consists of Web sites located on different computers around the world.

WYSIWYG Stands for "What you see is what you get" and refers to the Windows environment where you see the formatting while creating a document as it will appear in the final document.

Index

Index

Index

creating bookmarks, WIN I–16–17
creating internal links, WIN I–16–17
creating links to other Web pages, WIN I–18–19
defined, WIN I–1
formatting horizontal lines, WIN I–10–11
formatting paragraphs, WIN I–6–7
formatting text, WIN I–8–9
inserting graphics, WIN I–12–13
inserting horizontal lines, WIN I–10–11
opening Web pages, WIN I–2–3
saving Web pages, WIN I–2–3
Full format type, WIN C–5, WIN L–4–5
Full permission, WIN H–3

▶ **G**

GIF format, WIN I–12
Global positioning devices, WIN M–10
graphical user interface (GUI), WIN A–1
graphic images. *See* images
graphic links, WIN F–8–9
graphic objects. *See also* images
    in Web pages, WIN I–10

▶ **H**

hard copy, WIN B–14
hard disk. *See also* disks
    copying files to, WIN N–4–5
    saving files to, WIN B–5
hardware, adding, WIN E–15
    conflicts, WIN M–14
    installing devices, WIN M–10–11
    installing printers, WIN M–6–7
    legacy, WIN M–14
    managing, WIN M–1–17
    managing printers and print job, WIN M–8–9
    plug-and-play, WIN M–2–3
    removing hardware devices, WIN M–16–17
    viewing hardware settings, WIN M–14–15
    viewing printer properties, WIN M–4–5
    viewing system hardware, WIN M–12–13
hardware classes, WIN M–12
Hardware Conflict icon, WIN M–14
hardware devices. *See also* hardware
    defined, WIN M–1
    installing, WIN M–10–11
Help, WIN A–16–17
    command, WIN A–6
    context-sensitive, WIN A–16, WIN A–17
    Microsoft Outlook Express, WIN G–5
highlighting text, WIN B–4
History list, WIN F–15
hits, in searching, WIN F–16
home pages, defined, WIN F–14
    selecting, WIN F–14–15

Horizontal Line Properties dialog box, WIN I–10–11
horizontal lines, formatting, WIN I–10–11
    inserting in Web pages, WIN I–10–11
    size of, WIN I–11
host drive, WIN L–14, WIN L–16
HTML, WIN I–3
    markup tags, WIN I–5
http, WIN F–9
hyperlinks. *See* links
Hypertext Markup Language (HTML), WIN I–3

▶ **I**

icons, WIN A–1
images, aligning, WIN I–13
    for background patterns, WIN I–14–15
    background pictures for folders, WIN D–16–17
    external, WIN I–12
    inline, WIN I–12
    inserting in Web pages, WIN I–12–13
    linking, WIN K–14–15
    revising, WIN B–10–11
    Web page file formats, WIN I–12
Inbox Assistant, WIN G–11
Inbox folder, WIN G–10–11
Increase Indent button, WIN I–7
Increase Text Size button, WIN I–9
incremental backups, WIN N–2, WIN N–14–15
indenting paragraphs, in Web pages, WIN I–7
Index tab, in Windows Help, WIN A–16
inline images, WIN I–12
Insert File button, WIN G–9
Insert Image button, WIN I–12–13
insertion point, WIN B–2
Insert Object dialog box, WIN K–4–5, WIN K–6–7, WIN K–14–15
installing, hardware devices, WIN M–10–11
    Microsoft Network (MSN), WIN O–10–11
    plug-and-play hardware, WIN M–2–3
    printers, WIN M–6–7
    programs, WIN L–12–13, WIN L–19
Install New Font option, WIN E–11
Install/Uninstall tab, in Add/Remove Programs dialog box, WIN L–2–3
internal links. *See also* links
    for Web pages, WIN I–16–17
Internet. *See also* Microsoft Internet Explorer
    accessing from Active Desktop, WIN A–7
    calling others over, using NetMeeting, WIN O–18–19
    connecting to, WIN F–4, WIN F–5
    defined, WIN A–2
    history, WIN F–3
    using mouse on, WIN A–5
Internet accounts, WIN O–2
    managing, WIN O–2
    setting up dial-up networking connections, WIN O–4–5

Internet Accounts dialog box, WIN G–14–15
Internet Connection Wizard, WIN G–15, WIN O–4–5
    advanced settings, WIN O–6–7
Internet Explorer. *See* Microsoft Internet Explorer
    opening Web pages in, WIN I–18–19
Internet Explorer Channel Bar, customizing, WIN E–2
Internet Explorer link, Microsoft Outlook Express Start Page, WIN G–4–5
Internet Options dialog box, WIN F–14–15
Internet Protocol (IP) addresses, WIN O–6–7
Internet Service Providers (ISPs), WIN F–5, WIN I–19, WIN O–2
    advanced dial-up networking connection settings, WIN O–6–7
    connecting to, WIN O–8–9
    disconnecting from, WIN O–8–9
    online services *vs.*, WIN O–3
    setting up dial-up networking connections, WIN O–4–5
Internet (Web) style clicking, WIN A–5
interrupt request line (IRQ), settings, WIN M–14–15
IP addresses, WIN O–6–7
ISDN lines, WIN O–2
Italic button, WIN B–8
    in FrontPage Express, WIN I–8–9

▶ **J**

JPEG format, WIN I–12

▶ **K**

keyboard shortcuts, in menus, WIN A–11
keywords, searching with, WIN F–16–17

▶ **L**

Large Icons view, WIN C–7
legacy hardware, WIN M–14
line breaks, WIN I–6
link buttons, WIN F–14–15
linked objects, changing source, WIN K–17
    creating, WIN K–14–15
    finding, WIN K–17
    opening, WIN K–16–17
linking, defined, WIN K–2
    embedding *vs.*, WIN K–3, WIN K–14
    objects, WIN K–14–15
    using Paste Special, WIN K–14
links, colors for, WIN I–15
    defined, WIN F–2
    disregarding, WIN K–17
    external, WIN I–18–19
    graphic, WIN F–8–9

Index

newsgroups, WIN G–16–17, WIN O–3
   defined, WIN G–1
   deleting articles, WIN G–19
   filtering unwanted messages, WIN G–16
   reading and posting articles, WIN G–18–19
news servers, WIN G–14–15
normal backups, WIN N–2, WIN N–10–11
Notepad, WIN J–2
   viewing and printing backup reports in,
     WIN N–12–13, WIN N–14–15
NSFNET, WIN F–3
Numbered List button, WIN I–7
numbered lists, WIN I–6

►O

object linking and embedding. *See* OLE
objects, defined, WIN K–2
   embedding existing, WIN K–6–7
   embedding new, WIN K–4–5
OLE, WIN K–1–17
   basics, WIN K–2–3
   editing embedded objects, WIN K–8–9
   embedding existing files, WIN K–6–7
   embedding new objects, WIN K–4–5
   embedding video clips, WIN K–10–11
   features of, WIN K–2–3
   linking objects, WIN K–14–15
   modifying video clips, WIN K–12–13
   updating links, WIN K–16–17
online services, WIN O–2
   installing, WIN O–10–11
   Internet Service Providers (ISPs) vs, WIN O–3
   selecting, WIN O–3
Online Services folder, WIN O–2
Open command, Network Neighborhood, WIN H–17
Open dialog box, WIN B–4–5, WIN B–16, WIN B–18
   shared, WIN H–14–15
Open Source button, WIN K–17
operating systems, WIN A–1
optimization, WIN L–10
Outline Services folder, WIN A–3
Outlook Express, WIN A–3

►P

Page Location text box, WIN I–2
Page Properties dialog box, WIN I–15
Page Setup dialog box, WIN B–14–15, WIN F–19
Paint, WIN B–10–13
   editing embedded objects in, WIN K–8–9
   Toolbox, WIN B–10–11
Paint Color Box, WIN K–8–9
Paint objects, embedding into WordPad, WIN K–4–5,
   WIN K–6–7
Paint scraps, WIN J–12

panes, WIN A–16
paragraph breaks, WIN I–6
paragraph formatting buttons, WIN I–7
paragraphs, formatting, for Web pages, WIN I–6–7
   indenting, in Web pages, WIN I–7
paragraph styles, applying to Web pages, WIN I–4–5
passwords, WIN A–2
   for Internet accounts, WIN O–4
   for shared folders, WIN H–9
Paste Special, linking using, WIN K–14
pasting. *See also* copying
   data between programs, WIN B–12–13
   text, WIN B–6–7
patterns, background, for Web pages, WIN I–14–15
   desktop, WIN E–4
Pause Printing, WIN M–8
peer-to-peer networking, WIN H–2
Pencil tool, WIN K–4–5
people, searching for, on the Web, WIN F–16
Percent of window, specifying horizontal line size with,
   WIN I–11
permissions, defined, WIN H–3
   granting, for file sharing, WIN H–2
   types of, WIN H–3
Phone Dialer, WIN O–12–13
Phone Dialer dialog box, WIN O–12–13
pixels, defined, WIN I–11
   specifying horizontal line size with, WIN I–10–11
Play button, WIN K–10–11
plug-and-play hardware, defined, WIN M–2
   installing, WIN M–2–3
pointer trail, mouse, WIN E–12–13
pointing, WIN A–4, WIN A–5
point size, WIN B–8
Point to Point Protocol (PPP), WIN O–6
pop-up menus, WIN A–4
ports, WIN M–6
posting to newsgroups, WIN G–18–19
Power Management utility, WIN H–9
PPP connections, WIN O–6
Pre-Dial Terminal Screen dialog box, WIN O–8
preview pane, of Inbox folder, WIN G–10
Print dialog box, WIN B–14–15, WIN F–18–19
   hardware settings, WIN M–14–15
   report types, WIN M–15
printer drivers, removing, WIN M–16–17
printer icons, WIN M–4, WIN M–6–7
printer ports, WIN M–6
Printer Properties, WIN B–15, WIN M–4–5
printers, default, WIN J–14, WIN M–6
   installing, WIN M–6–7
   installing updated drivers for, WIN M–4
   local, WIN M–4
   managing, WIN M–8–9
   network, WIN H–3, WIN M–4
   shared, WIN M–4
printer shortcuts, WIN J–14–15
Printers window, WIN M–4–5
Printer's window, WIN M–6–7

printing, Address Book contacts, WIN G–13
   deferred, WIN M–8
   documents, WIN B–14–15
   e-mail messages, WIN G–13
   Web pages, WIN F–18–19
print jobs, managing, WIN M–8–9
   separator page for, WIN M–9
printouts, WIN B–14
Print Preview, WIN B–14–15
print queue, WIN M–8
programs, adding, WIN E–15
   defined, WIN A–1
   installing, WIN L–12–13, WIN L–19
   removing, WIN L–18–19
   sending documents to, WIN J–10–11
   starting, WIN B–2–3
Programs command, WIN A–6
Program Speed Dial dialog box, WIN O–14–15
properties, WIN E–1
Properties command, Network Neighborhood, WIN H–17
Properties dialog box, WIN C–16–17
   adding contacts to Address Book, WIN G–6–7
   network properties, WIN H–6–7
protocol, network properties, WIN H–6
proxy servers, WIN F–5
publishing, Web pages, WIN I–1, WIN I–19

►Q

QIC-compatible tape drives, WIN N–15
Quick (erase) format type, WIN L–5
Quick format type, WIN C–5
Quick Launch toolbar, WIN A–2, WIN A–3, WIN A–7,
   WIN G–2
Quick View, WIN C–2, WIN C–7

►R

random access memory (RAM), WIN B–5
Read Mail link, WIN G–4–5
Read News link, WIN G–4–5
read-only files, WIN H–15
Read permission, WIN H–3
Recycle Bin, WIN A–3, WIN C–12–13
   properties, WIN C–13
   restoring deleted files, WIN D–14–15
   sending documents to, WIN J–16–17
Regional Settings dialog box, WIN E–8–9
remote party, WIN O–12
Remove Compression? dialog box, WIN L–16
removing, hardware devices, WIN M–16–17
   programs, WIN L–18–19
Rename command, WIN H–17
renaming, folders in Windows Explorer, WIN D–8–9
Reply to Group button, WIN G–18

Index